UNEASY
NEIGHBO(U)RS

UNEASY
NEIGHBO(U)RS

Canada, The USA and the Dynamics
of State, Industry and Culture

David T. Jones & David Kilgour

John Wiley & Sons Canada, Ltd.

Library and Archives Canada Cataloguing in Publication Data

Jones, David T., 1941–
  Uneasy neighbors : Canada, the USA and the dynamics of state, industry and culture / David T. Jones, David Kilgour.

Includes bibliographical references and index.
ISBN: 978-0-470-15306-2

  1. Canada—Foreign relations—United States. 2. United States—Foreign relations—Canada. 3. Canada—Relations—United States. 4. United States— Relations—Canada. I. Kilgour, David, 1941– II. Title.

FC249.J65 2007   327.71073   C2007-902531-5

Production Credits
Cover design: Ian Koo
Interior text design and layout: Adrian So
Cover photography: Photodisc / Getty Images
Wiley Bicentennial Logo: Richard J. Pacifico
Printer: Friesens

John Wiley & Sons Canada, Ltd.
6045 Freemont Blvd.
Mississauga, Ontario
L5R 4J3

Printed in Canada

2 3 4 5 FP 11 10 09 08 07

CONTENTS

FOREWORD

Relations between Canada and the United States, although close and complex, are the subject of academic and press interpretation that sharply varies. One interpretation is that under the weight of proximity and a one-to-ten disparity in GDP and population size, the smaller partner, Canada, is succumbing to American values and political domination. In that view, Canada in its institutions and policies is becoming more like the United States; the very identity of Canada is in jeopardy. Inadvertently, according to such claims, Canadian culture is disappearing and with it the capacity of Canada to act autonomously.

Another interpretation is that globalization is causing these two countries to converge in outlook and value, not asymmetrically towards that of the United States, but mutually and equally in the direction of some global norm for rich, advanced-industrial democracies in which the multinational corporation and common political interests tend to drive these polities towards a market-determined sameness. Just as the North American car industry is no longer exclusively U.S. and Canadian, the distinctiveness and power of the nation-state is everywhere in decline.

A third interpretation, heard more frequently in the United States than in Canada, is that the two polities are actually diverging in social value, in ideological preference, and in outlook towards world politics. While the United States, for example, attempts to escalate the war against drugs in Colombia and Mexico, Canada decriminalizes marijuana use at home. While the United States pursues a vigorous policy of democratization in Iraq, Canada places its priority on the establishment of an International Criminal Court. According to this third interpretation, the two governments and societies are moving in opposite directions.

In contrast, the authors of this book hold a very different view. They believe that for reasons of history, geopolitics, and culture, Canada and the

United States are different and always will be. Kilgour and Jones see neither long-term convergence nor divergence. Nor do they see two polities at odds with each other over fundamental matters of foreign policy. For them, Canada and the United States represent alternative Americas, different yet compatible. For them, two visions of what North America is and ought to become is a salubrious expression of what democracy itself is in a modern, free, multi-party state. For these authors, opportunity, not negativism or ill-will, is the most remarkable attribute of Canada-U.S. relations.

What these authors bring to the discussion of Canada-U.S. relations is freshness and sanity. Their assessments, while frequently irreverent, are plausible and quite balanced. They draw upon their own long experience in the two respective governments to reveal both their confidence in the democratic process and their occasional frustration at its outcomes.

Their approach is to present a Canadian or an American assessment and then to bounce counter-responses off against that assessment. In approach, the analysis is a type of dialectic that eventually reaches synthesis. By no means does either author act as an official spokesman for the government with which he has been affiliated. Each is something of a maverick. Each is independent of conventional political labels.

There is a place for this type of book, written openly, by actors who have been on the inside of government. Signifying much of the best impulse in North America, this book reflects well upon the citizens of each polity and upon their largely successful effort to hold their respective governments accountable in an interrelationship that works.

Dr. Charles Doran
Professor of International Relations,
Paul Nitze School of Advanced International Studies,
Johns Hopkins University

PREFACE

Many across our shrunken planet now know, since U2's Bono voiced the thought, that the world needs more Canada. For that matter, it needs more USA too, although this proposition is certainly more controversial than the other in many corners of the earth. How to get the best of both of them is a question an observer might ask as all nations move more deeply into the 21st century.

Fused together like Siamese twins in North America, with Mexico as the third sibling, the pair both share and divide the northern part of the continent and a culture. Rather than merely highlight the negative in our relationship—or just trumpet the positive—there is a large in-between zone that has come to intrigue us both as individuals and now as authors.

Having encountered one another in 1992 in Ottawa, prior to 13 years of Liberal ascendancy and at the beginning of the interregnum between one George Bush and another, "David J." (the diplomat) and "David K." (the politician) found that they had a variety of mutual interests.

Although some of these connections were personal (both having fathered twin girls and married brilliant professional women) and some political (a shared love of history and electoral nitty gritty), others were substantive. There was considerable excitement in the early to mid-1990s, which saw the Charlottetown Accord defeated in a national referendum; GHW Bush defeated and Bill Clinton become president; Prime Minister Brian Mulroney resign; Kim Campbell become prime minister—and her Tories soon afterwards temporarily annihilated; a Canadian pizza parliament with a shattered opposition and federal Liberals rampant; the Quebec Liberals defeated by the Parti Quebecois; the Democrats ousted from U.S. House/Senate control for the first time in over 40 years; a presidential impeachment attempt; and the near-death Quebec referendum. It was a period of immense richness for the political junkies and policy wonks;

indeed, anyone not satisfied with that level of political activity would only be content with riots in the streets. One can be sure that a generation of graduate students will continue to feast over the period's entrails, just as journalists have expended galaxies of computerized electrons in their first cut at its "history."

And while the pace of our history has moved from the sprint of those middle-1990s to a long distance run, it continues to pose new questions and challenges virtually every day and in every sector of our shared continental experience.

While the foregoing account of the mid-1990s was hardly ephemeral, and the next decade (1996-2005) was equally full, it is still tactical and temporary. Today's "who and what's hot and who and what's not" media line rarely runs beyond 24 hours. In our discussions during the years, we mulled over the standard "where are we going" questions as we strode towards and then into the 21st century—and tumbled into the pit of 9/11 and its ongoing aftermath. While this catastrophe and its continuing bloody spinoffs in Afghanistan and Iraq are neither trivial nor short term, they also are still an essentially limited problem set. Terrorism has killed and will continue to slay by the hundreds, thousands, and perhaps—horribly—even tens of thousands. It may be the challenge of our and our children's generation, but it is not existential in the manner in which Nazi fascism and Soviet communism afflicted the western world for 50 years. With the defeat of Hitler and the end of the Cold War, we no longer face the specter of Armageddon tomorrow. Nor do we face the prospect of tyrannical slavery for future generations that would have been our prospect had our political will or our military forces failed when confronting either challenge. Under terrorism, death arrives "retail, not wholesale," and while to the individual violent death is always "wholesale," in societal terms the losses and their management are deeply disconcerting, but still probably endurable.

For David Jones, Ottawa was a change-of-pace posting after a long politicomilitary career focus as a U.S. State Department foreign service officer. In Washington, his career built on early experience as an Army intelligence officer and culminated as the Foreign Affairs Advisor to the Army Chief of Staff. Overseas, it was epitomized by a series of tours concentrated in Europe and NATO arms control negotiations: basing arrangements in Greece; missile deployments in NATO lands. A professional life was built around multilateral accommodation and the art of the possible—with problems usually "managed" rather than solved. Canadians were his day-to-day, working partners at Alliance Headquarters in Brussels, or tough military professionals who were part of the combat force deterring a Soviet invasion through the Fulda Gap. Never having been to Ottawa before his assignment as Political Minister Counselor at the U.S. Embassy, he saw Canada as a country—not a problem.

For David Kilgour, Ottawa in the 1990s was another period in a career marked by independence as a lawyer, writer, and politician. It seemed entirely appropriate that he concluded his political career, after giving the Progressive Conservatives and Liberals each a commitment of about 14 years, as an Independent. His life has been spent in public service as a lawyer and a representative in the House of Commons for the residents of Southeast Edmonton. He has frequently advanced the point that "the West wants in" so far as Canada is concerned—and attempted to convince the rest of Canada that it needs the West "in." Deeply concerned about the dismal state of human rights in many parts of the world, both as a Member of Parliament and as Secretary of State for Latin America and Africa and later the Asia Pacific, he sought to project Canadian (and North American!) insights onto the global stage.

The United States and Canada, as two of the three principal national inhabitants of North America, are related by a remarkable number of social, political, technological, and economic factors. As authors, we do not dismiss the presence of Mexico as a geographic member of North America but we acknowledge that, despite NAFTA, Mexico is more closely linked to the United States than to Canada; it remains a mainly bilateral rather than trilateral relationship. It is not "old think" but still "real think" that places Mexico in South/Central/Latin America. Over time such a judgment could be challenged, particularly if the Hispanic component of the United States generates greater national unity challenges (a point we investigate in the main text), but for the moment we set aside Mexico to facilitate our bilateral analyses. And, to be sure, the complexities of writing a tripartite text—that is, by incorporating a third author—were daunting.

To a degree, the current bilateral relationship between the United States and Canada suggests that our nations can endure anything except success.

In 15 years, we have moved from the afterglow of "When Irish Eyes Are Smiling" to distinctly less appetizing descriptions. Thus for some, George W. Bush is a mad cowboy driven by fundamentalist Christianity to invade/pollute/exploit wherever and whenever. And for others, Jean-Paul Chrétien-Martin was an indistinguishable duality. It has been a move from best friends to "best friends like it or not" (with the "not" portion of the cycle in ascendance). Each side is acting as an "injustice collector" more interested in nurturing grievances and totting up "points" than in devising creative solutions.

Consequently, we are not necessarily sanguine over the election of a Conservative government in Ottawa. A minority government is limited by definition: it is not a question of creativity or competence, but of simple head counts of MPs. Any near-term Canadian government is locked into the limits demonstrated by opinion polls that demonstrate popular distaste for U.S. policy; progress towards some abstract era of good feeling will be only marginal. It is also unfortunate that during the 2005-06 election campaign, the Liberals invested so heavily in anti-Americanism as the driver of their foreign policy and a major plank of criticism against Conservatives. Anti-Americanism may be the favorite dish for some Canadians to consume, but as a steady diet it can dull the palate.

A wide variety of Canadian authors, from S. F. Wise and Robert Brown (*Canada Views the United States*) to J. L. Granatstein (*Yankee Go Home?*), have examined the roots of anti-Americanism. Deplore it, explain it, flaunt it. For the near term at least, it is an element that must be factored in when the U.S. government calculates its bilateral policies. For the United States, the best that could happen from a Conservative government would be an end to the manure throwing from the sidelines. In practice, however, our countries are so enjoying their hissy fit that it is likely to last beyond the morrow. Just as the relationship did not deteriorate in a day, it will not be rebuilt in 24 hours.

We also need new metaphors for our relationship. The suggestion that Canada and the United States are "in bed together" on some issue or circumstance has that slightly titillating aspect to spark the intellectual prurient interest. That tired metaphor still applies, however, when it's given a crude Anglo-Saxon twist, since each side is always wondering who is getting screwed in the deal. We need to think more of the countries as business partners, facing a vast array of professional challenges. As is the case for many partners, we know all too much about each other: we've seen the pictures of each other's kids; we've heard old jokes and anecdotes; and replayed old irritations until the repetition becomes its own irritation. Sometimes, each partner would benefit from a long vacation. But the business isn't going to fail because Sam goes off to visit the Holy Land for a stretch, nor will it collapse if Joe has to spend some time enmeshed in family counseling to stave off a divorce.

One of the truisms of democratic society is that "to govern is to choose." Regardless of how rich our nations have become, we can't have everything—either as individuals or as societies. But we still do not know what we cannot have. Desires are infinite; resources are finite. Is it impossible, for example, to have the best, most technologically advanced health care rapidly available to all citizens without bankrupting the average taxpayer? Is it possible to have both a premier national defense and a world-class health system for the entire population? Will a multicultural society become something more than the sum of its parts—or nothing more than a cacophonous jumble, a 21st-century Tower of Babel?

It is easy in a dictatorship: everyone gets what the dictator wants them to get. Done. Discussion over. But democracy makes the answer harder and interest groups with competing experts are arguing virtually every social, economic, and political question with an intensity that used to be limited to religious wars.

Consequently, throughout our discussion, we will push a bit into the less traveled areas of public politics and look at some basic questions of national unity, political governance, and foreign affairs. Through topics such as optics on health care, crime and justice, and substance abuse, we hope to prompt thought while (perhaps) also roiling some intellectual waters.

As readers navigate the text, they will be aware that there are ostensibly "Canadian" and "American" sections in each chapter, reflecting the voices of both authors. Equally important, however, is that both of us engage in "cross talk" within these more national sections, and we take equal responsibility for the introductory and concluding chapters of this book. Again, at the peril of belaboring what is obvious to us, we are searching for productive paths for discussion (if answers are not immediately evident) for problems that afflict North Americans.

In so doing, we also hope to move beyond the hothouse of "Canada studies" both in the U.S. (a much larger domain than Canadians might think) and Canada. Although advancing beyond the proverbial cure for insomnia (reading about a "worthy Canadian initiative") is a challenge, we hope with this effort to generate a little heat, with the intent that some light might also result. It would be even more pleasant if this were a "green light" that led to greater mutual appreciation and understanding.

David T. Jones
David Kilgour

ALTERNATIVE NORTH AMERICAS I

What are we? Does conflict or cooperation best define the societal relationship between Canada and the United States? Are we, as suggested
by one possible title for this book, "Dueling Cousins," for which emerging incompatibilities trump genetic origins? Or, in an admittedly more
sanguine outlook, are there alternatives in each society that the other can
adroitly adopt/adapt and profit thereby? We are the proverbial work-in-
progress.

We have set aside the current Michael Adams conundrum of whether
we are "fire" or "ice" or some mutually melted slush. Likewise, the proposi-
tions advanced in Seymour Martin Lipset's *Continental Divide* juxtaposing
"collectivism" and "individualism" offer insights, but again specialize in difference as definitive. And, to be sure, the differences between the societies
south and north of the border become clearer the longer they are observed.
But it is important to avoid being trapped in an examination of differences.
We do not believe that microscopic examination of dueling dichotomies
or misleading juxtapositions is productive in the long term. There is much
more to our relationship than its differences.

Depending on how it is measured, Canada and the United States share
an 8,893-kilometer border or a 5,525-mile border. This geographic reality
has transmuted for some observers into the "world's longest undefended
cliché." For others, the "undefended" element is increasingly a 20th-century
artifact. Canadians and Americans share much beyond a common border, but there are major differences. Some are trivial: calculating distances
in miles or kilometers; fueling vehicles with gallons or liters; paying with
"greenbacks" or multicolored currency. One can make much of differences
and ignore similarities. In our exploration of how Canadians and Americans
perceive each other and their respective roles in the world, we discover that
each country practices, in effect, alternative visions of North America. The

differences are distinctive, defining—but not definitive. And like currencies and measurement, there are conversion factors.

Ever since Canada evolved into something other than a colony of Great Britain, it has puzzled over its relationship with the United States. The phenomenon can be viewed as akin to an accordion being played: regularly moving and squeezing closer and then changing harmony by pulling back. It is also analogous to the psychologist's "approach/avoidance" concept in which, as two bodies move closer, the forces to be overcome increase and push them apart again.

The Canada-U.S. bilateral relationship has been characterized by innumerable adages and pithy descriptive phrases. One of the most trenchant is attributed to John Bartlet Brebner: "Americans are benignly ignorant of Canada. Canadians are malevolently well informed about the United States." Another suggests that there is the sociological equivalent of a one-way mirror at the border. Canadians looking south see Americans as they are, but Americans looking north see only a reflection of themselves.

A wry anecdote, applied in this instance to Canada and the United States, provides another perspective. As this story goes, God gave Canada tall mountains, rich soil, and lovely lakes. Its population was to be thoughtful, hard-working, and kind. Someone then asked God why Canada was so favored. God replied, "Wait till you see the neighbors I'm giving them."

One might also say that geography has made us neighbors; history has made us allies; economics has made us partners; but we are friends by choice. More cynically, "we are best friends, like it or not;" if so, we are certainly in a "not" portion of the cycle as the relationship moves further into the 21st century, although many Canadians would say that the hostility is to the Bush administration rather than to the American people.

Rather than belaboring differences, another approach to examining our countries is to suggest that we are "alternative North Americas." Both Canada and the United States have similar political and historical origins in the United Kingdom, a commitment in differing degrees to free market capitalism, and a demography that began with indigenous tribes but now reflects worldwide immigration. Majorities in both countries speak primarily English, but each has a significant second language (Spanish is spoken by the largest U.S. minority; Canada's francophones, although a declining percentage of the population, are still over 20 percent). Both have technologically sophisticated, well-educated populations. And each is attempting to find solutions for basic questions of the 21st century: the most effective mechanisms of political expression for two peoples enjoying essentially the same human rights and freedoms; the most rational and effective manner to secure the safety of the population from external threat; the delivery of health services and care of the elderly; the education of children in a manner permitting them to address problems 50 years into the future; the exploitation of natural resources without significant environmental damage; the balance between the freedom and privacy of individual citizens with the societal objective of safety from violence; and creating the conditions for equality of opportunity—if not equality of outcome.

It is almost as if North America contains two bio-social/cultural Petri dishes into which the problems of the new century are being introduced for observation. There is virtually none affecting Canada that will not appear in the United States—and vice versa. The most ambitious objective of the following comparative analyses would be to identify solutions. Any such sanguine conclusion is admittedly unlikely, but even a recognition that the difference in approaches needs to be played out in a less politicized manner would be useful for our bilateral relations.

Canadians and Americans have taken different approaches on many issues. By exploring how Americans and Canadians differ on major social and political issues in these hypothetical "alternative North Americas," we can achieve a better understanding of both countries. These issues are addressed in the chapters that follow on national identity, democracy, economics, culture, education, religion, health care, crime, military defense, international relationships, and human rights.

Some of the major assumptions that underlie our discussions are that Canada and the United States have:

Essentially Different Views of Government

This point has been enthroned in the juxtaposition of "life, liberty, and the pursuit of happiness" from the Declaration of Independence and "peace, order, and good government" in the 1867 British North America Act. For Canadians, government is a friend; official authority is viewed positively; and it is lamentable and regarded as exceptional when individual politicians and governments do not live up to anticipated standards. "Adscam" is thus an aberration—almost an accident occurring in a fit of political absent-mindedness (and certainly not the norm). In contrast, Americans are not inherently hostile to government, but there is a distinctly skeptical edge in their view of its operation and the degree of authority it should hold over individuals. Historically, on too many occasions, governments have been pit bulls, endangering rather than protecting their citizens, and should therefore have a short leash, perhaps with a choke chain for extra assurance.

Basically Different Political Structures

The different political philosophies are reflected in the structures that implement them. Hence the Canadian parliamentary system (and Canada's Parliament is about as strongly centralized as any democratic state can be) maximizes the potential strength of a governing party. If government is believed to be "good," politicians can normally be trusted to do good. They will not abuse the powers that they inherently hold through practiced self-restraint and personal ethics, and Parliament will act efficiently and quickly to implement the will of the government (and the desires of the people who elected it).

In contrast, the American republic reflects the skepticism of its citizens about government. The Constitution virtually revels in checks and balances; the system may have been described as "dysfunctional" by the short-time and now-departed Canadian ambassador to the U.S. (Frank McKenna), but it was profoundly important to the founders of the American republic. Each of the three branches of government (executive, legislative, and judicial) has significant powers and authority to prevent action by the others. Within the legislative branch, the Senate can prevent action by the House of Representatives and *vice versa*. A significant action must have very substantial support throughout the government and reflect the desires of the general population to be implemented as law. The American system's weakness is the potential for deadlock; its strength lies in the degree to which it reflects the interests of the American people and the rights of individual states.

Differing Views on the Role of Labor

Canada remains significantly more unionized than the United States, particularly within all levels of government. Unions tend to be more politicized and stand further to the left on the political spectrum than those in the United States. Canadians, for the most part, hold that unions—like government—are designed to protect the little guy, not to damage business. In contrast, the prospect of striking health care workers—let alone diplomats—is still anathema to most U.S. citizens. Hence President Ronald Reagan could fire striking air traffic controllers in 1981 at no political price. The U.S. economy, enjoying prosperity throughout much of the past generation, has moved far from the 19th-century or Great Depression–driven fears of robber baron capitalism. Rather than being viewed as protecting the rights of workers, union officials are regarded by some Americans as vaguely respectable miscreants at worst or, at best, supporters of a featherbedding work force interested in preserving jobs rather than increasing productivity.

Contrasting Approaches to Social Problems

Both Canada and the United States seek a healthy, safe and secure, and well-educated citizenry that limits the use of addictive substances. Canada believes that health and education essentially should be delivered through government funding; Canadian taxes are higher to provide for the universal delivery of such services. The United States contends that the individual should have primary responsibility for obtaining health services and education at the postsecondary level. The United States remains deeply concerned over the use of narcotic drugs, starting with marijuana and moving through the ranks of addictive drugs, including cocaine, heroin, and other pharmacological creations, such as LSD. Canadian concerns appear somewhat abstract: more than having any moral or medical worry about drug use, Canadians seem to fear that the United States would react with draconian border controls if Canada decriminalized narcotics use. Of course, drugs often move from Canada to the United States, rather than vice versa, and thus there may be something of a "where you sit is where you stand" view of the problem by Canadians. Canadians appear to some American observers to be more concerned about the use of tobacco than marijuana.

American and Canadian views on the death penalty and gun ownership are 180 degrees at variance—at least at the official level. While the United States notes that the death penalty cures recidivism (and hence the Oklahoma City bomber, Timothy McVeigh, will not murder again), Canada appears to believe that it is morally superior by professing that the likes of a Karla Homolka and Paul Bernardo eventually should have fresh opportunities to enjoy freedom. Thus it is only with great reluctance that Canadian courts will extradite to the United States those accused of crimes warranting capital punishment within the U.S. And often the extradition process for those sought for crimes in the United States is excruciatingly protracted.

Coincidentally, the U.S. attitude towards firearms is embedded in its citizens' suspicion of authority and a historical bias that recalls the

Revolutionary War "Minuteman" as an essential element of its liberty. It is a myth, but a defining one. Hence, the likelihood of a U.S. national gun registry remains close to zero, and even the most unlikely political candidate is forced to demonstrate familiarity with weapons and joyfully slay unoffending wildlife. In contrast, many Canadians tend to believe that only aberrant individuals would want to own firearms and a 500-fold cost overrun in a national gun registry may be a lamentable waste of funds, but it remains a necessary control over the curious minority who want to possess weapons of individual destruction.

Significantly Differing Approaches to International Security and National Defense

As a superpower, the United States has wider—indeed global—interests and a greater ability to implement and defend its interests than does Canada. While Washington is willing to consult with others and even modify elements of its approaches and objectives if given convincing reasons to do so, it remains willing to act on its perception of its interests—alone, if necessary. Its willingness to act unilaterally reflects its ability to do so. Canada believes that significant international action—particularly force of arms—can only be taken in conjunction with allies and, if possible, with the sanction of the United Nations. By a systematic although somewhat absent-minded long-term neglect of its defense establishment, Canada virtually abdicated from significant military action. It is still to be determined whether Canada's venture into a NATO-Afghanistan commitment is a one-off exercise or a return to an earlier era. The intensely divided citizenry and very narrow May 2006 parliamentary endorsement of a continued participation suggests the former as Canada's future.

Consequently, to be able to defend and implement its global interests, the U.S. maintains a massive defense establishment at high expense and employs the most advanced technology both for offense and defense. In contrast, Canada's armed forces are marginal; they are now far below what its economy could maintain or what comparable countries do support. In effect, Canada has subcontracted its defense to the United States, making the actuarial judgment that it could never defend itself against attack from the south, but that any external threat to Canada would also threaten the United States—and the U.S. would have to address it. Hence, Canada can be defended badly at great expense or badly at little expense. With health care being more popular than a modernized military, the Canadian choice has been an antiquated military and it is likely to remain so, regardless of temporary upgrades of equipment or personnel increases.

In our discussion of such alternative North Americas, we intend to explore these various topics from our respective perspectives. The reader will certainly see the variances in approach and judgment; however, it is not our intent to be "shouting heads." Sometimes, there will be point–counterpoint and at other times clear coincidence of views.

American and Canadian Perceptions of Each Other

Over the decades, the lack of prior American experience with Canada has been a diplomatic and political constant. (It is relevant that the foreign ministries of other countries usually lump Canada and the United States into a "North America bureau.") The U.S. has specialists for other areas of the world: "China hands" deal with Beijing relations; a chrysanthemum club dominates bilateral relations with Japan; "Arabists" deal with the Middle East; and diplomats can still spend the core of their careers devoted to Russia, Germany or France. Indeed, there are others who have spent most of their study and careers in South America, where (with the exception of Brazil and Haiti, at least) there is only one foreign language to learn, albeit with multiple sharply differing cultures to master. And others have been fascinated with sub-Saharan Africa (the northern part of the continent belongs to the Arabists), despite the prospects of illnesses and isolated assignments.

There is no comparable "Canada corps." To be sure there is always a handful of individuals who, reflecting the predictable ties of birth, marriage, family relationships, and/or warm memories of summer cottages, have a continuing interest in Canada. But despite the healthy profusion of Canada studies courses in U.S. universities, not to mention the unprecedented bilateral economic relationship, U.S. diplomats assigned to Canada are generalists, virtually never with previous Canada experience. In contrast, Canada sends its A-team to Washington and a substantial element of its diplomatic corps specializes in managing the relationship.

Why should this be? The answer is obvious from the American perspective: "You are just like us." To be sure, this perception is completely wrong, and the first thing an American learns upon assignment to Canada is never to say, "You're just like us!" A favorite little exposition on this point was attributed to one of Canada's ambassadors to the United States, Derek Burney, and went as follows:

> Americans are proud of what they are—Americans!
> Canadians are proud of what they are not—Americans!
> Canadians are unrestrained in the advice they offer Americans.
> Americans offering advice to Canadians face a double whammy. If they say anything, it may be seen as provocative. It they say nothing, that can be even more offensive.
> Americans know they are Number One, but wonder whether it will last.
> Canadians know they are not Number One, but wonder if their country will last.
> Americans are still inspired by the American dream.
> Canadians are reluctant to dream, except with the benefit of federal/provincial consensus (*et dans les deux langues officielles*).
> Americans think the best compliment they can offer is, "You're just like us."
> For Canadians, the highest form of flattery is to be told, "You know, you really are different."

Nevertheless, many similarities are real. On a geographic basis, there is no reason for the existence of two countries in the northern portion of North America. Mountain ranges run north-south rather than east to west. The St. Lawrence River and the Great Lakes are more transport systems into the center of the continent rather than natural dividing lines. Other major river systems, such as the Missouri-Mississippi, run north to south.

Nor is Canada really the second-largest country on earth (next to Russia). In technical square kilometer/mile terms, that description may be true, but in socio-economic terms Canada is a country approximately 350 kilometers/200 miles wide and 6,000 kilometers/3,500 miles long, snuggled up to the U.S. border. Imagine a horizontal Chile attempting to keep warm. Approximately 85 to 90 percent of the Canadian population lies within that 350-kilometer/200-mile belt; indeed, there is only one significant population center (Edmonton) outside the imaginary boundary line.

On a region by region basis, Canada's east to west ties are significantly weaker than its north to south bonds. During the 19th and early 20th centuries, the difference between a Canadian and an American might well be defined as the difference between an immigrant who turned right rather than left while trekking across the continent. For an extended period, the population drifted back and forth across these borders drawn by the prospect of richer/cheaper land, better water, closer rail heads, etc. Whose label was on these empty lands was politically irrelevant to the economic immigrant.

Canada's Maritime provinces are thus closely connected with the "Boston states" and many of the same immigrant groups populated both areas. Historical information about the founding fathers and mothers of some of the Maritime provinces indicates how much they benefited from the American Revolution. The losing "Tory/Loyalist" populations frequently migrated to Canadian east coast sites. The demography of some of the New England states and upper New York reflects francophone Quebeckers pursuing early industrial/factory opportunities. The numbers incorporated in that "brawn drain" are of such magnitude that had they stayed in or returned to Quebec, the results of the 1995 referendum would likely have been different.

Similarly, the connections between Ontario, New York, Michigan, and other states of the old U.S. industrial heartland make it the greatest trading partnership in the world—exceeded only by the trade between the United States and Canada. The grain basket provinces of Manitoba and Saskatchewan connect nicely with the grain-producing states of the U.S. Midwest as an extension of the Great Plains.

Alberta could be Texas North so far as its concentration on cattle and oil and natural gas is concerned. U.S. financing and petroleum expertise were a significant factor in Alberta's early energy development, and U.S. investment in Alberta continues. At one point in the early 1990s, both the mayor of Calgary and the head of the Chamber of Commerce were or had been U.S. citizens. In the West, the Cascadia concept, including British Columbia, Washington, and Oregon, brings together timber, salmon, and a lifestyle that emphasizes the great outdoors with an enthusiasm undampened by too many days of rain per year. And if B.C.'s politics are "wacky," residents have yet to elect movie stars as their premiers as have Californians, but perhaps that is in their future as British Columbia further develops its film industry.

These geographic and economic relationships have been endlessly reinforced by marriage, dual nationality, and immigration. Canadians are well aware of their nationals who have been prominent in U.S. media (William Shatner, the late Peter Jennings, Michael J. Fox, etc.) or enormous cultural successes in both societies (Margaret Atwood, the late Robertson Davies, Pamela Anderson, Shania Twain). They are probably less aware of Canadians with previous U.S. citizenship or rights to it, figures as diverse as Conservative MP Diane Ablonczy, former NDP MP Svend Robinson, and *Globe and Mail* national columnist Jeffrey Simpson. Some years ago, it was noted that the third highest number of illegal immigrants in the United States came from Canada. Nobody noticed (or cared) because U.S. society is so diverse and multicultural and multiracial that not even the occasional "eh" was noteworthy. Thus the 2001 *New Yorker* cartoon featuring a man saying to a woman, "You seem familiar yet somehow strange—are you by any chance Canadian?"

And the obverse is tritely true. Nowhere else in the world can a U.S. citizen instantly blend into the demographic landscape, betrayed neither by "visible minority" status nor by cultural or linguistic comment. There are no racial, cultural, ethnic, or religious elements represented in one country that are absent in the other. Thus it could happen—and did—that a Chinese-American U.S. diplomat visiting a Quebec language rally was mistaken for an allophone (an immigrant whose first language is neither English nor French), mistaken in British Columbia for a native Canadian, and also informed that the diplomatic tax-free status identification was "not good off the reserve."

There are a limited number of countries in the world where the overwhelming percentage of the population speaks English. The benefits of life in the "First World" sometimes must be articulated to their citizens to be appreciated. First, Canada is a sophisticated political democracy with deep respect for human rights, the rule of law, free elections, and with constitutional guarantees in the Charter of Rights and Freedoms that largely mirror parallel protections in the United States Constitution. Countries such as these are in short supply. Indeed, in this regard, the world *does* "need more Canada."

Second, Canadian politics and elections are not only regulated by law but are essentially "free and fair." Despite the mindless vitriol spewed during a Question Period or an election campaign, the level of riotous disturbance in the streets, even after the most closely contested election, is less than after a Stanley Cup or World Series victory: the armed forces remain in their barracks. To be able to argue a position—and not be killed for deviance from the norm—is a given, appreciated more in its absence. Yet for those with personal or professional experience with the politics of other nations, this tranquility generates a daily silent blessing.

Third, Canada is very high tech; essentially any technology that exists in the United States is also available in Canada and vice versa. Living where your automobile, plumbing, or video system can be repaired—correctly, the first time—gives one a sigh of relief. One's children don't have to be sent to private schools away from home to get a competitive education or have parents gambling with correspondence courses and local schools rather than deprive themselves of the (mixed) pleasures of raising the next generation. Personal safety in your home, on streets, or highways is essentially a given. Even the variety of complaints that one hears from Canadians and reads about in the media reflects the complaints (medical services, school quality, public utilities, problems with children, potholes) that dominate the concerns of many U.S. citizens.

Moreover, doing business—bureaucratic as well as economic—is easy in Canada. An ostensibly trivial, but still important, reality is that Ottawa and Washington are in the same time zone. Our societies are not six hours "behind," as we are with European colleagues, nor do we have to wait for Tokyo to be up and running (or stumble about for the correct date in dealing with countries across the international date line). Officials at all levels, up to and including presidents and prime ministers, can talk to one another directly. There is not even the inconvenience of overseas dialing codes; the North American communications grid, with the same electrical voltage, allows instant access. Carry your laptop computer from Calgary or Vancouver to Washington or New York and you will still have no more problems accessing the Internet than you might have between the upstairs and downstairs of your home. The connectivity is social and cultural as well as technical.

Laws, regulations, codes, reports, and all of the impediments of litigious, lawyer-driven cultures are fully present in both countries. With the exception of Jean Chrétien in his younger days, lawyers do not punch each other out in the streets; they have it out verbally in the courtroom. Even many of our holidays coincide, ranging from obvious dates in the Christian religious calendar such as Christmas and Easter to historical points (Remembrance/Veterans Day). Canadian Thanksgiving roughly parallels U.S. Columbus Day; Victoria Day is close to Memorial Day. Our national days (July 1 and July 4) are close enough to make it a holiday vacation week for those close to the border.

Consequently, although paying polite attention to the "you really are very different" maxim, U.S. visitors frequently come to the mistaken conclusion that we are just about the same (Canadians are "disarmed Americans with health insurance").

Without question there is an enormous difference between a country whose population approaches 300 million and one of approximately 32 million. Moreover, there is a comparable difference in economic capacity and output and differences in military strength that are even more dramatic. Nevertheless, while the statistical differences attract the most attention, they are only one part of the matrix of differences.

Americans' Perceptions of Canadians

Americans think that Canadians are very sensitive. As an illustration of Canadian hypersensitivity towards the United States, recall the reaction during the 1992 World Series in Atlanta. A U.S. Marine color guard ventured forth with the Canadian flag upside down. Reportedly, when looking at the flag the Marine decided that the maple leaf normally would be falling or hanging downward and so arranged the colors. In the United States, to fly the stars and stripes upside down is a distress signal. Carrying the Canadian flag upside down certainly distressed many Canadians, and it instantly became an international incident. While a comparable error with the U.S. flag would have been laughed off, President GHW Bush felt compelled to telephone Prime Minister Mulroney to apologize personally, and the Marines requested the opportunity to carry the flag in the next game (normally the countries rotated color guards) to get it right. Unsurprisingly, somewhat later at a Pan American Games event, another nation paraded the Canadian flag upside down with not 1 percent of the commotion accorded the World Series error.

Canadian politicians, particularly the Liberals, also emphasize their independence from the United States. During the 1993 campaign, Liberal leader Jean Chrétien as part of his "cassette" stump speech regularly declared that Canada "would not be the 51st state of America" and announced that he didn't want to be "Bill Clinton's fishing buddy." The transparent tactic was to contrast Chrétien to the departed Mulroney, but it became baseless bombast to a U.S. political observer. Prime Minister Paul Martin duplicated this tactic in his 2004 and 2006 campaigns against Stephen Harper's Conservatives; the latter episode was more intense but less effective than the first. Such ritualistic rhetoric seems to be genetically imprinted on the Liberal forebrain when campaigning—especially against any party that suggests the United States is not a codeword for "Great Satan." In effect, the U.S. response would be, "Who asked you?" so far as becoming a state of the union was concerned. Why should the U.S. seek to add 32 million more liberal Democrats to its electorate at this juncture in its political history?

There is also a paranoid (and clearly limited) community that remains convinced that the United States is about to invade and conquer Canada. It is as if a skittish citizen living next door to a large muscular male is intellectually convinced that he is committed to law-abiding activity but constantly worries about what would happen to him or his property if the neighbor went over to "the dark side." In the early 1990s, this belief was illustrated by a toxic little tome (*Bordering on Aggression*) whose cover illustration superimposed U.S. Army Blackhawk helicopters against the Ottawa Peace Tower. Under this logic, the creation of the 10th Mountain Division at Fort Drum, New York, was to supply the lead combat element for the U.S. invasion force. In fact, the placement of the 10th at Fort Drum was an illustration of then Senator Patrick Moynihan's ability to rip some pork from the coalition of Southern senators who had overloaded Georgia, Mississippi, and the Carolinas with military bases throughout the decades. At the same time, those who are most strident in professed concern about the prospect of U.S. military aggression are uninterested in expanding the Canadian Forces.

Insecurity is a corollary to the sensitivity. Instead of deriving confidence from its unique accomplishments, Canada downgrades itself unnecessarily. Thus the suggestion is endlessly recycled that when the United States gets a cold, it is pneumonia for Canada. Another example is Pierre Trudeau's famous elephant and mouse metaphor, exclaiming that no matter how docile or respectful the elephant, whenever it moves, the mouse becomes nervous. However, with Trudeau gone, it is also time to inter this self-denigrating comparison. Canadians should consider the potential relationship between an 800-pound gorilla and an 80-pound chimpanzee as a better reference point. The objective of the chimp should be to out-think the gorilla and use its strength to its own benefit. Such a jujitsu maneuver might see the United States providing a market for 85 percent of Canadian exports and defending Canada gratis. From that perspective, it is hard to see why the "mouse" is quite as nervous as it is—or professes to be.

U.S. interest in Canadian sports also stimulates outpourings of angst. In the mid-1990s, there was a boomlet for Canadian-style football in the United States with a number of Canadian football franchises opening in a wide range of cities. Although this experiment ultimately failed, some of the teams, notably the Baltimore Stallions, were quite good. But instead of stimulating Canadian pride that their faster, more creative version of the sport was developing a U.S. audience, there was endless anguish over the potential for U.S. players taking over the sport and dominating it to the detriment of homegrown Canadian players.

Another variant has been the growth of interest in hockey in the United States and the transfer (or prospective transfer) of failing hockey franchises from Canada to the U.S. Somehow the United States was implicitly guilty of stealing these franchises—such as the Quebec Nordiques, who went on to win the Stanley Cup as the Colorado Avalanche—by the unfair practice of providing money. Did Canadians believe that professional hockey players should profess poverty as their objective? Perhaps the most amusing outburst was connected with the Anaheim, California, franchise naming itself the Mighty Ducks—after a highly successful Disney film. Apparently, the name was regarded as frivolous for something as sacrosanct as hockey. So instead of eagerly viewing the team as poultry prime for plucking by upscale Canadian teams, the response often seemed to be that the U.S. was compromising Canada's birthright and not paying due deference to the Zen of hockey. It would have been more appropriate to follow the suggestion attributed to former Quebec premier René Lévesque to "take a valium" and await developments.

Canadians' Perceptions of Americans

For their part, Canadians generate reciprocal stereotypes. Canadians view Americans as insufferably arrogant and indifferent to the interests of any citizen except a U.S. one. Americans are insular, self-centered, and hyperpatriotic flag-wavers. These Canadian attitudes are not regarded as "anti-American," but as reasoned judgments about southern neighbors whose deliberate penchant for wrong course selection is individually, nationally, and globally dangerous. Seeking respect and appreciation of themselves as good neighbors, allies, and friends, Canadians have been increasingly concerned over a unilateralist United States, convinced of the correctness of its decisions in virtually every foreign and domestic arena, bulling (and bullying) its way forward on the basis of brute military, economic, and cultural strength. Such historical American tendencies have been exacerbated by the presidency of "Dubya" Bush, who was widely viewed as essentially ignorant and anti-intellectual (regardless of his Yale and Harvard degrees) and whose born-again Christianity embraced socially archaic attitudes towards abortion, gay marriage, and soft drugs such as marijuana. According to this view,

George W. Bush was seeking to make the 1950s the "future" of the United States and drag Canada in the same direction as well.

If the British in the Second World War thought of American GIs as "over paid, over sexed, and over here," Canadians are comparably fatigued by a country whose economy is "over inflated," its military "over aggressive," and its culture "over plebian." Canadians shudder at the thought of more Americans without health insurance than the population of Canada, and of death statistics from the Center for Disease Control that show more Americans killed by firearms (approximately 30,000 in 2003) and in automobile accidents (approximately 40,000 in 2002) than the populations of significant Canadian communities.

In this view, if the United States now finds itself threatened by terrorists, 9/11 was at least partly Washington's fault for not being properly respectful to the interests of Arab states in the Middle East and Muslim concerns worldwide (coupled with its relentless support of Israel in disregard for Palestinian rights). The U.S. should be more responsive to the concerns of international organizations, not just the United Nations (which admittedly, even to many Canadians, has some flaws) but more recently developed organizations such as the International Criminal Court. Moreover, if the United States is to lead internationally in an appropriately ethical manner commensurate with its economic and military strength, it should endorse and fully support treaties such as those banning antipersonnel landmines and those that seek to improve the global environment such as the Kyoto Protocol. But ultimately the power of the mighty should be harnessed to the concerns of the many; the United States is ignoring this maxim.

Nevertheless, even under the circumstances of the early 21st century, Canadians generally like Americans—or at least so the polls (which admittedly are up and down) continue to indicate. They do not, however, want to *be* like Americans. Indeed, Canadians professing worries and concerns about retaining their culture and remaining distinctly Canadian can appear overwrought at best, paranoid at worst. To be sure, this attitude can be amusing—as epitomized by the rant by "Joe Canada" to sell Molson's beer. It was so successful that he got an offer from a U.S. agency and promptly decamped for Hollywood. (Subsequently, he returned to Toronto, where he has continued his acting career without further ranting.)

For Americans, the Canadian emphasis on their difference elicits only shrug-of-the-shoulder indifference. And, to be sure, it is just another facet of not paying attention to their northern neighbors. After all, what significant nation emphasizes that it is *not* another? But Canadians seem to need to rip up their social, political, and emotional roots on a regular basis to examine them. Such an exercise isn't conducive to growth.

At a point in history when our two countries are either agonizing over or reveling in bilateral differences, we believe it is useful to step back and take another look at this ever-evolving relationship. For the foreseeable future, when we get up in the morning, we will still inhabit the same continent. It is close to being historically unique that our differences have been more often benign than bloody. Most people are better haters than forgivers; most proximate relationships between the vastly more powerful and the vastly less powerful end invidiously for the latter. From one perspective, Canada is the equivalent of a disabled person in a solid gold wheelchair; happily the United States has not played the thug that history normally documents. But Canada wants (and arguably deserves) more than benign neglect. Can Canada make a difference, and, if so, how? Are its alternative approaches a useful and productive guideline into the forest of the 21st century? Or is it blazing a trail to nowhere with idealistic social, economic, and political/international approaches and policies that would require saints to administer and sinless congregations to implement?

Tough questions and tough answers need not be mean-spirited ones. We intend to pose and explore these questions, their answers, and some ramifications. On both sides of the border, there has been a plethora of unloving critics—and uncritical lovers. There are puzzling and often unapproachable shibboleths, such as water as a commodity, or sovereignty over the Arctic and its Northwest Passage in the North, or the generation-long struggle over when life begins and ends in the South. Those who claim a monopoly on truth, virtue, or the "right answers" are usually wrong on all counts. Black and white are such vivid colors; gray seems appropriate only for middle-muddle bureaucrats, but gray can make a fashion statement in its own right. It will be the reader's decision as to what color is preferable for the next stage of our relationship.

NATIONAL IDENTITY AND SELF-IMAGE 1

Individuals search for their distinctiveness, and so do nations. Both the United States and Canada have expressed identities by moving along different paths. The United States has emphasized (and is willing to enforce) unity; Canada has tolerated an almost unprecedented level of disunity and has remained one country. Indeed, a history of regional discontent, separatism, and alienation between its national government and both provinces and regions has marked Canada's existence since birth and may be a defining element of its nationality.

Thus, to some, the Canadian experiment in political diversity is the structure for the future: federalism permitting enormous local variance within a loose political structure. Some Canadians suggest that the United States has its problems ahead of it, rather than behind it, as various U.S. minorities appear less willing to adopt the longstanding "melting pot" concept. For others, however, the Canadian example has the fragility of spun glass. To some Americans, the Canadian model looks like a bear dancing; the criticism is not that the bear dances badly, but surprise that the bear dances at all. The question remains for them whether the bear will continue to dance.

For Canada the "bear" is primarily Quebec; its care and feeding are of primary political concern. Some surface-skimming observers have suggested that Canadians are Americans "with a French accent." The observation is neither profound nor accurate; nevertheless, the "Quebec problem" has been in reality the defining national issue for Canada. Unresolved year after year, it leaves Canadian unity in question and at risk in a way that cannot but hobble future decision-making on other topics, as it has done in the past. Canada may be groping towards a new self-image, a concept of "nations" in Canada with asymmetric federalism as the norm, rather than continuing to hope in vain that Quebeckers will ever again come to view themselves as essentially French-speaking Canadians.

The most recent iteration of circle-squaring has Parliament defining the *Québécois* as a nation "within a united Canada." What a question beggar is this formulation. Does the description imply that the province of Quebec, the province housing those *Québécois,* is akin to a kidney or a lung with no ability to survive on its own? And just what then is the rest of Canada? Is the ROC also a nation "united" around the nation of *Québécois* in some yet-to-be-defined socio-political manner? Or is Quebec more equivalent to an unborn child with an undetermined gestation period?

To be sure, if a new label ("nation") for the *Québécois* political reality proves sufficient to satisfy those francophones dubious about their extended life as Canadians, it will be a trivial adjustment in nomenclature. If a rose is a rose is a rose, then a French-Canadian, a Quebecker, a *Québécois,* is still a Canadian. However, it is more likely that Quebec separatists will simply pocket this concession and demand more specific substantive concessions to transform the national "name" into an independent nation "game."

In the United States, most Americans believe that the essential issue of national unity is behind them; the Civil War remains the seminal event of all U.S. history. There is no serious discussion of any element separating from the rest of the country, regardless of the level of mutual irritation. It is not prescient to observe that U.S. minorities are spread throughout the country and thus they have sought political power (and protection) on a federal level. And while non-European-origin communities have governed a state, no minority has ever obtained comprehensive political power in a state or region.

Consequently, the latest polarization in U.S. politics has been much bruited about, but it is more apparent than real. There is no expectation that these states (or their residents) are interested in independence. Indeed, for all the rhetorically heated announcements by celebrities ostensibly committed to leaving the United States if their desired electoral outcome did not eventuate in 2004, U.S. emigration to Canada in the year following the election was no greater than in the one prior.

The Canadian National Dilemma: Quebec

Much of the world probably thinks of contemporary Canada as essentially problem free—a peaceful, orderly land of harmonious human diversity and prosperity, with Canadians enjoying lifelong education, good social programs, first-rate technology and possessing a beautiful and clean natural environment.

The words "Canadian identity" entered on Google.ca currently bring up fully 4,360,000 entries. In the pre-digital world, countless barrels of ink and forests of trees were consumed by books and articles on the nature of Canadians.

Our renowned national historian William L. Morton first published *The Canadian Identity* 45 years ago. Understandably, his central point then was that if Canada wished to enjoy independence in concert with the Commonwealth and the United States, it would have to achieve a "self-determination of greater clarity and more ringing tone than it has yet done." This, for Morton, was a task for every Canadian; he urged us to assume it with "good humour and without animosity, as would benefit perhaps the most fortunate country on earth and times in which all sovereignties are becoming conditional and all nations something less than independent."

Little could Morton then anticipate that the European scholar-diplomat W. Robert Cooper would write in the first years of the 21st century, in *The Breaking of Nations*, that the encroachment of chaos, aided by technology, could result in catastrophe for the world. Fortunately, Cooper added that "better politics" could still build sustainable peace around the planet. The key argument in this chapter will be that first-class statecraft is going to be needed to preserve Canada as a single magnificent example for a turbulent world as well.

The Canadian Shield and the Creation of Canada

Like most Canadian historians, Morton always understood the importance of the Canadian Shield, which comprises about half the country's land mass and stretches from the east coast of Labrador almost to the mouth of the Mackenzie River in the Northwest Territories. Probably no one has ever described the Shield better than Jacques Cartier, the French explorer and founder of Montreal, when in 1534 he said of the bleak and rocky Labrador coast that it was "the land that God gave Cain."[1] It was perhaps more conducive to prosperity than it appeared to Cartier, however, since for centuries afterwards many Canadians earned their living from the fur and mines of the Shield and fish from its rivers and coasts.

French fur traders, fishermen, and missionaries followed Cartier up the St. Lawrence and by 1700, then numbering only about 16,000, had mostly driven their English rivals from present-day Canada. Peace negotiations in

---

1. Cartier journal, quoted in *Source Book of Canadian History*, Harry S. Crowe, J. H. Stewart Reid, Kenneth McNaught. Toronto: Longmans, 1959, p. 9.

Europe leading to the Treaty of Utrecht, however, soon undid most of their efforts when France ceded Hudson Bay, most of Newfoundland, and all of "Acadia" to the Anglo-Americans. Undismayed, residents of New France by 1750 had managed to recover and extend their fur empire to what is now Winnipeg. Negotiations and treaty settlements following yet another European war, however, removed much of these gains.

In 1759, General James Wolfe and the British army defeated Louis-Joseph Montcalm, commander of French troops in North America, on the plain beside Quebec City. The following year, the Anglo-American army captured Montreal; the subsequent Treaty of Paris left the once dominant France only a Newfoundland shore and the tiny Saint Pierre and Miquelon islands in the St. Lawrence River. Astonishingly, in hindsight, the French negotiators took the sugar-rich island of Guadeloupe in the Caribbean; Britain took Canada.

From 1759 until today, cultural and linguistic tensions have persisted between Quebeckers and other Canadians. Fortunately for contemporary Canada, the British colonial government, after a decade of declining to do so, finally accommodated the approximately 60,000 French-speaking residents who stayed on after the colonial officials returned to Paris. The British Parliament's Quebec Act of 1794 guaranteed Quebeckers their civil law systems and existing religious practices.

Almost two decades after the British conquest, following the American War of Independence, came an exodus of thousands of loyalists, mostly into what are not only today's Atlantic provinces and Ontario, but also Quebec. There are Americans who suggest that Canadians should be profoundly grateful for the War of Independence as it provided some of Canada's most vigorous and successful settlers. Imperial London eventually divided central Canada into largely French-Catholic Lower Canada and Anglo-Protestant Upper Canada.

Neither colony enjoyed representative self-government because the governors and executive council members were appointed from London, even though the assemblies were elected by the local residents. The French majority in the Assembly of Lower Canada, however, led by Louis Joseph Papineau, to its credit continued to push for the election of executive council members. In Upper Canada, William Baldwin and his son Robert argued for "responsible government" under which the executive council members must also be members of the assembly and be responsible to its membership. An armed rebellion broke out in Lower Canada in 1837, followed by another in Upper

Canada, which was led by William Lyon Mackenzie. Both, however, were put down quickly by British soldiers and local volunteers.

This crisis of democracy caused the British cabinet to send John George Lambton (the Earl of Durham, known as "Radical Jack") out to Canada as governor. Unhelpfully, Durham recommended uniting the two Canadas in order to allow an English-speaking majority to eliminate the French language over time. This failed largely because of the willingness of English-speaking legislators and others to respect their French-speaking compatriots in the assembly and courts. More prudently, Durham eventually accepted the Baldwin model of responsible government, provided Britain kept control of trade and foreign affairs, the constitution, and public lands. Our present national and provincial model of responsible government was finally achieved only after 1846, when the colonial governors began to accept political party ministries and to conduct themselves as constitutional monarchs.

The factors leading to Confederation in 1867 were complex, but one, the need for some provinces to hold strong legislative and administrative powers, is vital from the standpoint of Quebec continuing within Canada today. Partly driven by concern about possible fallout from the American Civil War, a union among the three Atlantic provinces and Canada began to seem essential in the early 1860s. Remarkably, given our subsequent national history, the proposed constitution was not strongly protective of provincial rights, a factor that was no doubt influenced by what strong states were then doing to themselves in the United States. Later, the judicial committee of Britain's Privy Council, as the final appeal court, did breathe real power into the provincial legislatures in a series of key decisions. By the spring of 1867, parliamentarians from Canada, Nova Scotia, New Brunswick, and the Imperial Parliament enacted and ratified the British North America Act as Canada's first constitution.

Linguistic and other shocks aplenty were to follow for francophone Quebeckers. First came the two Riel Rebellions, led by the French-speaking founder of Manitoba, Louis Riel, who understandably now wanted dignity for the Metis residents of the tiny new province. In due course, thanks to Riel's agitation, the Manitoba Act of 1870 confirmed that residents of the new province could speak French in their assembly and courts. Fifteen years later, overlooking the voices of French-Canadians across the country, Prime Minister John A. Macdonald made a colossal error from the standpoint of national unity when, after a deeply flawed trial ended in Riel's conviction for treason, Macdonald did not spare Riel's life. Nationalists in Quebec have ever since argued that this prominent national issue demonstrated their lack of influence in Ottawa.

Americans had no intellectual qualms about suppressing rebellion. The Civil War is the best example of this, but there were also several uprisings against federal authority soon after the conclusion of the revolutionary war; they were promptly ended by federal military action. In U.S. eyes, however, the Riel execution was a tactical error. In contrast, after the Civil War, the U.S. did not "hang Jeff Davis from a sour apple tree" as sought by many Northerners, but imprisoned him for a relatively short period. No Confederate political leader or prominent military commander was executed for the equivalent of war crimes. Although executions would have been momentarily satisfying (and certainly supported in the North), they would have further delayed the reconciliation that, nevertheless, took much of the next century to achieve.

The Riel debacle, from a national unity perspective, was quickly followed by another in Prairie Canada. After the Manitoba Act was enacted in 1870, thousands of English-speaking settlers flooded into the new province. The established French-speaking and Catholic majority in the province, which had been assured of equal language rights and rights to Catholic schools, watched with dismay as provincial legislators, now representative of the new English-speaking majority, removed both the official status of French and the separate school systems. Sovereignists in Quebec continue today to denounce both these measures enacted in 1890 although the Supreme Court upheld the Manitoba Act 80 years later.

Ontario's Regulation 17 had a similar effect on unity right next door to Quebec. The Quebec government had permitted its Protestant schools to operate in English continuously after Confederation, but in 1913 the Whitney government's regulation all but abolished the use of French in Ontario schools. When the courts in effect upheld the validity of the regulation, Canada took another severe linguistic blow to its unity. The regulation was eventually repealed, but not until a decade later.

Two other major English-French confrontations involved conscription in both the First and Second World Wars. Robert Borden's government resorted to mandatory military service in 1917 because volunteer recruitment was not producing enough reinforcements for a terrible war persisting in Europe. Many Quebeckers regarded the conflict as simply not Canada's business. When Borden attempted to enforce the conscription law a year later, a riot broke out in Quebec City. Four persons died and many were injured when the army attempted to end the demonstration.

From the all-important unity standpoint, the conscription crisis during the Second World War was much better handled, although many Canadians outside Quebec objected to what they felt was Ottawa's "game playing" with national security. Although Canada made its own decisions regarding the level of its military contributions in the First World War, by 1939 it was no longer a colony and the government of William Lyon Mackenzie King was free to be more cautious, in a constitutional sense, about sending soldiers to help defeat Adolf Hitler. In a plebiscite on the issue in 1939, four-fifths of the voters outside Quebec released King from his pledge not to impose conscription. In Quebec, however, fully 73 percent took the opposite view. In practice, the prime minister postponed implementing mandatory service until the war was virtually over.

In both American and Canadian eyes, Mackenzie King's fibrillations regarding the draft indicated a profound lack of leadership. During the American Civil War, there were riots against the draft, rioters died, and the draft continued. For Canada, combat losses during the Second World War fell disproportionately on English-speaking Canadians; the contempt that many of these soldiers and their families felt for King was demonstrated by their concentrated and successful campaign to defeat him in his own riding in the 1945 election. A comparable personal humiliation for President Roosevelt was not even conceivable.

Quebec's Quiet Revolution of the 1960s had a major impact on national unity as the government of Jean Lesage greatly increased the role of the provincial government, requiring much-increased tax transfers and jurisdiction sharing with the national government. Nationalists across the province wanted the legislative authority and other means to build a linguistically and culturally distinct nation, if not a country. A growing number of middle-income Quebeckers during this period began to question the province's continued role within Canada.

In Ottawa, however, Prime Minister Pierre Trudeau (1968-79, 1980-84) refused to see Quebec differently from any other province. He favored instead encouraging bilingualism across the national government and country. Conflict was inevitable and continuous between these two dominant visions. When a branch of the independence movement (the Front de Libération du Québec, or FLQ) turned to violence, including the kidnapping and murder of provincial cabinet minister Pierre Laporte, in October

1970, Trudeau invoked the highly draconian War Measures Act rather than rely on the probably adequate provisions of the Criminal Code. In fairness to the prime minister, he did so only after receiving written requests from Montreal mayor Jean Drapeau and Quebec premier Robert Bourassa. More than 400 non-violent supporters of sovereignty were soon jailed under the War Measures Act, without just cause. The FLQ was crushed, but the heavy-handed and undemocratic methods used became a real boost to the nascent sovereignty movement.

In the 1970s, despite Trudeau's centralism, the first government of Robert Bourassa in Quebec City gained provincial control over immigration and family allowances and extended French as the province's working language. The election of René Lévesque's separatist Parti Quebecois in 1976, however, shocked Canadians right across the country. His government's Bill 101 made French the only official language in the National Assembly and ultimately in practice elsewhere across the province.

The PQ referendum of 1980, on the question of pursuing "sovereignty association" with Canada, was rejected by a decisive 60 percent of Quebeckers, presumably at least in part because of the promise by Trudeau, Jean Chrétien, and other federal politicians to provide "renewed federalism." What followed were 18 months of federal-provincial negotiations, resulting in the 1982 Constitution Act, which clearly reflected the opinions of Pierre Trudeau rather than those of most Quebeckers. Both the Parti Quebecois and the provincial Liberal party rejected the decision by Trudeau and the other provincial premiers to impose the new constitution on Quebec.

By 1984 and the landslide election of Brian Mulroney as prime minister, partly in response to Trudeau's concept of federalism, there was a clear need for the rest of Canada to reach out to Quebec. Robert Bourassa, once again in office as Quebec premier, alienated many outside the province by resorting to the "notwithstanding clause" of the new constitution to legislate French-only outdoor signs across the province. (By 1993, bilingual signs were permitted on outdoor signs, provided the French text was larger than the English.) The Meech Lake Accord, intended to win Bourassa and Quebeckers back into the constitutional family, partly through recognizing the province as a distinct society, was not approved in the required time by the Manitoba and Newfoundland legislatures. Many Quebeckers were disappointed and support for sovereignty grew in Quebec. Several members of Parliament from both the Conservatives and Liberals joined Lucien Bouchard's new political party, the Bloc Quebecois, as Quebec sovereignists.

The next attempt at national harmony was the Charlottetown Accord, which contained most of the Meech Lake proposals, including distinct-society status for Quebec based on its French-language majority, civil law, and otherwise unique culture, and more powers for all provinces if they wished to use them. There would also be an elected Senate, similar to the one in Australia, and Aboriginal self-government. In a national referendum held on October 26, 1992, the result was 55 percent "no" and 45 percent "yes"—including 56.7 percent "no" in Quebec. The accord was dead.

In 1994, the Parti Quebecois returned to office in Quebec under Jacques Parizeau on a platform to take the province out of Confederation. In due course, a provincial referendum was called for October 30, 1995, on a highly unclear question. The Jean Chrétien government in Ottawa held to the myopic—in hindsight—view that a majority of Quebeckers would vote "no" if Chrétien could persuade them that a "yes" vote would mean separa-tion. Only in the final days of the campaign did Chrétien promise a rather vague recognition of the province as a distinct society, a Quebec veto over constitutional amendments, and decentralization of legislative authority to the provinces from Ottawa. Thousands upon thousands of Canadians from across the country staged a rally in Montreal shortly before voting day to tell Quebeckers that we wanted them to stay. A record turnout of residents—92 percent—voted: 50.6 percent "no" versus 49.4 percent "yes."

In an immediate response, Parliament passed a motion recognizing Quebec as a distinct society within Canada and enacted a law that gave each region of the country, including Quebec, a veto over all constitution-al amendments. Job skills training was also transferred from the national to provincial governments. Prime Minister Chrétien also referred to the Supreme Court of Canada the issue of whether a unilateral declaration of sovereignty by any province was legal. The unanimous decision of the court held, in part, that "a clear majority vote in Quebec on a clear question in favor of secession would confer democratic legitimacy." Chrétien then in-troduced his Clarity Act, which was designed to prevent deliberately vague referendum questions such as those posed in 1980 and 1995.

New Century

An opinion survey done in mid-2005 indicated that approximately 54 per-cent of Quebeckers then favored sovereignty for their province, although the question was not a "hard" one—that is, it didn't ask whether Quebeckers were ready to give up economic association with the rest of Canada. While it was reassuring for Canadians outside the province to attribute the rise in support for sovereignty to the effect on public opinion of some of the very troubling testimony being presented at the Gomery Inquiry, then being shown daily on television across the province, the reality was more complex. Quebeckers are a proud people, with great historical self-awareness. (Witness the slogan for vehicle license plates in Quebec: *Je me souviens*—"I remember.")

With a population of 7.5 million, approximately four-fifths of whom can speak French, Quebec is the center of francophone Canada. Many Quebeckers continue to believe that the current constitution places their culture and language under threat from the national government. Fully 60 percent of Quebec francophones, moreover, voted in the 1995 referendum in favor of provincial sovereignty. More than ever, it seems a forlorn, nostalgic hope to think that Quebeckers will ever see themselves as Canadians who happen to speak French.

What is to be done when so many earlier initiatives have failed? There are probably as many different responses as there are Canadians, but a good way to start is by reaching a consensus on the nature of our country early in a new century.

In his *Misconceiving Canada: The Struggle for National Unity*, the Ontario political scientist Kenneth McRoberts makes some important points. First, it is no longer possible—if it ever was—to integrate Quebeckers with the rest of the country through the Trudeau concept of a Canada based on the Charter of Rights, effective bilingualism, multiculturalism, and equality of the provinces. For better or worse, most Quebeckers now see themselves as a distinct community within Canada and only by abandoning the Trudeau vision in favor of a genuine attempt by all Canadians to accommodate Quebec's aspirations can we hold our country together in the new century.

The increasing reality of globalization, for better or worse, is that postmodern states such as Canada will never again be as they once were. As Robert Cooper points out, national borders are increasingly irrelevant in the 21st century. Are Canadians now prepared to accept a looser—even much looser—arrangement between Quebec and the rest of Canada? If it became necessary, would majorities in Quebec and the rest of Canada accept something just short of independence for Quebec? A good deal of the world is watching because similar situations exist in a number of other countries today. Can a cohesive linguistic or cultural community be a nation within a country—and yet not seek full independence?

A Multinational Country

It is now clear to many Canadians that we no longer inhabit a single nation and a more decentralized federalism offers a single sovereignty while giving Quebec (and our First Nations) autonomy for many purposes. As Kenneth McRoberts reminds us in *Misconceiving Canada*, Lester Pearson used the term "nation" openly in applying it to Quebec. Why not recognize our indigenous peoples as a third nation too with their own right to their languages and cultures? There is no certainty, of course, that this approach will work, but if Quebeckers are persuaded that the price of full sovereignty is economically too steep they might well be open to such an accommodation.

If, however, in response to a clear question (as now required by the Clarity Act), a clear majority of Quebeckers do at some point approve sovereignty in a referendum, the "autonomy option" will have failed. To be sure, very few of us in the rest of Canada see real similarities between the Canada-Quebec situation *today* and that of, say, Serbia-Kosovo; in mid-2005, Serb officials offered Kosovo "more than autonomy and less than independence"—an option that Kosovo has repeatedly rejected.

There is a vast range of options available short of full independence for Quebec, including asymmetrical models. With such models, if Quebec or another province has opted out of federal programs, its MPs and senators in Ottawa would not vote on issues relating to those programs. Differing Ottawa–Quebec City priorities could be accommodated by applying European models of partnership and joint–decision making.

If Quebec were to leave, the parts that remain would be fully viable as a country, having for instance one of the world's largest national economies.

The United States would never officially sponsor or encourage the breakup of Canada. It has supported the continued unity of a wide variety of countries that either successfully separated (Czechoslovakia); separated with much bloodshed (Yugoslavia); or remained united after much violence and suffering (Nigeria). While noting the right of peoples to determine their political fate, the U.S. government has made its preference clear for a united Canada. It has done so repeatedly, particularly during the 1995 referendum campaign, while attempting to avoid charges that it was interfering in Canadian domestic politics.

Nevertheless, unofficially, at least some neighboring residents appear to be relatively sanguine over the concept of an independent Quebec; a fractured Canada would be a sorrowful event, necessitating endless rearranging of bilateral relations, but it would not be a tragedy on the level of the great catastrophes that marked the 20th century. Assuming any separation occurred under democratic circumstances, Americans and their government would doubtless accept the results—as they have accepted other unpreferred but democratic decisions.

Canada does provide for some Americans a salutary negative example of the concept of multiple official languages. The Canadian example appears to suggest to some Americans that a second official language accentuates division rather than unity. It forces issues into linguistic frameworks rather than permitting them to be addressed as substantive national problems. Illustrating the U.S. attitude in this regard has been the repeated U.S. political endorsement of English as the language of national unity. The mastery of English is portrayed in the United States as a vital element for immigrant integration into society.

U.S. Self-Images and Values

The classic scholarly juxtaposition of U.S. and Canadian images has been to posit the objectives of the Declaration of Independence for "life, liberty, and the pursuit of happiness" against those of the Canadian founding act of 1867 for "peace, order, and good government."

From an American perspective, the United States certainly has not backed away from a commitment to "life, liberty, and the pursuit of happiness," regardless of how these might be defined or (mis)interpreted. Clearly, we see ourselves as inhabiting "the land of the free and the home of the brave." For those with low-range voices, our ability to sing the all-but-unsingable "Star-Spangled Banner" may be limited, but at least we don't need to navigate the lyrics in two official languages. However, our interest in patriotic songs ("America the Beautiful," "God Bless America," "Country Roads," etc.) is a constant—and not only in "red state" USA.

The Pledge of Allegiance and Building the United States

American bedrock patriotism is nurtured from the first days in elementary schools when the Pledge of Allegiance is recited by virtually every child and remembered by every adult. That pledge is reasonably short and worth examining in detail. Thus: *I pledge allegiance to the Flag of the United States of America, and to the Republic for which it stands, one Nation under God, indivisible, with liberty and justice for all.* This language covers the essence of American national unity.

Now more than a century old, the original pledge was published in the September 8, 1892, issue of *The Youth's Companion* in Boston. Authorship ultimately was credited to Francis Bellamy of the magazine's staff. The phrase "under God" was added to the pledge on June 14, 1954, and continues to generate legal controversy and commensurate political counterfire.

In passing one might note that the U.S. flag is both uniquely memorable (one of the few national flags with wide global recognition) and not an indistinct mix of various colored bars either horizontal or vertical. Also, through much of U.S. history, the flag has been a work in progress: an additional star was added for each state that became a member of the union. During the building of the United States, the addition of each star reinforced the unity of the new state with the old. It is probably the combination of the flag's unique physical design and the internalized commitment by every school child that made flag-burning so controversial over the past generation. Indeed, it took a Supreme Court decision to conclude that burning the flag was politically protected "free speech," and efforts to pass a constitutional amendment to prevent flag desecration secured congressional majorities, but not by the necessary two-thirds required for a constitutional amendment.

In its iconic position in the United States, the flag is almost in the same position as the sacred host in Christian communion. If a worshiper consumes the host in remembrance of Jesus Christ and his suffering to redeem mankind, Americans fly the flag as a symbolic representation of their belief in the United States and its virtues. Although the analogy might strike some (Christian) observers as verging on sacrilege, no democratic nation displays the flag more than does the United States or pronounces its commitment to religion more deeply.

Nor has there ever been a controversy comparable to that over Canadian veterans' desire to fly the "Red Ensign" either at the Vimy Memorial or elsewhere. U.S. troops in the First and Second World Wars and the Korean War fought under a 48-star flag. Yet all U.S. national and combat memorials, from the Marines' Iwo Jima memorial to the Tomb of the Unknowns, fly a 50-star flag that was not extant until Hawaii became a state in 1959. The only point for U.S. veterans is that the flag is an *American* flag.

Thus, the elements of the pledge can provide some insight into the bedrock aspects of U.S. values.

"A Republic, if you can keep it" (Benjamin Franklin)

A baseline question in those early days of creating the United States government was what kind of government it would be. It was far from clear what type of government would be designed: in practice, the national governing experience of the mid-18th century was limited to monarchy with some parliamentary controls. The colonies had operated for the most part under royal governors with elected parliamentary-style assemblies whose powers were highly limited and subject to dissolution by arbitrary action of the royal governor. The concept of a republic was vaguely known through historical examples (Venetian, Roman, Greek city states) and reflected in the writings of political theorists, but was far from the pragmatic experience of those "founders" of a new United States.

Indeed, the Revolutionary War was supervised by continental congresses whose representatives were selected by various means and whose powers were largely limited to what the individual states were willing to countenance. The post-Revolutionary War government under the Articles of Confederation wasn't much stronger or more coherent. Between 1781 and the Constitutional Convention in Philadelphia in 1789, the States more resembled a collage of temporarily and loosely allied tribes than anything like an organized state. Many Europeans were either contemptuous of these "United States" or anticipated that their many differences would quickly prompt their disintegration and expected that England would pick up the pieces.

To resolve the restless incoherence of the postwar United States, there were those who would have emulated European political culture by creating an American monarchical system. The obvious man to be king was George Washington: he was the most prominent military commander during the Revolutionary War, an inspiring leader from the most prominent state (Virginia), of imposing stature and flawless personal character. The monarchy was quietly offered to Washington. To his everlasting credit, he spurned the offer; his reasons are not on record, but one senses throughout the American revolutionaries a deep contempt for the intermittently mad George III and the feckless manner in which the English nobility comported itself. Revolutionaries are often puritanical; regency England was not.

Consequently, the United States was relentlessly egalitarian in its early years, at least so far as governance was concerned. And a substantial element of those who might be regarded as pro-royalist either returned to England or migrated to regions such as Canada. No U.S. official would bow to a foreign leader, regardless of what protocol demanded. These "stiff-necked Yankees" were mocked in polite European societies, but our indifference to rank-by-birth has become virtually a genetic political imprint for Americans. While there are certainly Americans who would have enjoyed a system of inherited nobility and become Duke Rockefeller, Baron Kennedy, or Count William Gates of Microsoft, the pretensions of our self-anointed and self-important social climbers have more often punctured awe than inspired it.

Americans find the peregrinations of the dysfunctional House of Windsor amusing and are happy to be able to flip the channel on the latest episode of the royal soap opera. More thoughtful Americans can appreciate the utility of separating the head of government from the head of state, if only to reduce the protocol drag of time-devouring, ritualistic activity that falls upon the president in his combined role as head of state and government. Nevertheless, the thought of a king who was once humiliated when his private expressions of sexual desire for his mistress (now wife) were leaked to the press would be even less palatable for the public than the vision of Monica Lewinsky's semen-stained dress. A president, at least, is gone in a maximum of eight years, but a monarchy can embarrass for generations.

Even in Britain, the utility of kings and queens and royal families is minimal. For U.S. citizens, the most memorable queen is as likely to be the Disneyfied "off with their heads" screamer in *Alice in Wonderland* as the long-enduring Elizabeth II. Americans take their republic and republican structure for granted now, although in 1789 it was a true anomaly. One becomes aware of how deeply it is in our political structure when a distinguished U.S. citizen must receive special approval to accept a British knighthood or a State Department protocol officer is denounced for dropping a curtsy to a visiting royal.

The U.S. National Crisis: Civil War

"Union now and forever; one and inseparable" (Abraham Lincoln)

The word in the pledge of allegiance is "indivisible" and the politics behind the word caused more death and destruction than any other political concept in U.S. history. The Civil War, doubtless the seminal event in U.S. national existence, resolved the issue of American national identity—for that moment, for now, and for the foreseeable future. Prior to the Civil War, one said "the United States *are*...." After the war, the United States became a singular rather than a plural noun: "the United States *is*...." Not a solution to be recommended, the war scarred U.S. politics and culture for a century, but it had the virtue of answering the question posed in Lincoln's Gettysburg address, whether a nation "conceived in liberty and dedicated to the proposition that all men are created equal . . . can long endure?"

It is difficult today to grasp the 19th-century emotion behind the concept of that indivisible union. Even 50 years ago it was difficult: to a boy growing up in northeastern Pennsylvania with a Union soldier among his ancestors and Gettysburg little more than 100 miles away, the word "union" was more likely to inspire a vision of a labor organization for defending workers' rights than an abstraction to die for. "Uniontown," "Union Street," and Washington's "Union Terminal" had already become names with no emotional freight. And if, 150 years after the Civil War, the union is so much a political given and so rarely mentioned that it has no modern resonance, one must provide other plausible explanations for the war—or risk it becoming as inexplicable as the fighting that took place in 12th-century Europe over the Albigensian heresy, or the War of the Roses.

To provide that explanation, Americans today tend to stress that the Civil War was fought to end slavery, an objective that is clear, concrete, and understandable in modern terms rather than the almost mystical abstraction of preserving the union. Freeing the slaves, however, was no more than a secondary cause for Abraham Lincoln. It may have been primary for abolitionists, who were consummate media experts, but for Lincoln and many others in the North, the Union was a unique and precious creation, still virtually without parallel throughout the world, and breaking it was quite literally unthinkable.

In truth, those who sought to leave the Union, for whatever reason, would appear, in the terms of today's political philosophies, to have the better intellectual case. They argued that they would never have created the United States if they had understood that they could never leave it. No one said in 1789 that the United States was the equivalent of a lobster pot wherein those that entered could not escape. Imagine, they argued, a men's club from which you could never resign—regardless of the provocation from other members. And given the evolution of political thought to embrace the Wilsonian concept of the self-determination of peoples, it would be hard to argue that the Confederacy was not a perfectly legitimate political creation. It fulfilled all the qualities necessary for a state: coherent geography; economic self-sufficiency; effective leadership; popular support. That is, it had all the qualities of a state except its inability to survive external military action.

Indeed, it was not until after the conclusion of the Civil War that the Constitution was amended to make separation in effect illegal (the 14th Amendment); a clear case of making sure that the horse will never legally leave the barn. Perhaps an *ex post facto* Clarity Act equivalent? And consequently the political and legal judgment was made that the states of the Confederacy had never left the Union, and thus did not have to be readmitted.

From this bloody historical base, the United States has been able to avoid the devolution pressures now afflicting countries such as the United Kingdom, Belgium, Spain, and Canada, let alone the disintegration of collapsing dictatorships such as the former USSR and Yugoslavia. The U.S. commitment to a "melting pot" assimilation of immigrants continues, with the recognition that ill-digested lumps in a country's demography lead to political discontent. That is not to suggest that U.S. social demography is homogeneous, but—at least at this point—it has not moved to the level of political discontent that would imply separatist pressure.

"In God we trust" (motto on U.S. currency)

Both in its history and its modern culture, religion has played a strong and persistent role. A number of U.S. colonies were founded by religious dissenters—both Catholic and Protestant—most famous among them the Plymouth, Massachusetts, colonists in 1620 and the Quakers in Pennsylvania led by William Penn. There was persistent resistance to an "established" Church, that is, an official, state-sponsored religious establishment, and one of the key elements in the U.S. Constitution is its first amendment, which *inter alia*, postulates the separation of church and state. That the ramifications of this separation continue in extended juridical cases indicates both the intensity of argument for "separation" and the commitment to religious beliefs by the majority of Americans.

Although revisionist historians have accurately noted that many of the "Founding Fathers" were religious skeptics ("Deist" was the parlance of the time), that reality does not detract from the religious element within the American Revolution. In its 1775 effort to demonstrate solidarity with Massachusetts, when the port of Boston was about to be closed as a consequence of the destruction of British tea, the Virginia House of Burgesses declared a day of "humiliation and prayer," a point made by lecturers at Colonial Williamsburg. There was no equivalent, for example, to the anticlerical focus of revolutionary France. Certainly, none of the American revolutionaries were systematically humiliating clergy, or sacking and burning churches, and it was from the steeple of the Old North Church in Boston that the famous lanterns ("one if by land and two if by sea") were displayed to prompt the alert that "the British are coming" to the armed resistance in Lexington and Concord.

While the Declaration of Independence was hardly a religious document, its primary drafter, Thomas Jefferson, invokes God in four different ways during the short document ("Nature's God," the "Creator," "the Supreme Judge of the world," and "Divine Providence"). Specifically, he attributes the "unalienable rights" of life, liberty, and the pursuit of happiness to the "Creator" and states that governments are instituted to implement such God-given rights.

Nowhere in the Western world does religion continue with the intensity that it did 200 years ago. Nor is the United States immune to the tides of secularism that have eroded the intensity of religious belief. Science and technology have vitiated unthinking belief; the literal interpretation of the Bible as the absolutely accurate word of God did not survive the famous 1925 Scopes "Monkey Trial" over the teaching of evolution in the origin and development of mankind. The new argument is one of "intelligent design" (implying a directing intelligence in the creation of life), juxtaposed against evolution (without such "intelligent" direction), but the importance of God/religion in American political, social, and cultural life is as vibrant as it has been at any point in the past 50 years.

It is not necessary to belabor this point to make it clearly. American presidents take their oath of allegiance with their hand upon a Bible. Lesser government officials are also sworn into office. Juridical testimony is "sworn" truth in which the witness swears to tell the truth, etc. And while there is the option of "affirming" the truth of a statement for those without religious faith, it is very much a secondary option.

In a more general way, most American politicians (either truthfully or diplomatically, in reflection of U.S. domestic reality) express clear commitment to religion. They regularly attend church services and will end every significant public address with "God bless America." Even more striking in the U.S. public has been the emergence of born-again Christians who profess a deeper commitment to their religious faith following a personal religious experience, usually associated with a new appreciation of the role of Jesus Christ in their individual lives. Several recent U.S. presidents have professed to having been "born again" and secured some insulation from attacks over past peccadilloes from such profession. (Previous U.S. presidents, one might assume, had no need to indicate a rebirth of their Christian commitment.) Strong religious believers play a major role in U.S. politics or are believed to do so, according to polls and statistical analysis. While certain shibboleths of the past (for example, that a Catholic or a divorced individual could not become president) have been set aside, no non-Christian has yet become president, and the likelihood of that happening (despite the presence of Senator Joseph Lieberman on the 2000 Democrat ticket) remains rather remote. Nor is Senator Barak Obama's early exposure to Islamic instruction regarded as a multicultural benefit for his campaign for the Democratic presidential nomination.

It is not surprising, then, that many of the most furiously debated elements of the current socio-political domestic scene in the United States (abortion, homosexual marriage, death penalty, prayer in public schools) are essentially rooted in the role of God in America.

Nor has the influence of religion been absent from foreign affairs. There was a touch of the "white man's burden" in the Spanish-American War of 1898, despite the fact that the Philippines were already Christian (albeit Catholic). And missionaries in China doubtless influenced U.S. support for Chinese Nationalists (and their Methodist leadership) over the Japanese alternative. Even the resistance to "godless communism" was at least partly prompted by communist attack on religion generally ("the opiate of the masses"), and on religious believers and leaders specifically. The Cold War era was replete with stories of communist persecution of religious believers, from the 1949 "brainwashing" show trial of Hungarian Joseph Cardinal Mindszenty to the attempted assassination of Pope John Paul II, primarily due to communist efforts to eliminate the otherworldly influence of religion, and the natural resistance of religious believers to those efforts. The collapse of communism has been followed by a renaissance of religious activity throughout the former USSR, a development supported by U.S. religious groups.

If anything, the end of Soviet-directed communism has prompted new U.S. concern for religious freedom. Since 1998, the Department of State has prepared a detailed annual report regarding the state of religious freedom throughout the world, with the potential for legal sanctions against persistent violators of this human right as an element of the report's implementing legislation.

So analysts will see the continuing, sometimes implicit but nevertheless real, U.S. commitment to a republican form of government, national unity, and religious freedom as American political and cultural baselines.

A New Century: American Exceptionalism Continues

Just as everyone is a hero in his or her own autobiography, it is a rare country that is not heroic in its own history texts. In its own legend, the United States reflects the individual Boy Scout virtues (trustworthy, loyal, helpful, friendly, courteous, kind, obedient, cheerful, thrifty, brave, clean, and reverent) on a national level. Consequently, Americans up to and beyond former president Ronald Reagan have cited the Puritan leader John Winthrop's description of a future America—"a shining city upon a hill"—as a reminder that the United States is to be an inspiration for the world to emulate. As the United States takes its first steps into the 21st century, there is much that has been learned from the past as well as a willingness to embrace the new.

Thus there is a constant theme of American exceptionalism, the belief that because of unique historical origins, tremendous economic and politico-military successes and consequent strength, the United States is both uniquely blessed by God and uniquely worthy of God's blessing.

A less pleasant side effect of this belief in American exceptionalism has been an element of braggadocio, the "Ugly American" stereotype (both at home and abroad) for whom everything American is better than anything elsewhere. Homes are bigger; cars faster; culture more vibrant; technology more "high tech;" and on and on (and on). "Keeping up with the Joneses" was a full-time job for individual Americans (although, in America's view, keeping up with the good old U.S. of A. really wasn't possible for any other nation). Likewise, for the most part, Americans set aside concern for certain elements of U.S. society that are less advantaged. The average American feels little or no guilt over the status of the Native American, for example. Although the reasons for this indifference are speculative, it reflects the minimal Native American population (in 2003, the U.S. Census Bureau estimated there were approximately 2.8 million Native Americans or about 1 percent of the total population), its isolation in remote areas of the country, and the historical judgment that in the real-life game of Cowboys and Indians that played out until almost the end of the 19th century, the "cowboys" won and the "Indians" have to take the consequences of having lost. That the fighting was extended and bloody, and nowhere as one-sided as 21st-century critics might imagine, only reinforces the inherent lack of sympathy. (Such conflict is recounted in substantial detail in T. R. Fehrenbach's seminal account of Texan history, *Lone Star.*) Other nationals of non-European origin need only commit themselves to the elements in the self-image detailed below to assure their individual and/or group success.

AN OPEN SOCIETY

Some American self-images are dated. The suggestion inscribed on the Statue of Liberty, for instance, that the United States is open to the wretched refuse of the teeming shores of other nations would no longer be endorsed. But the image of Lady Liberty's electric torch beaming from New York harbor, indicating a safe haven for those escaping persecution and seeking freedom, is still regarded as absolute truth. And, to be sure, the theme of immigrants and refugees finding security and success in the United States is reflected throughout the social fabric of the country. There is virtually no U.S. citizen who does not know personally an immigrant or a child of immigrants who has benefited from the American Dream.

If the aftermath of 9/11 has moved U.S. society to a "trust but verify" attitude towards foreign visitors and prospective immigrants, the evolution of protection for minorities in the 50 years between Pearl Harbor and 9/11 is startling. After the multiple attacks by Muslim fundamentalists, there was not even a suggestion that Muslim-Americans should be rounded up; indeed, there was ostentatious attention directed to assuring Muslims that their rights would be protected equally.

FREE TO BE ME

If security from political persecution is one image that persists, personal liberty is another. Two generations ago, Americans were far more socially and personally conservative. Law and regulation restricted large elements of the media. Books were "banned in Boston," and depiction and description of human sexual activity was implicit or non-existent. The government was very much in the bedrooms of its citizens regarding access to contraception and abortion, interracial marriage, and the rights of gays and lesbians. Over the past generation, there has been a huge surge of sexual openness, especially in the popular media, such that virtually every current movie with more than a "G" rating would have been prohibited under the Hays Code of the past. Today, virtually no limits on language, beyond the notorious "F-word," are imposed on radio or TV commentators. Nor are there any practical limits on what can be written or published; there are no more books "in brown paper wrappers" or available only through clandestine purchases overseas (as was the case for American writer Henry Miller's *Tropic of Cancer* and *Tropic of Capricorn*, published in France in the 1930s but banned from publication in the States until the sixties). Perhaps the only remaining restraints on sexual activity are those associated with child sexual abuse and pornography.

Indeed, one practical way to measure this increased openness is to recall previous restrictions on obtaining federal government access to work with classified (secret) material. A generation ago, a married woman could not be a diplomat, a naturalized citizen could not be a diplomat for at least 10 years after naturalization, an open homosexual would be dismissed, an intimate liaison with a foreign national was highly questionable, and previous use of a narcotic such as marijuana was disqualifying. What previously was deviance has now become diversity.

To be sure, there is an active counter-current reflected in religious pressure against political efforts to obtain legal sanction for same-sex marriage and to reverse the Supreme Court decisions on abortion-on-demand. These "defense of marriage" and "pro family" movements are being worked out in the courts in state-by-state juridical action. But not even the starkest conservative would anticipate or endorse a return to the restrictions on personal life that existed during the 1950s.

THE SKY'S THE LIMIT

Throughout the United States, the population believes that hard work will be rewarded and anyone can get rich. According to one immigrant, all he had to do to get rich was to work as hard in the United States as he had worked in Vietnam just to survive. (As side benefits, his son would not be involuntarily impressed into the military, the tax collector was honest, and his daughters were safe from rapacious officials.) A popular book called *The Millionaire Next Door* suggests tactics regarding how an ostensibly average person can end up with a million-dollar estate by prudent saving and investing. With this basic philosophy, Americans have less class envy and less interest in class war; many expect to rise in "class" terms during their lifetimes, and if that isn't possible, for their children to rise in social and economic status. The enemy is not the rich; it is more likely to be the government. Such thinking leads to general support for lower taxes and has fueled the desire to eliminate the "death tax" (on inheritances) which obviously benefit the wealthy but which average Americans think will benefit them too some day.

Fueled by Education

Americans expect to be upwardly mobile and ultimately wealthy, and they also seek these objectives through education. Statistics are repeatedly cited in the media to demonstrate how much more money a college graduate can anticipate in lifetime earnings when compared to an individual with only a high school diploma. Citizens have noticed: unprecedented numbers of people—amounting to well over 50 percent of high school graduates—are heading to postsecondary education. Moreover, America is educating women at unprecedented rates. Currently, a higher percentage of women than men matriculate in universities, and women are the majority in entering classes for law, medicine, and veterinary schools. There is a clear appreciation that only through education—and the best available education—can the next generation maintain its current social and economic position and move upward. Consequently, bookstores are filled with self-help texts: everything possible to improve your ability to cope with the challenges of life, short of *Brain Surgery for Dummies*.

But No Special Status for the Educated

This commitment to education, however, must have a purpose. In contrast to European or Third World university-titled elites (the German *Herr Doktor Professor*), where special societal status is associated with education for its own sake, the United States pays no institutionalized respect for a PhD. (If anything, there is a touch of contempt for academic dissertations that suggests the educational manure is just "piled higher and deeper" with that advanced degree.) This lack of specialized status disconcerts the professorial class but reflects a contrarian element in U.S. attitudes: the craftsman who works with his hands (auto mechanic, plumber, carpenter) has more status than one who works with his mind (lawyer or diplomat). The dignity of labor is an essential element among Americans; there is no such thing as a low-class job, and many university graduates will talk of how they washed dishes, stood on factory assembly lines, held construction jobs or the like with pride rather than embarrassment. Perhaps because there is an essential societal respect for someone who works with his hands, the labor movement has never had the political strength as in other countries in creating a "them against us" attitude—all of us are "us."

A Country of Infinite Second Chances

Americans are constantly reinventing themselves; the American Dream is in Technicolor. Failure frequently is simply another opportunity to start anew.

Automobile baron Henry Ford was a multiple bankrupt. Ulysses S. Grant failed repeatedly in economic endeavors before returning to military service in the Civil War. Abraham Lincoln served only one term as a congressman (and was defeated for re-election) before becoming president.

There are endless stories of individuals returning to college or changing careers after long experience in one profession. An immigrant woman retired as an industrial worker, entered college after her children had graduated from university, and became a nurse. In the same light, a retired diplomat decided at age 50 that he wanted to become a lawyer and entered a respectable law school. That he concluded, after only one semester, that the U.S. had enough lawyers was irrelevant—he had the opportunity to check out a dream. Americans pick up and change jobs, change homes, change personal vehicles, change schools, and change spouses. There is nothing that cannot be improved: a "new you" with different hair color, enhanced (or reduced) physique, a personal trainer, or upgraded personal computer. "Total makeover" appeals to the voyeur, but it also reflects the belief that ruts are to be gotten out of, and you have no one to blame except yourself if you let a rut become a sunken road with no exit.

RISK TAKING BUT LAW ABIDING

Again, there is a dichotomy between American images of themselves as pushing the envelope in developing the geographic extent of the United States in the 18th and 19th centuries, and pushing forward technical and scientific frontiers ("Space: the final frontier") with the affirmation that we are a peaceful and law-abiding nation. Others might suggest that these self-labels persist only as long as Americans get their way. Americans are closer to vigilante justice; the great American movie is *High Noon* in which a man stands alone against outlaws while various so-called supporters scuttle away. John Wayne died in 1979, but his persona of the man who is slow to anger but relentless in extracting retribution has endured. Only in Canada are there Mounties who "always get their man" as a national institution; in the United States, a man who stands alone against challenge and adversity remains a revered ideal.

A Multinational Country?

The United States *is*—that consequence from the Civil War continues to hold. There remains no question about the political loyalty of racial and/or ethnic minorities in general although individuals, regardless of their racial, ethnic, or religious origins, are always capable of treason.

The United States believes that a multiplicity of voices and opinions leads to strength, but a multiplicity of special interest communities leads to conflict. Whether the special interest is racial, ethnic, religious, etc., its leaders focus on getting "more" for their clients, are often uninterested in the concerns of others, and are hostile to developments that would reduce their personal power over their constituents.

While the United States has never had greater numbers of immigrants (legal and illegal), the challenges in integrating these immigrants into American culture is not new. Indeed, it is the same challenge that has been faced by each generation, with different ethnic groups; the same play is staged, with different actors. It is the rare new group that has been welcomed with open arms by previous arrivals.

There are, however, unique challenges associated with some new immigrant groups. Historically, immigrants, regardless of their motivations (religious, political, economic), have arrived in the United States with no anticipation of returning to their countries of origin. The rationales for departure (political and/or religious persecution, war, famine) were imperative and long term. Travel was so slow and expensive, communication so laborious and delayed, that the immigrant was committed to life in a new country—there was no turning back.

Today, however, the prevalence of rapid and relatively inexpensive global transportation and instant communications makes the commitment of many immigrants more transient. The post-9/11 statements by Muslim-Americans have more than occasionally seemed to reflect personal concerns rather than fears for the fate of the United States. As well, the vast influx of Hispanic immigrants—driven by economics rather than more abstract concerns—has reached the point where they are now the largest U.S. minority. They are a special challenge, particularly as elements of Mexican society continue to reject the legitimacy of the southwest as U.S. territory. The divided loyalties of such immigrants raise the question—still unanswered—of whether they will be fair-weather citizens.

This issue was engaged anew during 2006 and 2007 in social and congressional debate over revision of immigration law. Fresh appreciation of the magnitude and ramifications of illegal immigration, epitomized by rallies of immigrants (illegal or not) waving Mexican flags and calling for a translation of "The Star-Spangled Banner" into Spanish, prompted a national backlash. The first priority for immigration has become border control with, in mid-2007, the corollary issues of addressing the status of immigrants (illegal or prospective legal) still unresolved. In the process, the role of English as the "common and unifying" U.S. language was touted in Congress.

For some observers, some of the foregoing assessments and self-images are simplistic to the point of being insulting. For such observers, the United States has been successful only due to the good fortune of having an amazingly rich continent to exploit and several centuries to do so, largely without external interference. The U.S. benefits from being the international equivalent of the rich child, "born on third base, who thinks he has hit a triple." Obviously, the opinion of the majority of U.S. citizens (and the U.S. government) is contrary. If the United States has benefited from great natural resources, others have been comparably blessed with less success (think of Brazil and Russia). If U.S. assistance to others has also benefited itself, nevertheless, others *did* benefit. When the United States, following the Second World War, could have imposed its will by force of arms, it instead interred its dead and put its citizens and treasure on the line for further sacrifice.

Every country is a hero in its own history books (and a villain in those of its opponents). In the end, there will be defining histories written and Americans, as those who have gone before them, will be weighed. Americans hope and believe that the United States will be found less wanting than others—but that will likely depend on who writes the history books.

DEMOCRATIC CULTURE AND PRACTICES 2

Tolstoy quipped that all happy families are alike—with the implication that they were thus uninteresting for fiction writers. One could similarly argue that all authentic democracies are alike. Such societies all have governments that are ultimately responsible to the residents of their country, in elections that would be characterized by neutral observers as free and fair.

Within that generalization is enormous variation on topics such as the structure of government, the division of and limitation on its powers, the timing and execution of its elections, the division of its resources, and many other vital governance issues.

Canada and the United States are among fortune's favorites as functioning democracies. To be sure, purists will find nicks and scratches in their practices; those designing perfect political science constructs will tut-tut over various elements of Canadian and U.S. practice. Each could benefit from re-structuring. Nevertheless, the Canadian and U.S. models both work and are open to change, albeit slowly and perhaps more in theory than in fact. The suggestion that those who love cooking and government should keep out of the kitchen and political backrooms is more truth than fiction. Still, massive electoral fraud and corruption are not the political norm in either country; corruption (either "Abscam" or "Adscam") and other abuses of power are uncovered, prosecuted, and/or rectified by new laws and regulations. The citizens of both countries are far better served by their governments than most alternatives, either current or historical.

Nevertheless, our governing models reflect popular attitudes: trust versus suspicion. While this dichotomy can be overdrawn and demonstrated inaccurate in particulars, it remains a useful overall characterization. For many Canadians, government is a good thing—you cannot have too much of it, and those who govern can normally be trusted to act in the public interest. The parliamentary system permits swift action based on rigid party discipline; it is responsive to leadership by public opinion—and the voters are not involved to a significant degree other than at election time. For Americans, government is a necessary evil—with the emphasis on "evil." The maxim "that government is best which governs least" remains a significant subtheme in U.S. politics. In contrast, a Canadian might say "that government is best that governs well"! Essentially, the U.S. government is designed for deadlock, its checks and balances so extensive that a major effort must be made to gather a majority on any significant decision.

Many of the issues at stake in Canada are inherent in its parliamentary structure. If "Outer Canada" (those who live beyond the Toronto-Ottawa-Montreal corridor) is dissed, "Inner Canada" may well believe that the regions should be grateful they are not being even more extensively exploited. If the Senate is as useful for average Canadians as teats on a boar, it is probably easier to eliminate it than attempt its reform. Of course, if the Senate was to be abolished, patronage would find another outlet (American administrations send their equivalents to foreign capitals as ambassadors).

For its part, the United States political structure effectively represents states both small and large, permitting the less populated West to block much of what it might regard as exploitative. Over time, due to demographic shifts, states in the South and West (for example, Florida, Texas, California) have gained power as well in the House of Representatives. Since there has been more alternation of power during the past 50 years, there appears to be a slowly diminishing anxiety in the United States over the "first past the post" electoral system; the various political science constructs regarding proportionate representation and/or single transferable vote have remained imprisoned in academic ivory towers for the most part.

The Canadian Experience

About 20 years ago, I attended a conference of parliamentarians, mostly from Latin America, about the nature of democracy and its many forms and practices. On that occasion, and at various times since, I've heard legislators and others speak about many issues of democratic government, including those occasions when a long-anticipated free and fair election (such as the 2006 election in the Democratic Republic of the Congo) is unlikely to be enough to create significantly better lives for the population of a country.

At one such conference for new and restored democracies, which took place in 2003 in Ulaan Baatar, Mongolia, delegates from about 120 countries heard about the prospects for democracy across the world. At present, there are more than 120 multi-party democracies among approximately 200 sovereign countries, compared with probably fewer than 35 as recently as the 1970s. A sobering message, however, was read from then-UN Secretary-General Kofi Annan, saying it was not a moment for triumphalism by the world's democrats. The rule of law is essential to any well-functioning democracy; Annan's message expressed concern about declining voter turnouts in some democracies, asking if the cause might be feelings of "exclusion and marginalization" among those opting not to vote.

Even as we delegates discussed the real enemies of democracy—unemployment, poverty, bad governance, corruption, and so on—news came that Anna Lindh, Sweden's respected foreign minister, had been attacked in a Stockholm department store. When confirmation of her death reached the conference, there seemed to be unanimity that democratic governments, in combating terrorism, should not retreat a single step from the best practices of open societies everywhere.

Akouété Akakpo-Vidah of the Canadian NGO Rights and Democracy pointed to the tendency of new democracies to morph from one party to several and then essentially back to one, partly because opposition parties are often left at a competitive disadvantage because parties in power have access to government resources. The importance of cultivating strong civil societies was flagged by several delegates, as was the general need for women and minorities to play larger roles in national parliaments. There was considerable support too for the need for a free and independent media to provide substantive information to voters.

As we listened to tributes to Anna Lindh, I thought back to September 11, 2001 (Lindh died two years to the day after 9/11), when approximately two hours after the two passenger aircraft struck the World Trade Center in Manhattan, we delegates from the governments of virtually every nation in the Americas except Cuba, meeting in Lima, Peru, unanimously adopted the Democratic Charter of the Organization of the American States (OAS). Those attending that assembly seemed more determined than ever that democracy, including the well-known features of our societies which protect citizens, must continue to be a source of inspiration across the world.

WHITHER DEMOCRACY IN CANADA?

How are Canada's democratic practices holding up in terms of public confidence at the national level today?

A representative democracy, including the Westminster parliamentary model, is supposed to function as a means for the nationals of a country to have their opinions and concerns reflected in policy and legislation. Members of Parliament (MPs) are elected by constituents to represent their interests. They can only maintain legitimacy by acting in accordance with the wishes of their electorates most—if not all—of the time.

In our current practice, the ability of a Canadian MP to represent constituents is seriously impaired by the high degree of party discipline in our system, which developed after about 1900. Some degree of party discipline is clearly necessary in order to maintain the coherence of political parties as viable institutions; this should not preclude a member from representing his or her constituents on issues of real importance to them.

Currently, this role is seriously compromised by the fact that the only real political power lies with the prime minister of the day. Alone, he or she has the power to dismiss a member of caucus at any time; to make all cabinet appointments, all appointments to the Senate, to the Supreme Court; all ambassadors—to name but a few. The combination of the prime minister's explicit power to discipline through censure or expulsion and the implicit power to discipline through denial of cabinet appointments or other appointments creates an environment in which it is severely hazardous to one's political career for members of a government caucus to deviate from any agenda set by the prime minister.

In early 2004, the rules on votes for the then-governing Liberal MPs were overhauled and a "line" voting system was put in place. It categorized all House of Commons votes as one-, two-, or three-line votes. *One-liners* were to be truly free votes, which would allow all members, including cabinet ministers, to vote as they saw fit. *Two-liners* would compel cabinet ministers and relevant parliamentary secretaries to vote with the government and encourage all other caucus members to do likewise. *Three-liners* were to be considered matters of confidence and would thus require all members to vote with the government. Items such as the Throne Speech, the budget, and important spending motions would be considered three-liners.

The declared aim was to create more opportunity for free votes by making more explicit what constitutes a matter of confidence. In theory, it allowed for more free votes by increasing transparency with regard to government prerogatives, but the prime minister still held the power to designate what *category a vote would fall under* on a vote-by-vote basis. The new system did not appear to change the longtime practice very much at all. In the case of three-line votes, moreover, a member could be expelled for following the contrary wishes of constituents.

An expelled MP is forced to sit as an independent and is to a degree excommunicated from the political process. He or she must try to work with diminished resources and a reduced ability to ask a question or raise an issue in the House of Commons, which in theory at least diminishes the ability to serve constituents. Such members have little means of influencing government policy to the benefit of their constituents in any way because they can no longer count on the support of their former party. While true that any non-cabinet MP has the right to put forward a private member's bill, this technical ability is of little practical value because very few such bills pass the House.

It is very difficult for an MP on the government side to vote against any issue a prime minister has designated as a matter of confidence even though one's constituents are demonstrably not in favor of it. One is faced with a choice in which one's ability to serve as representative is undermined regardless of what choice is made. If one toes the party line on a piece of legislation constituents have deemed undesirable, one loses the faith and trust of the electors and is seen as a political figure who lacks legitimacy. If one obeys the wishes of the constituents, one's ability to serve them becomes severely constrained as a result of being dismissed from one's political party.

The reality of our present system, then, is that the will of the constituents is often trumped by party discipline. Ironically, members of the governing party, who should theoretically be in the best position to serve the interests of constituents, are in practice probably the least empowered.

Private member's bills are allocated a limited amount of time for consideration and are highly prone to failure since they require either the support of the governing party or broad-based support across party lines in order to be passed. During the Thirty-seventh Parliament (2000-04), for example, out of the 880 private members' bills tabled, only 11 substantive bills (those bills which are not merely constituency name changes) received royal assent. None of these bills had any significant socio-economic impact.

Another consequence of the current system is that it often effectively closes the door to any sort of cooperative efforts in the policymaking realm among parties unless there is a minority government. Where parties dominate the process as they do now, there is no real forum for substantive policy dialogue to take place among members of different parties when one of them has a majority.

Some assert that the daily Question Period in the House serves such a role, but "Q.P." is rarely seen today as a constructive policy forum. It is pointless for a member of any party to try to lobby members of other parties during Q.P., given the reality that virtually every vote will result in each party's respective members voting with their party. The lobbying that goes on in the House of Commons is really directed towards the public as the parliamentary parties jockey for position in anticipation of the next election.

In the U.S. Congress, where there is a constitutional separation of powers between the executive and the legislative branches of government, laws are passed with far less party discipline. The separation of powers and the weakness of party discipline in voting on Capitol Hill greatly facilitate effective regional representation. Unlike the situation in Canada, where a government falls if it loses the support of a majority in the House on a confidence vote, U.S. presidents and Congress are elected for fixed terms. Neither resigns if a measure of any kind is voted down in either the Senate or the House of Representatives.

The voting practices in our two countries are so different that *The Congressional Quarterly* defines party unity votes as those in which at least 51 percent of members of one party vote against 51 percent of the other party. Under this definition, itself astonishing to Canadian legislators, the *Quarterly* notes that for the years 1975-82 party unity votes occurred in only 44.2 percent of the 4,417 recorded Senate votes, and in only 39.8 percent of those in the House of Representatives. This sample, moreover, includes the years 1976-80, the last period before 1992-94 when Democrats controlled the White House and both branches of Congress.

REGIONAL REPRESENTATION

Another feature of the American system that fosters effective regional input in national policymaking is territorial bloc voting—something quite unknown in Canada's House of Commons. Representatives from both political parties from the Mountain, Sun Belt, New England and others regions vote *en bloc* or work together in committees to advance common regional interests.

A good example of how effective regional representatives can influence the geographic location of federal government procurement, which affects the geographic distribution of the manufacturing sector, is the southern influence in Congress. It played a major role in the postwar concentration of federal military and space expenditures in the South and in the general economic revival and growth of the Sun Belt. During 1981-82, for example, the height of the "boll-weevil era," the long-time legislative coalition of southern Democrats and Republicans was successful more than 85 percent of the time, due to mutual areas of agreement and interest. What this point also illustrates, however, is that U.S. party labels are a weak indicator of political philosophy. During that period, some political scientists argued that there were really at least four parties in the United States: Liberal Republicans and Democrats and Conservative Republicans and Democrats.

The point of this comparison is only to emphasize that, unlike the American Congress, Canadian bloc voting makes bi- or tripartisan agreement on anything in our legislatures, except in minority government situations, exceedingly rare. In our current political culture, if a government or opposition MP's loyalty to his/her region clashes with the instruction of the party whip, placing constituent or regional considerations first when voting implies considerable risk to one's prospects for party advancement.

Private MPs in Canada are thus far less able to represent regional interests effectively on an inter-party basis than are their counterparts in Washington, where there is freedom allowing effective regional representation when an issue has clear regional implications.

In rare cases, independent MPs in Canada can play a significant role, but it is usually only in minority parliaments, perhaps most notably in recent times in the parliament that sat between 2004 and late 2005. Having left the Liberal party in April 2005 over further revelations at the Gomery Commission of criminal conduct by Liberal partisans and some fundamental differences over policy, I was able to push hard for Prime Minister Paul Martin to provide leadership against the appalling crimes that continued to occur in the Darfur province of Sudan. We met twice on the issue, but in the end could not agree on what Canada should do, and I voted against the government on a clear confidence vote. The vote was tied, so the Speaker of the House, as required by convention, broke the tie in the government's favor.

This is not to suggest that Canada should duplicate the American style of government. It is to point out that the best solution to ongoing problems of representative democracy in Canada might be to adapt attractive features from various systems, including the American one.

Another system that is useful to examine is Germany's. In Berlin, a vote of non-confidence requires that the opposition on the same motion also propose a candidate of their own whom they wish to be appointed chancellor by the federal president. A motion of non-confidence is required to be made at the same time as one for a new chancellor. The idea behind this was to prevent crises by always maintaining a chancellor in office. Unlike Canada's current application of the Westminster model, the chancellor does not resign upon the passage of a non-confidence motion and must instead be dismissed by the federal president.

To place this in a Canadian context, in the case of the Joe Clark government as an example, the defeat of the Clark minority government's budget in December 1979 would not have ousted him from office under the German practice unless the Liberals, New Democrats, and Social Credit MPs had agreed simultaneously on a new prime minister who could hold the confidence of a majority of MPs. The adoption of a similar measure in our own practices might weaken party discipline and facilitate greater independence for MPs to vote on the merits of issues without fear of toppling a government. Alternatively, a more active governor general (which might require a change in the selection process for the GG) could refuse a prime minister's call for election—and require his continuation in office.

In an increasingly interdependent world, many Canadians in our outer eight provinces and territories want new or altered institutions that will represent the interests of both "Inner Canadians" and "Outer Canadians" effectively. Unless we move away from the notion that "the national interest" is merely a code phrase for the two most populous provinces (Ontario and Quebec) dominating all corners of the country, frictions between Inner and Outer Canada are likely to remain or worsen.

In the January 2006 election, the minority government of Stephen Harper failed to win a single seat in the two largest citadels of Inner Canada: Toronto and Montreal. The practical consequences for Outer Canadians of the Harper government remain to be determined. Outer Canada did enjoy significant representation in both the cabinets and parliaments during the Mulroney years in office, but ultimately obtained very little specific satisfaction for those who wanted "in." Political demographics force any party that wants to hold power to cater to the pair of provinces where most voters live. Understandably, the Harper government to date has, if anything, rather shorted the West, specifically Alberta, to demonstrate to the Inside (Ontario and Quebec) that it represents all Canadians. There has been no indication, aside from insisting that senators in future will be elected and a proposal that new senators be limited to an eight-year term, that the specific problems of Outer Canadians are going to be addressed.

If party discipline is relaxed, representation for all areas of Canada would be improved. It would be easier for, say, Ontario MPs to defy their party establishments, if need be, in support of provincial issues. Coalitions composed of members of all parties could exist for the purpose of working together on issues of common regional or other concern. The present adversarial attitudes and structures of Parliament, or legislatures in which opposition parties oppose virtually anything a government proposes, might change in the direction of all parties working together for the national good.

At present, few government or opposition MPs have any real opportunity to put constituents first in votes in the House of Commons. Real power is concentrated in the hands of the three party leaderships. Canadian democracy itself would thus benefit if we put our present mind-numbing party discipline where it belongs—in the history books.

COMPARATIVE PHILOSOPHIES OF GOVERNING
The English Canada historian William Morton believed, as of 1960, that the fundamental political differences between Canada and the United States lay in our radically different self-perceptions. America is a nation of covenant, claimed Morton, which means at least three things. First, there is a need for a degree of uniformity because covenants can only exist among like-minded communities. Second, Americans separate themselves from the uncovenanted, whether abroad or at home. Third, Americans are messianic, which means that where they think it warranted they will enter other countries to fulfill their mission. Whether this is more true today under the Bush administration than it was in 1960 under Jack Kennedy is debatable.

Indeed, for an American, such a characterization is simplistic and misleading. To believe in U.S. covenanted unity is to ignore the extensive U.S. history of disputatious political and social dissent, which has led to substantial change in almost every element of U.S. social policy throughout its national history, including the Civil War. Likewise, whether Americans are more "separate" than citizens of other countries (the Japanese, for example), is more likely to reflect geographic isolation than political philosophy. The willingness to intervene in the affairs of others is a reflection of the power to do so (for example, the imperial exercises of 19th-century European powers).

Morton characterized Canadians, on the other hand, above all by loyalty to the British monarch, and attachment to parliamentary democracy and its notion that all governing is done in the name of the monarch. Our people, whether of British, French, or any other background, feared America in the 1860s, during the Civil War and earlier. We feared it in the past as a world power and even more in recent years as the world's only superpower, at least for the moment. Morton goes on: "they (Americans) are not in their heart of hearts convinced that Canadian nationhood is perceived as a moral significance comparable with that of their own nation."[1]

An American, however, might well be puzzled over the "moral significance" comment. If Morton is suggesting that the U.S. believes itself to be exceptional and other countries less so, that is hardly surprising—it is a reflection of nationalism, which is certainly not unique to the U.S. World powers including the French, British, the old USSR, pre-1945 Germany, and other great powers of any era, believed their country to be of greater significance (economic, political, cultural, moral, etc.) than other countries. Nevertheless, whatever the "moral significance" may indicate, there is no question of the U.S. acceptance of Canada's legal nationhood.

There was no Canadian way of life as such for Morton. For him, any Canadian, regardless of origin or time in Canada, could be a citizen of Canada and subject of the queen "without in any way changing or ceasing to be himself. This is a truth so fundamental that it is little realized and many, in fact most, Canadians would deny its truth, but it is central to any explanation or understanding of Canadian nationhood."

Allegiance to the reigning Queen Elizabeth has for various reasons—having little to do with her admirable personal qualities—diminished considerably in most parts of Canada over the past half-century. Today, a former ambassador of Austria to Canada, Walther Lichem, speaks of the plural identity of Canadians, by which he means that, while Europeans can rarely think of themselves as other than nationals of their respective countries, Canadians can, more than any other nationality he knows on earth, have loyalty to many identities. If correct, this is a long way from the covenant concept of our American neighbors.

Part of the cultural world view of Canadians is rooted in the history of the 20th century and beyond. Ramsay Cook, in a brilliant essay written a decade ago on Morton's book, reminded us that ethnic nationalism can be a

---

1. William L. Morton, *The Canadian Identity*. Madison, WI: University of Wisconsin Press, 1961, p. 84.

profoundly nasty experience. He quoted three Europeans to make this case. Vaclav Havel of the Czech Republic (1992): "the sovereignty of the community, the region, the state . . . makes sense only if it derives from the one genuine sovereignty of the human being, which finds its political expression in civil sovereignty." Bernard-Henri Levy of France (1992): "But Europe is exactly what people don't seem to want today. They want identities. The great modern and murderous delirium in Europe is the folly of ethnic identity." And, most bluntly of all, Zlatko Dizdarevic, in *Sarajevo: A War Journal* (1993): "Because somebody somewhere decided that the bestial concept of a herd, composed of only one colour, all speaking the same language, all thinking along similar lines, all believing in the same god, must wipe out everything else."

So where are Canadians' values and our political culture in 2007? One can assert a number of almost universally held Canadian values. We are certainly democrats and believe that our representatives, elected normally for four years either provincially or nationally, can make legislative decisions.

We believe strongly in the rule of law, but there appears to be no clear national consensus on where the line should be drawn on law-making by judges purporting to be making decisions under the Charter of Rights and Freedoms. As I understand it, the courts in most EU member countries are unable to invalidate national statutes, even when those statutes in question violate the European Human Rights Conventions. The Supreme Court of Canada and the U.S. Supreme Court, on the other hand, can invalidate any measure they hold conflicts with the current members' view of the Canadian Charter of Rights and Freedoms and the U.S. Constitution and its amendments. Indeed, this reality is presumably the basis for the U.S. rejection of the International Criminal Court: the USA would not be the USA if it surrendered its citizens' rights to the rulings of judges from other countries. The most commonly cited mantra on the differences between Canadian and American political values is still valid: "Canada's 1867 constitution speaks of 'peace, order, and good government' whereas the American Declaration of Independence calls for 'life, liberty, and the pursuit of happiness.'" The reality today is much more complex.

It is often claimed that Canadians are more deferential to police officers, judges, teachers, clergy, and others. There is probably still some basis in fact to this perception, partly based on our very different beginnings as different peoples, but with each passing year it is now probably becoming an overgeneralization.

Whether Canada still suffers from a national inferiority complex is a more serious issue. Certainly, in travels around Asia, Latin America, the Caribbean, Africa, and the United States, I've seen many references to this. "My country respects Canada. Why don't you stand up and be counted internationally?" is a refrain I've heard in many capitals. Of course, these countries are looking for allies, and their actions regarding "standing up and being counted" do not necessarily match their words. Nevertheless, it is sad to admit, I think a national inferiority complex does persist far too often and diminishes our role across the world. Politeness and courtesy are excellent qualities. The Norwegians, for example, practice them within a population that is small, relative to Canada's, but are still able to make a significant difference on matters in many parts of the world, including Africa and Asia. To be sure, however, the United States does pay more attention to Canada than to Norway.

There are, of course, a number of other widely known Canadian features. We are celebrated in many countries for having two official and many heritage languages, although we are still not currently exploiting either well enough in our international trade. We rejoice in our leadership and other roles as a northern people, still attached—even if only for vacation purposes—to our rugged land, mountains, and lakes.

WESTMINSTER MODEL QUESTIONED

Until quite recently, many Canadians were rather proud of our Westminster model of parliamentary government at both the national and provincial levels, perhaps unaware that few of Britain's other former colonies adopted it following their independence.

Signs of discontent, if not major disaffection, have been emerging in recent years. One reliable indicator, registered voter turnout at elections, was only 61.2 percent in the 2000 national election—approximately the same as in the mid-2005 election in Iraq, where voting cost some people their lives. (Indeed, some neighboring residents in parts of Iraq formed tightly knit platoons to attend the voting stations so as to reduce the risk of infiltration by terrorists with bombs.)

Back in Canada, during the lively and hard-to-predict election of 2004, participation rates nationally actually fell to 60.5 percent. Opinion surveys indicated that participation was much lower among younger Canadians, particularly those in their 20s. More encouragingly, the overall voter participation rate in the 2006 election rose to 64.9 percent.

A number of Western democracies have experienced a similar trend. During the 1990s, according to the International Institute for Democracy and Electoral Assistance, which uses census numbers for citizens eligible to vote rather than voters lists in its calculations, Canada was joined in the 60 percent or less category by France (60.6), Japan (57.0), the United States (44.9) and Switzerland (37.7). The countries that maintained voting levels above 80 percent in the decade included Italy (90.2), Belgium (84.1), Australia—with compulsory voting (82.7), and New Zealand (80.4).[2]

Definitive reasons for the differences in participation rates are unclear, but Canada's first-past-the-post voting system (FPTP) is probably part of the explanation. There are certainly many other reasons, including voter dissatisfaction with the national government generally and the perceived ineffective roles of parliamentarians in Ottawa. But the sense that votes are wasted is pervasive. Why bother to vote in a national election if you're a Liberal in almost any part of Alberta, or a Conservative or New Democrat in parts of Montreal? The time and effort to visit the voting station must seem to some, who know their candidate will lose, unwarranted. On the other hand, two of the oldest democracies, the U.S. and Britain, have also maintained the winner-take-all FPTP model for the most part. In both of them, and in Canada, the historic close link between voters and their national representatives is reinforced by the voting system.

PROPORTIONAL REPRESENTATION

Proportional representation (PR) has been adopted in dozens of other democracies on the premise that no one's vote is wasted if some (or all) of the legislative seats in a predetermined region are distributed in accord with the overall percentage of the party's vote in that region. Advocates claim that women are marginally more successful in winning seats in PR democracies than in FPTP ones. Smaller parties, such as the Greens or NDP, have a better chance to win both legislative representation and places in the coalition governments, which PR clearly encourages. If Canada adopted a form of PR, regional polarization might be reduced, although I personally doubt if any voting system would seriously alter regional party preferences, at least over the short term.

The major practical objection to PR for Canada is that most models of it combine locally elected constituency representatives with regionally elected "list" ones. The latter normally owe their selection and all-important

---

2. Rand Dyck, *Canadian Politics: Critical Approaches* (Fourth Edition). Toronto: Nelson, 2003, p. 229.

placing on their respective ballot party lists to party bosses because the strength of a party with regional voters determines how far down the party list candidates will be successful. List members clearly have less democratic legitimacy than the former. As one successful list candidate in Europe noted to some visiting Canadian parliamentarians last year, referring to his own regional party hierarchy, "I have only 40 electors in my elections."

Another concern about PR is that in a number of European countries where it exists, elections are held regularly but the coalition governments frequently created by it rarely seem to change. The counter is presumably that under FPTP, the national Liberals in Canada held office for much of the 20th century as well. Voters under PR ultimately decide whom they want to form their government, and for how long.

Most Canadians have had little knowledge of, or experience with, PR since the last vestiges of it were abandoned in our three most westerly—and most populist—provinces about five decades ago. The British Columbia Citizens Assembly of 2004, comprising 153 provincial residents chosen at random, recommended electing members of the provincial legislature through a version of the single transferable vote (STV), which essentially means that a voter ranks the candidates on the ballot. A subsequent provincial referendum in mid-2005 indicated that a majority (57.4 percent) supported the concept, including majorities in 77 of the province's 79 constituencies.

There are, however, objections to the STV, which is presumably why it has been adopted in very few jurisdictions. The main one is that many voters prefer big-tent parties to form majority governments rather than through STV allowing tiny parties or movements—which can obtain, say, 5 percent voter support—effectively to decide which larger party forms the government with its support.

Finally, there is the issue that if Canada went to PR nationally with the model used in Germany—probably the most likely result—but retained our current 308 members of Parliament, half of them would continue to represent single-member constituencies. It would also mean that, since half the MPs would be elected from a regional party list, the number of constituents in each of the constituencies for the first category of representative would double to about 200,000—a prospect many voters and MPs alike are unlikely to welcome.

The PR half of the MPs from every province and territory, moreover, would presumably be elected from province-wide districts, except for the large provinces of Ontario and Quebec. This would tend to mean in practice that most of them would be residents of larger cities. Constituents from less populated communities would be likely to see their access to both their constituency and "list" MPs to be minimal. The representatives in turn would engage in a continuous competition for legitimacy with constituents, who would probably complain a lot about the reduced standard of service to constituents with the adoption of PR.

Among the other major problems in the practice of Canadian democracy in the early 21st century is the appointed Senate, and the continuing inferior political, cultural, and economic position of Canadians living outside the Toronto-Montreal-Ottawa triangle.

One of the hoariest ongoing issues of democratic legitimacy in Canada is our unloved Senate because our senators, while having almost the same legislative authority and salary as MPs, continue to be appointed in practice until the age of 75 at the sole discretion of the prime minister of the day.

In one opinion survey a number of years ago, I noticed that only about 11 percent of Canadians then approved having the Senate in its present form. The efforts over many years of the Alberta legislature, and residents of that province, to elect senators in province-wide elections have been mostly frustrated by prime ministers who preferred to favor political cronies. In 2004, the three successful candidates in the provincially held Senate Alberta election, two of whom won over 300,000 votes in these elections, were passed over in favor of three unelected persons for three vacancies in the Senate from Alberta. Former prime minister Martin later insisted that it would have created "tensions" if he had appointed any of the three elected. Indeed, the only time Albertans were successful was in 1990, when Prime Minister Brian Mulroney did appoint Stanley Waters, who had handily won a province-wide election the year before. Many said Mulroney did it only because he needed the Alberta government's support for the Meech Lake Accord, but whatever the motivation at least he attempted to reduce the governing democratic deficit in the Senate. However, Prime Minister Harper's decision in April 2007 to appoint Bert Brown, an elected "senator in waiting," has put new energy into the issue of Senate reform.

Defenders of the present model argue that two sets of elected parliamentarians would cause problems, forgetting that another parliamentary democracy, Australia, has long had an elected Senate. Twelve senators are elected from each of six states, plus two each from the Northern Territory and the Capital region. The preferential ballot used to do so is complicated, but the result historically is that members of the two major political parties only rarely hold a majority of seats in Australia. This means that it is normally an independent upper chamber, which does its best to improve bills, hold inquiries, and the like.

Reform of our Senate continues to be a major concern in various parts of the country, but it is now impossible to change it by constitutional amendment because the 1982 amendment formula, whether by intent or not, in effect makes it impossible to achieve the necessary consent of seven provincial legislatures and the Parliament of Canada. Too many of these bodies do not want major reform of the Senate in favor of making it elected, effective, and equal by province. It remains to be seen whether the proposal by Prime Minister Harper in mid-2006, specifying limited eight-year terms for new senators following provincial elections, can be agreed upon (as Liberal leader Stephane Dion has denounced the concept)—or is constitutional. As a result, the unloved Senate continues like a beached whale as the most blatant example of Canada's democratic deficit.

FURTHER REDUCTIONS IN DEMOCRATIC DEFICIT

Another major national embarrassment is the continuing plight of our First Nations communities that live in bands across the country (although about two-thirds live in Western and Northern Canada). Much good will, patience, flexibility, true inspiration, and open-mindedness are needed on both sides if real progress is now to be made in the coming years. Most social indicators indicate that only uneven progress has been made to date.

Regional alienation also persists. As one European ambassador put it recently, not long after his posting to Canada, "Your national government accommodates Ontario and Quebec and hopes that the West will not be too upset." In two books, I have documented this phenomenon, concluding how over many decades policies, attitudes, and spending have favored Inner Canadians. Those living elsewhere, Atlantic Canadians, Quebeckers living beyond Greater Montreal, northern Ontarians, Prairie and B.C. residents, and those living north of 60° are "Outer Canadians." Our executive democracy, in which the prime minister, his advisors, and the central agencies of the national government have long dominated parliaments—except in times of minority governments—is a major reason why some Canadians over time have remained more equal than others. These practices and attitudes must end in favor of policies and institutional reform that will foster more political, cultural, and opportunity equality for all members of the national family.

RECONCILABLE DIFFERENCES

Canada's national governments must represent the general interest as distinct from provincial interests. However, as "national interest" concepts are usually elusive, successive federal governments in pursuing this concept have often acted in ways in accord with the wishes of one particular region while subordinately forsaking the others.

David Elton and Peter McCormick, professors of political science from the West and prominent advocates of Western issues, offer an Outer Canadian view on "national policies": "There seems to be a strange convention of federal political language that when a program is labeled 'western,' it means the benefits are distributed fairly evenly across the country, and when it is called 'national,' it means the benefits go disproportionately to Central Canada."

Discussions of regionalism in Canada invariably boil down to arguments over which should prevail: regional interests or "the national interest." Nobody disputes that on some issues—those that reflect the aspirations of most citizens—the larger interest should take precedence. However, by choosing a federal system of government, Canadians rejected the notion that the national majority should always prevail. Federalism means that on some issues, at least occasionally, the will of the majority of the population will be frustrated. If the biggest battalions of voters were to prevail over smaller ones under any and all circumstances, we should drop the charade that we have a federal system of government that respects minorities in times of stress. The notion that the national majority will prevail has resulted in much regional discontent and accompanying feelings of regional irrelevancy.

In an increasingly interdependent world, Canada must imaginatively create or alter existing institutions in order to represent the interests of both Inner and Outer Canadians effectively. Unless we move away from the notion that "the national interest" is merely a code phrase for the most populous region dominating all corners of the country, frictions between Inner and Outer Canada will probably worsen.

The year 1989 witnessed spectacular developments in Eastern Europe. After 45 years of totalitarian rule, new governments, inspired by democratic principles and impulses, redrafted their constitutions and introduced sweeping changes affecting almost every aspect of daily life. Why has Canada, a country fortunate to have been governed since its beginnings by democratically elected governments, taken so long to initiate an effective process of reforms? They would not lead to such revolutionary changes as in Eastern Europe, yet they are of comparable importance to many Canadians, especially to the residents of the outer regions of the country.

Outer Canadians need to know that however far from Toronto-Ottawa-Montreal they live, they matter in Ottawa as much as their compatriots in Inner Canada. National policies and institutions must begin to reflect their needs and be targeted to meet their requirements and aspirations as well. They need to know that they will in the future be effectively represented during the process of national policymaking by those elected to defend the interests of their communities, provinces, or regions. This role can no longer be subordinated to other political considerations. In order for this notion to become a reality, we need as a people to renew our federalism. We need to do so now as badly, or perhaps more so, as when Prime Minister Trudeau promised "renewed federalism" to Quebec during the 1980 referendum campaign.

The first initiative should be Senate reform, combined with improved regional representation in many federal government institutions, agencies, and wherever policymaking affects certain regions. There is also a need for fair and generous financial assistance and federal government procurement funds that might show a bias this time towards disadvantaged regions of the country. The ongoing nation-wide debate on Senate reform and the repercussions of the failure of the Meech Lake Accord had already started the process of renewing Canadian federalism, but has now unfortunately effectively stopped since the 1995 referendum and the subsequent passage of the Clarity Act. Nor should we wish it to be averted. However, if it is lost now, future generations of Canadians will blame their parents for losing possibly the last opportunity to strengthen our sense of common purpose and unity.

Democratic Practices: The American Experience

There are those who suggest that the United States is a "bottom up" rather than a "top down" democracy. These observers have a point that deserves analysis.

THE REPUBLICAN-FEDERALIST MODEL OF REPRESENTATIVE DEMOCRACY

The United States is characterized by its federalist governing structure, both at the national and subnational level. The U.S. is the oldest currently operating federal state, and its design as originally drafted was as much a practical as a philosophical matter. With the country's population spread throughout a wilderness, communication was extremely slow. On land, nothing traveled faster than a horse, and roads were poor at best. Sailing vessels were quicker, but once a ship reached port, communication immediately slowed. The attempts to gather the various "continental congresses" prior to and during the Revolutionary War took months of advance notice and preparation. George Washington could require an entire day to travel the distance between his Mount Vernon home and local villages on horseback. Even admitting that he didn't rush, Washington needed seven days to travel from Mount Vernon to New York City, where he was inaugurated as the first president.

The United States at its inception was indeed primitive; in comparison to Europe, it was rudimentary in its ability to communicate information, with substantial parts of its population spread over the countryside. Much of the country was modestly literate at best; printing presses were expensive and clumsy (Benjamin Franklin made a significant fortune by franchising his print shops in several colonies). Even in the mid-19th century (according to Mark Twain in *Roughing It*), the Pony Express took eight days to cover 1,900 miles; the stagecoach took 18 days. American political activity was primarily local; the traditional New England town meeting reflected the adage still endorsed today that "all politics is local." There was no pre-set governing tradition, established over the centuries, that could operate semiautomatically because its standards and rules were known. In this evolving frontier society, political decisions were made without benefit of governing officials—and Americans became accustomed to making such decisions without guidance from on high. Although this condition can be overstated (as the primary political actors were in closer communication and limited in number), it also reflects the reality that Americans were not interested in tight, "in your face" government.

Immediately after the Revolutionary War, independence, freedom, and liberty were felt viscerally; people had just finished dying for these words, and for their colleagues and families the words were more than intellectual constructs. Consequently, American willingness to accept direction from a distant "top," just after a rebellion against such rule, was also limited. Whether that direction was English or American didn't seem to make much difference for many citizens. They just wanted to be left to their own devices. Moreover, the differences among individual American states were greater than the differences between many nations of the 21st century. That the United States would eventually fight a civil war over the limits of "states' rights" was more than 70 years into the future. Getting along with one another on the basis of what they were "for" rather than what they were "against" (English rule) was a learning process. So the emphasis was on local autonomy, local experimentation, and local control, since it was at this level that people could be found who would best understand the specialized local circumstances.

At its inception, the United States indeed may have made a virtue of necessity, but the ensuing 200 years have not resulted in the degree of centralized control that technological advance could permit. There is an enormous range of public and private life, for example, marriage/divorce law, law bar examinations, qualifications for a driver's license, primary and secondary school curriculums, zoning ordinances, building codes, etc., that could be made more efficient by a single national standard; however, U.S. citizens have relentlessly insisted on the constitutional delineation that rights not directly given to the federal government are reserved for the individual states. Doubtless the 50 states at the dawn of the 21st century are infinitely more unified and coherent than the 13 states were in 1789; however, regional and local differences remain a major characteristic of the U.S. sociopolitical landscape.

Separation of Powers: Checks and Balances

Federalism by definition has at least some elements of separation of powers. There is no ultimate authority "king" who embodies in his person executive authority, the power to create legislation, and juridical oversight; no one, in short, who proposes, weighs, and disposes the legal consequences. A federal system at a minimum will have governments at different political levels, with different levels of authority. Every local official at every subfederal level is not a federal official. Thus, while the postal clerk for a small county in Pennsylvania may be a federal official, the policeman and school teacher are not. And at no political organizational level are the courts required to respond to the direction of local or federal political officials at that level—or a higher level. But the separation of powers in the United States is just the beginning of its democratic practice.

Far more important is the U.S. attitude towards checks and balances. At almost every level, but most noteworthy and obvious at the national/federal level, the U.S. political system emphasizes checks and balances. That is, each branch of government can prevent action by another. The executive (president), legislative (House of Representatives and Senate), and judicial (Supreme Court) can reverse or prevent action by another branch.

To enumerate very briefly: Both the House and the Senate must agree before legislation can be presented to the president. The president can veto any legislation; however, the presidential veto can be overridden by a two-thirds vote by both House and Senate.

The Supreme Court can declare any law—state or federal—to be unconstitutional, regardless of its popularity or degree of domestic support. Thus, for example, burning a U.S. flag is "free speech," while public prayer in schools is unconstitutional. Each of these illustrations would probably have been supported in a national referendum—a political mechanism that exists only on the state level in selected states. The Supreme Court can discover previously unknown rights, such as the right to privacy, to buttress its decision on "choice" abortion. The only recourse the legislative and executive branches have to counter Supreme Court decisions is to amend the federal constitution—an extraordinarily protracted and convoluted effort requiring a three-quarters majority in both House and Senate and agreement by three-quarters of the states. As an illustration of the difficulty, since the first batch of 10 amendments (the Bill of Rights), only 16 additional amendments were agreed between 1791 and 1992 (and two of these—regarding prohibition on alcohol consumption—cancelled one another).

To be sure, over an extended period of time, presidential appointments with congressional support can alter the philosophical views of the federal courts. However, lifetime/good behavior appointments can make the most senior appointments few and far between. For example, in mid-2005, the composition of the Supreme Court had not changed for 11 years, a circumstance close to unique, but with the deliberate selection of younger judges, more likely to be closer to the rule than the exception. Thus the subsequent selection of two relatively young justices: Chief Justice John Roberts (51) and Justice Samuel Alito (55) could have juridical influence for the next 30 years. (As of mid-2007, the oldest justice, John Paul Stevens, is 87.)

Perhaps Most Important Are the Checks and Balances

The legal and political equality between the U.S. Senate and the House of Representatives is the defining element in U.S. politics. It is the ultimate check on federal political power as it gives the smallest state (Rhode Island), or least populated (Wyoming), or poorest (Mississippi), equality with the largest, most heavily populated, and wealthy. It was the essential compromise that permitted the ratification of the U.S. Constitution in 1789 for exactly the reason that persists today: the smallest states refused to be dominated by the votes of the large and the powerful. Without that agreement, there would have been no United States.

In practical terms, this arrangement moves power and influence from the "big battalion" states to the smaller, less economically important ones and dilutes the power of the executive branch even further. Those diplomats attempting to understand the U.S. government err if they assume that influence on and access to the executive branch will accomplish their objectives. First, they must understand the great limits on executive power in comparison to the legislative branch—one of the most obvious being the ability to reject or modify, at will, any and all legislative proposals presented by the executive branch. All expenditures are authorized by Congress and subject to congressional oversight. The president cannot name many of his most intimate advisors (his cabinet, many of his senior governing executives, such as the directors of the FBI and the CIA and ambassadors) without agreement by the Senate. Any or all of his nominees to the federal courts can be rejected. Agreements (treaties) contracted in good faith with foreign governments must have approval by the Senate. The only strength that the executive branch retains in these circumstances is that defeat does not mean that the government must face election. But the executive branch cannot alter the timing of federal elections—they are set and have been held without fail during our deepest historical crises: the Civil War and the Second World War (when a democracy such as the United Kingdom postponed elections).

Second, these outside observers must understand the internal power of the congressional committees—whose members can present legislation that is likely to be voted upon and determine which amendments will be adopted. Every money bill must be both "authorized" and "appropriated"—and having funds authorized is only the halfway mark to obtaining them. Whether a member of the majority or the minority, every congressional representative and senator is important 100 yards from Capitol Hill. There are no "trained seals" and while a combination of seniority and personal effectiveness are politically important, the requirement to gather a majority to pass legislation reinforces the importance of every elected representative.

Designed for Deadlock
The consequence is that any serious legislation requires coalition building. It is far easier to prevent something from happening than to get it to happen. As elections are not fought on platforms to the extent that guide many

parliamentary governments, there is little guidance, direction, or "mandate" for much of what a government may propose in legislation subsequent to election. To be sure, each U.S. party produces a "platform" document, but these are forgotten almost before they are drafted and the thought that a political opponent would criticize failure to implement something in a party's "Red, White, and Blue" book is risible. There is no political accountability associated with a political platform; it is a political science rather than a political policy exercise. A government has a mandate to attempt; it has no automatic majority to implement any policy.

There are no easy victories for the executive branch. In effect, every member of every party is a free agent and every vote is *de facto* a free vote. Unless a proposal is instantly and universally popular (for example, a "National Do Not Call Registry" limiting the activity of telemarketers), it requires painstaking political management. Although there are individual politicians who regularly vote with their party and adhere to the "party line," this support is a matter of personal philosophy and choice rather than an imposed discipline. Each congressman and senator has been elected through personal effort; there are no directed nominations or star candidates. Consequently, a congressman or senator responds first to his local constituents, and only secondarily—or not at all—to a party leader. These congressional representatives are closely attuned to the interests of their constituents, who pour their views into congressional offices with the expectation that they *will* be heard. Thus the United States in some ways operates as a continuing minority government. To assemble the temporary coalition necessary to pass legislation, individual representatives and senators are "bought"—often with "pork" (projects that will deliver spending to their state or district for which they can take credit with their constituents). The hope, often futile, is that an individual will "stay bought" at least for the given vote.

It is the enormous flexibility of this system that has permitted it to avoid the problems of regionalism and nationalism plaguing Canada. The West is "in"—as are the South, North, and East. The system guarantees all regions a voice and the geographic distribution of racial/ethnic minorities means that they seek federal/national rather than local backing. The most populous and most powerful states (California, Texas, New York, Florida, and Illinois) are sufficiently regionally diverse that their interests don't coincide to "gang up" on the rest of the United States—and the powers of small states in the Senate reinforce this reality. Philosophically, it makes it somewhat easier to think "nationally"—and governors of large states are viewed as national figures. (By contrast, Canadian premiers appear to be "provincial" in both senses of the word, and no premier has ever become prime minister.)

REPRESENTATION, PROPORTIONAL OR OTHERWISE

As a congressional representative faces the electorate every two years, there is quick approval or sanction for most decisions. While a senator may hope that the voter's recollection of an unpopular decision early in a six-year term will fade, a representative has no such luxury. It is virtually impossible for an essentially unpopular proposal (for example, a national sales tax) to be "whipped" through Congress by party discipline in face of local domestic opposition. It would simply be political suicide for an American politician to take such an approach. The reverse of the coin, however, means that Congress is unwilling to take preventive domestic measures that may be technically recommended or wise (adjustment of social security pension planning, for example, or energy conservation measures) that are not immediately obvious in their necessity but immediately obvious in their unpopularity for being expensive and/or restrictive. Far sighted the U.S. government is not; it is more likely to read the writing on the wall only when its back is up against it.

The nominee for the general election is selected in a "primary" election; normally, any individual registered as a party member can seek the nomination for any office. An individual can declare a party choice and run for office as a representative of that party, regardless of the agreement of official party leaders. How little control national leaders have over who runs under their party label was illustrated by the case of David Duke. A former local leader of the Ku Klux Klan, Duke contested and won the Republican primary in 1989 for a seat in the Louisiana House of Representatives. Anticipating that his nomination as a Republican would tar the party as racist, Duke was opposed by mainstream Republicans within the state and around the country, but he still ran as a Republican and could not be stripped of this right. Indeed, he won that race and continued to campaign as a Republican for other Louisiana offices (governor in 1991) against individuals endorsed by Republicans in the state.

POLITICAL PARTIES: SOME OBSERVATIONS

Political practice in the United States is both more limited and more coherent than in many other countries. Although anyone looking at a presidential ballot can find a wide variety of parties beyond the Republican and

Democrats, ranging across the spectrum from communist to libertarian, historically "third parties" have been virtually irrelevant. The U.S. has not developed niche markets for third parties, although the occasional "independent" is elected—often chosen as a "none of the above" candidate. The gaggle of third parties is not regarded seriously beyond the parents of their candidates. Although the voting percentage taken by "Reform" party leader Ross Perot in the 1992 election was significant (at 19 percent), Perot did not win a single state. And, while it can be argued that the Perot vote tipped the election to Clinton, others have argued with comparable justification that Perot's votes came equally from Republicans and Democrats. Likewise, while it can be argued that in 2000 the independent candidate Ralph Nader drew votes, particularly in Florida, that otherwise would have given the election to Al Gore, this conclusion remains speculative, and in 2004 the presence of Nader and a "Green" party had no effect. The last serious third-party effort was mounted by former Alabama governor George Wallace in 1968; Wallace won five southern states, but did not affect the election outcome.

Historically, both Republicans and Democrats have been big-tent, umbrella parties with intellectual room for both conservatives and liberals. While this observation is more historically true than currently valid, it remains generally accurate. As the United States enters the 21st century, there are fewer conservative Democrats or liberal Republicans, but both liberals and conservatives persist in both parties—and all parties, through polling and close observation of their local politics, are acutely aware of what the public wants and believes. The presence of several strains of political philosophy in each party means that leadership is more eclectic and willing to offer a broad set of polities to the electorate. Of course, one could also conclude that the U.S. political spectrum is more generally "conservative" than the political range in other democracies, and hence the political parties are philosophically closer to one another in general policy. One will not find, in either party, significant proponents of, for example, tax increases, ratifying the Kyoto Treaty or the International Criminal Court, reduced support for Israel, nuclear disarmament, a military draft, national, federally funded health care, gun registration, marijuana legalization, or homosexual marriage.

For a system of this nature to operate effectively, and stifle the evolution of third parties, the rule must be co-option. Thus, if an idea looks popular, it will be taken up and/or stolen from a prospective opponent. Consequently, both national parties express firm commitment to national defense, limited (but compassionate) government, balanced budgets (regardless of the reality), fair taxes, civil rights for minorities, and concern for the environment. It is up to the individual voter to decide whether the historical records of the parties and their candidates match the "campaign bed conversions" evident in their rhetoric. A "single interest" voter either decides that neither serious party is worthy of the vote or ignores other problem positions of the party if it meets the "single interest" requirement.

A Secondary Problem: Decline in Voting

The United States has been puzzled for decades over the relatively low (and often declining) percentage of voters. Historians, however, as noted in a PBS special prior to the 2004 election, have observed that the U.S. has never had high percentage of citizens voting—even when the franchise was restricted to white, property-owning males, eligible voter participation rarely reached 50 percent. Nor did lowering the voting age to 18 stimulate the electorate (the youngest voters continue to be the least likely to vote). Likewise, the 1994 "Motor Voter" act that eased registration procedures had no significant political effect. In one survey, the U.S. ranked 139th of 172 countries in voter turnout. Although the 2004 election showed a slight increase in the percentage of those who voted, to 64 percent, it still reflected historic traditions: higher percentages ranking from youngest to oldest; greater voting by the best educated and most affluent.

While some political scientists view this low level of voting with alarm, others suggest that it reflects essential satisfaction with the sociopolitical situation in the United States that does not galvanize the potential electorate to the polls rather than alienation/indifference to politics and/or politicians. Nor is there any interest in implementing mandatory voter registration and poll appearance of the kind that has existed in Australia since 1924. In that regard, it is interesting that even on a mandatory level, with fines for non-registrants, only 82 percent of Australians go to the polls. On the other hand, individual states have experimented with devices such as voting by mail (Oregon), but also without a radical increase in voter participation.

It may be that people value the secret, contested ballot only when they are deprived of it.

These various voting devices suggest that there is sufficient political flexibility in the existing U.S. structure to make creative experimentation in political abstractions such as proportional representation and the single transferable vote generally unattractive. These mechanisms are associated with fringe elements that are "out"—and whose ideas are not sufficiently attractive to persuade individual representatives or senators, let alone major parties, to endorse or adopt them. Nor are their proponents sufficiently politically charismatic to gain personal electoral support.

Essentially, Americans conclude that their system isn't broken—so why break it? When over 200 years of experience indicates that "first past the post" provides a clear winner, there is no incentive to mess with success. From every hopeful team (read "party") that starts a sports season, there emerges only one World Series, Stanley Cup, or Super Bowl winner. The person who places second has a clear title: loser. One does not share the results of a track meet on the basis of how close the fifth-place contestant was to the first-place victor. So if you want to win—run faster next time.

Moreover, most U.S. political observers have concluded that minority/coalition governments are a recipe for incoherent governments. And the United States already has sufficient internal limitations in its structural power that it doesn't need more constraining factors. In coalition government, the factions maneuver for factional advantage rather than national benefit. In contrast, in a two-party system, the "outs" conceive of themselves as just an election away from exercising power. In a PR government, most of the parties will never exercise authority and thus have no impetus to be responsible in their demands or to consider the concerns of the nation before the interests of their faction.

CULTURE AND COMMUNICATION

The United States lacks one of the great parliamentary institutions: a forum for serious debate and/or a "question period." Oratory designed to persuade an opponent within the confines of congressional debate has virtually disappeared; there are severe time limits on speakers in the House, and, if a senator is speaking at length, it is more likely to be a filibuster to prevent action than to convince others of the legitimacy of a position. There are no "great debates" (or, for that matter, great congressional speakers). The thought that anyone would listen to a two-hour speech beggars the 21st-century imagination; a two-minute televised presentation would be stretching the audience's attention span, and a 20-second sound bite is what is really desired.

For his part, the president normally does not directly engage with Congress. It is, for example, exceptionally rare for a president to testify personally and formally before a congressional committee. The most recent illustration was the carefully scripted and negotiated joint appearance of President Bush and Vice President Cheney before the Commission inquiry into the 9/11 events.

Indeed, communication between the branches of government is almost always formal, such as the traditional presentation of the federal budget (which the opposition invariably pronounces "dead on arrival"). The annual State of the Union address now is as scripted as a stage play. In this instance, Congress *is* a collection of trained seals with the president's supporters clapping on cue and his opponents sitting on their flippers.

In the absence of a question period (or formalized point/counterpoint between the president and an official opposition leader), the United States does not benefit from the opportunity (beloved in its abstraction by political scientists) to hold the government to account on a daily basis. On the other hand, the citizenry also avoids the reality of hearing puerile exchanges between cavorting jackanapes on the level of "your mother wears combat boots" that suggests answers are the last thing anyone should expect from a question period. Instead, the United States exercises two mechanisms for public accountability of government: through the media and congressional committee hearings.

The Media

The president (and other cabinet members) will "meet the press" in formal or informal exchanges, often nationally televised. The liability is that the executive branch has no requirement to respond to the media on any given schedule; the president may go for months without a serious or extended media encounter. He is least likely to meet the press when the press most wants to call him to account. Cabinet officers are more available in multiple forums. Nevertheless, these exercises are traditional to any serious democracy: a certain amount of information is delivered and a certain number of questions posed. Occasionally the information delivered is something useful to the wider public; occasionally the information delivered even matches questions asked. Occasionally.

The government, however, is legally required to respond to Freedom of Information requests that permit inquiries for documents and other information. Enacted in 1966 and extensively updated 30 years later, the Freedom of Information Act states that requesters need not even be U.S. citizens, but the information sought may be denied on grounds such as official secrecy or privacy, or extensively edited/restricted prior to being released to the public. Nevertheless, it is a device evolving over the past generation that has fostered greater access to government decision-making and information previously regarded as confidential.

U.S. television has no equivalent to the Canadian Broadcasting Corporation (and no government-supported second language network). Public opinion sees no need for a special government organization to support national unity—national unity isn't an issue. The U.S. Public Broadcasting System (PBS) runs leftward, and on a shoestring. Consequently, it struggles against both ritualistic political hostility based on its perceived bias and the economic philosophy that the government should not be running a media system in competition with private industry. Government funding without government control is regarded as a waste of taxpayer money; if the PBS is producing something "popular," it should be funded by private sponsors. If it isn't popular enough to be supported privately, it isn't worth being produced at public expense. Moreover, in a 500-channel media universe, it is the rare idea or opinion that cannot get air time—again, without expending taxpayer money.

Congressional Committee Hearings

The many congressional committees and subcommittees hold regular hearings into every subject of conceivable interest, domestic and global. Most of these hearings are open to the public and listed in newspapers and websites. Senior representatives of the government, notably cabinet secretaries, flag-rank military officers, foreign affairs officials, and a full range of government and civilian experts of every description, provide frequent and extensive information and comment, ostensibly to ensure that Congress is better informed. The resulting committee reports may provide the basis for legislation (or for political attack/criticism of the administration). Or, even more likely, they will serve as door stops and dust catchers.

Political Debates Amuse More than Persuade

Presidential, vice-presidential, and other "debates" between political candidates at all levels are a reflection of traditional U.S. politics. The most famous debates in U.S. history were between Lincoln and Stephen Douglas in 1858 for the U.S. Senate (Douglas won the election). Although not due to that outcome, political debate fell into disuse as communication became more effective and citizens didn't have to come to the county fair to learn what competing politicians had to say.

The rise of nationwide television, however, prompted a revival of debate. The 1960 Kennedy-Nixon debates proved pivotal to introducing JFK to the U.S. population, while Nixon underestimated the need to master the medium as the message (rather than just debate his opponent). Subsequent presidential-level debaters learned from Nixon's debacle (even if no further debates were held until 1976), and they are watched by U.S. audiences more to determine whether the candidates meet minimal thresholds of competence (don't babble, drool, or transform into Wolfman Jack) than to evaluate their political stance. Candidates, for their part, answer the question that they wish to answer with pre-drilled sound bites rather than what may be asked by the questioner(s). Consequently, while each side's media "spinners" proclaim that their candidate wiped the floor with the other (or "kicked some butt" as GHW Bush memorably said following his 1984 vice-presidential debate with Geraldine Ferraro), the public almost always concludes that the exchange was a draw.

What the debates have demonstrated, however, is that U.S. politicians are total professionals and that it takes many years to master the parameters of their craft. You can start late in U.S. politics, but you cannot be untutored. Who can forget, for example, how the late Admiral James Stockdale (Ross Perot's running mate in 1992), Medal of Honor winner, Vietnam POW, and scholar of Greek philosophy, was eaten alive in the vice-presidential debate when matched against luminaries such as Dan Quayle and Al Gore. Stockdale's abject failure simply demonstrated that intelligence, courage, personal probity, and the like are distinctly secondary to mastering media moments with a mental disk drive that dispenses 20-second sound bites on command.

SOME PRESSURE POINTS

Systemic Problems

The reality is that the United States remains embedded in an 18th-century political artifact experimentally designed for a country profoundly cautious about the ramifications of democracy: one in which no woman voted, property qualifications limited the franchise for white males, and senators were selected by state legislatures. Only the House of Representatives responded directly to popular vote. The presidency was carefully insulated from popular enthusiasm. Thus the creation of "electors" emphasized the federal element of the new republic and installed a level of responsible citizens who would serve as a potential bulwark against rampant republican democracy. Although not widely advertised, they stood ready to vote for the "better" man, regardless of how the citizens of their states may have voted. And indeed, they retain that authority to this day.

The U.S. political train went off the tracks in 1876 when the disputed Hayes-Tilden election was not resolved until inaugural day. In that contretemps, most historians now will quietly admit the convoluted decision process that awarded all disputed electoral votes to the Republican Hayes (and hence accorded him a one-vote victory) was badly biased. The United States, in 2000, was fortunate that no one survived from that 1876 experience to communicate the intensity of yesteryear's bitterness; imagination about that period had to suffice following the 2000 election.

Already there is more than enough in anecdote and reality to stimulate a generation or more of bitterness for the loser: the presumed bias of the Republican Florida attorney general; the questionable evenhandedness of Democratic leadership in the counties conducting arcane hand recounts under regularly changing ground rules; the perceived political preference of the six Democrat-appointed justices on the Florida Supreme Court; the partisan Republican majorities in the state legislatures. All was finally concluded by a 5-4 vote in the Supreme Court not to take further action and to let the George W. Bush victory in Florida (and thus in the country) stand.

Having stumbled through the Hayes-Tilden fiasco, the electoral college system underwent some minor technical fixes, but any attempt to abolish it and move to direct popular vote for the president was futile. Indeed, despite the bleats of outraged irritation still echoing from the 2000 election, the Electoral College will not be abolished or even modified. Essentially, the system gives disproportionate weight and hence political influence to the voters in small states—power that they will not surrender. In the 2000 election, for example, in the District of Columbia (with the smallest number of voters: approximately 190,000), only 63,000 votes were required to deliver an electoral vote for Al Gore. In contrast, for California (with the largest number of voters: approximately 9.7 million), 180,000 votes were needed to provide one electoral vote for the vice president. And in Texas (the largest state to support Governor Bush), over 198,000 individual votes were required to generate one electoral vote. To amend the constitution, an amendment must be agreed upon by at least a two-thirds majority of both the House of Representatives and the Senate, and then approved by three-quarters of the states. Twenty-three states (with 46 votes in the Senate) have seven or fewer electoral votes. Thus the likelihood that there will be direct popular vote election of the president is zero.

Not Bottom Up in Some Dimensions

There were great political reform efforts at the end of the 19th century. These incorporated creative political devices: referendum (putting a specific question directly to the people); recall ("dis-electing" a politician prior to a formal election); and initiative (a proposal presented for popular vote based on a demand by the voters). Although these innovations are reflected in a number of state political systems (most obviously in California, which notably recalled its governor in 2004, and which has held a series of referendums for a generation), there are no federal/national illustrations to parallel the state-level mechanisms.

In this regard, the Canadian institution of a national referendum has attractions. To be sure, the issues likely to be put in play are going to be divisive, but it is the nature of the topic, not the mechanism for resolving it, that creates the divisions. An "up or down" vote can compel an agreement to a problem that 100 nuanced legal decisions leave festering. One can imagine national referendum topics for the United States on issues such as prayer in school, abortion, homosexual marriage, and gun ownership (despite the Second Amendment). Canadians' reluctance to employ their referendum authority (along with the almost pathological refusal to invoke the "notwithstanding" clause in the charter) deprives them of answers for such questions. Enough unanswered questions can be as societally damaging as hard answers.

Political Attitudes in the States

While it is not true that "a Republican is a Republican is a Republican" (or the same for a Democrat), one does not find great differences from state to state. A Massachusetts Republican will be more "liberal" than a Texas Republican (and a South Carolina Democrat more "conservative" than a California Democrat), but the party labels produce a generally recognizable politician. Political parties at the state level are reasonably close analogues to those at the national level. There is no equivalent, for example, of Quebec politics where "Liberal" really means "federalist," regardless of personal political philosophy. Nor is there an equivalent of British Columbia where the provincial "Liberal" party was, in effect, a hostile takeover of the small Liberal party by assorted provincial conservatives looking for a vehicle after the wheels came off the Social Credit party; B.C. "Liberals" have little more than a nominal connection with federal Liberals.

An Older Person's Game

While there is always a bow to "youth" in U.S. politics and election campaigns, there are clear limits to how much youth will be served. There are Young Republicans and Young Democrats, and candidates recognize that youthful activists are always useful. Nevertheless, there are no reserved voting blocks of delegate votes for youth in selecting a candidate at the party presidential conventions and there are no illustrations of candidates specifically revising policy to cater to a "youth" position or to deflect anticipated "youth" criticism. If anything, social policies of interest to the young, such as raising the age to consume alcohol legally, engage in sexual activity, smoke tobacco, or enjoy full driving privileges, have militated against youth interests—at the same time that the age to vote was lowered. Moreover, the youth vote is also split; although U.S. youth are more "liberal" than the rest of the population, they do not act with the degree of coherence on topics ostensibly of their interest that other blocs of voters do (for example, the elderly on social security).

In effect, federal politics is an adult game. And this should be no surprise; a reality check suggests the unlikelihood that an individual would be ready to lead as complicated a society as the United States at the constitutionally permitted age of 35. The youngest man ever nominated to be president was William Jennings Bryan (at 36) and he ended by losing three times. The youngest ever elected was John F. Kennedy (at 43); the average age of vice presidents is 54.

Although many of those seeking the presidency and other senior federal offices are career politicians, others come from full or partial careers in business, law, the armed forces, and even acting! Observers might argue that the United States is a firm believer in the Peter Principle—allowing individuals to rise to their level of incompetence. One need not spend all one's life within political circles in order to enter politics. This flexibility in U.S. politics is partly possible because there are no specialized skills that must be mastered prior to seeking national office. For example, while an ability to hold a casual conversation in Spanish with the United States' largest minority will doubtless become increasingly useful, it is not a make-or-break factor for a candidacy. Nor does one have to be an elected political figure to serve as a cabinet minister (indeed, it is rather rare for a president to appoint a currently serving federal political official to his cabinet). Nor do cabinet officers subsequently enter politics with any frequency. If you have become successful enough to qualify as "famous," that fame factor will suffice. If your primary accomplishment has been making a considerable amount of money, it will serve to hire media manipulators who specialize in transforming amphibians into royalty.

And Still a White Male Milieu

Women are not proportionally represented in U.S. politics. At this juncture, this point is neither a problem nor a value judgment, but simply a fact. There are no formalistic requirements for either major party to present female candidates in some proportion. At the same time, U.S. society does not agonize over the circumstance that, as of 2007, 70 members of the 435-member House of Representatives and 16 members of the 100-member Senate were women. Nor for that matter is much attention given to the numbers of the "Black Caucus" (at 43, approaching their percentage in the U.S. population), the distribution of other visible minorities, or the presence of Jews, Hispanics, or Asians in Congress. These numbers have steadily increased, but have done so as a reflection of greater interest by women and minorities in the political process rather than a mechanistic design to increase gender/racial distribution. It is hardly that race, gender, sexual orientation, and religion are irrelevant in U.S. politics, but it is closer to permitting individuals to succeed (or fail) on their own merits and through their own choices. The United States does not accept that one must be represented by your "own kind" for the representation to be legitimate; affirmative action does not carry into politics. Thus the millions of males in California and Maine do not complain that they are unrepresented in the Senate because both of their state senators are women (they are more likely to complain in Maine that both senators are Republicans and in California that both are Democrats).

The Role of Money

Former Californian assemblyman and speaker Jesse Unruh is credited with saying that "money is the mother's milk of politics." He could have said that "money is the mother's milk of everything" and been no less accurate. His truism about money and politics, however, becomes more valid with every election. An FDR-era Democrat once said that the Democrats would "tax and tax; spend and spend; and elect and elect" and, while he meant that public works projects attributed to the Democratic party would prompt voter loyalty, he might as well have been referring to campaign funding. Incumbents tend to attract the most campaign funding (they are also more likely to be re-elected than defeated), and while money is not the *only* factor in the equation, it is hardly irrelevant.

U.S. campaign financing rules have attempted to balance a spectrum of views: reformers who believe that large campaign donations implicitly "buy" political influence; traditionalists who suggest that the monies spent reflect the difficulties in reaching a large population and are proportionate to generally rising costs; and legal opinions regarding constitutionally protected free speech. A baseline 1976 Supreme Court legal judgment held that political spending is the equivalent of free speech, essentially not to be restricted although "reasonable" limits on spending are possible. While a variety of laws manage the funding for U.S. presidential campaigns, the amount of money spent rises steadily.

The most obvious element of U.S. public presidential campaign financing is reflected in the "check-off" on the federal tax form. Begun in 1971 with a $1 check-off, the mechanism in 2007 permitted a taxpayer to designate $3 ($6 for a joint return) for campaign financing. The tax form clearly states that the contribution will not affect the individual's taxes (or a refund). Nevertheless, U.S. taxpayers have remained highly skeptical of public financing, being either hostile to the use of tax revenue for political campaigning, hostile to using their funds to support parties or ideas they reject, or just hostile to politics and politicians generally. Consequently, participation rates have been low from the beginning and have declined steadily—from a high of 28.7 percent on 1980 returns, when 40 million tax returns were checked, to less than 10 percent in 2006. (The remainder of taxpayers have either checked "no" or left the box blank.)

A review of campaign funding law and practice for this study is not of particular use; it changes with virtually every election as partisans seek "fairness" (that advantages them) and highly adroit political practitioners seek legal mechanisms to permit maximum funding. Thus the 2002 McCain-Finegold law supposedly shifted the focus of fundraising towards individual contributions to candidates ("hard" money) and away from contributions by wealthy individuals, political action groups, and other vague associations to political parties ("soft" money). The dominant device for the 2004 election, however, became the "527" groups, which could spend unlimited money if they did not specifically endorse the election or defeat of a candidate, and were prohibited from coordinating with a candidate's campaign. To be sure, the juxtaposition between issue advocacy and candidacy advocacy is heatedly debated. The reality is that anyone smart enough to accumulate the funds of the dimensions expended by a 527 is sufficiently intelligent to back a preferred candidate without clandestine, Deep Throat-style campaign coordination.

It is difficult, however, to measure the effectiveness of the money spent. One might contend that money spent by one side is designed to offset the money spent by the other rather than attempting to convince any significant part of the population to vote in favor (or against) a candidate. The three largest 527 groups were regarded as Democrat-oriented and spent over $200 million. The most effective 527, however, was arguably the Swift Boat Veterans for Truth, which ultimately spent over $22 million in raising credible questions about Democratic Party candidate John Kerry's service in Vietnam. Indeed, it is difficult to argue that either major candidate in the 2004 election had any shortage of funds. But ultimately the costs of the campaigns are not a factor in public thinking. The United States electorate notes, but does not obsess over, the costs of a political campaign. To be sure, each election is more expensive than the last, but the "viewing with alarm" over the prospect of spending a billion dollars on the 2008 campaign has no popular resonance; it is a cost of democracy and, as some note, often comparable to the costs of a major advertising campaign for a new automobile model or a new brand of athletic shoes. It's useful to note as a comparative that major cigarette makers spent a combined $15.2 billion on advertising in 2003.

The conclusion would be that the United States has a very wide range of effective democratic procedures for those who wish to employ them.

ECONOMIC AND RESOURCE MANAGEMENT 3

Both Canada and the United States are blessed by economic circumstances and opportunities that are unparalleled in the world.

North America was replete with virtually unexploited and extraordinarily extensive resources when Europeans arrived on the continent. These resources, developed under democratic, free-market systems, and largely unthreatened by enemies within or without the continent, have resulted in unparalleled wealth for the residents of North America. The United States has more rapidly exploited its resources, partly due to easier access to them and the imperatives of a population ten times that of Canada. Nevertheless, the economic relationship has been symbiotic; Canadian and U.S. wealth and prosperity have reinforced each other.

The economic relationship is reflected mostly in trade: the bilateral trading system is the world's largest and most intensive. Characterized technically as "free trade," the current emphasis is directed towards the restrictions rather than on the freedoms. Although 95-plus percent of these exchanges are friction free, 95-plus percent of the political and social focus is on areas of disagreement.

The most pointed economic challenge of the 21st century revolves around energy: obtaining it, using it, conserving it. The United States is the world's largest energy consumer; Canada, potentially, is the world's largest petroleum producer—and already the largest energy exporter to the U.S. Although the current arrangements are enormously profitable and effective, problems that are more than theoretical are easily discernible.

One of the most obvious challenges is the tension between energy use and conservation. For many Canadians, despite the carefully couched skepticism of the current Tory minority government, the strictures of the Kyoto Treaty are guidelines for conduct; for most Americans they are prescriptions for economic disaster—and rejected out of hand. Nevertheless, conservation is a "conservative" as well as a "liberal" issue, and the economics of conservation are more relevant to its success than any philosophical commitment.

The Canadian Economy and Energy Situation

Canada has long been a land of abundance in the form of arable land, fresh water, minerals, vegetation, and wildlife. Europeans who came to Canada's shores found two key differences from what lay farther south: the rugged terrain of the vast Canadian Shield and the harsh Canadian winters. Their experiences contrasted sharply with those of American settlers, who, with the exception of those who settled in close proximity to what is now the Canadian border, encountered mostly highlands and vast plains and on the whole a far milder climate. These two facts of geography had a profound impact on Canada's development, which is evident today. First, they limited population growth. Second, they had major impacts on the settlement patterns.

Examining a map of Canada on the distribution of our population, it quickly becomes obvious that the great majority of Canadians lives in a relatively compact area that extends about 160 kilometres from the American border. These populated regions hugging the border hold approximately 90 percent of our population today, leaving the rest almost empty by the world's contemporary standards. Our overall population density is about 3.1 people per thousand square kilometers, the lowest of any major industrialized nation.

The Canadian Shield, which proved to be such a formidable obstacle to settlement, is enormously rich in mineral deposits and forestry resources. As a result, the national economy was built initially by supplying raw materials to the world. Canada has always been and will doubtless remain a trading nation.

Canadians are dependant on trade to an extent unparalleled by any of the world's other affluent economies except for Australia and New Zealand. In 2004, exports of goods and services as a percentage of GDP were 38.2 percent, while the imports of goods and services reached 34 percent, thus making Canada the most trade-dependant nation in the G7 by far. Historically, trade in commodities fueled economic growth, but this has changed dramatically over the past two decades. A majority of Canada's exports today are finished goods with high added value. Among Canada's total exports of products in 2004, almost 60 percent were finished industrial goods, machinery and automotive products. Trade in commodities, however, remains important: about 30 percent of merchandise exports are still energy commodities and forestry products.

SHIFTING TRADE PATTERNS

The overall condition of the global economy has always been and continues to be central to Canada's economic prosperity. More specifically, it is the economic gyrations of the American economy to which Canada has been most acutely attuned in the post-World War II era. Despite continuing efforts to diversify exports, Canadians still rely on the American market to absorb most of them. In 2004, for example, Americans took fully 84.5 percent of our exports and remain our customers of choice. The reverse is also true: we are America's single largest group of consumers for their exports as well. A little more than 23 percent of all American exports are consumed by Canadians. (The EU as a whole, however, is now the United States' largest trading partner.) The total of the bilateral trade between the two countries is so great that it constitutes the world's largest trading relationship, not including the EU.

Given the deeply integrated and interdependent nature of the two economies, many assume that Canada and the United States developed in a largely symbiotic manner. In fact, it was only with the advent of the post-World War II era that the two economies began to operate synchronously. Earlier, our trade relationship with the United Kingdom was of paramount importance; trade with America was seen for a long period as being of subsidiary weight. Even at the beginning of the 20th century, the majority of Canada's exports were destined for Britain, which was an especially attractive market due to the preferential market access that Britain granted Canadian exports. At that time, north-south trade was even seen as a threat to the development of Canadian industry. A plethora of protectionist measures were adopted in Ottawa to ward off the threat of American economic dominance.

Unlike the United States, which early on developed a large internal market due to rapid population growth, Canada always needed export markets to absorb its goods. It was in Canada's interest to maintain the commercial relationship with Britain when the Americans declared independence. We could thereby continue to enjoy privileged access to the British market. In America, leaving the British Empire proved to be far more attractive in part due to the rapid development of a very robust domestic economy. In fact, Americans had received little benefit from the preferential market access afforded them by their affiliation with the empire and lost much due to the restrictions on economic development imposed by British mercantilist policies and by having to pay taxes to the British crown without representation in the Westminster Parliament. America was capable of being its own engine for growth and so it became national destiny to unfetter itself from the imperial controls it saw as impeding progress. Of course, the American Revolution was far more than an illustration of economic determinism; specific political differences were exacerbated by British economic policies. In Canada's case, the market access granted by Britain more than made up for the economic restrictions and the tax burdens that came with it.

Natural resources laid the foundation for the modern economy of Canada. Our economic history can only be understood by examining the historical pattern of resource exploitation and development. The recognition of the vital role these resources and commodities played led economist W. A. Mackintosh to propose his now famous "staples thesis," which was later enlarged upon by Harold Innis.

According to Innis, Canada's development followed patterns dictated by the exploitation of different natural resource endowments to produce certain staple commodities. These staples, which constituted the raw materials required for the manufacture of more sophisticated goods or of goods for direct consumption, were then exported to Europe, primarily through Britain. Innis argued that because of the exploitation of certain natural resources to produce particular staples, each of Canada's regions followed a developmental path dictated by its unique allotment of resources.

The staples thesis is useful in understanding the Canadian economy and its development until it began to industrialize rapidly in the 1850s. It was in fact a single resource, fish, that lured Europeans to the shores of northern North America in the first place; it was the exploitation of fish stocks that eventually encouraged the rise of permanent settlements and the development of other industries. As early as the pre-Columbus 14th century, the Portuguese were fishing off the Grand Banks. (Legend has it, however, that when these fisherfolk were asked what was out there, the response was "Ca nada mas" or "nothing much.") When the explorer John Cabot first navigated Cape Bonavista and Cape Breton Island in 1497, he found schools of cod so numerous that they impeded the movements of his ship. Returning to England, he spoke of fish so plentiful that they could be caught with buckets lowered into the ocean. These reports induced the first wave of European fisherman, from Britain, France, and Portugal, to begin the tradition of annual fishing expeditions across the Atlantic that would endure for centuries.

In the early years of migratory fishing, which developed principally around Newfoundland in the early 1500s, it was the Spanish and the

French who moved fastest to exploit the new resource. While the English were active in the coastal fisheries, they were not as vigorous as the Spanish and French, mainly because of the disadvantage they faced by not being able to procure large amounts of salt. At the time, salt was essential for the preservation of the fish harvest so that it could survive the journey to Europe in edible condition. French and Spanish fisherman had access to abundant domestic supplies of salt, so they engaged in what was known as the "green" fishery. The green fishery relied on the use of large amounts of salt to preserve fish as they were caught and allowed for drying to take place later. The British had to rely on the "dry" fishery due to their limited supplies of salt, which involved drying the catch on land in the open on a wooden platform called a flake. The drying process was lengthy and required a considerable amount of space as well as access to timber to build the flakes for drying the fish.

The difference in cost for large quantities of salt faced by the British in comparison with the French and Spanish had profound consequences. It necessitated the construction of temporary settlements on the part of the English, which were occupied during the fishing season in spring and summer. These settlements eventually evolved into permanent settlements and laid the basis for the English claim to Newfoundland.

The cod fishery remained the primary economic activity in northern North America until the early 1600s, when it began to be supplemented by the fur trade, which has its origins in the early 1500s and came into being as a consequence of the cod fishery. During the summer months when fishermen from Europe were operating in the waters around Newfoundland, they would have little to do between fishing expeditions and processing caught fish. In their spare time, they explored the coastal areas and encountered indigenous people with whom they traded metal implements, glass beads, and blankets for furs. When the fishermen returned to Europe to sell their catch, they also sold the furs for what proved to be large profits. By the mid-16th century, French ships had begun trade with the coastal Algonquin Indians, involving the exchange of European goods for furs. Tadoussac on the Saguenay River near the mouth of the St. Lawrence became the site of an annual meeting between French traders and indigenous peoples for the express purpose of trading. This early French involvement helped to establish the dominance of its traders for over a century until the English through the Hudson's Bay Company came to control virtually all trade in furs across British North America.

TRADE—FREE AND OTHERWISE

As the fur trade gradually came to a halt due to changes in European fashions, a new resource fortunately emerged as the driver of Canada's growth: timber. As Britain's domestic supplies of timber ran out in the 18th century, it was forced to look for new sources to maintain its large navy and merchant marine fleets. At first, it turned to imports from the Baltics, but due to Britain's mercantilist economic policies at the time, the importation of Baltic timber was subject to heavy tariffs. Britain instead preferred to source timber from its own possessions, with which it could exchange finished goods for timber. This had a positive effect on the domestic economy and also eliminated the need for payment to the Baltic states. For most of the 18th century, the policy had been to encourage the New England colonies to supply Britain by giving the timber exports preferential tariff treatment. However, with the advent of the American Revolution in 1775, as well as the fact that most of the easily accessible quality timber in New England had already been harvested, the British increasingly looked to Canada to fulfill their growing needs.

From the beginning of the 19th century until the 1840s, timber exports from Canada boomed under the preferential tariff treatment. Another consequence of the trade was an influx of British immigrants into Canada. Due to the low bulk-to-value ratio involved in the timber trade, it required the use of large ships in great numbers. The ships were filled with timber on their journeys east, but they often made the return journey carrying ballast. The population of Canada at the time was very small so the market for goods from Britain was limited. To maximize returns, shippers resorted to offering passage to Canada on their westward voyages. After the repeal of the preferential tariff regime in 1840, there was much worry that the timber industry would collapse. This did not come to pass, as British demand for long specimens of high-quality Canadian white pine continued to be excellent. Canadians also began to ship timber south, as forests in the eastern United Sates were depleted.

Canadians soon began to increase exports of other commodity goods to the United States, which marked the beginning of what would blossom into the world's most prolific trading relationship. While the trading relationship continues to be vitally important today, this by no means implies that it was always amicable. The relationship has been characterized by alternating bouts of free trade and protectionism. Even during periods of free trade, there have always been disagreements; the relationship remains prone to spasms of American and Canadian protectionist sentiment.

Our modern trade relationship began to develop in earnest in the mid-19th century when the British moved away from mercantilism towards free trade. This involved the abolition of preferential tariffs, which had favored trade from the colonies of the British Empire and discriminated against goods from outside the empire. The policy shift suddenly cost Canada its privileged access to its single largest export market, with devastating economic consequences. The economic depression that soon began in Canada forced it to look to its neighbor to the south for economic salvation.

While trade between Canada and the United States was already significant, it had been impeded by tariffs on both sides. In the late 1840s, lobbying began for a free trade agreement. The Americans resisted for a number of years, due to the influence of protectionist lobbies, but in 1854 they finally signed a 10-year free trade agreement, commonly known as the Reciprocity Agreement, largely because one of its provisions allowed American fisherman access to the rich east coast fisheries. After 10 years, the Americans reviewed the treaty and decided not to renew it, due to protectionist pressures and despite persistent lobbying by Canada. This refusal to endorse a new treaty forced Canada to seriously contemplate its economic future and was a factor in the negotiations among Canada, Nova Scotia, and New Brunswick that eventually led to Confederation. With its ratification, all customs duties that had been levied on trade among the three jurisdictions were abolished, which helped to bolster the new national economy.

Even after the rebuff from the Americans and the advent of Confederation, Canada continued to push for a new free trade agreement. As late as 1871, a full five years after the U.S. had abrogated the original agreement, John A. Macdonald, as first prime minister, attempted to resuscitate it within the context of the Washington Treaty. He was again rebuffed. Thereafter, Macdonald advocated a protectionist policy for Canada, which came to be known as the National Policy. It was intended to promote Canadian economic interests and bolster the confidence of Canadians in our economy. It protected domestic industries from foreign competition by establishing a tariff regime that made importing manufactured goods prohibitively expensive while simultaneously easing customs duties on imported raw materials and semi-processed products used in manufacturing.

The policy proved a boon to manufacturing concerns in Ontario and Quebec, which were granted a captive market, but had an adverse effect on Westerners. All Canadians subsidized the National Policy by foregoing access to cheaper manufactured foreign goods, but it was Westerners who suffered most. They were forced to purchase manufactured goods made domestically at a higher cost compared to the pricing of similar imported goods, while being subjected to world prices for their own output, which was almost entirely composed of commodities like wheat. This squeezed Western producers due to their higher cost base, while enriching central Canada, where most manufacturing took place.

From about 1879 until the 1930s, the National Policy continued to be popular in Ontario and Quebec. It was not until 1935, when the Mackenzie King government negotiated a trade agreement with the United States of a less comprehensive nature than the original Reciprocity Agreement, that a policy shift towards free trade began. The implementation of the 1935 agreement, and a subsequent agreement in 1938, marked the beginning of a gradual period of easing tariff restrictions, which eventually led to a complete dismantling of the National Policy.

The last remnants of the policy were finally disposed of with the creation of the General Agreement on Tariffs and Trade (GATT) after the Second World War. During the negotiations among 23 participating nations, those between Canada and the United States were by far the most extensive. With the ratification of GATT, the original trade agreements of 1935 and 1938 were subsumed and a foundation was laid for even greater economic integration. This trend continued with the ratification of the Auto Pact in 1965, which eliminated tariffs on cars, trucks, buses, tires, and automotive parts between the two countries. This effectively created a unified North American market with regard to the manufacture and sale of automobiles. However the agreement also contained safeguards for Canada's auto industry. Chrysler, Ford, and General Motors agreed to build one car in Canada for every one sold in Canada and that 60 percent of the constituent parts and labor of every car manufactured in Canada would be of Canadian origin. This managed trade agreement was a significant step in that it recognized the need to rationalize the burgeoning trade relationship between Canada and the United States to the benefit of both countries.

The increasing recognition that the two economies had become interdependent to a degree unprecedented anywhere else in world, and that this pattern was likely to continue, finally led to negotiations aimed at establishing a comprehensive bilateral free trade agreement. The signing of the Canada-U.S. Free Trade Agreement (FTA) in 1988 finally put an end to oscillation on both sides between protectionism and free trade, and recognized once and for all that both are trading nations and that the economic interests of both are best served by facilitating the free flow of goods and services. Canada has maintained a commitment to free trade since the signing of the 1988 agreement and its successor, the North American Free Trade Agreement (NAFTA), which came into effect in 1994 and includes Mexico in its terms. The United States has done so more selectively, most recently in 2004 and 2005, when the Bush administration chose to ignore the ruling of a NAFTA tribunal and WTO rulings on softwood lumber and argue for selective interpretation of other rulings. Although the softwood lumber dispute was resolved—at least temporarily—in 2006, its extended and fractious course illustrated how persistent, ostensibly economic issues can evolve into national-level political concerns.

ENERGY COLOSSUS

Canada's energy situation is vastly different from that of the United States in that our neighbor is a large net energy importer. In 2004, Canada's proven reserves of oil were officially upgraded from 4.9 billion barrels, which referred only to conventional oil, to 178.8 billion barrels, including oil sands, by the responsible agency of the U.S. government. This upgrade reflects the capability of Alberta's oil sands to become one of the world's major production areas, given the expectation that oil (as of "futures" for June 2007 trading at $72 a barrel) seems likely to continue to trade above $30 per barrel indefinitely.

While the U.S. Energy Information Administration (an independent reporting body) in mid-2006 put Canada's reserves at almost 180 billion barrels, there is in fact much more oil. The total amount of oil trapped in the sands is estimated to be about 1.7 to 2.5 trillion barrels. The current reserve figures only reflect that part of the oil sands which is economical to extract with today's available technology. As technology advances and the worldwide demand for oil continues to put upward pressure on its price, the remainder of Alberta's vast resource are likely to become economically viable.

The relatively recent realization of the full economic promise presented by the oil sands has resulted in a massive investment boom in Alberta as companies compete to secure access to what will prove to be one of the world's single richest reserves of oil. Over the next decade alone, it is expected that as much as $87 billion will be invested to exploit the oil sands. This will result in a near tripling of output to about 2.7 million barrels a day. Some observers think Canada's oil output—mostly due to new oil sands output—could rise to five million barrels per day by 2020.

Billions of dollars in related investments will also be made to build pipelines and other infrastructure to transport the oil to markets. Most of the new production from Alberta seems likely to end up going south to the United States, putting Canada in the enviable position of being the main supplier to the world's number one consumer. Canada already accounts for about one-sixth of American oil imports. As investment in oil sands production continues to increase output, Canada's importance to Americans as a secure and rule-of-law-respecting supplier of oil will continue to grow. This is especially so in light of the fact that so much of the world's current oil supply is located in politically unstable or potentially unstable regions of the world.

Out of the top 10 countries with the world's largest oil reserves, Canada is the only stable democracy. Furthermore, Canada is not a member of OPEC, which means that no artificial restrictions will be placed on Canadian supply expansion over time. As Canadian supply capabilities have been increasing, moreover, so has our distribution capability. Pipeline projects under consideration would make possible the large-scale export of oil sands petroleum to Asian markets as well. The primary destination for most of this oil is likely to be mainland China, but India and Southeast Asia will grow as markets as well. Beijing has been aggressively pursuing opportunities to invest in oil sands projects or to secure access to their output.

The implications of this continuing development are serious for the United States, which has been heavily dependent on unimpeded access to Canadian oil. Given that American energy needs will only continue to grow, while domestic supplies of conventional oil are shrinking, it will be of paramount importance to the energy security of the U.S. to safeguard its access to secure foreign supplies. Already Americans must import 58 percent of their oil requirements. As demand continues to grow and supply continues to diminish, the dependence on foreign oil will grow to the point where even a small disruption in supply could have devastating consequences for the American economy and in turn the global economy itself. Furthermore, given current production rates of non-OPEC producers and the current pace of new discoveries, approximately 80 percent of remaining global oil reserves will soon be controlled by Middle Eastern governments. Without securing alternate sources of supply, the U.S. will find itself beholden to undemocratic and increasingly unstable Middle Eastern states for economic survival.

The United States may soon find itself in direct competition with China for Canada's oil exports. This will leave Canadian policymakers with the difficult task of balancing the competing interests of the United States and China in order to prevent a further escalation of geopolitical tensions between the two that could have disastrous consequences for the entire world. Canada must also actively encourage cooperation on energy issues between Washington and Beijing. It must cooperate with China on energy conservation and efficiency and the development of alternative energy sources to reduce the pressures on the planet's limited resources. As Thomas Friedman points out in his 2005 book, *The World Is Flat*, Beijing alone is adding about 30,000 new vehicles to its streets each month. Cooperation on energy efficiency will be especially important given that China currently still consumes twice as much energy per unit of output as other industrialized nations.

CONSERVATION AND KYOTO

The foregoing offers some of the positive aspects of Canada's oil sands endowment, but I must also point out that they pose unique challenges as well. Even given the continued debate over whether Canada's Kyoto commitments are realistically obtainable, it will still be necessary to take major steps to reduce the environmental impact of increasing oil sands production. What can be done to mitigate these emissions is under intense investigation. There is profound concern by Albertans, whose memories of Trudeau's National Energy Program have not been softened by time, that Central Canada would be sanguine about riding towards Kyoto compliance on the backs of an eviscerated Alberta energy industry. Nevertheless, currently the production of each barrel from the sands creates more greenhouse gas emissions than the amount created by four cars in a day. The process is also energy intensive and uses large amounts of precious natural gas as feedstock for bitumen conversion. Production processes will have to continue to be improved in order to lessen the demand for natural gas, which is desirable as clean-burning fuel for power plants and residential use. One encouraging sign on this front is the recently unveiled proposal by one of Canada's major oil sands producers to implement in its next expansion project a technology that does not require the burning of any natural gas in the conversion of bitumen into synthetic crude oil. Another suggestion moves towards carbon sequestration underground. In any event, considerable ingenuity will be required to avoid transforming an economic issue into an unmanageable semi-ideological one. In that regard, accusations that Kyoto skeptics are "global warming deniers" is not a useful contribution to dialogue, let alone likely to prompt political flexibility.

Economics and Resource Management in the United States

Throughout its history, the United States has operated under the assumption that there were no limits to its economic potential or the natural resources at its command. And, certainly until the middle of the 20th century, that judgment was true to all practical extents and purposes. From the arrival of colonists/citizens on North American shores, there was a fabulously wealthy "new" continent ripe for exploitation, and the wealth appeared limitless. Animal, vegetable, or mineral—if the United States didn't have it readily available, what was absent was of marginal importance and/or could be easily imported.

At every point in early U.S. history, there was what the individual needed either for existence or for trade. Thus colonists farmed—and moved onward to better land, virtually cost free, if what they were farming was exhausted. Trappers provided furs for the beaver hat (or buffalo hide blanket) industry of Europeans. Tobacco was a "cash crop" that made Virginians wealthy. Tobacco was followed by cotton, which made other southern planters rich and prompted textile production in the North as well as supplying European manufacturers. Southern plantation (and smaller farm) agriculture was fueled by low-cost labor, first indentured servants and then slaves, which were a significant part of the "capital" of the pre-Civil War South. In the Northeast, excellent timber was available for ships, fish were abundant, and water power drove small industrial mills. The great natural waterway of the Missouri/Mississippi rivers and their subsystems opened the center of the country, provided vital north-south transportation, and was the economic link between the North and South for the states surrounding the rivers.

By the mid-19th century, a long string of gold and silver strikes, starting with "the 49ers" gold rush in California, prompted the development of the U.S. West. For those looking to farm, "God had cleared the trees" west of the Mississippi, and the prairie sod yielded to steel plows creating corn and wheat harvests that appeared to be a limitless breadbasket, complemented by cattle and sheep herding throughout the West. The 1862 Homestead Act provided free land for settlers (and government grants stimulated the expansion of the railroads, with attendant speculation and corruption). There was so much potential wealth and so much physical security from external attack that the United States could believe that isolationism was a practical political policy. The U.S. economic self-sufficiency was closer to a reality than was conceivable for European countries packed cheek by jowl, and its growing wealth and regional power resulted in a "What, me worry?" attitude by Uncle Sam when contemplating the rest of the ill-favored globe.

Until the Second World War, the involvement of the United States with the world at large was by choice, not necessity. Although the Great Depression of the 1930s was a global phenomenon, the United States looked internally to resolve its economic problems, with little concern for the rest of the world.

For its post-World War II economics, the United States reached beyond its territorial boundaries to obtain less expensive resources; however, it remains a major producer (as well as the largest global consumer) of most natural resources. Combining unique inventiveness, the most modern technology in manufacturing, and vigorous entrepreneurial energy, the United States has exploited its resources and created the world's most wealthy and technologically advanced society.

This wealth and an unprecedented level of resource consumption for a population approaching 300 million have generated a substantial number of challenges. Although at 300 million the U.S. has the world's third-largest population, its consumption of the world's resources is disproportionately first on a per capita basis. This reality has generated a number of basic questions, including:

- Can the United States continue to consume world resources at its current rate?
- Can the United States continue to serve as the consumption engine for world manufacturing?
- Can the United States continue to serve as the implicit repository for global investment, to the extent that the U.S. dollar is held by other countries (despite its declining value)?
- Is there an outer limit to energy production/consumption or, if there are relatively near-term limits to oil production, what will replace it?

INVESTMENT

There are only two sources for investment: domestic and international. For the latter, a country must be sufficiently attractive to prompt the investors of another country to devote money and resources to invest in less familiar circumstances than "at home." The attraction can be easily exploited riches offering a quick reward, regardless of potential political risk; a collegial joint opportunity with a reliable partner; or the security that the foreign country offers. A country could be owned outright by another (a colony) with the foreign investment designed to secure the ownership as well as profiting the colonial master. And, without examining the circumstance in detail, many advanced economies are both investors and recipients of investment. Globalization allows free flows of capital that permit foreign investors opportunities that previous restrictions on foreign ownership prevented. Not all countries are so open, nor are all sectors for prospective investment (banks, media) open even in permissive countries. For the United States, foreign investment is a major element, both as a recipient and as an investor.

Although purchases of major corporations (or offers to make such purchases) attract the most media attention, the largest "investment" item by foreign countries in the United States is holding U.S. currency, primarily in Treasury notes/bonds, etc. At the start of 2004, for example, foreign direct investment in the United States was $2.4 trillion, while U.S. direct investment abroad was about $2.7 trillion. The largest holders of American debt instruments are China and Japan. The United States is now the world's greatest debtor and has the largest net liabilities in world history. Since foreign claims on the United States ($10.5 trillion) exceed U.S. claims abroad ($7.9 trillion), the net international investment position is now negative: -$2.6 trillion at the start of 2004, or -24 percent of GDP. The reasons for these holdings remain varied: extremely safe investment; guaranteed return on the investment; and, notably for China and Japan, a mechanism for keeping their currencies artificially undervalued and consequently providing continued stimulus for their exports to the U.S.

Alternatively, a country can rely primarily on its own resources for investment. It can defer consumption, restrict foreign investment, "force" domestic savings on its population, and/or control investment through heavy taxation and government investment into the economy. As a subset of this concept, a population in recognition of its history (war, famine, flood, plague) can culturally conclude that it must save for that proverbial "rainy day," and such saving is not directed towards consumption. There are societies in which a single saved silver coin provides the food that means a child doesn't die—that fearful prospect is an incentive to save.

Such has not been the paradigm for the United States. The U.S. has been so rich and food so easy to obtain that there has never been a famine on the level of those current and/or historic in Europe, Asia, and Africa. There has been—at least until the New Orleans catastrophe in 2005—no U.S. equivalent of televised images of starving Ethiopian children with flies walking on their eyes (or, for an earlier generation, the vision of starving Chinese after a Yellow River flood). There was no 19th-century equivalent of the Irish potato famine to emboss an indelible imprint on U.S. culture. The result has meant a cultural willingness to spend rather than save (with the always low U.S. savings rate falling even lower in the early 21st century), and consumption rather than saving has driven the economy. Thus production, profits, and subsequent further investment by those who have profited, have repeated in an upward spiral of larger manufacturing facilities and greater productivity. It is an investment pattern that reflects U.S. economic optimism since citizens are confident that they will be able to obtain well-paid jobs, the value of the currency is unquestioned (that is, essentially low inflation has never replicated the hyper-inflation of a post-World War I Germany or post-World War II China), and saving for one's old age will be covered by social security, private pensions, and/or continued work.

Rather than the government directing or allocating investment, the "market" has done so. One can sigh over the amount of investment into the equivalent of R&D/production of Barbie Dolls or lavish vacation homes rather than tenured professorships for the study of Sanskrit or funds for protecting the habitat of the snail darter. Nevertheless, this is free market choice, and the U.S. government relentlessly refuses to "pick winners" so far as industrial investment is concerned. The U.S. government is more willing to fund a substantial variety of basic scientific, medical, and technical research at the private university and federal laboratory level; however, with the exception of military and aerospace equipment, government investment in products for manufacture is limited.

TRADE—FREE AND OTHERWISE

The concept of "free trade" is a basic of economics. The argument is that every country has natural advantages in certain products (natural or manufactured) or services. It is to the profit of all if these advantages are maximized and a natural balance between countries in goods/services/labor develops as a consequence of such trade.

At every point of history, for every country, the free trade ideal has struggled with (and often been strangled by) specific national interests. The most obvious category might be military security production. The most efficient munitions producer in the pre-1939 world may have been the German Krupp armaments factories, but the French were unlikely to depend upon German exports for their armed forces. During the Cold War, the United States was unlikely to look to the Belgians for a better rifle, the Germans for a better tank, or the Soviets for a more powerful rocket engine—despite the unquestioned excellence of these military producers. Instead, we persisted with arms development and, arguably, there are no weapons systems made outside the United States that are significantly better than those that now are U.S. produced.

More generally, in historical terms, countries have attempted to protect their "infant industries" from external competition to give them a secure and profitable domestic market, albeit at greater expense for the domestic population. At best, when these industries have developed, the protection is reduced or eliminated. Competition with external sources then both makes domestic industries more efficient and reduces prices for consumers.

In general terms, the United States has followed this approach. It protected its emerging industries after the Revolutionary War from far more efficient British production. High tariffs throughout much of the 19th century provided the bulk of federal government revenues. As there is always a special interest with political clout seeking protection, it was always easier to keep tariffs high than to reduce them.

The easiest point to reduce tariffs is when a nation's economy is booming, domestic wealth is climbing, and job opportunities plentiful. At such a juncture, particularly if the tariff reductions are reciprocal, a country accentuates its opportunities to export while obtaining raw materials/manufactured products more cheaply. When the economies are complementary, as is the case for Canada and the United States, there is more incentive for tariff reduction. Consequently, as noted above, at different junctures either the United States or Canada advanced "free trade" proposals; however, until the 1988 Free Trade Agreement (FTA), these suggestions were rejected or ended after brief experimentation, usually due to domestic opponents' facile use of the proposal to demonize the idea.

The success of the FTA and its subsequent expansion in 1994 into the tri-national North American Free Trade Agreement (NAFTA) has resulted in a bilateral trading relationship running approximately $2 billion per day as of the end of 2005. It is one of the frustrating aspects of NAFTA that while the great expansion of trade would appear implicitly to be the positive consequence of the agreement, it can be argued that trade would have expanded commensurately with—or without—NAFTA. Such remains an unknown alternate universe. Still, the various calamities that were predicted for Canada under NAFTA (for example, an end to the Canadian health-care system, U.S. control of Canadian media, and sale of Canadian water) have simply not occurred. With proponents of the agreement able to say "I told you so," for many positive results, NAFTA's success (or at least lack of dire consequences) has muted if not silenced its critics. It has definitely not silenced them, and the issues that roiled the domestic scene in 1994 have not been resolved; indeed, the congressional debate in mid-2005 over ratification of the Central American Free Trade Agreement (CAFTA) with its exceptionally narrow victory in the House of Representatives (217-215) demonstrated anew how intensely divisive and politicized free trade remains. Likewise, the question of a free trade agreement with the Republic of Korea remained in play early in 2007. For the United States, a series of free trade issues remain:

• the loss of "good" manufacturing jobs that have been moved and/or "off-shored" out of the United States. While jobs continue to increase and manufacturing productivity rises, according to a 2003 Economic Policy Institute Study there was a decline of approximately 2.4 million manufacturing jobs between March 2001 and October 2003—a loss that persists. There have been many factors involved in this decline, and manufacturing jobs have been declining in many countries; however, there is sufficient anecdotal evidence of jobs that have moved south (to Mexico) or been exported (to China/India) to discomfit union activists. There is a probably accurate appreciation that U.S. consumers would pay a few dollars more for clothing, electronics, autos, etc., if the result were that U.S. workers would not lose their jobs. The abstract economic response that better jobs are available, those losing jobs find new ones, that the efficiencies of the system are making goods cheaper are just that—abstract. For the 50-year-old assembly line worker, the factory relocated in Mexico is a job gone and a "McJob" is not a satisfactory substitute.

• the agreements lack protection for labor in third countries where labor costs are extremely low. The argument by union leaders in the U.S. that NAFTA/ CAFTA agreements don't protect safety or health of Mexican or Caribbean country workers is a red herring, but it doesn't mean that it isn't accurate. These countries *do* lack the intensity of union protection for workers that has evolved with over a century of union activism in the United States. Consequently, the anti-free trade argument becomes, "not only do we lose our jobs, but globalization exploits the poor worker elsewhere."

• the agreements fail to include environmental protection elements, although some claim that the North American Commission for Environmental Co-operation, created as a "side agreement" to NAFTA, is effective. Again, this professed concern is both a red herring and true. American union leaders/environmental activists have more concern for U.S. jobs than for the environment; however, it is also accurate that environmental protection in Mexico and the Caribbean is less stringent than north of the Rio Grande.

More generally, trade agreements have become increasingly politicized in the United States. Although NAFTA was negotiated by a Democratic administration, it had significant Republican support. The far less important CAFTA (all Caribbean countries combined have 1 percent of the U.S. GNP) had virtually no Democratic support and was used as a rallying point against the Bush administration. The continued frustration over the loss of manufacturing jobs and the very high trade deficits with primary trading partners (Canada, China, Japan) continue to erode U.S. public support for free trade. The benefits from free trade and globalization are harder for the average citizen to identify than the liabilities (and certainly the liabilities are politically easy to exploit, for example, closed factories).

It is not that renegotiation of NAFTA for worker rights and/or environmental issues is probable, but any expansion of World Trade Organization agreements appears limited. What was earlier regarded as an "ambitious" commitment to hemispheric free trade in the near term now recedes into the never-never. The WTO topics of interest to the United States, for example, intellectual property rights and opening markets to U.S. media, banking, and agricultural products, were of limited interest to other Doha Round WTO participants. And now Doha is regarded as doornail dead. Some economists sense that there is a crunch coming because the United States cannot continue to absorb the excess production from new world economies at the cost of greater and greater trade deficits. Conversely, the willingness of the world to hold ever greater amounts of U.S. debt to permit continued American consumption (and foreign exports) can be questioned.

Canada–U.S. Trade

Switching from the general to the specific, Canada–U.S. trade is the most intensive and successful in the world. It is far, however, from conflict free. There is a rolling laundry list of complaints that range from the most hardy of perennials (softwood lumber, Pacific Coast salmon) to the middle-term neuralgic ("mad cows" and bad potatoes) to the fleeting and transient that the case-handler or action officer of the day will recall years later but no other living soul will remember.

Even if 95 percent of the trade passes without the slightest concern, that still leaves billions of dollars of trade each year for which there are problems. What is difficult for U.S. citizens to stomach (when it is noticed at all) is the level of outraged virtue that Canadians direct towards each trade issue. It is not that the United States does not have pointed trade complaints about Canadian action. The Quebec exclusions of U.S. dairy and poultry products are simply designed to protect (expensively) Quebec producers. And, regardless of decisions concerning the legitimacy of the Canadian Wheat Board control over grain exports, there are Canadian farmers willing to go to jail to protest government interference with their desire to sell grain directly to U.S. purchasers (as well as those who fervently want to retain the board).

To look at a specific issue, it did not seem to matter to Canadians how many cases of mad cow disease were uncovered (or the fact that the first such Canadian BSE case destroyed the U.S. beef export market to Asia at the cost of billions of dollars per year). For Canadians, the error lay with the U.S. for not accepting unlimited Canadian beef. Nor did there appear to be any significant Canadian interest in the type of comprehensive testing that the Japanese have instituted. Nevertheless, anyone who has seen the televised video of the BSE afflicted cow thrashing *in extremis* can extrapolate it to a human condition—and be unenthusiastic (despite assurances) about importing such cattle. That an exclusion decision was implemented during a presidential political campaign made the decision to re-open the border even less likely—and the ultimate decision after the election by the Bush administration to push for resumed trade still had political costs. These costs, incidentally, remain unappreciated in a Canada generally unappreciative of the Bush administration. The decision in mid-2005 to accept Canadian beef for U.S. slaughterhouses, and the discovery of a homegrown U.S. mad cow and sporadic discoveries of other BSE cases in North American herds, mean that there is a larger pool of beef that will probably not be acceptable for Asian export for at least another decade. The continued discovery of the occasional afflicted bovine, both in Canada and the United States, now appears to have been accepted as a socio-economic hazard-as-usual; however, popular reaction to the first human case connected to a North American animal is still pending.

A comparable, albeit brief, review of softwood lumber is also in order. The issue has been intensely debated and in play bilaterally for over a century. In the most recent iteration, battalions of lawyers and negotiators engaged in the dispute until the announcement in April 2006 of a bilateral agreement—an agreement that appears more a consequence of exhaustion than conviction. At the risk of oversimplification, the most recent difficulty stemmed from the expiration of a bilateral agreement in the mid-1990s. Subsequently, the United States placed unilateral tariffs and export limits on Canadian lumber; Canada rejected these U.S. restrictions and during protracted effort and multiple appeals won NAFTA rulings in dispute resolution panels. Conversely, the U.S. won WTO decisions that it regarded as more pertinent—and urged a negotiated settlement rather than enforcement of judicial/panel decisions. Arguing that they had "won" the legal case, Canadians declined to engage in diplomatic discussion, and the issue remained both unresolved and increasingly politicized—at least by Canadians. The tentative April 2006 negotiated agreement, which survived legal challenge from various dissatisfied elements on both sides of the border, will provide access to the U.S. market for specific quantities of lumber after which steep tariffs are imposed. Most, but not all, export fees collected by the USG were to be returned. After more pulling and hauling on elements of the agreement, resulting in side letter elaborations, it came into effect in October 2006 and received royal assent in December. More skeptically, it is an agreement that probably could have been reached years ago—had there been the political will to accept the obtainable rather than the ideal agreement.

Doubtless there are U.S. companies that would happily accept every stick of lumber until Canada was clear cut to the Arctic Circle. There are others that wouldn't take Canadian lumber if they had to build their homes from pressed mud as the alternative. Nevertheless, the trade disputes over softwood lumber have predated the creation of Canada and show no likelihood of permanent resolution as long as a twig grows on either side of the border. To a degree, the dispute illustrates that it is cheaper to hire lawyers than to adjust economic practices. In another dimension, it illustrates the intense complexity of balancing costs from essentially privately held timber and primarily publicly owned forest resources. Nevertheless, regardless of the amount of any tariff or the heated charges of subsidies, the vagrant question remains: if the U.S. actions were so invidious, why did Canada continue to sell to us? Canadians were not compelled by force of arms to ship lumber south. The argument on the Canadian part seemed to be over the size of the profit they make from the trade, which is a useful economic concern but perhaps not worth all the expended rhetoric, exacerbated bilateral relations, and general ill feeling. Moreover, Prime Minister Martin, having invested in diatribe, apparently could not accept an agreement (particularly as a minority government during a campaign) not viewed as a "victory" over the United States. Unfortunately, too, given the history of disagreement, the current agreement (assuming it holds) is more likely to be a reloading break prior to the next round of softwood combat.

Alternatively, Canadians might consider a slightly different perspective. The amount of political capital invested by Canadian politicians in the softwood lumber issue appeared disproportionate to the financial values involved—it was closer to an exercise in national pride and political posturing than an economic concern. Perhaps, Canadians might consider some of these tariff difficulties as a "defense tax"—payable to the U.S. Treasury as implicit compensation for U.S. defense expenditures for the North American continent.

ENERGY

For most of human history, energy was restricted to that provided by human or animal muscle. The energy available to the richest and most mighty was not qualitatively better than that available to the most lowly; it could be quantitatively greater if the ruler controlled herds of animals or legions of slaves. Substantial effort was directed to breeding larger, stronger animals and devising harnesses or other systems to most effectively exploit their energy. During this same period, the energy of falling water was tapped on a microscale, with individual small waterwheels driving grindstones to convert grain into flour and saws to rough cut lumber. Again, much human ingenuity was directed to properly positioning waterwheels (and worry over whether the stream would dry up—or flood) and creating effective millstones, saws, and the like.

The movement away from muscle mass energy into combustion energy began seriously when James Watt designed steam engine improvements in the last quarter of the 18th century. From that point forward, global energy has expanded exponentially, with intense investigation and subsequent exploitation of energy sources. As one energy source appeared less efficient (or more expensive), societies moved to others. Hence, the use of wood to fire steam engines for river boats or rail engines was initially cheap and convenient in the United States. Rather quickly, easily available lumber had gone into the fire boxes and coal was substituted. Within short order (in historical terms), coal, oil, natural gas, and the nucleus of the splitting atom have been tapped to provide energy.

The United States economy for over a century has been driven by cheap, readily available, and secure sources of fuel. Probably until 1973, with the fuel crisis stemming from the Arab oil embargo to the West following the Middle East war between Israel and assorted neighbors, the United States did not consider the question of energy vulnerability or begin to take deliberate government action associated with maintaining assured access to energy supplies. The issue is now epitomized by the statistic that, despite remaining one of the world's largest oil producers, the United States imports more than half its oil requirements.

POLITICIZED ENERGY

There is no issue in the United States that lacks for intense political difference and energy is no different. In the old description for a controversial problem, "Everyone has a dog in the fight." In rough terms for the energy debate, these might be described as minimalists versus maximalists. The minimalists believe the future will see less and less energy available (or they believe that its potential sources, such as nuclear energy, are the equivalent of poisoned apples); consequently, energy use must be reduced on both a per capita basis and society wide by greater efficiencies in all industrial and transportation energy uses, while simultaneously eliminating dangerous, polluting energy sources (such as coal-fired electric generators) and restoring the environment (through, for instance, the elimination of dams that produce hydroelectric power but restrict fish movement).

In contrast, the maximalists believe that economic progress is closely tied to rising energy use. The United States must act first to locate and secure energy sources, particularly oil and gas, and exploit these sources as they become available. Energy security is possible both through emergency storage of oil and development of good relations with foreign partners within and outside the Western Hemisphere that would guarantee access to oil reserves. They view oil and gas as finite—but hardly finite in any near-term manner that would require draconian use restrictions. They are proponents of vigorous oil/gas exploration and drilling and believe that it is possible to protect the environment (to a reasonable extent) and still obtain the desired resources. If there is to be conservation, it should be driven by the free market: that is, when it is profitable to use less energy, less energy will be used.

The juxtaposition of these opposing philosophies most recently was manifested in the Energy Bill passed by the U.S. Congress in summer 2005. It was a dog's breakfast of the "something for everyone" school. That is to say that in a bill that ran 1,724 pages there were provisions and funding for energy conservation; fuel efficiency for automobiles and various appliances; research and development of both nuclear energy and "clean" coal energy, renewable energy (wind, solar); hydrogen fuel cell research, improvements in the national power grid, domestic oil production/deep drilling; breaking the bureaucratic logjam that has stymied work on approximately 40 liquefied natural gas facilities nationwide; and (last but not least) extending Daylight Savings Time by a month—a mixed pleasure that came into effect in spring 2007. But naturally it did not fully satisfy all special issue contenders and some were not satisfied at all.

Critics suggest that there was much left undone in reducing U.S. dependence on imported oil; some demand greater miles per gallon requirements for automobiles while others wanted immediate authority to drill for oil in Alaska's Arctic National Wildlife Refuge.

CONSERVATION

The idea of conservation in resource management has not so much been a late addition to U.S. thinking as a spotty one. Yellowstone, the first U.S. national park, was created in 1872, and a century ago President Teddy Roosevelt (1901-09) was a significant figure in the conservation of scenic wild areas and natural wilderness. The total area covered by U.S. national parks and federally protected lands is larger than many countries. Nevertheless, the 20th- and 21st-century U.S. "green" environmentalist is viewed by the average U.S. citizen not as a self-sacrificing idealist but rather as a tree-hugging, economic obstructionist endorsing expensive solutions to theoretical problems. Indeed, the skeptics assessing environmental or conservation issues note the past apocalyptic predictions ranging from global overpopulation and famine to nuclear winter and conclude that such "greens" have no connection to pragmatic political reality. Their apparent vision of a fat-free society, whose members bike everywhere, compost their garbage, and power their homes on solar energy, might work for a country the size of Lichtenstein but lacks applicability to a continent-sized country.

Conservation for its own sake is a "goodie-goodie" objective. To have any resonance in the United States, conservation must be demonstrably profitable or designed to counter a blatant health risk. Hence if Lake Erie is sufficiently polluted that it burns, water quality needs to be addressed. If Los Angeles smog and air pollution begin to damage the region's economic attraction, rigorous laws to control smog will be implemented. But the thought of preventing logging to protect a spotted owl or stopping a major hydroelectric facility to save a snail darter is hostile to much of U.S. public opinion. Moreover, the enormous costs of public transportation, with its interminable tax subsidies, are unattractive to many U.S. citizens. The limited nature, inflexibility, inconvenience, and high costs of public transportation (outside the largest urban areas) combined with the ubiquitous nature of the private automobile and the vast driving distances facing many citizens reduces to zero the willingness of Americans to accept the tax-driven gasoline prices paid by Europeans. Such gasoline prices might prompt greater fuel efficiencies, but would effectively eliminate most of the older, heavier, high-performance vehicles for those drivers with average incomes—and these voters are unwilling to surrender their vehicles. It was unsurprising that the rise in gasoline prices during 2005 and 2006 prompted high decibel and much reported laments, but did little to affect U.S. driving habits; nor are future incremental gasoline increases likely to discourage current driving patterns.

Kyoto and Kyoto Substitutes

The current U.S. administration remains skeptical of the science behind "global warming" and even more skeptical of the motivations and mechanisms behind the Kyoto Treaty. Some scientists say the science behind global warming is as much ideology as replicable experimental science; others, of course, say the opposite. In essence, as long as Earth exists, the climate will change—as it has changed massively and dramatically in the past without human participation. Even if the globe is presently "warming," the cause and duration of this circumstance is far from known and the transformation of an issue into an ideology will not advance agreement.

Even the most partisan U.S. supporters of the Kyoto Treaty refused to bring it to the Senate for a vote, and in July 1999, the Senate voted 95-0 in a "sense of the Senate" resolution against the Treaty. Eight years later, U.S. government attitudes have not changed substantially: the Treaty is considered fatally flawed through its exemption of the very heavy Third World polluters, India and China, which are also major economic competitors for the United States; it appears likely that meeting the objectives would hobble the U.S. economy substantially while providing for massive economic transfers to Third World states; it is best designed for a small country with a highly developed public transportation network, or a country such as Russia or Germany with failed industrial plants that can be closed and "credited" as a reduction in pollution when the reality is that they are economic failures. Moreover, the overwhelming likelihood is that Kyoto adherents will not adhere to its provisions for reducing various greenhouse gases. The American government concluded that it was better not to commit to impossible objectives than to be castigated for not meeting them.

Recognizing that a "just say no" response to Kyoto, regardless of how inimical it appears, had become a public relations sore spot, the government in Washington has hypothesized a variety of alternative, voluntary objectives for reducing greenhouse emissions, based on the argument that encouraging economic conservation is a more effective approach than attempting unenforceable fiats. In mid-2005, the United States announced agreements with several Asian states and Australia directed towards voluntary conservation measures. The administration was not particularly amused when, during the Canadian election campaign, Prime Minister Martin twitted the United States at the December 2005 Montreal UN Climate Conference about lacking a "global conscience." Martin's comment appeared both condescending and sanctimonious, particularly when Canadian greenhouse gas emissions had risen more rapidly than those in the United States. Whether the Conservative minority government will move more definitively towards the U.S.-Asian position on voluntary reduction of greenhouse emissions was still unknown in early 2007; however, its public recognition that Kyoto Treaty objectives could not be met was a useful reality check. At this point, Canadian politicians (like others in the West) are maneuvering to look as "green" as possible through palliative measures such as tax credits for homeowner energy reduction without draconian regulations that would perceptibly affect the economy or cost the taxpayer.

There is a military axiom that goes, "Don't just stand there; do something." And such appears to be the current political attitude towards climate change. The hope is that doing something (and something will be done) can proceed rationally rather than reflexively. Whether the earth is facing centuries of warming; whether today is a warming blip in the course of centuries of prospective global cooling; or whether circumstances will remain "about the same," there are still areas of agreement that Americans (and Canadians) can embrace. These include greater energy efficiencies, in production and in use; further exploration—and exploitation—of known reserves; encouragement for technological innovation.

Hard Choices Ahead

Through a combination of vast natural resources and massive societal wealth, the United States has been able to avoid many of the unpleasant economic (and associated political) choices that some other countries have made. If no one wants, for example, to live near an oil refinery because of the prospect of pollution, it can be avoided—if the country is rich enough to afford to import gasoline rather than refine crude oil into gasoline. If a country is wealthy enough to run its huge electric generators on oil or natural gas (some have said this use of natural gas is the equivalent to washing windows with champagne), it can avoid building nuclear reactors (and avoid political battles with those who cannot tell the difference between a nuclear reactor and a hydrogen bomb). If a country lacks such natural resources, it will build nuclear reactors (as has been the case for South Korea, France, Japan, and other nations) to supply its electric power. If a country's sociopolitical preference maximizes personal freedom as epitomized by the individual automobile, it may choose to subsidize this societal preference implicitly by financing a national superhighway system and not heavily taxing gasoline.

But these are all expensive choices; some or all of them may have to be modified, if not eliminated in the years to come. If renewable energy sources (wind, solar, ocean waves, ethanol) are regarded as amusing oddities rather than vital future energy sources, R&D funding for them will fall into the "sops to Cerberus" category rather than receive the priorities of a "must-have."

CULTURE, EDUCATION, AND RELIGION 4

Canadians have a quiet confidence that their education and culture are both in the world's top tier; this circumstance is created and enhanced at least partly by having two official languages and approximately 200 ethnocultural traditions and heritage languages in active use across the country.

Americans view their culture with a self-satisfaction that can easily be mistaken for arrogance. It is not as if they believe no other cultures exist, but rather that such "cultures" are the equivalent of museums for specialists in the arcane, while their own is a shopping mall for the world. American culture has been globally successful across every element of the political, economic, social, and artistic spectrum. It is probably the most pervasive and vigorous culture in history (whether it is also the most enduring is still to be determined). Probably partly due to its ubiquitous success, Americans (in contrast to Canadians) see no need for self-conscious state sponsorship of culture. In the free market, culture will survive—or not—on its merits; it should not receive hot-house treatment to thrive. For that reason, even the most prominent of U.S. officially supported cultural organizations, such as the National Endowment for the Arts, are essentially marginal operations.

If Americans are satisfied with their culture, they are frustrated by its educational component. As is the case for health, education is an endless draw on public funding, but the results have been disconcerting for 50 years, reflecting mediocre performance for the average U.S. student when compared with other industrialized countries. One can realize easily that something is wrong; however, fixing it is infinitely more challenging, and Americans cannot even agree on where to start. In contrast, despite a variety of shortcomings, Canadian education is producing marginally superior testing results for the average student. Canadians are essentially satisfied with the quality of their basic education, although increasingly and properly concerned at the costs for a university degree and the debt load of many graduates.

Americans are also viewed as more religious than other industrial democracies. U.S. religiosity is hardly surprising, considering its national origins. For most, such a conclusion would reinforce U.S. belief in its exceptionalism. For a nation so blessed by God, it would be almost sacrilegious to fail to recognize this blessing. Coincidentally, many Americans are profoundly perturbed by the "liberal" variations of marriage, abortion, and assisted dying—social relationships which for the religious believer are defined by theology rather than social convenience. Canada for its part is now full of vibrant religious communities.

The Canadian Experience

CULTURE

Most Canadians, unlike Americans, distinguish culture from our work, professions, and commerce. If so, it's worth noting some findings of a federal government study completed about a quarter of a century ago:

• Virtually all (93 percent) of television dramas then watched by English-speaking Canadians were non-Canadian-made, whereas the share for French-speakers was only 60 percent.
• Virtually all (92 percent) of Canadian theatres then ran non-Canadian-made films. (This appeared to continue to apply in 2007.)
• Not far off two-thirds (60 percent) of the books in our bookstores were American, with Canadian titles comprising only about 35 percent of the books sold.
• Eight in ten (81 percent) English-language consumer magazines on our newsstands were imported; Canadian ones comprised about 14 percent.
• About nine in ten (88 percent) of sound recording releases were from elsewhere; Canadian ones: 9 percent.

Culture should not be confused with mass communications, but in practice the linkage is often strong. If it is, at least in the early 1980s, our culture was essentially that of our southern neighbors.

Historically, this pattern set early on among most of our media. For example, some U.S. radio stations by the late 1920s engaged many Canadian listeners across the border. A Royal Commission on Radio Broadcasting, appointed in 1928 by the government of Mackenzie King and headed by John Aird, proposed a government-owned radio system. The rationale was best caught by a rather facile quip in its report: "the state or the United States." Since 1932, the government-owned Canadian Broadcasting Corporation has competed with private radio and TV stations.

Other royal commissions and studies over the decades since have tended to adopt a similar view. In order to have Canadian cultural voices heard at home in both official language communities, non-market devices seem necessary. One of our continuing national challenges is to find ways of having two languages and cultures cohabit within one country. Victor Rabinovitch, formerly assistant deputy minister at the federal department of Canadian Heritage, quoted the late René Lévesque, the first sovereignist premier of Quebec, speaking in 1968:

> We are the heirs of the fantastic adventure which first made America almost entirely French, and of that collective stubbornness which enabled part of it to remain alive in Quebec . . . . This is how we distinguish ourselves from other people, particularly other North Americans, with whom we have most other things in common . . . . This means that we must be able, in this place, to earn our living and lead our careers in the French language. It also means that we must build a society, as effective and as "civilized" as all the others . . . we must give ourselves enough reasons to be confident in ourselves and proud of ourselves.[1]

Whether Levesque's points now apply as fully in the rest of Canada as in Quebec is debatable, but the need for cultural assertion appears to now be greater outside Quebec.

The real challenge today in comparing the cultures of the two nations is isolating what is meant by culture in the context of ethnically diverse nations. The cultures of Canada or the United States, for example, are not the sum of the cultural practices by residents in each, but are rather the procedural and substantive policies their governments apply to cultural practices within each territory. A nation then can be gauged by its laws and practices on cultural diversity, promotion of intercultural dialogue, protection of intangible history, aid to cultural industries, and the consideration given for cultural preservation in the process of economic development.

---

1. R. Levesque, *Option Québec*. Montreal: Les Éditions de l'Homme, pp. 20-5. Quoted by Rabinovitch, *Queen's Quarterly*, Summer 1999, p. 221.

The major difference between Canada and the United States here is the entrenchment of cultural protection and promotion in Canadian law and its lack thereof in the United States. In language, for example, Canada has legally established the equality of English and French, but the United States does not recognize any official language at the federal level, thus deferring to English as the sole official language in practice. While Canada has an official policy of multiculturalism codified in its 1985 Multiculturalism Act, the United States has no comparable document. And while Canada has normally had a cabinet position dedicated to multiculturalism, the U.S. does not.

Although there is a staggering difference in the outward promotion of cultural diversity between the two countries, it should not be confused with the protection of multiculturalism. The United States does not go out of its way to encourage multiculturalism the way Canada does, but it has deeply entrenched anyone's right to practice whatever culture one chooses. While the First Amendment prohibits the government from endorsing any particular religious tradition, it protects a citizen's right to practice as they choose and gather peaceably. The citizenship rights in the Fourteenth Amendment are not explicitly pro-multiculturalism, but due process prohibits any government from restricting cultural practices as long as they do not harm others. Thus, while Canada may take an active role in protecting culture, the United States cements the right of its citizens to practice as they choose and leaves the promotion of culture to individuals and nongovernmental organizations.

In spite of these different approaches, the outcome in practice is roughly the same. Whether called a cultural mosaic or a melting pot, both countries have thriving immigrant communities that continue to speak their heritage languages, wear their cultural dress, and prepare their cultural dishes. With or without state-sponsored cultural dialogue, people are exposed to different traditions by their neighbors, classmates, friends, films, and music. Whether or not there is a comparable top-down approach to multiculturalism and cultural dialogue, it is happening in both countries' classrooms, parks, and grocery stores.

EDUCATION

In the 17th century and earlier, education in what is now Canada was a process by which most families informally passed on necessary skills and values to their children and grandchildren. Formal education was organized by the Roman Catholic Church in New France in the early 17th century. Following the British conquest of Quebec in 1759-60, the imperial government in London saw formal education as a means of encouraging identification with the English language, British customs, and Protestantism. Little success in any of these areas was achieved in the province of Quebec between 1759 and 1791.

Only in the mid-1800s did early educational leaders make real headway in primary, secondary, and tertiary education, although it appears that the major motivator then was not academic knowledge, but solving social problems, including unemployment, poverty, and crime during a social transition from agriculture to industrialization. This was made more complicated by the arrival of large members of immigrants.

As Chad Gaffield points out in the *Canadian Encyclopedia*, concerns about the United States as a country born in revolution were for a long period sufficiently great in Ontario that American textbooks were effectively banned in favor of readers imported from Irish schools.[2] In Quebec, the primacy of the Catholic Church over education was established firmly by the 1870s and prevailed until the 1960s.

In British Columbia, a predominantly British-origin population living in urban areas resulted in a number of measures aimed at excluding Asian immigration. During the Second World War, the Mackenzie King government in Ottawa even brought in measures for the relocation of Canadian-born citizens of Japanese ancestry into camps. In the educational spill-over, some educators in the province for a period even sought vainly to use "scientific" intelligence tests to demonstrate that British-origin students were more teachable than their classmates of origin in Asia. It was, in short, not a pretty scene on the governance side on the West Coast.

Only during the emergence, in the 1960s, of francophone economic and political power characterized as the "Quiet Revolution" did the Quebec provincial government and denominational school boards take over the administration of schools. Budgets were increased greatly. High literacy and school attendance were thereafter stressed in the province, partly to achieve modernity. In a controversial attempt to reverse the traditional pattern by which immigrants to Quebec usually integrated into the anglophone community, the National Assembly of Quebec in the 1970s required French-language schooling for immigrant children. Skills in mathematics were also stressed more than the humanities in an effort to ensure economic competitiveness and to overcome what was seen as British-origin suppression of francophone

2. http://www.thecanadianencyclopedia.com/index.cfm?PgNm=TCE&Params=A1SEC819818

Quebeckers, dating from the 1703 Treaty of Paris. There was a significant divide in Quebec, from the 1950s to the 1970s, between the largely well-educated anglophones, who were in positions of authority—managers in large companies or within the ranks of government, for instance—and most other Quebeckers, who were generally not as well educated. The revelation of this fact was the beginning of the Quiet Revolution.

The rest of Canada, which had not had such close ties between church and education, developed standard textbooks, teacher training, and curricula in the late 1800s. Following Confederation, established separate Catholic and Protestant systems were given a constitutional anchor in some provinces, when education became a formal provincial responsibility. Minority language education became an ongoing point of contention in some provinces and school districts.

The 19th-century notion of males as breadwinners and women as responsible for home life continued far into the 1900s. The effort to assimilate indigenous peoples has continued unabated from the period of French rule almost to the present day. This included residential schools intended to separate First Nations children at a young age from their families, languages, and culture. More recent efforts to teach programs that respect cultural identity, including languages, appear to be gaining ground briskly.

THE TWO SYSTEMS COMPARED

Given that the differences between the two countries are subtle with respect to student performance, an examination of a variety of measures is required. While the average years of education may be comparable, public approval of the government's performance with regards to education can differ greatly. While overall secondary education achievements may be similar, the gender differential in performance may be shocking. And while the quality of education available may be the same, the cost of such an education may be staggeringly different. Thus, we will approach the evaluation of education in Canada and the United States by comparing a variety of results that will lead to a conclusion more nuanced than the proclamation of a clear winner.

In terms of methodology, the fact that two countries are being compared inherently limits the usefulness of the data. Absolute measures, such as government spending per capita or average years of education, are straightforward, but comparisons of performance are more complex. Performance can only be compared if the same tests were administered; as such, valid data is restricted to the rather small number of international performance tests that have been conducted. Furthermore, this data tends to treat countries as homogeneous units. Consequently, little can be said about performance on the margins. This is particularly unfortunate because what a government does to educate its most marginalized citizens is a tremendously important social indicator.

This section is broken into three themes: the performance of students; the education systems themselves; and public perception of education. Much of the data is from the UNESCO Institute for Statistics, the OECD Programme for International Student Assessment, and several domestic sources and public opinion polls.

Student Performance

In terms of educational attainments, the two countries are quite similar. The United Nations Statistics Division reports that in 2001-02 men and women in Canada and the United States had roughly the same "school life expectancy" or expected number of years of formal schooling.[3] Although the gap has narrowed significantly in the past 15 years, the percentage of each population attaining postsecondary education is now similar. While in 1991 the UNESCO Institute for Statistics found that 21.4 percent of Canadians had a postsecondary education, as compared to 32.2 percent of Americans, more recent studies, using a different definition of postsecondary education that now includes university and non-university postsecondary degrees, found that 39 percent of Canadians as opposed to 35 percent of Americans attained some form of postsecondary degree.[4]

Although the absolute level of education attainment is roughly the same, various international performance assessments conclude that Canadian students are outperforming their American counterparts. The Programme for International Student Assessment (PISA) is an OECD initiative to measure 15-year-olds' reading, mathematics, and science literacy every three years. All three subject areas are tested each cycle with one studied in depth—in 2003 it was mathematics. Canadian students performed particularly well in math, ranking 30 points above the OECD average and being outperformed by only two countries, Finland and Hong Kong. The United States, however, performed well below the OECD

---

3. Women in both countries were expected to average 16 years, while men differed by one year with Canadian men prevailing at 16.

4. OECD, *Education at a Glance: OECD Indicators.* Paris: OECD, 2001. Cited by Human Resources and Services Canada:
http://www.hrsdc.gc.ca/en/cs/sp/hrsd/prc/publications/research/2002-000014/2002-000014.pdf

average, placing approximately 20 points below the OECD average and 50 points below Canada's. While the United States met the OECD average for reading and fell only slightly below in science, Canadian students excelled well beyond these averages in both categories.[5] Another international study, the Progress in International Reading Literacy Study, assesses specifically reading comprehension in the upper of the two grades with the most nine-year-olds (usually fourth grade). In 2001, Canadians students outperformed American ones overall and well outperformed them with respect to information derived from reading.[6]

This data indicates that, while Canadians and Americans are getting roughly the same number of years of education, Canadian students are doing better at various stages along the way. This does not, however, suggest that the Canadian education system is better. The difference could be due to a variety of factors totally unrelated to education: Canada doesn't have the same problems with notorious socio-economically disadvantaged neighborhoods. We do not have the same kind of racial tensions; nor do we have a large population of uneducated immigrants. Having said that, in the next section, we will discuss the various aspects of the education systems that may have an impact on this difference in performance.

On explaining the change, I discard the view that Canadian postsecondary education (PSE) enrolment fell in the 1990s by pointing to OECD data which showed that the enrolment drop was only two percentage points between 1995 and 1999. I think the major reason for the change is due to the introduction of the new ISCED-97 criteria. They exclude apprenticeship, trades certificates, and short-term diploma programs, which are now classified as non-tertiary. The implementation of the new criteria, in contrast, had little effect on the determination of American PSE achievement. In short, the overestimation of non-university attainment in Canada prior to 1997 is the cause of the change.

For non-university postsecondary education (PSE) attainment, a fifth of Canadians "achieved a Level 5B education (e.g., community college) by 1999, compared to only 8 percent of Americans," presumably because we have a better developed community college system that grants diplomas and certificates instead of degrees. Conversely, as of 1999, a little more than a quarter of Americans (27 percent) aged 25 to 64 had earned university degrees, compared to about a fifth of Canadians (19 percent).

5. PISA Canada: http://www.pisa.gc.ca/brochur_e.pdf; PISA USA: http://nces.ed.gov/surveys/pisa/
6. http://nces.ed.gov/pubs2004/pirlspub/3.asp

Education Systems

One of the problems in comparing the education systems of the two countries is that it assumes they have uniform systems. In both countries, education is not controlled on a federal level. In Canada, it is a provincial responsibility, while in the United States, it is even more locally governed by school boards that roughly correspond to counties. Furthermore, numbers like class size are unhelpful because they vary tremendously from place to place in both countries, particularly in the United States where roughly 10 percent of children getting private educations distort the average of children in the poorest public schools. Although private schools are far less prevalent in Canada, there is a disturbing difference in public education between have and have-not provinces that can be seen in performance results. While students in Alberta perform well above the Canadian and OECD averages on PISA mathematics tests, Prince Edward Islanders perform well below both.

In terms of postsecondary education, the public versus private divide becomes even more problematic. While Canadian students pay much less for a high calibre of public university education, American students have a much greater range in choice. There are affordable state schools offering a very good education as well as private universities offering the very best at a premium. Schools such as Harvard, Stanford, Cornell, University of Pennsylvania, Princeton, and Yale have access to a tremendous wealth of resources, resources that Canadian schools simply cannot compete with, yet they are accessible only to a small elite in America.

While it would be easy to accuse the United States of having a greater socio-economic gap in education because of its public-private divide, Canada suffers from a similar gap between its have and have-not provinces. The systems themselves both have flaws, but it is not apparent that one is defective in a way that would account for the difference in student performance.

Public Opinion on Education

Recent studies indicate that Canadians are in general satisfied with the quality of education but want more government funding for postsecondary education to reduce the tuition burden on students and their families. Americans appear to be unsatisfied with the quality of public education. A 2004 Decima poll taken for the Canadian Association of University Teachers found that a strong majority of Canadians agree the federal government should provide a free university or college education to any qualified student who can't afford it, with a majority agreeing that every qualified student should be guaranteed a university or college spot even if that means spending more tax dollars on postsecondary education.[7] Recent polling of Americans done by Public Agenda, a non-partisan opinion research and civic engagement organization, found that racial segregation and violence in schools rank among their top concerns with education in America.[8]

Given that both systems have distributional inequities and that public opinion data points to underlying social issues being a problem for education in America, it is unclear that the difference in performance is due to an inherent failure or success of any education policy. More in-depth studies need to be done about performance on the margin, the distribution of performance, and how students perform when there are controls for various other social influences.

In a contrarian mode, co-author Jones notes that one could also argue that both the U.S. and Canada are educating essentially all of their citizens almost at the level they are willing to accept. Perhaps both societies are obsessing over that which cannot be rectified: there are significant numbers of individuals who remain hostile to learning. The "bringing a horse to water" adage is not irrelevant; the society's objective through providing lifetime learning opportunities should be to encourage greater academic accomplishment at every stage of life.

RELIGION

The 2001 national census by Statistics Canada dealt in part with the state of religion across the country; its conclusions released in mid-2003 provide many interesting insights.

Despite large immigration from mostly non-Christian countries since the 1970s, seven out of ten Canadians as of the time of the census still identified themselves as Catholic or Protestant. Almost 13 million claimed to be Catholic; 8.7 million self-identified as Protestants. Those who said that they were simply "Christian" more than doubled from the 1991 census to 784,000.

The denominational patterns among Protestants are mixed, in part, concludes Statistics Canada, because their members are mostly descendants of immigrants who arrived before 1961. Between the 1991 and 2001 censuses, Baptists increased by one-tenth to 729,500 across the country. The number of United Church adherents dropped 8 percent to approximately

---

7. http://www.caut.ca/en/issues/funding/decima_summary_eng.pdf
8. http://www.publicagenda.org/issues/pcc.cfm?issue_type=education

2.8 million. Anglicans fell 7 percent to about two million; Presbyterians, 36 percent to about 409,800. Pentecostals rather surprisingly fell 15 percent to 369,500. Lutherans dropped by one-twentieth to 606,600.

In 2001, 16 percent of Canadians, or about 4.8 million individuals, reported having no religion. The country of origin was no doubt a factor because a fifth of the immigrants who came to Canada between 1991 and 2001 reported having no religion, particularly those born in China, Hong Kong, and Taiwan. Interestingly, males were more likely to report no religion than females. The jurisdictions with the highest proportion of "none" were Yukon (37 percent), British Columbia (35 percent), and Alberta (23 percent), which contrasted noticeably to Newfoundland and Labrador (2 percent) and Quebec (6 percent).

Statistics Canada went further to sample persons over 15 living in private households in all 10 provinces on their frequency of attendance at religious services. Nationally, one-fifth of those sampled—or about 6.4 million individuals, assuming, probably to err substantially on the high side, that the same attendance level applies to those under 15 as over—attend religious services on a weekly basis. Even if there is exaggeration in the total of those reporting weekly attendance, no other voluntary activity across the country would appear to attract anything like this number of regular participants. Most of our media continue to overlook this phenomenon.

Religion Today

Canada's religious situation in fact contrasts strongly with that of our southern neighbor. In *The Churching of America: 1776-1990*, authors Rodney Stack and Roger Finke assert that fewer than one-fifth of Americans were active in churches in 1976, compared to more than 60 percent in 1990. The ongoing link between faith involvement and "the American way of life" remains very strong. Weekly church attendance in the 1990s among Americans—40 percent nationally—is higher than in the 1930s (35 percent). Congregational membership at 69 percent is only slightly lower than in, say, the 1950s (73 percent). Reg Bibby of the University of Lethbridge (Alberta) notes that about 30 percent of Americans belong to conservative Protestant churches, which manage to stay in close touch with the spiritual concerns of their members—compared to only about 7 percent of Canadians. He notes the now well-known phenomenon that both attendance and religious belief are stronger in countries like Canada and the U.S. where there are numerous competing churches.

Just over four in five Canadians nationally continue to believe in God. The Project Canada survey conducted by Reg Bibby found that about 70 percent of Canadians across the land, as of 1990, believed there is life after death, with only 14 percent ruling out the possibility completely. The same percentage—70 percent—said that there is a heaven and almost half—46 percent—of Canadians say there is a hell.

Europe, however, is at the opposite end of the spectrum. In Britain, only 3 to 5 percent of the population attended church weekly in 1990. On the continent, regular church attendance is estimated to be no higher than 5 to 10 percent in France, Belgium, Holland, Italy, France, and the Scandinavian countries.

Faith Renaissance Afoot?

One of the nine books Bibby has published, *Restless Gods*, sets out how Canada's various religious communities can build on an emerging religious renaissance which he and others are documenting. On the important weekly attendance at services by members of selected faiths, for example, Bibby compares surveys done in 1990 and 2000:

	1990	2000
Nationally	24 %	19 %
Catholic	31	23
Outside Quebec	35	29
Quebec	26	14
Protestant	24	28
Mainline Protestant	16	18
Anglican	14	18
Lutheran	18	21
Presbyterian	24	25
United	15	14
Conservative Protestant	50	48
Baptist	38	38
Other Faiths	26	27
Jewish	12	8
Other	33	36

Bibby adds that two Statistics Canada surveys, with samples 10 times larger than the two he used, corroborated these findings. In a question asked in

2000 of persons who attend services once a month or more on whether their own congregation is growing or declining, the trends were mixed:

	Growing	Staying the Same	Declining
Nationally	36 %	32 %	32 %
Catholics	24	33	43
Outside Quebec	33	35	32
Quebec	11	32	57
Protestants	47	31	22
Conservative Protestant	59	28	13
Mainline Protestant	32	36	32

The approximate weekly attendees of various faith communities across Canada in the mid-1950s, according to a March 1957 Gallup poll, and a 2000 survey were as follows:

	Mid-1950s	2000
Nationally	10,000,000	6,300,000
Catholics	6,600,000	3,700,000
Outside Quebec	3,000,000	2,500,000
Quebec	3,600,000	1,200,000
Protestant	3,300,000	2,500,000
Conservative Protestant	700,000	1,500,000
Mainline Protestant	2,600,000	1,000,000
Other faiths	120,000	85,000

Bibby here refers to the American congregational expert Lyle Schaller and his argument that a new religious renaissance is taking place in both Canada and the U.S. Schaller's list of indicators of this trend includes:

• many worship services are changing, going from dull to exciting
• new era in religious music
• emergence of megachurches
• more ecumenical initiatives coming from congregations and ministers
• increased number of independent congregations
• laity more involved in ministry
• positive impact of television on churches
• bestselling books having religious messages

- growing interfaith cooperation
- priority given by adults and teens to prayer groups.

Other faith communities, including Sikhs, Muslims, Hindus, and Buddhists, have also added numbers since the 1960s, presumably in part because of enlarged immigration by newcomers from Asia and the Middle East. These groups, combined with Eastern Orthodox and Jewish immigrants, have caused the numbers in other religions to grow from less than 500,000 in the mid-1950s to approximately two million across Canada by 2000.

Internationally, Canada is now seen as a land of many vibrant faiths. There is even an All-Party Inter-Faith Parliamentary Friendship Group on Parliament Hill in Ottawa, which meets quite regularly and is well-attended by representatives of numerous faiths. Among other activities, its members meet with parliamentarians to build bridges between various faith groups and to equip MPs to address the concerns of religious groups in public policy. All faith communities represented at its meetings to date appear to accept that there will never be sustainable peace in the world until its myriad faith communities can learn to live in harmony.

Bibby has explored how faith communities can attract more Canadians. He quotes the late Queen's University historian George Rawlyk, using national polling data gathered a decade ago:

> A large number of Canadians would return to the Church if they were given specific guidance on how to live their lives—two or three specific things they could remember from a church service concerning how they should live their lives. A large percentage (also) would return if they felt that their spiritual needs would be met in the church. When you get down to it, they're looking for guidance and there is this aching for spirituality.[9]

This is consistent, asserts Bibby, with factors detected about 15 years ago in the U.S. by pollster George Gallup. The veteran American pollster concluded then that the future vitality of American faith communities would depend largely on their response to several basic needs of the American people. He listed them as the need to believe that life has a purpose; a sense of community

---

9. Dennis Gruending, *Revival: Canada's Christian Churches* (video). Ottawa: Carleton University, 1996. Quoted in Reginald W. Bibby, *Restless Gods: The Renaissance of Religion in Canada*. Toronto: Stoddart, 2002, p. 225.

and deeper relationships; the wish to be respected; the need to be heard and listened to; the need to mature spiritually; the need to obtain help in closing the deficit between belief and practice. Gallup reminded Americans in the early 1990s that most of their churches and synagogues were not then effective in helping their members to "find meaning in life … the fact is, significant numbers of people find churches irrelevant, unfulfilling and boring."[10]

Concluding Thoughts on Religion

In the final chapter of *Restless Gods*, Bibby notes that a majority of Canadians now say faith groups have a role to play in their spiritual, personal, and relationship needs—"precisely the three emphases that have been central to religion throughout history. Religion has much to say to people who are trying to come to grips with spiritual restlessness, who are looking for personal hope, resources, and the possibility of new beginnings. Religious groups also have much to say about how interpersonal relations at all levels of social life can be enriched . . . . It sounds like a match made in heaven."[11] It is difficult for anyone but the most jaundiced to disagree.

Bibby's surveys and resulting prescriptions for growth among all religious communities across Canada can be summarized in two parts: First, Karl Marx, Emile Durkheim, Sigmund Freud, and many other proponents of the "God is dead—or should be" school have now been proven wrong by history. The vast majority of Canadians, along with societies of varying sizes in much of the world, continue to hold supernatural beliefs.

Second, on which religions will flourish in the 21st century in Canada, Bibby thinks the ones that have been around for a long time are best positioned. Recent evidence is strong that, for better or worse, the 21st century will be one of enormous religious activity, requiring real attention by all who seek peace in the world. For example, Bibby thinks that the Catholic Church in Quebec, while obviously now in a difficult period, will survive. So will the national branches of other multinational churches, including the United Church, which has 4,000 congregations across Canada and "a core of staunch supporters, an enviable pool of affiliates, a real tradition, and young and upcoming leaders who are determined to see congregations flourish. Denominations that are smaller will have tougher times, but only a handful will actually disappear altogether."[12]

---

10. Gallup (1992) pp. 15-16.
11. *Restless Gods*, p. 225.
12. *Restless Gods*, p. 233.

Bibby thinks that established religions such as Islam, Hinduism, Judaism, and Buddhism will also be able to avoid assimilation and acculturation and to flourish in parts of Canada. I agree with him too and others, such as noted theologian Don Posterski, that the congregations of any faith that seem likely to thrive the most are those that champion both a love of God and genuine compassion for people. In *Future Faith Churches*, Posterski, for example, concludes that "when soul care and social care are fused together, the church is truly the church and the people of God are truly the people of God."[13] Members of all faith institutions, however, will have to work hard to enjoy the renaissance foreseen by Bibby.

The United States: Culture, Education, Religion

CULTURE

The United States is aware of only one global culture: American culture. Intellectually, U.S. citizens are aware of other cultures, just as they are aware of countries outside U.S. borders. Nevertheless, for many Americans, this awareness is vague and abstract, while viscerally, it is American culture that they recognize as valid and ubiquitous. And this judgment is not without some merit.

More than a generation ago, the admittedly ethnocentric question was posed, "What language should Jesus Christ speak during a 'Second Coming' if he wished to reach the greatest number of people?" The answer was "English"—an answer that has only become more accurate over the years. English is an official language in every world organization. It is the required language of communication for international air traffic control. It is the primary language for scientific publication and communication and medical studies. It dominates the Internet. And when more people speak English than any other language (and it is the second language of choice throughout the world) as the new *lingua franca* or the equivalent of Latin in medieval times for virtually anyone with a decent education, citizens of the United States are reinforced in their belief that American culture is global. Foreigners flood to the United States for tourism, education, medical treatment, investment, or commercial activity of every type. Partly because Americans are more likely to meet a foreigner speaking "their" language than not, Americans tend not to learn a foreign language—or learn it badly

---

13. Don Posterski and Gary Nelson, *Future Faith Churches: Re-Connecting with the Power of the Gospel for the 21st Century.* Winfield, BC: Wood Lake Books, 1997.

at best. After all, which foreign language could an American learn that would serve half as well as the language (s)he already knows?

This conclusion reflects practicality rather than arrogance. English is not more virtuous than other languages; it is simply a "convertible currency." If one has English among one's intellectual credentials, it is a more useful tool on a global basis in the 21st century than any other language. The circumstance may be transient—or not. (A generation ago, a joke went that "the optimists study Russian; the pessimists study Chinese," but now one might have the pessimists studying Arabic.) For their part, U.S. citizens are hardly hostile to foreign languages—there is no country where more linguistic expertise is represented. However, Americans are also intensely pragmatic, and time spent learning another language is time not spent on another academic or professional discipline.

More subtle is the point that when non-Americans learn English, read English, speak English, develop the ability to think in English, and have U.S. points of reference for political, social, and economic thought and action, their culture becomes "American." No official recognition is required for what is a popular reality. Much of American culture is particularly seductive for young foreigners, who often find its avant guard elements, emphasis on personal freedom and liberty, and general permissiveness for youth (particularly sexual permissiveness) far different than the conservative strictures in their native lands. This judgment does not imply that American culture is more valuable, valid, or better—simply that it responds to the needs and desires of many non-Americans.

Just as at previous points in history an individual seeking the most advanced level of the civilization of the day might have journeyed to Athens, or Rome, or Paris, or London, the primary choices at the beginning of the 21st century are in the United States. And, for U.S. citizens, a handful may seek personal affirmation or knowledge in specialized topics or esoteric religion/philosophy outside the United States; however, there is no "must see" civilization to compete with their own.

In historic terms, the United States is "young"—barely 230 years old. But as a representative democracy, it is arguably the oldest. Consequently, American political history has become part of world culture: major U.S. political figures, Washington, Jefferson, Lincoln, FDR, JFK, Martin Luther King are parts of world culture. They have served as positive inspirations for those seeking liberty and human rights; U.S. political documents (the Declaration of Independence, the U.S. Constitution) and speeches ("I Have a Dream") have sparked the cultures of others. Americans who recognize this reality reinforce their own sense of exceptionalism.

During the 20th century, American culture jousted with both fascism and communism. Each alternative philosophy had its attraction: fascism appealed to order and discipline; communism to a desire for revolutionary change that would comprehensively redistribute societal wealth under the direction of an elite directorate (the communist party) working for the good of the many. These ideological and philosophical clashes were pivotal for future history; the outcome was never foreordained. Fascism was defeated only after a catastrophic world war; communism collapsed from internal economic and social inconsistencies as well as from invidious comparison with the successes of the United States. As the leader in this protracted conflict, the United States has benefited from the general appreciation that its society and culture were indeed principal elements in the defeat of communism—and thus worthy of emulation. Who now rhapsodizes over Marx, Stalin, or even Ché? Whether American culture is envied, admired, or hated, it has been victorious and cannot be ignored.

Everywhere American culture is evident: in movies, music, videos, literature, art, architecture, clothing styles; consumable goods are American. Major U.S. personalities in these fields are global rather than national figures—for good or not. Thus around the world, one can identify American culture figures by initials or first names: OJ; Michael; Liz; Jackie O. Who is comparable? Diana, before she died? You travel the world, and you can feel that you've arrived at another American strip mall: McDonald's, Burger King, Pizza Hut. First-run U.S. films fill the cinemas—Disney productions delight the global child and the Star Wars saga taps universal themes of good versus evil. Your computers in the Starbucks Internet café will be U.S. designed (if perhaps built around the world); information technology and software is written in the U.S.; you fly on Boeing aircraft; your heavy construction equipment is U.S. designed and built. Most of the panoply of activity in extra-atmospheric space is U.S. produced or directed, ranging from moon landings to Mars explorers, to interplanetary probes, to a slowly developing space station. The result has been described with dismay, "The Coca Colonization" of the world. And an American might reply, "If you don't like it, drink Pepsi!"

And not to belabor the point, but still to make it, the U.S. Armed Forces are part of American culture. Combat competence is impressive and the armed forces of every nation want to reflect the most current and effective military technology and tactical/strategic thought and training. To copy comparable elements from states that have lost their wars is to risk comparable failure. Those who want world-class military establishments must look to the United States for this "culture."

No Official Interest in Culture

In contrast to the self-conscious self-promotion of culture by many nations, the United States is one of the few countries without a ministry of culture. Indeed, in 1998 at a global meeting in Ottawa of culture ministers, Canada's then-Minister of Heritage, Sheila Copps, declined to invite the United States to the conference, giving as her rationale that the U.S. had no minister of culture (and thus presumably no culture or at least no interest in same). The absurd audacity of that position was noted by some Canadians at the time, but unless they were Canadian specialists, no U.S. citizens were aware of Copps' non-invitation. Presumably, official umbrage might have been taken at what could have been interpreted as an insult (or at least a snub). The United States not only was not insulted, it didn't even notice. If it had actually noticed the event, Washington probably would have been amused at the presumption of those who were meeting to discuss culture as if the global elephant of U.S. culture could be ignored. On the other hand, as the results of the conference seem to have been ephemeral, perhaps Washington can retrospectively express appreciation for not having been invited and hence not wasted the time or money attending.

Indeed, Americans are skeptical to the point of hostility regarding government support for the arts or media. They are not philistines: they simply believe that the proper role for support of the arts lies with private funding rather than public tax revenues. Consequently, although there is a National Endowment for the Arts and a level of government financial support for a Public Broadcasting System (PBS), there is a basic attitude that says (a) if it is worth doing, there will be a private sponsor to support it; and (b) if there is no private sponsor, it must not be worth doing—and certainly not worth doing with taxpayer revenue. Taxes should not be committed to projects that are essentially a question of personal taste, for example, an artistic display or a musical group. Naturally, there is also intense public criticism of controversial "artistic" exhibits that are supported by public funds. Thus the exhibit of a crucifix in a beaker of urine and a portrait of the Virgin Mary splattered with elephant dung were deliberately "in-your-face" exercises by their creators, but regarded as particularly offensive because they were supported by public funds.

The result has been a steady series of "conservative" challenges to public funding of the arts. The 500-channel television universe has also resulted in specialized broadcasters covering (with advertising) many of the most interesting shows that previously were broadcast uniquely by the PBS. The PBS funding was threatened and the system's officials, as well as pointing out with alarm, rallied its subscribers to lobby Congress—and accepted a greater amount of private advertising. "Big Bird" was saved from being plucked and roasted by barbarians.

Nor is there any equivalent of a Governor General's Award for U.S. literature; our literary prizes are measured by weeks on the *New York Times* bestseller lists and selection for commercial book clubs. Awards such as the Pulitzer and the National Book Critics Circle awards are private recognition rather than government-sponsored prizes. It has not been since the desperate Depression days of the 1930s that government has paid significant numbers of writers to write or painters to paint. And rightly so; while presumably such Work Projects Administration largesse prevented some writers and/or artists from literally starving in garrets, nothing memorable resulted from these efforts, although some public buildings of the era still show the fading exemplars of the social realism school of painting then prevailing.

There is no end to the variation and individuality of culture in the United States, but it is almost totally privately sponsored and supported. No nation is more multicultural or multiethnic, "multi-multi" than the United States, but its individual elements are viewed as a community, not a community of communities. Thus if the descendants of Welsh immigrants in Scranton, Pennsylvania, hold a Saint David's Day dinner, it has been financed from the subscriptions of its members. The re-enactors of Revolutionary and Civil War battles and historical life pay for and/or make their own equipment and uniforms. The Chinese dragonboat races on the Potomac River are locally sponsored events. And the marching bands, floats, and horse-riding groups that appear in our annual Rose Bowl and other festivals, and the presidential inaugural parade in Washington, D.C., have raised the funds for their participation by bake sales, private donations, and the like. There is no U.S. Department of Multicultural Affairs; Americans believe that their culture—whether riding Harley motorcycles as "Rolling Thunder" participants on Memorial Day or Veterans Day, attending a local violin concert specializing in atonal compositions, seeing *Revenge of the Sith* for the "nth" time, or whatever—is their personal choice.

Americans can appreciate the interest in a country such as Japan in identifying individuals who are "national treasures" and paid to preserve selected cultural traditions, such as making kimonos or samurai swords. Nevertheless, such is not the U.S. approach to their cultural legacy. Happily, with a shorter history, it is less difficult to continue traditions such as quilting, gun making, wood carving, and other handicrafts with private means. Colonial Williamsburg was started with private (Rockefeller) funds and continues to be sustained largely by private donations.

Culture Is Money

Culture, however, is also money. American culture is one of the most profitable and largest U.S. exports. By 1996, cultural items (movies, TV programs, music, books, computer software) were the largest U.S. export and generated over $60 billion in international sales, according to Commerce Department data and industry figures. Official interest in American culture is more than an abstract appreciation; it is a vitally important element of U.S. exports—at a time when our export balance is highly negative. A corollary element is strong U.S. interest in intellectual property protection. The illegal piracy of every facet of U.S. culture, but most notably DVDs, videos, music CDs, books, and computer software costs billions of dollars.

U.S. trade negotiators are highly skeptical of those who wish to impose trade restrictions to "protect" their national culture industries. It is seen as on the same protectionist level as when a country excludes more competitive U.S. wheat, aircraft, computers, etc. Cultural exclusions or "carve-outs" from free trade agreements are viewed comparably. If such arrangements are accepted, it is as the consequence of negotiating agreement, not because of U.S. recognition that culture is unique or deserving of exceptional protection against competition.

In U.S. eyes, culture is a product; it should be subject to free market rules. If a population wants to watch "The Very Most Modern Mindless Sitcom" or the latest excretion from a film festival, it should be free to do so without government interference or regulation. To be "popular" does not mean that a book, play, movie, or music lacks intellectual merit; Shakespeare was popular. His competitors have disappeared for all but the archival specialists in 16th- and 17th-century English theater. And those who believe that a panel of experts can determine what will last historically need only to review what garnered critical acclaim a century ago—and what subsequently has happened to these critically anointed masterpieces.

A culture will survive and thrive (or not) according to its ability to attract and maintain supporters. Not every culture that "dies" was worthy of support. We do not mourn for those cultures, and, to be fair, Americans do not expect to be mourned when we disappear. Across history, probably more cultures have died and disappeared than are currently extant. Although seeking the origins of language in Sanskrit might qualify it for revival, exhuming Carthaginian or Aztec culture (unless there was a world audience for televised human sacrifice) doesn't seem particularly attractive.

EDUCATION

Education in the United States attracts enormous attention and generates almost equally enormous frustration. As a bottomless receptacle for funds, education vies with health care; likewise, American dissatisfaction levels with its education system appear to be at the same intensity as its irritated dissatisfaction with health care.

To some extent, Americans are even more puzzled over education than over health care. After all, the progress of life ends in death; better medical care can counter death at all stages of life—but in the end, nobody gets out of life alive. It (along with taxes) is regarded as one of the great inevitabilities of existence.

But education is not supposed to have a negative end. Greater financial commitment should bring greater educational achievement. In the United States, education is not an end in itself or a pleasant abstraction, but rather the pathway to success—particularly financial and social success. Each level of education is associated with increased lifetime earnings. A March 2005 U.S. Census Bureau study indicated, for example, that the average worker with a bachelor's degree earns $51,206 per year while someone with a high school diploma earns $27,915. Workers with an advanced degree average $74,602 while those with no high school diploma average $18,734. Over a lifetime, the differences are even more dramatic. In 2002 the Census Bureau calculated that a high school diploma garnered $1.2 million over a lifetime; a BA earned almost $2 million, and a professional (medical/law) degree pushed earnings above $2.8 million (all calculated in 1999 dollars).

More essentially, as society and economics have become increasingly complicated, additional education is regarded as necessary to take appropriate advantage of new technology. The earnings differentials are advertised to suggest to those struggling with their existing level of education that it is wiser to continue to struggle further and defer gratification from immediately getting a job and earning money. Consequently, there are substantial sacrifices at all levels, individual and societal, to improve education. It is regarded as both the vast integrative device for immigrants and the mechanism for upward mobility for all classes. However, education in the United States at the opening of the 21st century is not performing as desired—despite massive societal investments.

Education has been a societal basic in the United States from colonial years. The most educated and respected members of colonial society were preachers and teachers. If there was a book in a colonial home, it was likely to be the Bible; being able to read the primary Christian text was a major incentive for education. One of the iconic U.S. folklore tales is of Abraham Lincoln learning to read by the light of the family fireplace, being instructed by his stepmother, and becoming a lawyer by "reading for the law" from the textbooks of another lawyer. The most revered U.S. leader was a "nobody" at birth; education provided the stepping stones towards greatness. His example isn't missed by many.

Stories of the American West often featured the one-room schoolhouse or the arrival of the new "schoolmarm" in the small town. Although students paid for their education at early colonial schools, the concept of a free public education, ultimately through secondary (high) school, was rapidly embraced—even by those without children. If the price of education is high, the price of ignorance is higher. Likewise, education became mandatory; children (regardless of their sex) had to go to school, and could not leave school (regardless of their level of intellectual attainment) until reaching a specific age.

Although the observation is impressionistic, there appears to have been, during the 1950s, a sea of change in both educational requirements and societal satisfaction with U.S. education. In the 1930s, a man with a primary school education could still cope effectively with U.S. society, hold a decent job, and raise a family. By the 1980s, an individual without a university degree was regarded as educationally handicapped and unlikely to have a fully successful economic future. A generation ago, less than 10 percent of the U.S. population had a university degree; currently, 60 percent of high school graduates go on to take postsecondary education.

Despite such ostensibly increased educational competence, the United States is far from satisfied with specific attainment. Starting in the 1950s, a popular book, *Why Johnny Can't Read,* began the effort to grapple with functional illiteracy and whether phonics was a more appropriate approach to the most basic educational tool: reading. The 1957 Soviet launch of the Sputnik orbiting space satellite stunned Americans, prompting the conclusion that they were falling behind in science education and associated technology and engineering. The dual problems of literacy and numeracy have been in the forefront of U.S. education for 50 years without resolution.

On a variety of international tests, most recently the 2003 Trends in International Mathematics and Science Study (TIMSS), American fourth and eighth graders scored below Taiwan, Japan, and Singapore, and the eighth graders scored below 14 countries (out of 46) in math and 8 in science. The TIMSS tests did not include major OECD countries such as Canada, the UK, Germany, and France. Although national rankings differ according to the test and the participants, the United States does not score at the top of such exams.

However, it is hard to ascribe this shortcoming to lack of funding. There is no obvious corollary to spending more money and getting greater academic accomplishment. In 1999, U.S. per capita expenditures on elementary/secondary students was approximately $7,400; in 2003, it had risen to slightly over $8,000. The District of Columbia spent over $13,300 per student, followed by New Jersey ($12,200), New York ($12,140), and Connecticut ($10,370). The lowest was Utah ($4,860) and other low rankers were Arizona ($5,670), Mississippi ($5,800), and Idaho (slightly over $6,000). On the other hand, the states with the highest percentage of high school graduates are Minnesota, Montana, Wyoming, and Nebraska (all over 90 percent). And when children taking the Standard Aptitude Tests (SATs) in North and South Dakota, Idaho, and all of the other states ranking low in per capita financing score substantially higher than the students where the highest funding was provided, clearly there is more in play than money.

Nor is the public school system serving the immigrant community in the same manner as in the past. Early 20th-century urban school systems were replete with immigrant success stories. Leo Rosten's 1937 humor classic *The Education of H*y*m*a*n K*a*p*l*a*n* was light-hearted, but designed also to show the effort by European immigrants to master the sometimes impenetrable intricacies of English. It was amusing—but also an inspirational success story. There are many comparable 21st-century success stories, notably among Asian immigrants; it is almost standard to hear of an Asian child who arrives in the United States without speaking English and graduates 15 years later from a "name university" with a PhD in science. By early 2005, the Census Bureau noted that Asians had the highest percentage of their population (49 percent) with a bachelor's degree or higher. For these students, the objective is "an iron rice bowl"—a career that the U.S. economy will value for their lifetime. On the other hand, Hispanic immigrants have been less successful. Research suggests that third-generation Hispanics have obtained high school degrees at an even lower rate than their parents, and all Hispanics drop out at a higher rate than peers from other racial or ethnic groups.

The United States educational system is flailing as well as failing. The most recent perception has been that boys are now more at risk of being left behind than girls are. Boys are failing in ever greater numbers. They are statistically more "troubled," stricken with attention deficit disorder and likely to have academic and behavioral problems. They are the ones doing drugs, doing crime, doing time. They kill each other through urban street wars and themselves through suicide and auto accidents. Although absolute numbers at universities continue to rise, the percentage of young men enrolling is steadily declining; in only a tiny handful of niche areas, essentially science and mathematics, do they still prevail.

The "what to do about boys?" question appears to have no obvious resolution. The United States has no 21st-century need for large numbers of unskilled (citizen) laborers. There is an absence of role models for many young males; "broken" homes or homes that never had a full-time male in residence are further complicating factors. So also is the relative shortfall of male teachers in primary and secondary education. Even the most caring and attentive female teacher can find the exuberant energy of little boys (or the sullen hostility of male teens) unattractive when compared with the usually more biddable nature of girls.

Indeed, one of the most significant advances of the last generation has been the massive rise of women as a percentage of those attending university and obtaining advanced degrees. As of 2005, more women than men over age 25 had obtained a high school diploma. Women are now a majority (56 percent as of 2001) of those matriculating at U.S. colleges and more than a majority of the entrants in graduate school generally and for law and medical schools in particular. Surprisingly, they are also the majority in veterinarian schools, previously an unquestioned male preserve. In all areas where the culture of the coming society will be created—law, liberal arts, education—women are positioned to command this future.

On a secondary note, the numbers of foreign students matriculating at U.S. universities has slowed, a trend that began immediately following 9/11. In mid-2005, the American Civil Liberties Union published a study claiming that foreign student enrollment declined 2.4 percent in 2003; the ACLU also argued that most of the reduction was in the physical or biological sciences and engineering. The Bush administration dismissed the ACLU study as politicized and "lack[ing] credibility." Moreover, increased restrictions on working with scientific information also reportedly inhibited foreign student study. The effort to obtain a balance between security and academic freedom/openness when dealing with foreign students has become as much a political as a technical issue. And, by early 2006, the number of Saudi students was above 9/11 levels, suggesting the phenomenon was reversing.

Who Are the Teachers?

The rise of women throughout all elements of society has created a more subtle problem. Little more than a generation ago in the United States, the stay-at-home mom was the standard for emulation, and a woman who wanted a career was largely limited to being a secretary, a nurse, or a school teacher. Today these women are in business, medicine, law, engineering, and, as a consequence, the woman of exceptional intelligence who elects a career teaching in primary/secondary schools is rare. Indeed, as an anecdotal illustration of this phenomenon, one teenager, who was impressed with the stellar quality of her about-to-retire high school chemistry instructor, expressed interest to him in teaching. His instant response was, "You're too smart to teach." Taking the point to heart, she earned a PhD in chemical engineering.

Consequently, the impression, reinforced by the academic test scores of those entering as education majors at university, is that U.S. teachers are drawn from the intellectual mid-levels at best. Course work is often not intellectually challenging, and the emphasis is on learning the techniques of teaching rather than the academic subject matter to be taught. Teachers are defensive about their abilities, and unionization has made it difficult to pay the most highly qualified teachers commensurately with their abilities. This is particularly true in math and science where there are endless anecdotes about the bright high school student correcting a teacher's errors. Or the better teachers departing for higher-paid positions in industry. Moreover, the unions resist teacher testing after hiring and obtaining career status; the public impression is then that the teachers are afraid of being tested because they doubt their qualifications. A study such as Steven Levitt's *Freakonomics* demonstrates devices that some teachers employ to manipulate more positive test results for their students. However, if students were perceived as performing successfully, teachers would not be in question. As in sports, you can fire the "manager," but you cannot fire the "team." While the primary schools may involve a good deal of the equivalent of child care/babysitting, middle and high schools have higher intellectual challenges—and the inadequate teacher is a substantial liability.

No National Norms

One of the basic political structures in the United States is the school board, and, for many citizens, it is the only political body in which they have any interest. Often the school board will hire a superintendent of schools and monitor performance closely. The results may be good or bad, but they always vary due to the absence of agreed-upon national standards. Likewise, the texts chosen for schools vary in quality; what can be taught (and how) is subject to local argument. (The issue of teaching "evolution" versus "intelligent design" in high school biology is one of the current imbroglios.) Likewise, the standards for teacher hiring, retention, and promotion are idiosyncratic; obtaining teacher's certification in one state does not automatically qualify one to teach in another state.

In contrast with many countries where every child has the same textbook for specific disciplines and grade levels, the United States has no national standards for its state and local educational curriculums. In this regard, both Canada and the United States agree and take the same approach—facilitating systemic comparison. For the U.S., there is intense resistance to any national curriculum, and draft models, for example, a prototype for U.S. history, have attracted furious criticism for "politically correct" selectivity or emphasis. This circumstance reflects American commitment to federalism and to local control of public schools. It can be a great strength, permitting a thousand flowers to bloom and then selecting the most vibrant; however, incoherence (akin to having every instrument in the orchestra play without a conductor) in outcome can also be the result. A student who moves three times to separate states during high school might have to take "state history" three times (and consequently omit general U.S. or world history).

Consequently, as all local forms of evaluation for high schools are impressionistic and/or relative to local circumstances, colleges and universities put considerable weight on the SATs, which are national exams that have provided a baseline for judging prospective success at the university level. The SATs have been operational for over 50 years and, while repeatedly tinkered with and revised, are all but universal U.S. standards for measuring high school accomplishment.

Trying Everything

The frustrated recognition that public schools are inadequate has sparked both national and local efforts. The federal government's 2001 No Child Left Behind Act is an ambitious effort to raise academic scores for *all* students in every U.S. school district. Schools are ranked and scored against one another; increased federal funding has provided a goad for more precisely measuring specific reading and math accomplishment. States enjoy the increased federal funding, but are increasingly irritated at meeting the federal benchmarks for student accomplishment and complain about having to "teach to the test." However, the first lesson to be learned is "There is no free lunch."

Although there have always been private schools, which are run for profit based on fees from students, they have become more prevalent in the past generation. Although some are "elite" schools, attended for generations by richer and/or more socially prominent students, many are institutions where education may have a greater religious orientation. Although private schools must be academically accredited through inspection and review of their curriculums, they will hire teachers without the "union card" who may well be more academically qualified for the subjects that they teach. However, as private businesses, they may also close from lack of funds.

School systems throughout the United States are also experimenting with "charter" schools and special programs ("basics" or "no walls") that obtain public funding, but are permitted greater flexibility in their curriculums and greater control over who attends the school. Some individual parents are home schooling their children in a reflection of a back-to-basics approach by those who are dissatisfied either with the discipline, academic quality, and/or secularized education in their local public school. Although the parent must adhere to a basic curriculum (and often the child has the option of participating in some programs in the local public school), the essential requirement is to pass standardized tests reflecting what should be learned at the child's academic level.

Significant numbers of those parents committed to the public school system intervene intensely in their children's education to the extent that they become "parents from hell" for teachers and administrators, or "helicopter parents" hovering over their children. These parents often are focused on their children developing a resume that will gain them entrance to an elite university and view any grade less than A+ as the equivalent of failure.

The alternatives to the public school system are looked upon with either skepticism or direct hostility by public school administrators. The charter schools drain some funds on a per pupil basis, but more importantly, the public schools conclude that they attract the better, more disciplined, motivated students who have more concerned parents. When such parents and children opt out of the public schools, the question becomes whether the remaining students will learn or can be taught effectively.

The argument reflects the continuing battle over how children learn. The 1954 Supreme Court decision decreed that "separate but equal" school systems for blacks and whites were inherently unequal. An exhausting sociopolitical effort to create an integrated U.S. school system was only marginally successful; a *de facto* segregation largely based on urban/suburban housing patterns is now the norm. Segregation is now socio-economic rather than racial.

Infinite Opportunity

Despite its problems, one of the great continuing strengths of U.S. education is the chance for anyone to get an education beyond high school. To be sure, this is not a "free" university education, and at one end of the spectrum are the much-bruited-about private universities of the Harvard, Princeton, Yale, University of Pennsylvania, Stanford variety, with ever rising costs now over $44,000 per year (2007) for combined tuition and living costs. Attendance at these schools can be considered as sending a smoke signal to the Internal Revenue Service that you have too much money. Nevertheless, a significant percentage of attendees at these schools benefit from scholarship and/or loan packages. More generally, there is an extensive complementary system of relatively low-cost, state-financed universities and community colleges that permits almost any motivated student to obtain an inexpensive education. These colleges and universities can provide a full degree, a two-year technical degree, serve as a "feeder" for a four-year university, provide supplemental/retraining studies, or simply allow leisure study of the part-time, follow-your-own-interests nature.

An almost unnoticed educational system is that in the U.S. Armed Forces. The armed forces has become a rung in the upward mobility ladder, both for what the soldier can learn directly and for "GI bill" equivalent funding for subsequent education. Not that there is much of a civilian market for a combat infantryman or a tank gunner, but the wide variety of logistical support specialties in electronics, aviation maintenance, medical services, and the like, are almost instantly applicable to the civilian world. Moreover, many of our commercial pilots started with military training and education.

The reality is "lifetime learning" or "continuing adult education" in U.S. society. Americans are continually reinventing themselves. The United States is at the forefront of night schools—those who put in heavy-duty study after a full working day, seeking a law degree or a master's degree in business or some other discipline. The United States invented the system of adult home learning, starting with the International Correspondence Schools (whose origin was for Pennsylvania coal miners at the turn of the 20th century training to be foremen), in which participants pay for courses delivered by the postal system or the Internet. The latest innovation has been the *For Dummies* books, a series that began by covering information technology topics but has subsequently dealt with almost every topic except brain surgery.

RELIGION

It has become a topical truism that the United States is the most "religious" of modern democracies. There is almost a sneer at times in this observation, which is invariably cast as a semi-criticism. It is either couched as a pseudo-sophisticated intimation that the observer has outgrown such primitive idol worship or the latest illustration of equivalency thinking. The previous generation of these chatterers enjoyed juxtaposing the United States and the Soviet Union as moral equivalents (while not spending any time as work camp colleagues of Alexander Solzhenitsyn). The current generation suggests that born-again Christian U.S. political and social figures are equivalents to Islamic leaders whose adherents practice (on a one-time-only basis) suicide bombing. These are also individuals who view the word "crusader" as the international political equivalent of "pedophile," while carefully forgetting that the Crusades of the Middle Ages sought to recover lands that had been conquered by Muslim invaders.

Nevertheless, the religiosity of the United States should hardly be surprising. Several of the original North American colonies, such as Massachusetts, Rhode Island, Pennsylvania, and Maryland, were founded primarily by those who sought to escape the religious strictures of the established Church of England. In current parlance, they wanted to "do their own thing," and religious freedom is a consciously observed element of U.S. society. Although it is fashionable to recount the religiously skeptical nature of some leaders of the U.S. Revolutionary War, the absence of clear protection for religious freedom in the U.S. Constitution as originally drafted was rectified in the first words of its first amendment ("Congress shall make no law respecting an establishment of religion, or prohibiting the free exercise thereof . . . .").

Nor would every nation, when faced with its greatest national crisis of a civil war, compose an equivalent of "The Battle Hymn of the Republic." Still a part of the standard hymnal in Protestant churches across the United States, God is implored to support the republic in its time of testing. The Union forces have "read a fiery Gospel writ in burnished rows of steel" and God is implored to "crush the serpent [the Confederacy] with His heel." As Jesus Christ "died to make men holy," Union soldiers were called upon to "die to make men free" while "God is marching on." And, in conclusion, Christ is "wisdom to the mighty" and "honor to the brave." In contrast to the grim resolve of these stanzas, which were sung in American churches with fervor in the weeks after 9/11, the lyrics of the traditional Confederate song "Dixie" sound light-hearted and nostalgic.

Another clear theme of American religion has been its missionary commitment. There has been a constant societal effort to promote Christianity and democracy to people and areas where it was not known. Religious denominations writ large and churches individually have historically supported missionaries, and U.S. foreign policy has been influenced by missionary activity. Whether, for example, the United States would have backed Chiang Kai-shek and the Republic of China with such dedication if he had been an observant Buddhist rather than a devout Methodist can be debated. More currently, the annual State Department International Religious Freedom report is a comprehensively documented assessment of the state of religious freedom in countries throughout the world that incorporates a graduated system of penalties for states deemed as violators.

Ramifications of the First Amendment

From the few words cited from the Bill of Rights have come the "separation of Church and State" principle and, during the subsequent two-plus centuries, an unending battle over the position that religion may hold in public life. Consequently, the reading of a religious text in school or prayer (other than that of a student silently petitioning the Almighty prior to an examination) has been banned. Likewise, public prayer at public school sporting events or graduations has been outlawed (although some schools have simply defied these bans without subsequent juridical prosecution).

Religion in Today's USA

It seems invariable that major social questions will also have a religious dimension and an associated litigious prospect. Consequently, there has been a more than generation-long sociopolitical dispute over abortion rights. Does a child have a "right" to life and government protection for this status from the instant of conception or at some latter point in gestation, or not until the first second after birth? Is a woman no more than a host (willing or unwilling) for a fetus or is her "right" to choose to continue or terminate a pregnancy at any point the determining factor? Annually, the Roe v. Wade Supreme Court decision of 1973 is commemorated or deplored. A lawyer's or judge's position on Roe is a political litmus test for the bench—as it is a defining question for every politician whose ability to dodge artfully while answering forthrightly has become a basic element of political jargon. "Choice" versus "life" is far from fading in U.S. debate, although technology in the form of still more prevalent contraception and effective morning-after pills may eventually put a practical, if not philosophical, conclusion to the debate.

More recently, the issue of a "right to die" and even more currently "gay marriage" have roiled the religious-social-legal spectrum.

Right to Die

It is said that societies are comfortable with sex or with death—but not with both. The United States is increasingly comfortable with sex; however, death is a different problem. Most Americans resist death with the same passion that they resist military defeat; both death and defeat are un-American failures. And those for whom religion plays but a small role in their lives want to be able to control the last act of their lives personally, and, if there is a God who judges such actions, they will accept the consequences. With the right to life at one end of society, the right to death now becomes the other bookend in theocratic-political discourse. So questions comparably as hard as those associated with abortion have religious belief smashing against secular views. Does an individual have the right to choose death?

Can some other person (or the medical establishment, or the government) choose death or abet/participate in "assisted suicide"? And at what point in the life/death process can the decision be made? Or must death be resisted with every "heroic" technological measure that society has at hand until the brain wave is flat and/or insurance funding runs out?

If life is "God-given," then only God can determine the time of death; however, if life is an accident of a cosmic nature and/or religion has no relevance for the beginning or ending of life, then government can justifiably decide these issues. Consequently, the judicial system has been called into the fray (as government is loath to define death or allocate responsibility in other than criminal cases). The Terry Schiavo case in 2005, which pitted parents against husband and called upon doctors and lawyers to determine whether the woman could be deprived of fluids to die of dehydration, was clearly unsettling, regardless of the observer's philosophical or religious beliefs. The United States is still far from reaching a conclusive societal judgment on the legitimacy of a "right to death."

Gay Marriage

During the course of the past generation, U.S. state and local government has exited the bedrooms of its citizens in regard to the sexual activity of consenting adults. This departure has been slow, with a medley of juridical decisions ending legal racial restrictions on heterosexual relations and then on homosexual relations. And when the Supreme Court on June 6, 2003, ruled state sodomy laws as unconstitutional, these laws were still in effect as felonies in both Maryland and Virginia. Indeed, Virginia also remains one of seven states with a law prohibiting cohabitation of unmarried couples (heterosexual as well as homosexual)—although the law is not enforced and would be highly unlikely to withstand any legal test.

Nevertheless, while religious fundamentalists reject homosexual behavior, the U.S. government has implemented laws and regulations militating nondiscrimination towards homosexuals in the full range of hiring, property rental or purchase, commercial activity, access to social services, adoption, inheritance, etc. The current issue in the United States is whether homosexuals have a legal right to marriage in a form, either religious or civil, that is recognized by the government as precisely identical to that enjoyed by heterosexuals.

At this juncture, the U.S. population is profoundly uncomfortable with the question. Although the Supreme Court in Massachusetts declared gay marriage legal in February 2004, the state currently (in mid-2007) stands alone. In the 2004 national U.S. election, the electorate overwhelmingly endorsed differently worded amendments, to 11 state constitutions, that marriage could exist only between one man and one woman. Comparable legislation was presented in other state referenda during the 2006 election. Currently, 26 states have constitutional amendments specifically barring recognition of same-sex marriage, with civil marriage restricted to a legal union between a "man" and a "woman"; 43 states have statutes defining marriage as between two persons of the opposite sex.

At this juncture, the U.S. electorate has barely come to grips with the gay marriage issue. It has not seriously begun to examine alternative sociosexual arrangements such as polygamy (a husband with multiple wives) despite the practice being part of the doctrine of the original Mormon faith (and still practiced quietly in some sections of Utah and other parts of the U.S.). A prime-time TV sitcom featuring polygamy scheduled for 2006 release attracted predictably alarmist criticism prior to airing. Equally relevant, albeit still less discussed, is polyandry, which is a legal sexual relationship between one wife and more than one husband. To a degree, the polygamy issue has been a red herring in the current debate. Those opposing same-sex marriage insist that polygamy/polyandry would also quickly become legal—an argument likely made in order to generate revulsion against same-sex marriage. Those supporting same-sex marriage claim that it would not. But no one knows.

A perhaps more delicate and thus not broached question would be the remaining legal barriers to incest. For example, if my daughters could marry other women, why could they not marry each other? Indeed, why should not all three of them be able to marry each other in a group marriage?

Why should a brother be restricted from marrying his sister, particularly when the individuals in question are past the age of conceiving children? Or a son marrying his mother? Or his father? Or a father or mother any/all of his/her daughters or sons?

Or why should any combination of males and females in any genetic combination be restricted from marriage?

We assume, of course, that all involved are "consenting adults," perhaps even counseled by a representative of the state in private to assure that "consent" is real. Indeed, consent, rather than the number or the distribution of sexes of the partners, would be the imperative. We are not discussing an endorsement of child molestation—adulthood and informed consent would be absolutes. So far as the genetic problems associated with incest are concerned, modern birth control and genetic counseling should be able to manage this aspect of the relationship.

These are serious, not frivolous, questions for society to examine. They are inconvenient rather than inconceivable. Humanity has experimented with every physically possible form of sociosexual relationship during its history. Polygamy continues in Utah (and Bountiful, BC). There is polyandry in Nepal. In ancient Egypt, brothers and sisters married. In many places in the world, first cousins marry. In the communes beloved of "summer of love" counterculture lore, group sexual relationships were more than salacious rumor.

Ultimately Americans—and Canadians—may want to move in these directions, but they should be aware what will (and will not) be regarded as "legal." Surely not even a decade ago would the most prescient have envisioned that homosexual marriage (and not just the private relationship of the bedroom) would have legal sanction. In determining the legal framework of these alternate futures, Canadians have a tremendous legal advantage that the United States deliberately rejected: Canadian governments can request a formal opinion from their Supreme Court without having to present a specific case for judgment. Canadians can pose these questions on any conceivable sociosexual relationship under discussion—and see if they wish to live with the answers.

APPROACHES TO HEALTH CARE 5

There is a systemic problem for health care: in the end, we all die. No matter what level of funding society commits, the ultimate consequences are still the same. Thus, there is an essential frustration to medical expenditure—particularly as national funds are not infinite and medical funding quickly comes into competition with other social goods: education; law enforcement; infrastructure; scientific research; defense. How much do you steal from the future to minister to the present?

This expenditure is particularly frustrating for Canadians who have paid "up front" for their medical services through taxes during their working lives. Consequently, delays in service (treatment) damage public faith in the national medical system.

Canada has made an enormous psychic investment, equivalent to national self-definition, in its health care system; discussion, let alone criticism, often ventures into theological rather than problem-solving substance. The term "two-tier" is closer to being a pair of four-letter words than an alternative medical practice. Nevertheless, Canadian medicine is not meeting the welfare state objectives that citizens believe have been promised.

Everyone recognizes that this gap between promise and performance must be resolved, and Canadians are studying their medical system with great intensity. The "theologians" say "more of the same but better," which essentially means spend more money. The critics offer a wide range of doing medicine differently.

In contrast, U.S. psychic investment is in national security; it, rather than health care, is the area of greatest national concern and, to date, it has not failed.

The United States—or at least those Americans with health care insurance—is perhaps more pleased with its medical system as fitting its national philosophy of "you get what you pay for." Americans are not always pleased by how much they pay, but they are satisfied that services are rapidly available. And, despite the "legend," Americans without health insurance are not devoid of medical treatment—or invariably bankrupted by its costs.

The respective demonization of medical practice north and south of the border is counterproductive. Greater accessibility, reduced administrative overburden, and improved medical technology are neither "Canadian" nor "American" issues. Far more could be accomplished with personal behavior modification than with bureaucratic reform.

Health Care in Canada

Two incidents I witnessed personally say a good deal about this subject. Having sat on the Health Committee of the House of Commons for a period during 2004, I became increasingly concerned about some health care issues, partly because our much-praised-outside-Canada system does not look as good at times to those of us living and dying with it. As one health professional quipped, paraphrasing Winston Churchill about democracy, "Our health care system is the worst—except for all the others."

The first incident involves a visitor to Canada from a developing country, who through a series of errors arrived without any form of health care insurance applicable in Canada. Watching a concert in one of our larger cities, he collapsed. Those reaching him first thought it was a heart attack. An ambulance rushed him to the emergency department of a nearby hospital, where some excellent heart and kidney specialists determined quickly that it was kidney failure. Approximately two and a half weeks later, he was taken to the home of his wife, who had been a resident of the province at issue for several years, and daughter. Initially, the three of them faced a bill for all services of approximately $100,000, but to their later enormous relief and gratefulness he was subsequently found to be covered under his wife's provincial government health coverage.

The second incident involves a woman in her mid-80s suffering from pneumonia who, several years ago, was taken by ambulance from her home in a senior citizens residence to the emergency wing of a large hospital in another major Canadian city in a different province. In the emergency wing, she was given numerous tests to see if she was admissible. Fully nine hours later, the medical staff in emergency decided she could be admitted, at which point staff from the ward she needed to go to upstairs came down to conduct further tests. She was finally taken upstairs, where she died a few days later.

In my view, the first case shows our system at its very best in one sense. Excellent medical care, including advice from both heart and kidney specialists, saved a life without imposing a severe financial burden on the patient or other family members. Others, however, in fairness might assert that those paying for health care in the province in issue should not absorb the costs because a visitor failed to obtain insurance before arriving. In the second case, I'm not at all certain today whether faster active treatment of the woman in the emergency ward would have saved her life.

But to evaluate where we are now and to calculate where we are going and should go, it is useful to review some history.

SASKATCHEWAN LED THE WAY

On the bright side, life expectancy in Canada since 1950 to the present has risen a full decade, from 69 to 79. Why? One reason is certainly our health care system, whose genesis was in Swift Current, Saskatchewan, in 1947, when its residents (not health care professionals or politicians) created the first public health care insurance program on the continent. In that community, health care was henceforth to be a publicly run service rather than a service to be purchased in the market place. A year later, Premier Tommy Douglas of the Canadian Commonwealth Federation (now the New Democratic Party) extended the Swift Current model to the entire province with the support of farmers, churches, many other grassroots agencies, and most of the voters across the province.

A full decade later, the Liberal national prime minister, Louis St. Laurent, introduced North America's first national hospital insurance plan; his successor, Conservative John Diefenbaker, implemented another national bill that applied to all health services due in hospitals across the country under a 50-50 cost sharing between the federal government and the provinces.

In 1962, the Saskatchewan legislature again stepped into the lead by covering all services provided by doctors—even if outside hospitals—on a fee-for-service basis.

In 1968, the Federal Medical Care Act was implemented. It required universal medical and hospital insurance coverage, government administration, portability between provinces, and reasonable compensation for physicians. The 50-50 cost sharing by the federal and provincial governments was maintained, but a subsequent explosive growth in the building and use of hospitals saw federal costs escalate so much that in 1977 the

Established Programs Financing (EPF) was introduced, with federal funding to be provided in equal parts through a tax transfer and a cash transfer. EPF replaced cost-sharing programs for both health and postsecondary education; however, in 1984, this program changed again and the health portion was tied to the Canada Health Act.[1]

CANADA HEALTH ACT

In 1980, the Hall Commission found that user fees and extra billing by physicians, which were still permitted at that time, were creating accessibility obstacles for lower-income Canadians. The Canada Health Act (CHA) of 1984 banned user fees and required all provinces to abide by federal regulations to receive federal funding. It's worth mentioning some of the features of that legislation:

1. Provincial insurance plans had to be run by public authorities on a non-profit basis—even though the roles of payer and provider were in practice joined.
2. Comprehensiveness required that all medically necessary services provided by hospitals and physicians must be insured. "Medically necessary" was not defined by the CHA, but today approximately 2,300 services are provided in some provinces and deinsured behind closed doors in others. The CHA focus on hospitals and medical services all but ignored health promotion and disease prevention.
3. "Universality" demanded that all residents of a province be eligible for public insurance coverage.
4. "Portability" meant that the coverage is maintained if a resident of Canada moves within the country or travels outside, although the coverage is restricted to what the insured has in their province.
5. "Accessibility" demanded access to medically necessary hospital and physician services, unimpeded by financial or other barriers, with no discrimination based on age, health status, and income. Line-ups, however, were permitted.

Overall in the 1980s, our health care was a major source of national pride across the country. We were mostly delighted that, unlike America, we provided equal access to our entire population. Many of our attitudes towards the system, however, began to change with media stories and personal and

1. http://dsp-psd.communication.gc.ca/Pilot/LoPBdP/BP/bp264-e.htm

friends' experiences with it. By 1999, an Angus Reid national opinion survey on health indicated major public concern about government cutbacks, long waiting periods, availability of services, shortages of nurses and physicians, specific illnesses (AIDS, cancer, heart disease) and caring for our aging population.

Since 1984, there has been huge growth in what can be done to lengthen and improve patients' lives, as well as changes in virtually all aspects of communities, technology, and demographics. Almost eight in ten Canadians indicated, in 1999, that they believed the level of waste, duplication, and overlap posed a major threat to the viability of the health system.

The Mulroney Conservative government (1984-93) granted 20-year patent protection to brand name drugs. It also reduced the federal part of health spending from 30.8 percent on its election to about 23.5 percent when it left office nine years later. Its successor, the Liberal government of Jean Chrétien, in the 1995 austerity budget of then-Finance Minister Paul Martin, effected severe reductions in federal funding to health and some programs. Janice MacKinnon, Saskatchewan's NDP minister of finance from 1993 to 1997, asserts in her book, *Minding the Public Purse*, that Martin's 1995 budget cut federal spending across the country by more than $25 billion in health, education, and social programs. By fining several provinces for extra billing and user fees, the Chrétien government in time forced all provinces to stop these practices.

In 1999, a report by the premiers made a number of important points about health spending. First, provincial expenditures had skyrocketed from $11 billion in 1977-78 to about $56 billion in 1999-2000. In the premiers' view, Ottawa's contribution towards health care and other source programs as a portion of their spending had declined from approximately 27 percent in 1977-78 to about 13 percent in 1999-2000, thereby requiring the restoration of the cash funding lost in 1995. An escalator was needed because they projected that their spending would rise from $56 billion to over $85 billion within a decade. The federal government disputed this finding; by their accounting, 33 percent of health funding comes from the federal government.

FUNDING AND EFFECTIVENESS

The most current health spending figures are always behind the times, but it's worth looking at how Canadian and American health care funding compare, even several years ago. In 2002, public spending on health care in Canada totalled about 7.3 percent of Canada's gross domestic product versus 6.8 percent in the United States. Philippe Le Goff of Canada's Parliamentary Library, in a study he published in 2004, however, concluded that private spending on health care in America amounted to 8 percent of GDP versus only 3 percent in Canada. Accordingly, Americans were at the time spending almost 15 percent of their yearly output on health care, compared to 10.3 percent in Canada and an average of 8 percent in other OECD member countries.

Canadians are quick to notice in analyses such as Le Goff's that much of American private spending is consumed by administrative costs. Our eyes light up when the study concludes that such costs, paid by insurers, employers, and health care providers in the U.S., reached an astonishing US$294 billion even back in 1999. Astonishingly, this represented virtually one-third of all American health care spending, compared to 16.7 percent of Canadian spending on health care. In approximate terms, Canadians spent US$9.4 billion, or $307 per capita, on administrative costs versus US$1,059 per capita in the U.S. A study reported in the *International Journal of Health Services* concluded that reducing American administrative costs to Canadian levels would save our neighbors at least $209 billion a year, "enough to fund universal coverage."[2] The single-insurer system in Canada obviously results in much lower administration costs.

The frustration for Canadians arises from the chronic shortage of health services created by the rationing of many of those services across our country and caused by what many think is chronic underfunding. In Canada, any improvement in health services, or access to them, is likely to come from increased taxes or compulsory provincial government premiums. In the U.S., residents who want more services must usually pay higher premiums to private insurance plans if they can afford them. Le Goff also points to a recent study indicating that the average health insurance premium for a family of four in the U.S. in 2004 was US$9,602, with employers generally covering about three-quarters of it.

A CRITICAL ANALYSIS OF HEALTH CARE IN 2005

In 2004, Nadeem Esmail and Michael Walker published for the market-oriented Fraser Institute a comparative analysis of our health care system relative to most other OECD countries. The study did not include the U.S. and Mexico because neither has a universal access and publicly funded health care system. Among the conclusions of their report:

2. *International Journal of Health Services*, 2004, Vol. 34(I), pp. 65-78.

Comparative Spending

After adjusting the data for the average age of a member country's population, the authors conclude that Canadians in 2004 spent more on health care than any other industrialized OECD country, having publicly funded and universal access health care, except Iceland and Switzerland. Those spending less included the UK, Sweden, Ireland, France, Norway, New Zealand, and Australia.

Not surprisingly, Esmail and Walker conclude that health costs can be significantly lowered if patients are required to participate in paying for the services required. Most of the countries they studied, while providing universal access, charge user fees for access to hospitals, GPs, or specialists—in many cases to all three. Interestingly, Canada is the only member of the OECD to bar the privately funded purchase of core services. All other members use one species or another of user-pay private provision of health care. Many OECD nations insist that only public hospitals offer publicly insured services, but more than half of them allow private providers to deliver publicly funded care.

Value for Health Money

Does Canada's health care system provide good value for the spending? The Fraser Institute study draws a number of conclusions, which are not very positive. On health care performance, which applies tests for health longevity, low levels of mortality from disease, and effective treatment for terminal illnesses, Canada does not rank in this study where most Canadians would expect us to be. For example, ranked in comparison with other OECD members, Canada was 16th in healthy life expectancy, 21st in infant mortality, 24th in doctors/1000 of population, and 17th in MRI and CT machines/million population.[3] We are certainly not leaders, despite all the public and private funds we spend on health care.

Roles of Doctors

On a comparative age-adjusted basis, says the Fraser Institute study, Canada has a low number of medical doctors relative to comparable nations: we rank 24th out of 27 countries with only 2.3 doctors per 1,000 persons and a total of 66,289 physicians, no doubt very unevenly distributed across the country. The study concludes, in short, that Canada has fewer doctors than most other OECD countries and that Canadians report longer waits for access

---

3. http://www.fraserinstitute.ca/admin/books/files/HowGoodHealthCare2006.pdf

to treatment. Only the UK, Japan, and Turkey have fewer doctors per 1,000 persons (age-adjusted) than we do.

The study quotes a recent survey by Harvard University in which Canadian respondents were more likely than any other universal-access country surveyed to wait more than one month for non-emergency surgery, although there was little difference between Canada and the UK. Canadians were also most likely to find it somewhat, very, or extremely difficult to see a specialist. As well, in terms of income and access, Canadians with below-average incomes were 9 percent less likely than ones with above-average incomes to rate care as excellent and 6 percent more likely to rate care as poor.

Canadian doctors are normally paid on a fee-for-service basis, as is the case in a majority of OECD member countries. For specialists, however, 70 percent of OECD members rely in whole or in part on salary compensation, with 37 percent relying on it exclusively.

Inflexibility in many of our practices is probably the biggest obstacle to continuing improvement in Canada's health care system. Part of this, paradoxically, is the insatiable rise in health spending, which is already consuming almost 42 percent[4] of provincial budgets (versus about 32 percent a decade ago). Various efforts at cost restraint have been attempted to reduce incremental increases, including creating rationing through waiting lists and reducing the number of insurable services. Neither, of course, corrects the problems over the longer term, which can only come from high-quality health management and better delivery of services.

CAN HEALTH CARE BE IMPROVED?

The Supreme Court of Canada, in mid-June 2005, held in the case of Chaoulli and Zellotis versus Quebec that the Quebec Charter of Rights, which in part guarantees life, liberty, and security of the person, was violated in denying private sector funding through private insurance for health care. In effect, as Senators Wilbert Keon and Michael Kirby, both health care experts, argued in a newspaper piece they wrote after the court made its ruling, "governments cannot have it both ways—legislating their own monopoly and then failing to deliver timely access to necessary care." Shortly thereafter, however, Quebec was excused by the court from taking any action on the decision for a year.[5] The prospect of any significant change based on

---

4. Linda West, *Trends and Issues in Health Care* (Third Edition). Toronto: McGraw-Hill Ryerson, 2005.
5. http://casselsbrock.com/publicationdetail.asp?aid=1172

the decision—flatly opposed by the federal government—remains problematic. In June 2006, responding to the court decision, the Quebec National Assembly introduced legislation that would, among other revisions in the health code, provide patients with guaranteed access to certain procedures, currently limited to total hip or knee replacement and cataract surgery. The bill was not officially assented to until December 2006.

Through mid-2007, Quebec has moved tentatively to reduce waiting times for the specific medical procedures identified in the Supreme Court decision; minor (and arguable) levels of success have been reported in this regard.

However, among the Keon-Kirby suggestions to save and improve public health care are:

1. Provincial and federal legislators should abandon their fixation with the ownership of health care agencies in favor of a range of delivery options in order to obtain the best results for Canadians from a mix of public and private features. (The senators were probably too polite to remind Canadians that aside from North Korea and Cuba, Canada is evidently the only nation of any importance on earth to prohibit or discourage, in a number of provinces, private insurance for health services covered by public insurance.)
2. Hospitals must be given the flexibility they need to make the most efficient use of their resources. This includes "eliminating the complex and rigid work rules that permeate the hospital sector."
3. It is long overdue for members of the medical profession, such as the Coalition of Family Physicians in Ontario, "to stop dragging their feet on reforming primary care delivery. Every report over the past decade has recognized the critical importance of having primary care services delivered through multi-disciplined clinics that are mainly funded on a capitation rather than fee-for-service basis."[6]

To take a related example—my own, not the senators'—someone recently queried why the men and women who, say, clean toilets in public hospitals in at least one of our provinces, should earn an hourly rate estimated to be at least twice what persons doing the same work in hotels receive. Indeed, isn't this taking public ownership of health care to an unreasonable, even ideological, extreme?

---

6. Senators Michael Kirby and Wilbert Keon, "Still Time to Save Public Health Care," in *National Post*, June 16, 2005.

Similarly, when a province's minister of health claims that the Canada Health Act (CHA) bars anyone from staying overnight in a private hospital, to what section of the legislation is he referring? The correct answer is no doubt "none." One of the strengths of the CHA is that it does not make such statements, instead encouraging maximum flexibility in provincial health management.

In 2005, we had Ujjal Dosanjh, as federal health minister, telling the opening session of the annual meeting of the Canadian Medical Association that giving patients more "choice" in treatment could violate the Canada Health Act. Essentially ignoring the recent Supreme Court decision, the federal minister, who was a practicing lawyer before being elected to Parliament in 2004, insisted that better health care and shorter line-ups for Canadians be done only through reforming the public system.

Delegates at the meeting were clearly not impressed. Almost two-thirds of them subsequently passed a motion that read, "The Canadian Medical Association supports the principle that when timely access to care cannot be provided in the public care system, the patient should be able to utilize private health insurance to reimburse the cost of care obtained in the private sector."

The incoming CMA president, Dr. Ruth Collins-Nakai, noted after the passage of the resolution that it was not the "preference" of the association to see the development of a private system, but members were motivated by fatigue. She added, "I think doctors are very, very frustrated at not being able to provide timely care to their patients."

Kirby and Keon, for example, insist that Canadians who seek better health treatment must be willing to accept some new realities. One they mention is that, in order for expensive diagnostic equipment to function 24 hours a day and thus to help patients sometimes waiting months for results, patients should be required to have such tests run at inconvenient times when necessary.

Another piece of health care reality they mention is the overall impact of an aging population, new technologies, and new drugs. The result will be rising health costs even if every inefficiency is wrung out of the system.

The two senators eloquently query why none of the professionals involved in service delivery of health care has been willing, following the Supreme Court of Canada decision, to say what they would do to save public Medicare. If progress on wait times, for instance, is too slow, the senators urge that the Senate's Standing Committee on Social Affairs, Science, and

Technology's proposed "care guarantee" should be enacted. It would allow the use of public funds to ensure that treatment is received in a timely fashion—"even if public funds must be used for patients to receive treatment in another province or in the United States."

Finally, the two legislators conclude that Canadians generally owe our Supreme Court a huge debt of gratitude for upholding our charter rights: "No Canadian should suffer unduly—let alone die—because vested interests involved in the health care system refuse to change their attitudes, refuse to make the system more efficient or refuse to fund it adequately." They also applaud the justices for cutting through the "myths, untruths, and distortions on which debates about health care have been heard for years."

Professor Linda West, who teaches at the Faculty of Nursing at the University of Manitoba, points out that there is both universal access to health care and virtually no waiting lists in some other jurisdictions, including Austria, Belgium, France, Germany, Japan, and Switzerland.

Looking Outside the North American Box

WORLD HEALTH STUDY

The World Health Organization (WHO) says there are "three key goals to any health system: improving the health of the population served; providing protection against the costs of health problems; and responding to expectations."

The WHO review, in 2000, of 191 countries for the quality of their health care services placed France first and Sierra Leone last. Many Canadians were probably surprised to see that we placed 30th, not far ahead of the United States at 37th. Canada ranked 21st in availability of CAT-scan machines, 19th in availability of MRIs, and sixth in availability of cancer radiation units.

Having provincial governments as single payers clearly reduces management costs, as we see in the case of such expenses in the U.S. model. There is also the advantage that because taxes or mandatory premiums are paid in advance, there is no additional burden at a time when someone is ill.

FRENCH MODEL

Patients in France can choose their own doctors and treatment centers (public or private). The compulsory health insurance plan finances health care services and pharmaceuticals, but individuals must pay 26 percent of their total health care expenditures. In Canada, the private sector share is approximately 30 percent (15 percent for private health insurance and 15 percent for out-of-pocket expenses). Public and private hospitals co-exist in France to maximize the access to necessary services. Both kinds of hospitals are subject to government approval for their locations and medical equipment, including MRIs, scanners, etc. On the other hand, during the summer of 2004, more than 15,000 French (primarily the elderly) died of heat-related causes without significant subsequent action. Following an initial media outcry, the absence of follow-up or juridical action is startling—the equivalent of a Gallic shrug. It is hard to endorse a medical system that generates such a catastrophe, regardless of its ostensible ranking in the WHO study; indeed, the magnitude of this medical failure puts the utility of the WHO study's rankings into serious question.

Kirby Committee

Senator Kirby's Senate Standing Committee on Social Affairs, Science, and Technology made the important point, in a 2002 report, that because health care is entrusted with public money, it has a duty to provide services as efficiently and in as timely a manner as possible. It reminded Canadians that our health care currently has no means within it of evaluating the health care industry as a whole, adding some incendiary (to some) words, "The committee concluded that continuing government micromanagement of health care would make reform of the health care system impossible."

It strikes me personally that as Canada will soon be coping with 10 million aging baby boomers, the role of the private sector in care delivery is a key question, especially when France, the Scandinavian countries, Belgium, Switzerland, Germany, and other nations all have both universal coverage and a private component that appears to augment the standard of care delivery rather than harm it.

Many senior Canadians, however, believe that increased privatization will result in two-tier health care in which they will be among the major victims. Others argue that a publicly funded system with private supplements can ensure as good equity and better service than our current system. In short, they argue that without competition between the public and private sectors, improvement is almost impossible to achieve. With it, dollars will tend to move to the more efficient areas of health care.

One additional model is the current UK system, which evolved out of the post-World War II National Health Service in which the government employed on salary most of those in the health care sector, including doctors, and owned all hospitals. The no-competition structure is now gone. Hospitals were given discretion over their operations and fee schedules, with doctors becoming free to contract with independent purchasers of their services. The goal was an efficient internal market without impairing universality or equality of the tax-financed system.

In Canada, there have been initiatives in some provinces in favor of greater efficiency, including privatized surgical centers (both with and without overnight stays), privatized diagnostic centers, clinics, and health care practices with expanded services of diverse kinds, and growing numbers of private alternative medical companies.

It seems overwhelmingly obvious that the Canada Health Act ought to be modernized to focus on timely access to high quality care and life-enhancing interventions, in ways that are results-based and accountable. More of what is termed "evidence-based medicine" would lead to better decision-making in a host of areas, including whether a procedure or product really reduces time in hospital, doctor rates, or the need for surgery.

The WHO certainly appears to believe that governments should develop explicit health policies that set benchmarks, outline parameters, delineate the expected roles of health care professionals, and build public consensus.

ROMANOW REPORT

Much has been written and said about the fairly recent $15-million federally funded study on health care by Roy Romanow, the former longtime premier of Saskatchewan. One commonly expressed concern is that it is essentially a defense of the status quo in health care. Janice MacKinnon, Romanow's finance minister in Saskatchewan for four years, has for one parted company with him because she thinks his recommendations are too much "inside the box" to provide the kinds of innovative solutions needed to improve health care across the country while not shortchanging other important areas.

MacKinnon also worried that most of the new money called for in the Romanow Report would go to health care professionals rather than to increased health quality for patients. Her thoughtful book, *Minding the Public Purse*, notes that between 1998 and 2000 health care costs rose by almost 28 percent while federal revenue rose by less than 12 percent. In the provincial field, she cites the Alberta experience. In 1990-91, 24 percent of the provincial budget went to health care; by 2000-01, it was about one-third; by 2008, the estimate is that fully half will be going to health care. She asks, responsibly, if a similar pattern prevails across the nation, will all provincial governments before long be closing schools in order to pay for health costs?

Like MacKinnon and many others, I share the view that unless something effective can be done about skyrocketing health spending, other important priorities—education, research innovation and development, poverty reduction, environmental protection, human resource training, and infrastructure—will increasingly suffer. She and I both see more sustainability in the health recommendations by Senator Kirby's committee and former deputy prime minister Don Mazankowski than in some of those by the Romanow Commission.

The U.S. Experience with Health Care

THIRD RAILS IN CANADIAN AND U.S. POLITICS

Most readers will be familiar with the "third rail"—the electrified rail in a subway system that powers the subway trains, but is fatal for one who falls from the subway platform and lands on such a rail. In politics, the "third rail" is the analogy for an issue that candidates deliberately, even desperately, avoid discussing or acting upon from fear of being "fried" by the electorate. Of course, what electrocutes one candidate often empowers another, and hence some of the most exciting maneuvering in politics is watching one candidate attempting to trip an opponent into falling across that third rail.

In the United States, the third rail is social security; in Canada, it is health services, but in both societies, discussion of health care is increasingly prominent in politics.

For both societies, to stretch the analogy a bit further, the third rail is part of a social infrastructure that badly needs rethinking and perhaps substantial repair. However, because it is still "working" (just as is the North American power grid), all are loath to absorb the electoral risks associated with its repair. And, unlike other politically poisonous issues such as prayer in school, "God" in the Pledge of Allegiance, homosexual marriage, flag burning, self-expression through pedophilia, or the legality of marijuana use, neither social security nor health care can be adequately transferred to the judiciary, as proven by the June 2005 Canadian Supreme Court decision that did little to clarify the debate over private health care options.

In the United States, social security pension rights have evolved since their implementation over 70 years ago. Once derided as another tax grab, since the benefits didn't begin until age 65 in an era when life expectancy was in the low 60s, social security has become an iconic element of U.S. politics—and a major source of financial support for the elderly. There is a general recognition now that with the combination of higher pensions, greater longevity, and a smaller working population base, social security needs to be restructured. The health elements of social security, notably the ramifications from the increased longevity of recipients, are just beginning to be appreciated. It is not that the scare stories of "running out of money" are accurate or even politically relevant; funding from general revenues rather than social security taxes is always possible. This prospective revenue drain, however, needs to be addressed, and the answer may lie in a combination of higher social security taxes on workers, reduced benefits for some or all recipients (or at least a slower rate of increase), beginning pensions at older ages (already in process), or providing other options for workers to invest their payments throughout their working lives.

In this regard, Republicans—particularly conservative Republicans— who have always been skeptical of social security, have for decades proposed mechanisms to reduce costs to the federal government such as making social security optional or permitting workers to invest some of their social security taxes in government-regulated, but privately managed, mutual fund stocks. Democrats, who know the fiscal realities as well as Republicans, have always berated Republicans for trying to take social security away from the poor and elderly. It is a useful political cudgel, for no matter how hard the Republicans protest that they love, respect, and appreciate social security, citizens—particularly the poor and/or elderly—are suspicious.

Does this litany sound familiar to Canadians?

In Canada, the third rail is health care. From any perspective, the problem is obvious: extended waits for essential services. Many months, frequently a year of painful (or anxious) waiting for hip, knee, or heart surgery. For Canadian citizens, this circumstance can only be infuriating since they have paid up front for years, indeed decades, through higher taxes, with the anticipation and the explicit promise that when they need medical attention, it will be quickly available.

Likewise, the 2005 report that 3.5 million Canadians do not have a primary care physician is daunting; they must resort to hospital emergency rooms for their medical problems. Canadians enjoy comparing their health circumstances with the invidious example of 44 million (circa 2003) or so Americans who don't have health care insurance and must resort to hospital emergency rooms. However, both figures are about 10 percent of our societies.

It is hard to see the practical difference between Canadians who have the right to free health care, but can't get it, and Americans who must pay for the care—and can get it.

Yet any Canadian politician who suggests a solution other than spending more public money torpedoes his election chances. And health funding already is the equivalent of *Jaws*, devouring all else in the budget. Nevertheless, regardless of how passionately a Conservative politician professes commitment to a single-tier, all-Canadian solution to health care, Canadians remain suspicious of this promise. They seem to view it as akin to the "lobster pot" that Quebec separatists promised following a referendum victory—once in, you would never get out and you would be cooked in the process. For health care, the Conservative lobster pot would be the horrors of combined public and private medicine—the dreaded "two-tier" system. It was indicative of this concern that throughout the 2005-06 election campaign, Conservative leader Stephen Harper never missed an opportunity to emphasize his affection for Canada Health as it exists. And, after his minority victory, he has steadfastly criticized any alternatives, for example, Alberta Premier Ralph Klein's hypothesis of a "third way" for provincial health care. The prime minister, to his credit, has made shorter waiting times one of his five key priorities; however, transforming this commitment into fact will be a tremendous challenge. And, indeed, by mid-2007 this much-bruited-about priority had become the unmentioned ugly relative in the Tory political campaign family.

Two sophisticated societies such as Canada and the United States should be able to move beyond finger-pointing over whether the "pot" or the "kettle" is blacker.

Perhaps the only conclusion is that Canadian and American societies must wait until social security and health care have collapsed to the extent that citizens are willing to accept the fiscal sacrifices and/or social changes that accompany restructuring. Then all parties—Liberal, Conservative, Democrat, Republican—can heroically claim credit for victory over the problem. But don't hold your breath waiting.

HEALTH CARE CHALLENGES IN THE UNITED STATES

The lives of Americans and, indeed, more generally, the citizens of Western democracies, grow ever richer in material goods. Despite the very real problems posed to domestic security by terrorism, these challenges are not existential: we do not face foreign invasion or the prospect of nuclear annihilation that dominated the protracted conflict against fascism and communism during the last half of the 20th century. Individual rights are comprehensively protected by legitimate political systems. If this is not the "best of times," the times are still very good and certainly not "the worst of times." Our complaints, albeit not trivial, are those of success and wealth; indeed, there is never an end to wanting, and the desire for "something better" is a universal constant.

The most obvious next goal for someone who "has it all" is to enjoy it longer, and with the full ability to appreciate this good fortune physically and mentally. This objective is where the real crisis for Americans in the early 21st century emerges. Although we are no longer as directly limited in our expected lifespan to the biblical "threescore and ten," we are clearly outliving our design specifications, and it is increasingly expensive and complicated to maintain our bodies while they do so. Biology prepared humans to mature in their teens, procreate at that point, and die in the fourth or fifth decade of life, when our reflexes, eyesight, and hearing lost hair-trigger reactions and something hungry and faster caught us. The most obvious illustration of this point is the normal failure of our teeth—they just wear out without careful dentistry, and the result for the toothless in a state of nature is a diet not conducive to long life. Although through technological ingenuity life expectancy continues to inch upward, the substantial "leaps and bounds" increases that marked previous generations are not going to happen again. Most of the improved life expectancy of the 19th and early 20th centuries was obtained not by having adults live longer, but by preventing early childhood mortality and death in childbirth through better sanitation, immunizations, and basic antibiotics.

Consequently, while life in its final decades is less painful and debilitating than even 50 years ago and there are more centenarians than ever, we are not seeing individuals living longer than the longest previously recorded lifetimes (let alone to those recounted in biblical text, such as Methuselah's 969 years). And those who do creep into the years above 100 do so with much diminished physical—and often mental—capacity. This reality is particularly disconcerting to the U.S. "boomer generation"—those born during the baby boom immediately after the Second World War. This cohort, the largest in U.S. demography, regretful admits that "you can't take it with you." Its response has been, however, "We're not going."

Nevertheless, it does not appear as if there are any easy answers to boomer (or other) reticence about death. Indeed, the longer and more intently we examine the nature of life, the more complicated it appears. The proverbial "mad scientist" of the 1930s cinema created life with a mix of chemicals blasted by a lightning bolt, or revived the dead through scientific creativity. Three generations later, although we have pushed the limits of human fertility and cloned animals, we are as far from creating life without a human genetic base as we were 75 years ago. And, so far as ending disease is concerned, a generation ago in books such as Bernard Glemser's *Man Against Cancer,* there were rather blithe predictions of how long it would take for cancers of various varieties to be cured or prevented. To be sure, there have been tens, even hundreds of thousands of individuals "cured" of cancer; however, in many instances, the reality is that death has been protracted rather than a condition cured.

Likewise, the astonishing technical feats of organ transplants, hip and knee replacements, microsurgery, kidney dialysis, heart bypass, and so on, are miracles at the margins. If all heart problems and cancers were cured, life expectancy would only increase by a few years. The problem of basic debility remains; slow, systemic failures of multiple organs mutually interacting, with no "fix" and only palliative measures to alleviate the conditions. Instinctively, one hopes that technical efforts such as transplants and microsurgeries are the equivalent of attempting to get greater effectiveness from human and animal muscle power by using more intricate pulley systems prior to the invention of the internal combustion engine. Popular health and science offer stories of miracles-just-about-to-happen from stem cells, gene therapy, antioxidants, a vegan diet, or pyramid crystals. So far as scientific predictability is concerned, however, we still do not have the controlled fusion power that excited environmentalists 50 years ago. While we are probably happy that the computer intelligence of Hal, from Arthur C. Clarke's *2001: A Space Odyssey,* has not emerged, neither have the ostensibly sober 1950s expectation of moon colonies and trips to Mars. If anything, the past generation has taught us that "the possible" may have limits, and whatever is possible is going to take much longer than those in need of immediate medical answers might hope. And much, much more money.

Expensive

What we can say with confidence is that health care in the United States is expensive. Very expensive, and going to become more so. Every element of health care, from research and development to the ministration of terminal illness, appears open-ended in its financial demands. It has become a truism that a disproportionate amount of medical expense occurs in the last year of life. Unless one dies suddenly in a funeral parlor, substantial expense is going to be devoted to that "last year"—whether it occurs in the first hours or days after birth when doctors struggle against congenital problems or birth-related complications; those hours when the riddled victim of a drug turf-war shootout is delivered to the ER trauma center and maximum medical effort is devoted to preventing death; or whether it is an octogenarian undergoing heroic measures to stave off the ravages of multiple ailments accumulated over a full life.

Fostering, sustaining, and prolonging life (or protracting death) is high-tech, cutting-edge technology, and those who have mastered its intricacies in the medical services come at proportionate price.

That circumstance would not be objectionable if resources, private and societal, were infinite. But they are finite, and those unwilling to expend personal or societal money to cure physical or mental problems or preserve and extend life (for relatives and friends, if not for themselves) are few indeed. The truism that everyone hopes for life after death, but none are eager to try it prematurely, increasingly holds forth, particularly during an era when the intensity of religious belief and a desirable "hereafter" is fading, but secular attractions are increasingly pleasant. Americans do not want to die; death is not "natural," but rather an illustration of failure and defeat in a society that sees success and victory as "natural." And while there is a movement, often religiously based, to return death to a religious orientation and to desecularize death through formalized legal rejection of heroic measures to sustain life, most people continue to reject death and seek all possible measures to prevent it and to preserve and enhance life.

This means the bane of politicians in a democracy: choice. While a dictatorship might decree that there would be no medical support other than palliative pain relief for individuals over 70, such a view is not an option in a democracy. Even Colorado governor John Love waited until he was no longer in office to suggest that the elderly had a duty to die; the elderly virtually unanimously rejected the suggestion, and Love's suggestion has faded into "don't go there" political lore. Love himself is now dead, and no one has picked up his thesis.

Public Rejection of "Socialized Medicine"
But the choice issue remains real. Public monies expended on health care can not be expended on the wide variety of other societal needs, from primary

education to culvert repair. There is a blunt fact that if money is spent on infrastructure—such as universities, bridges, dams, airports, electrical transmission lines—at the end of several decades, society still has a tangible product. On the other hand, you can spend an infinite amount of money on health, but still everyone will die.

Indeed, the estimate of money expended on health care varies considerably, but there is no question that it is rising, and there is no prediction that it will decline. Each population wants the best possible care for the least cost, so the myth of "free" medical care is attractive. Consequently, the amounts spent, the percentage of GNP that health services consume, and the expenditures from state and federal budgets has become an increasingly political rather than a technical issue. The public is inundated with comparative studies, each designed to prove the superiority of one system over another. However, the United States is not navel-gazing over health care costs to the degree prevalent in Canada. There are no U.S. equivalents to the dueling documents from Senator Kirby and former premier Romanow, etc. The basic judgment appears to be that the United States pays more per capita on health than any other OECD country, but still ranks low on a variety of health indicators. To a degree, these studies illustrate not that figures lie, but that selective employment of statistics is an ideological and political reality. However, rather than debate decimal points or "view with alarm" from one point of the political spectrum or another, it is more useful to attempt to examine basic U.S. beliefs, attitudes, and social circumstances.

To be sure, there is the possibility that a society simply cannot afford both a 21st-century military/defense establishment and full-coverage public health care. Or, at least, cannot afford both without massive deficit spending or taxation that verges on confiscation. Although U.S. citizens are not taxed at levels commensurate with Canadian or many European polities, the population is highly resistant to higher taxes. Indeed, U.S. politicians promise the opposite—tax reductions and lower taxes—having noted that when President GHW Bush broke his "read my lips; no new taxes" commitment, he was punished by the electorate.

In the United States, the higher tax option is not politically acceptable—certainly not in the near term. And an essential suspicion of big government (unless it is engaged in defense/security) has left Americans with a profound skepticism of sweeping national programs. Such are characterized as "socialism" (a label which for decades was close enough to communism to be a fatal description) or even "fascism" (which was, after all, "national socialism"). More currently, national medical programs are associated with failed socialist states of the former Soviet Union and Warsaw Pact or European states whose socialized medicine shortcomings appear structural (the United Kingdom) or who have had catastrophes (the thousands of deaths associated with the 2004 French heat wave) that can be attributed to socialized medicine.

Two other societal elements find the current system quite acceptable. These, at different ends of the spectrum, are the HMOs and the trial lawyers. Socialized medicine (or medicine with a large, institutionalized government presence) would certainly squeeze the private insurance firms. And, if the government were a major player in health services, the likelihood is high that it would regulate and limit legal awards in cases of malpractice or negligence.

And, to be sure, U.S. medical practitioners are all but unanimous in their rejection of a "socialized" system. In such a system, they conclude that they would be hired help rather than independent professionals, subjected to niggling bureaucratic rules and restrictions. Without question, they despise the current iteration of bureaucracy associated with insurance companies, but they instinctively believe that full government bureaucracy would be even worse. Probably, and more importantly, their income would be limited as civil servants, and the very substantial incomes that doctors and medical technicians receive would fall. Many doctors and medical technicians view themselves as small businessmen and free market capitalists, with their skills as the product presented in the marketplace. They have made enormous personal investments of time and money in university study to reach professional competence, and, consequently, wish to benefit to the maximum from their investment. As highly educated, articulate, and politically aware individuals, doctors have substantial influence on the electoral system through professional organizations such as the American Medical Association.

THE U.S. MEDICAL SYSTEM

There are as many U.S. medical systems as there are legs in a nest of millipedes. That is, every American has a "medical care program," but it is personally selected (even if by default); however, there is nothing akin to a national health services system. One could conclude that the U.S. system is a total mishmash of options—including having no formal medical care at all for many individuals. And that judgment would be accurate to a degree, although perhaps not relevant.

There are, to be sure, huge public medical systems that are virtually ignored in the discussion of U.S. health care. The entire cadre of the U.S. Armed Forces and their dependents are covered by a government-financed and -run medical system with military health personnel providing the care (or reimbursing civilians when military medical services are not available). Likewise, there is an extended system of hospitals for veterans (162 in 2004), run by a cabinet-level secretary for veterans' affairs, which provides for those (and their dependents) who have completed a career of professional military service.

Additionally, government medical services are provided for a number of special groups, for example, Indians on reservations, and diplomats assigned outside the United States. Furthermore, extensive medical assistance is given to the elderly and a number of disadvantaged and/or low-income groups under Medicare and Medicaid.

Many private companies provide health insurance plans to their employees; often these non-salary benefits are the consequence of detailed union bargaining over decades with major industries, such as the auto workers. Some are paid partly by the employer and partly by the employee. In any event, they are significant expenses: General Motors, for example, contends that health-related costs, at $1,525 per car, are a greater percentage of the cost of each vehicle than steel, and that these costs are bankrupting the company.[7] Indeed, one observer suggested that GM was a medical care service (for its retired employees and their dependents) that sold cars as a sideline. Other major manufacturing companies argue vigorously that the United States is becoming uncompetitive because the national health care systems of other countries relieve their industries of health costs that U.S. firms must absorb.

Nevertheless, the bulk of medical care comes through systems of private (or government-sponsored) insurance. Again, while the U.S. system offers almost infinite choice in such private medical care, the basic point is straightforward. The individual selects a system of insurance coverage and pays a fee for this coverage.

Then it becomes complicated. Coverage can be for self and/or family. Conditions and degrees of care vary. Qualification for insurance coverage may exclude pre-existing conditions; that is, insurance companies may not accept (or accept only at increased fee) an individual who already has a medical condition requiring extensive continuing expense. Most coverage

---

7. George Will, *Chicago Sun-Times*, May 1, 2005.
  http://www.suntimes.com/output/will/cst-edt-geo01.htm

includes a deductible (an annual initial amount of medical expense—usually several hundred dollars—that the individual pays in full) and requires the individual to pay a percentage of the total cost (usually 20 percent). Many insurance companies have a "catastrophic" clause wherein the company assumes all expense at a certain point. Many insurance plans have an extensive listing of physicians who are associated with their company (most physicians are associated with many insurance companies), and whose fees are regulated by the insurance company. For non-emergency medical services (for example, optional surgery), the individual is often advised to seek assurance from the company that such action is covered by the insurance company.

By and large, Americans have accepted that you get what you pay for. Since one pays the fee for the service performed—at the time of service—the connection between personal payment (even if through insurance) and value received is clear. Americans have not, like Canadians, paid up front through decades of higher taxes only to be unable to obtain the service desired at the time of need. And waiting for these services is usually relatively brief. To use an analogy, one may have to wait for customized aspects in a new model of automobile, but virtually all models can be driven off the lot.

The Uninsured

An individual may be uninsured. For some, this is a matter of choice. While to many observers, such a choice may seem an unacceptable risk, there are individuals who will decide against health insurance on rational, logical, or philosophical grounds. These include religious believers who eschew traditional medical care and seek healing for medical problems through prayer or nontraditional practices. Others are young, healthy adults who do not anticipate any medical needs and choose to spend the money they save on products (cars, plasma televisions, clothing, etc.) or services (vacations, education, concerts). Others put the money they would expend on health insurance into financial investments. Some "hedge" their medical bet, seeking insurance only for catastrophic and unlikely accidents or illnesses. Some, who can easily afford insurance, practice "health care by emergency room." They do not have a doctor, so if they have a problem, they go to the nearest hospital ER for treatment. Yes, this approach has risk, and doesn't allow for an extended relationship with a doctor of choice or the ability to plan and schedule specific treatments, but based on percentages it is not irrational. It also reflects the societal free choice that the United States epitomizes—and who can object to a system that maximizes free choice over tax-driven compulsion?

Nevertheless, the worst case is what dominates politicized discussion. That is those individuals who need and/or desire medical insurance but cannot afford it. These figures vary according to the source and the degree to which "viewing with alarm" is driving the judgment. Nevertheless, the number is always significant; the most frequently cited figure is slightly higher than 16 percent of the U.S. population, that is, approximately 44 million persons (in 2003). There is frequently the intimation associated with the figure that these individuals are dying in gutters outside locked hospital doors, denied any care because they lack insurance.

The reality for the medically uninsured, however, is vastly different. Society at large pays for their medical care, albeit invisibly. Almost invariably, they are treated in hospital emergency rooms. There is a substantial amount of "charity" work done, particularly in the large teaching hospitals, and if the major surgery is of an emergency nature (for example, in the case of a traumatic auto accident) it is simply performed. To the extent possible, these patients pay their charges; additional sums are handled in the hospital financial accounts as charity. Their care ends by being prorated across the services given to those who pay personally or have insurance. In effect, they receive free care. Is this the optimal approach for providing medical service? To be sure, not; however, it is far from the highly publicized horror story so often heard.

At Its Best . . .

At its most proficient, the U.S. medical system delivers to those with appropriate insurance astonishing, timely care, regardless of age. In modern, urban areas all technological support is available for the most highly skilled professionals to employ extensively. At one juncture, there were more MRI machines in a single university teaching hospital than in the province of Ontario. Scheduling procedures or tests isn't always instantaneous but waiting is minimal. Some illustrations:

• An 85-year-old Asian-American male received triple bypass, valve replacement with a pacemaker less than a month after being diagnosed with what would have been short-term fatal cardiac problems. Surgery and subsequent care were delivered by Chinese-speaking medical personnel. Five years later, he continued to actively enjoy the company of his grandchildren.
• An 82-year-old Asian-American female received knee replacement surgery three weeks after it was determined that palliative care would no

longer resolve the problem. Within less than six months, she was fully active and pain free.

• A 50-year-old American male suffered from chest pain. Checking into a hospital, he was diagnosed as requiring heart bypass surgery—and was taken directly to the operating room, even before his wife was informed. He survived, and 16 years later was enjoying the company of his grandchildren.

The obverse was the case of a man who was judged as requiring bypass surgery, but consigned to a waiting list. He died waiting—but that was in Montreal. And there is the instance of an American woman in Montreal who required a minor gynecological procedure; after more than six months of discomfort, while the surgery was repeatedly rescheduled, she arranged with brief prior notice to travel to Plattsburg, New York, where the operation was performed without incident. To be sure, these anecdotes are trivial in systemic terms, but an observer can appreciate how a U.S. citizen would decide if asked which system is superior.

Indeed, the United States is the "second tier" for the world—and notably for Canada. That is, if there is a medical need for rapid service for someone with the ability to pay, the need can be met in the United States. Where "experimental" medicine is needed, as was the case for Jordan's King Hussein or Quebec Premier Robert Bourassa, people turn to U.S. research hospitals. A high percentage of global medical research is performed in the United States; arguably, the U.S. also has the best medical schools in the world.

The result is a constellation of diamonds. All too often, however, the setting for these gems is brass rather than gold.

And at Its Worst . . .

Indeed, no medical system has a shortage of horror stories. The wrong leg amputated; the wrong medication dispensed; exhausted interns and residents providing inadequate or incorrect care, resulting in extended discomfort or death.

Some statistics suggest that as many as 100,000 deaths per year are the consequence of medical lapses (the conclusion of a 1999 study by the National Academies Institute of Medicine), and that a significant percentage of drugs are incorrectly prescribed.[8] Other studies indicate that there are

---

8. "To Err Is Human: Building a Better Health System," Institute of Medicine, November 1999. Cited in "Iatrogenic Disease: The 3rd Most Fatal Disease in the USA" by Ronald Grisanti, at http://www.yourmedicaldetective.com/public/335.cfm (8/28/2005), and elsewhere.

shortages of medical service personnel for inner cities, Indian reservations, and rural towns and villages.

The unpleasant reality is that some people are killed by direct error and others when a malady or a condition is "missed." Of course, for every individual whose life is ended in such a way, even a reasonably capable doctor saves hundreds, perhaps thousands of individuals—and alleviates the discomfort and concerns of countless others. Nevertheless, this recognition that error is a constant and that "there, but for the grace of God, go I" makes doctors reluctant to judge errors of commission or omission by others. Consequently, the level of doctor error must be high, blatant, and persistent before colleagues will institute sanctions. The combination of systemic refusal and inability to hold doctors to account has fostered a medical malpractice legal subspeciality that has become highly contentious and politicized. The astronomical and still rising cost of malpractice insurance in areas such as obstetrics and gynecology has driven some doctors into retirement and others to transfer their medical practice to states with lower costs.

Doctors spend (waste) extensive time in dispute with insurance companies regarding whether a medical action desired by the physician is justified and covered by the insurance company. This endless, frustrating exchange between the medically desirable path (for doctor and patient) and that acceptable to insurance professionals has been one consequence of the effort to hold medical costs in check through Health Maintenance Organizations (HMOs).

Nor can Americans be pleased at drug costs. For many reasons, drugs are being used more frequently and at greater costs. Some are certainly life-enhancing, such as those to reduce high blood pressure, lower cholesterol, or resolve psychiatric problems. Others, such as Viagra or assorted antihistamines, are quality-of-life related. Still others are "the latest thing" whose benefits over an earlier medication or "generic" product may be marginal, but whose costs are distinctly higher than the alternatives. The result, however, without a drug insurance plan, is often very high costs. These costs have resulted in the nationally embarrassing exhibition of impoverished senior Americans taking bus trips to Canada to buy their medications at far lower costs. These activities have also fueled the battle over prescription Internet pharmacies that send drugs to U.S. purchasers—an argument with increasingly bitter overtones that could result in U.S. drug companies limiting sales to Canada.

INVIDIOUS COMPARISON

In early 2005, a senior Canadian journalist used a selection of medical case histories to illustrate differences in Canadian and U.S. medical practice. Among other accounts, the story juxtaposed the poignant case of a young U.S. university student whose medical condition was fatally misdiagnosed in a Waterloo emergency room against that of a Canadian girl in a tobogganing accident in Vermont who was skillfully and comprehensively attended by U.S. emergency room medical services.

· On one level, the comparison is invidious: Canadian medicine obviously failed; the young woman died. On the other side of the border, the Canadian parents were fulsomely pleased with the caring, professional medical service their daughter received.

On another level, one could complain that the comparison is between watermelons and walnuts. The U.S. student's problem was not immediately obvious (in an ER, if you are not bleeding, still breathing, and conscious, the attention you get often is not immediate). The little girl in Vermont benefited from the defensive X-rays and follow-up CT scan that are a medical norm following a traumatic accident, even without obvious injury.

As noted above, one could use these dueling anecdotes to spin further stories of medical problems in Canada and triumphs in the United States. But regardless of what a U.S. observer may believe personally (for example, that the Academy Award-winning *Barbarian Invasions* is an accurate documentary of Canadian medical practice), our bilateral differences over medical practice lie at a deeper level.

To wit, in the cases above, the Canadian mother was quoted as saying, "We were terrified about being in the hands of the American system," when her daughter was injured. Yes, "terrified." In Vermont.

Something is seriously wrong in our mutual, bilateral perceptions if a presumably well-educated, upper middle-class Canadian professed terror when faced with the U.S. medical system. Did she believe that Vermont medical students majored in witchcraft? Or that U.S. hospitals were staffed with brutal incompetents practicing vivisection? Did she think that her daughter would be held for ransom until astronomical medical bills were paid?

Indeed, it was all but insulting for an American to read how she reportedly exulted over the "care, attention, and compassion" that her daughter received. As if a group of presumed cannibals had morphed into vegetarians or a covey of Hells Angels had come to her rescue, returned funds stolen by miscreants, and escorted her to safety. Ultimately, did Canadian readers conclude that such care was "the exception that proves the rule" of standard horror in U.S. medicine?

To be sure, there are places throughout the world where the medical system may be more dangerous to you than no medical care at all. There are some African states where embassies stock their own blood supplies to ensure that AIDS-contaminated blood products are not used for a diplomatic patient. U.S. diplomats are regularly medically evacuated from such locations to hospitals where the highest quality medical care can be identified. But blue-state Vermont?

WHAT CAN BE DONE?

In some respects, the near-term answer is not much. We are groping in 100 directions to improve technology, expand research, deliver services more efficiently, train more and better personnel, and emphasize the new buzzword, "wellness." Until the secret of eternal life and concurrent health (at an affordable cost) is unlocked, there will be argument over which system medicates best at the least cost.

Nevertheless, the degree to which the number of medical practitioners can be expanded does not appear very wide. The number entering U.S. medical schools has recently declined, perhaps partly because students now appreciate just how long the process has become. In one example, a highly skilled radiologist in 2006 was in the 19th year of study and had just obtained full certification in the profession. In the process, the doctor had obtained a Bachelor of Science and Master of Science in electrical engineering; completed a combined MD and PhD (in biomedical engineering) from a leading U.S. medical school; done the standard year of medical internship; completed four years of a radiology residency (again at a leading U.S. university); and was completing a year of "fellowship" study in radiology. Admittedly, this doctor was a leading particle at the cutting edge of radiology, but it also tells the observer that if you want to be a board-certified radiologist, you must allot 13 to 14 years (minus the PhD) to become one.

The concern is similar for nursing, given the recognition that many of the current members of the profession are "boomers" and headed for retirement. For several generations, the medical service profession benefited from implicit societal limitations on female careers. Being a nurse was one of the few professions available to an educated woman who sought full-time work with some flexibility for family. Today, these women are entering medical school. In fact, better than 50 percent of new medical school students are women. The downside to this gender equality has been the new appreciation that some female doctors are uninterested in working the 100-hour weeks that doctors worked in the past. Family and personal interests reduce their working hours—and thus the amount of health care that they will deliver over a lifetime.

Consequently, the United States has been harvesting the English-speaking world in search of nurses, and we may be obtaining all that will be available. It is, however, easier to expand programs to train nurses and, for example, recruit more males into the profession. Moreover, to a degree not possible for doctors, technology can supplement what nurses normally have done.

Behavior Modification

The most important approach that could be taken to improve longevity is not in R&D, not in nanosurgery, not in pharmacology, or in any other high-technology area. The most effective life enhancer is applied psychology: behavior modification. This label is a collective to include: stop smoking; lose weight; exercise more; end drug/alcohol abuse; avoid early pregnancy and risky sexual behavior; don't drink and drive (and drive more slowly); stop shooting your associates in criminal confrontations. In short, live in your teens and twenties as if you were already in your forties and fifties—it is a bit dull, but significantly safer. In short, if you don't smoke, keep your weight on the lean side, exercise regularly, consume alcohol in moderation, practice "safe sex," and keep your guns at home, you are likely to live longer—and live better while living longer.

While in the long, long run we may develop genetic programs to determine specific physical weaknesses at birth and implement gene "fixes" to cure such problems before they occur, this is a "not in my lifetime" prospect. However, through steady education, we may teach individual citizens to modify their risky behaviors (and be alert to prospective problems).

This problem is not solved by "free" medical services. Proponents of free medical care argue that any fee, even a nominal one, would discourage individuals from seeking treatment until their symptoms are at crisis level. Of course, the obverse is that citizens do not value "free goods" and abuse the service for trivial reasons. However, there is another class of patient: those in denial of their symptoms who would not see a doctor if services were free and the hospital located next to their home. Every doctor knows of cases in which the individual doesn't see a doctor until the throat tumor is so large that it is no longer possible to swallow; or won't go to a hospital because people die in hospitals (and hence they die at home from treatable problems).

In the end, however, we are all at the mercy of our genetics and our luck.

CRIME AND SUBSTANCE ABUSE 6

No matter how low the overall crime rate in a country, for a victim it is always at least one offense too many. No matter how few drug addicts are present in a community, the damage to each one is much more than economic. Dealing with crime and substance abuse is a baseline—and profoundly frustrating—challenge for 21st-century democracies. Getting the answers "right" is critical for any society.

Starting with a shared historical base in English common law, Canada and the United States have developed somewhat different legal traditions. The former at this point appears to be more willing to experiment beyond the traditional views of crime and punishment. If Canadians suggest that the punishment should fit the crime, Americans are more willing to argue that one size fits all and conclude that acceptance of minor crime breeds major crime.

Even more striking are the variances in the official view of gun control and capital punishment. Canadians are moving towards implementing rules that would make it so difficult to own firearms that no reasonable or logical person would endure the process. And, if only illogical or unreasonable individuals want to own firearms, they are the very ones who should be prevented from owning them under any circumstances. This blatant contrast to the U.S. constitutional right to own firearms does not need belaboring; it is a defining societal difference.

Likewise, government-directed elimination of capital punishment in Canada may fly in the face of popular preference. But there is no likelihood of it being reinstated. Official Canada appears willing to avert its eyes from Bernardo-Homolka depredations and, regardless of the number of victims ultimately uncovered on that former pig farm in British Columbia, no murderer will ever pay a capital price. In contrast, in the United States, several particularly brutal crimes that resulted in mass casualties have reinforced public support for capital punishment.

Both societies are clearly frustrated by the ramifications of substance abuse, especially that involving only "soft" drugs such as marijuana. Unofficially, Canada appears on the verge of throwing in the towel so far as taking criminal action against small-scale use or possession of these drugs. The United States continues to believe that production is driving demand rather than vice versa, and that drug use is a significant social evil. However, as a policy, "just say no" has had less effect with other drugs than the comparable, generation-long campaign against driving under the influence of alcohol. The U.S. policy of "more of the same" in the War on Drugs appears to be doing little better than holding its own; it has certainly been filling U.S. prisons with low-level drug retailers rather than drug barons. Creativity in addressing the problem appears at low ebb.

Canadian Criminal Justice

Canada's legal system was not achieved overnight or without conflict. In particular, the criminal justice part has been strongly influenced by international practice and, in particular, the common law of England. Under King Henry II, a system developed in which the decisions of judges, based on the "King's law," gradually replaced laws based on local customs. As judges began to exchange information about their decisions on laws passed by government to apply to all citizens, they also began to decide cases based on decisions made in similar cases. This practice resulted in the principle of *stare decisis*, which means "to stand by that which is decided."

In Canada today, judges still use *stare decisis* in making decisions; this type of law is generally known as case law. The Constitution, statutes, and administrative law make up the other three sources of contemporary Canadian criminal law. The Constitution embodies the bedrock principles that direct the enactment and application of laws across Canada. The power to enact criminal law statutes is vested solely in Parliament by the operation of section 91 (27) of the Constitution Act, 1867. Administrative law consists of regulations that carry the power of criminal law, but have been made by regulatory agencies of government, rather than judges or legislators. Statutes are enacted by the Parliament of Canada, the provincial legislatures, and municipal councils.

The advantages of codification began to be accepted at the end of the 18th century in Britain because, in the words of Canadian Federal Court justice Allen Linden, criminal law had evolved into a "bottomless pit of complex case law, petty anachronistic offences, and harsh punishment." While England resisted all efforts to codify the criminal law, her colonies began to experiment with it. In the 1840s and 1870s, draft criminal codes were seriously debated in the Westminster Parliament, but were defeated. Out of these debates, Canadians' desire for a unified criminal code developed.

Before Confederation in 1867, there was no uniform criminal justice system across what became Canada. Initially, Canada's pattern of westward settlement, like that of the United States, resulted in frontier justice. When the West began to open, defendants were regularly taken to the more established parts of Canada for trial. During the settlement period, an infrastructure for justice existed in Ontario, Quebec, and Atlantic Canada, while law was being administered by circuit judges in log buildings in Western Canada. The military was the first to maintain law and order, especially in places where there were naval ports. Over time, the construction of prisons as places of punishment began. So, too, did training of a professional police force.

Eventually, crime control was centralized in the national parliament by the Constitution Act of 1867. Parliament was given the exclusive power to create criminal law. The provinces, however, were responsible for the administration of justice. Subordinate legislation would take the form of municipal bylaws, provincial regulations, and orders in council.

The criminal justice system was codified in Canada's first Criminal Code of 1892. Common law offenses were abolished in the revised Criminal Code of 1953. (The only exception was Quebec, which uses a version of the Napoleonic Code, a civil code that is a set of principles to guide civil disputes. For any alleged criminal act in Quebec, one must always look to the Criminal Code or some other relevant federal statute.) An initial set of nine statutes was passed by Parliament in 1869, which consolidated the law for coinage offenses, forgery, larceny, perjury and procedure, offenses against the person, and malicious injuries to property.

When the provinces of Canada were confederated in 1867, Canada's first prime minister, the Scottish-born John A. Macdonald, was determined that the new country would not suffer from the disparate system of law that England had. At the time, all provinces more or less had their own forms of criminal law. Believing in a uniform body of law for the entire country, Macdonald gave effect to this idea in the Canadian Constitution, which he helped write. The Constitution gave to the federal parliament exclusive power to codify the criminal law for the entire country.

In 1873, the Police of Canada Act created what became national police. The North-West Mounted Police (NWMP) were created, with jurisdiction over the regions that ultimately became the prairie provinces. In 1920, they became the Royal Canadian Mounted Police (RCMP) and the pattern was set for municipal, provincial, and national police services. In Western Canada, there was no organized system of law enforcement at the time of Confederation. The Hudson's Bay Company used its employees to enforce its own penal code. The North-West Mounted Police were sent to protect Indians living in Canada from the Americans and to bring the Queen's justice to a dangerous territory, thus becoming an instrument of federal economic policy and an important force in the eventual subjugation of indigenous peoples. The NWMP was able to use criminal sanctions in the name of law and order to repress political dissent, control the indigenous populations, and maintain sovereignty. The maintenance of order in the West was essential for settlement and the simultaneous creation of new markets for manufactured goods made in older parts of Canada.

A complete Criminal Code was enacted in 1892 under the leadership of the minister of justice and soon-to-be prime minister, John Thompson. It was later revised often to accommodate the needs of changing times, such as the creation of drunken driving offences. In 1955, a major overhaul of the Criminal Code took place, reducing it from 1,100 sections to 753.

Although the intent of the codifiers was to incorporate all criminal offenses into one body of law, there are now other federal statutes that establish criminal offenses. For example, the Controlled Drugs and Substances Act of 1997 proscribes offenses relating to the sale and use of illegal drugs as well as legal ones. Although the Code provides for the procedure to be followed in a criminal case, the Extradition Act of 1999 and the Youth Criminal Justice Act set out procedures to be followed in special cases involving extradition and crimes committed by minors (persons under age 18).

Canada has one of the lower crime rates in the world and is comparable to the average in Western Europe. In 2002, for example, Canada had 7,590 reported incidents per 100,000 people. As noted earlier, criminal legislation falls under federal jurisdiction, with the provinces being responsible for its enforcement and prosecution. It is thus the provincial governments that are responsible for the hiring and supervising of prosecutors and provincial court judges, who hear most criminal cases. Punishment is supposed to be more or less uniform across the country, although different levels of enforcement and sentences prevail in the various provinces. Judges in British Columbia, for example, appear to sentence more leniently for illegal drug convictions than in Alberta.

Compared to the United States, Canada has a far lower rate of violent crime (such as murder, rape, assault) with the homicide rate for 2004 in the United States indicated as 5.5 per 100,000 and in Canada as 2 per 100,000. Another area in which rates in the United States far surpass Canada is the per capita number of arrests for drug-related offenses. Studies indicate that rates of drug use in the two countries are actually quite similar, but it is clear that the amount of resources directed towards combating drug sales and use are far higher in the United States as evidenced by its War on Drugs policy.

CRIME CONTROL IN CANADA

The most common complaint made against the criminal justice system in Canada is that it is too soft on criminals. Critics point to a series of perceived weaknesses—criminals on parole who commit more crimes, lenient sentences resulting from plea bargaining (the Karla Homolka case being the most glaring example), and police officers who warn offenders instead of arresting them. There are others who feel that parole boards, federal and provincial, make reasoned decisions based on information that the public does not have access to and that plea bargaining is a necessary evil that makes the system workable. This school of thought argues that many complex social issues, such as poverty or family breakdown, contribute to crime in ways that cannot always be controlled or managed by the criminal justice system.

There is no single, clear policy objective that guides the operation of Canada's criminal justice system, though it may be said that the Canadian justice model is founded on the notion that justice, in a broad sense, must not only be done in the courts but must be seen to be done. Four major features underpin the system: deterrence, retribution, selective incapacitation, and rehabilitation. None alone dominates criminal justice; they are usually used in combination with each other to guide legislators. All four have in common that they seek to reduce crime in Canadian society. It is clear that the use of one alone will not achieve that goal; as a result, the criminal justice system in Canada can be seen as a mix of all four philosophies. The main challenge is how to balance the different objectives of the different philosophies. For example, while the rights of victims and the ideal of a crime-free society are both important, the treatment and rehabilitation of criminals also matter to Canadians. The approach to crime in the United States often seems more focused on punishment. Canadians want to see criminals punished for their crimes (the Conservative party's 2005-06 election campaign, emphasizing fixed-term sentences, highlighted this desire), but they also want to see respected the due process rights of accused persons as laid out in the Charter of Rights and Freedoms.

The suggestion in the foregoing that the United States is interested in punishment but not in "due process rights of accused persons" is provocative to Americans. The "Miranda" warning and right to a lawyer are so ingrained in U.S. society that they are all but genetic elements of the legal system. However, having been afforded their rights, U.S. citizens do desire that criminals be swiftly tried and, if guilty, surely and comprehensively punished.

In Canada, the federal Parliament in theory controls the relationship between crime and punishment by the use of maximum sentences. However, as in the United States, it is the courts that often interpret what the federal Parliament legislates. The use of broad judicial discretion in Canada means that courts are often the final arbiters of the proportionality between crime and punishment. Many Canadians feel that since the introduction of the Charter of Rights and Freedoms in 1982, the courts have gone too far to protect the accused. Much criticism has specifically targeted the Supreme Court of Canada and some of its decisions that protect and expand the rights of the accused. Those who think that governments, Parliament, prosecutors, and the courts should be "tough on crime" argue that the Supreme Court focuses too heavily on the vague principle of justice when making decisions and not enough on the consequences of crime. This, they say, is exemplified by the deterrence and selective incapacitation models of crime control. There are many others, however, who feel that the Charter has been good for Canadians in general.

Beyond the four philosophies that generally underlie criminal justice in Canada, there is another that lies outside the conventional models. Many First Nations communities across Canada have traditionally emphasized "restorative justice." It is an approach in which it is understood that all things are interrelated and that crime disrupts the harmony that existed prior to its occurrence, or at least which it is felt should exist. Sanctions are determined on the basis of the needs of the victims of crime, as well as the broader community and the offender. In the 1990s, the idea of creating formal First Nations justice systems throughout Canada was widely discussed. The Law Reform Commission in its 1991 report discussed the case for an indigenous peoples' legal system:

From the Aboriginal perspective, the criminal justice system is an alien one, imposed by the dominant white society . . . not surprisingly, they regard the system as deeply insensitive to their traditions and values: many view it as unremittingly racist.

Soon after this report was released, then-justice minister and soon-to-be prime minister Kim Campbell promoted an integrated system that mixed traditional indigenous values with the Western legal system. Five years later, the federal government of the day adopted Campbell's position and rejected the proposal that First Nations peoples establish their own separate system of justice. To date, most indigenous systems in Canada have functioned within an existing legal framework in order to have their own approaches to justice counted. Most provincial governments have also rejected the idea of a separate legal system for Aboriginals.

The problem with separate culturally or religiously based justice systems (for example, Sharia law for Muslim Canadians, which was for a period under discussion in Ontario) is that they divide rather than unite society. Such justice systems appear inherently potentially open to if not specifically designed to exploit the weaker, less influential members of these societies, particularly women. They foster societies of men, not of laws, and make "equal justice under the law" a matter of culture and tradition. Moreover, there are as many variants of Aboriginal justice as there are Aboriginal communities, and as many variants of religious community justice as there are religions. One system of law—for all individuals living within the territory of a country—avoids the "soft bigotry of low expectations" (in George W. Bush's familiar phrase). An individual should not be able both to select his crime and then to select the system under which he will be judged.

THE CANADIAN PRISON SYSTEM

It is only in recent decades that Canada, like the United States and some other Western nations, has increased the use of incarceration as a last resort to dealing with criminal offenders. Previously, society did not have the resources for long-term imprisonment (and human labor was economically more important) so many convicted criminals quickly received corporal or capital punishment. The first federal prison in Canada was built in 1832 in Kingston, Ontario, one of seven to be built between 1834 and 1950. From the 1950s to the 1980s, the number doubled, with a total of 17 new prisons being built in that period. Prisons in Canada mirror those in the United States, with the Auburn prison system (which is based on the belief that the best way for offenders to rehabilitate themselves is through hard work) being the most prevalent form of prison architecture in Canada today.

In 2001, for example, it was estimated that the prison population in Canada totaled 31,624, giving a rate of 102 prisoners per 100,000 residents. Canada's prison population thus hovers around the median worldwide, but, when compared with the United States, the number of people incarcerated in Canada is relatively low. In 2001, it was estimated that the prison population in the United States was 1,962,220, with a rate of 686 prisoners per 100,000 people, the highest official rate in the world. The reasons for this disparity between the prison populations in Canada and the United States is unclear, although it is commonly thought that high crime rates, the philosophy of selective incapacitation (most notably embodied in the "three strikes and you're out" legislation used in the United States), and the War on Drugs policy all contribute in full measure.

Canada and many Western European countries have experimented with privatizing prisons, but the United States is the only country to have implemented such a system to a considerable extent. It is estimated that about 3 percent of prisons in the United States are now privately run. They are thought to be a less attractive option in Canada because citizen approval of debt for capital projects is not required in this country. Thus, Canadians find privately funded prisons to be less enticing because the cost of raising capital is higher when debt instruments are not backed by the full credit of the government. The growth of private prisons in the United States is also attributed to the view that prisons run by private companies could relieve the government of the costs of running prisons while maintaining the same standard of quality. The studies that have been done on whether privately run prisons offer the same quality of service and protection have produced mixed results.

On the other hand, there is criticism that Canadian prisons are "country club" equivalents where the primary punishment is the absence of freedom rather than significant material deprivation, let alone physical hardship. The concept of "hard time," epitomized by chain gang prisoners breaking rocks with sledgehammers or performing exhausting physical labor in harsh climates, has entirely disappeared.

GUN CONTROL AND THE DEATH PENALTY

With the passage by Parliament of the Firearms Act in 1995, Canada established a national registry for all firearms in Canada and their owners. The act required all firearms owners in Canada to apply to a center for a license by January 1, 2001, and to register their firearms with the RCMP by the beginning of 2003. In 1996, corresponding amendments to the Criminal Code were made, which increased the penalties for the use of guns in the commission of crimes and the illegal smuggling and trafficking of firearms. The registration of all handguns has been required since 1934. Permits to carry them have been issued only in certain circumstances, such as protection where police protection is inadequate and in some security jobs. Fully automatic weapons have been banned since 1977.

In 1996, for example, the total number of deaths resulting from the use of firearms across Canada amounted to 1,131, of which 815 were deemed suicides; 45 were accidents and 156 were homicides. In stark contrast to the attitude towards firearms in the United States, where the right to bear arms is regarded as fundamental, the Supreme Court of Canada declared in 2000, "All guns are capable of being used in crime. All guns pose a threat to public safety." This statement is representative of the way many Canadians view firearms and their role in crime.

The province of Alberta challenged the federal government's constitutional authority to require the registration and licensing of all firearms in Canada, claiming that Parliament was infringing upon the provinces' jurisdiction over property and civil rights. The Firearms Act has met with much controversy in Western Canada and elsewhere, as well as from First Nations peoples whose land agreements with the federal government entitle them to hunt and harvest wild game on reserves without regulation. The massive cost overrun associated with the implementation of the Firearms Act (some media estimates of $2 billion, against original projections of $2 million) has exacerbated criticism. Responding to the persistent intensity of this dissatisfaction, the Conservative government in mid-2006 indicated that it would suspend registration requirements and fines associated with non-compliance. Whether eventual parliamentary action will eliminate the registry is likely contingent on the Conservatives retaining power.

Another area of criminal policy in which Canada and the U.S. differ is the death penalty. Between 1892 and 1961, the penalty for murder in Canada was death by hanging. The first private member's bill calling for the abolition of the death penalty was introduced in 1914, but did not pass. From 1954 to 1963, private members' bills calling for the abolition of the death penalty were introduced in each parliamentary session. In 1966, after the first major debate on the issue, Bill C-168 was passed, which limited the use of the death penalty to situations in which either an on-duty police officer or corrections officer had been killed. In 1976, the death penalty was abolished from the Criminal Code and replaced with a mandatory life sentence without the possibility of parole for all those convicted of first-degree murder. The death penalty remained in place for military offenses, such as mutiny or treason, but was abolished in 1998 with legislation removing the death penalty from the National Defence Act. The last instance of capital punishment in Canada took place in 1962, when two men were hanged in Toronto.

The homicide rate in Canada decreased slightly after capital punishment was abolished in 1976; the general trend has been downwards since. Interestingly, the overall conviction rate for first-degree murder doubled in the decade following the abolition of the death penalty, which implies to some that Canadian juries are more willing to convict when they do not have the weight of a life-or-death decision over their heads.

All of Canada's national political parties oppose the reintroduction of the death penalty. A national poll conducted in 1995, however, indicated that 69 percent of Canadians strongly or moderately supported the reintroduction of the death penalty, which suggests that Canadian attitudes towards capital punishment may be more similar to those held by Americans than some might think. Other surveys have indicated that this "support" is a mile wide and an inch deep. In one nationwide survey of 1,500 Canadians, not one identified the reintroduction of the death penalty as a priority issue. An opinion poll taken in 1998 showed a dramatic decrease in the number of Canadians supporting the death penalty to 48 percent. An April 2007 Associated Press poll noted that, regarding capital punishment, "One-third felt the murder rate would decrease if the death penalty were instituted while nearly two-thirds felt the number would stay the same."[1]

Since the death penalty was abolished, there have been at least six cases in which persons convicted of first-degree murder were later found to be innocent and released. In two cases, the prisoners had been incarcerated for 10 years before their wrongful convictions were overturned; had the death penalty not been abolished, almost certainly both would have been executed before their innocence was established. For whatever reason, there has been no recent case in the United States in which an executed individual was subsequently found innocent.

Canadian research on the death penalty has reached similar conclusions as research done on the topic in the United States: the death penalty has not

1. http://www.chron.com/disp/story.mpl/nation/4750347.html

been found to increase deterrence when compared to other punishments. Counter comment suggests that proving a negative is impossible. It appears that the greater emphasis on the punishment of criminals in the United States may play a greater role in the use of the death penalty in the U.S. than does the theory that capital punishment deters criminals from committing crimes. In Canada, there are no plans to provide for the reinstatement of the death penalty.

SUBSTANCE ABUSE

It is impossible to measure accurately the extent of alcohol and drug abuse in Canada. One comprehensive study by the Canadian Centre on Substance Abuse more than a decade ago estimated that substance abuse cost more than $18.45 billion yearly in Canada. Such costs are attributed to direct losses in the workforce, administrative costs, prevention and research, law enforcement, and health care. The largest was lost productivity due to illness and premature death. The overall rate of drug offenses in Canada has certainly increased since 1993, but the long-term trend has generally remained stable over the past 15 years. Rates of cocaine offenses peaked in 1989, but have thankfully dropped by about one-third since then. The rate for heroin offenses increased for a number of years, peaking in 1993, but has also fallen by more than one-quarter in recent years. The use of drugs such as crystal methamphetamines, Ecstasy, and marijuana has grown substantially in recent years.

The serious situation in several Canadian cities concerning injection drug use, including high rates of overdose and contraction of HIV/AIDS and hepatitis C, is of major concern to Canadians. There are approximately 50,000 to 100,000 injection drug users in Canada. It is estimated that half of the 3,000 to 5,000 new cases of HIV in 1996 were due to injection drug use. Of the newly identified hepatitis C infections, 80 to 90 percent are estimated to be due to injection drug use.

In comparison to the War on Drugs model in the United States, which seeks to reduce the supply of illegal drugs, Canada takes what it terms a "balanced approach," based on the belief that the most effective way to address the problem is to deal with both supply and demand. Canada's policy seeks to reduce the harmful effects of the problem on individuals, families, and communities. Law enforcement agencies put an emphasis on going after traffickers and confiscating the proceeds of their crimes as an effective way to reduce the resources available to continue their activities.

In 1987, the Mulroney government adopted a harm reduction approach as the framework for Canada's National Drug Strategy. It was a five-year program with a budget of 210 million dollars, 70 percent of which was allotted for demand-side reduction and the balance to supply-side reduction. The strategy was renewed for five years in 1992 with a budget of 270 million dollars. The demand-side reduction allotment was reduced to 60 percent with the supply-side increased to 40 percent. The United States, known for supply-side actions, such as spraying the fields of drug crops in developing countries, spends about 60 percent of funding for its War on Drugs on supply-side reduction.

The long-term goal of Canada's National Drug Strategy is to reduce the harm associated with alcohol and other drugs. Seven strategic components form the foundation of the strategy: research and knowledge development; knowledge dissemination; prevention programming; treatment and rehabilitation; legislation, enforcement and control; national cooperation; and international cooperation. The national government works with a variety of partners, including provincial and territorial governments, nongovernmental organizations, community groups, the private sector, health professional organizations, law enforcement agencies, and target populations.

The policy of harm reduction has been controversial, but countries such as Britain and the Netherlands have been promoting this approach aggressively in recent years. The primary objective is reducing the negative consequences of drug consumption and addiction. Harm reduction sets up a hierarchy of goals, with the more realistic and immediate ones to be achieved as first steps towards risk-free use and eventually abstinence where possible.

Safe injection sites are one recent and very controversial application of the harm reduction approach Canada has adopted. They are controlled health care facilities where drug users take drugs under supervision. In some cases, they may also receive health care, counseling, and referral to health and social services, including drug treatment. Safe injection sites are an immediate harm reduction measure and visitors are often given harm reduction teaching and counseling in order to prevent the ongoing spread of HIV/AIDS, hepatitis C, and drug overdoses and deaths, and other drug addiction issues. Opponents say it only encourages the use of drugs, including unsafe ones, when no one tests the drug consumed.

Vancouver has become well-known across Canada for its huge substance abuse problems and has one of the largest concentrations of injection drug users in North America, centered in Vancouver's downtown eastside. HIV/

AIDS and hepatitis C infection rates for Vancouver's heroin users have reached epidemic levels. In 2003, Vancouver became home to North America's first legal supervised injection site pilot project. Health Canada granted Vancouver Coastal Health an exemption under Section 56 of the Controlled Drugs and Substances Act, and provided $1.5 million to support it.

Safe injection sites have been criticized roundly in the United States. The U.S. "drug czar," White House director of the Office of National Drug Control, John Walters, said that harm reduction sites are havens that will only encourage heroin use. Vancouver Mayor Larry Campbell replied, "I think all (the Americans) have to do is take a look at (their) prison system and (their) law enforcement to see if the drug war is being won in the States. It's an unmitigated disaster and they know it, but they can't back out of it." What cannot be disputed is that Vancouver has embarked on a North American first, for better or worse.

To address the supply issue, Parliament has responded with new instruments intended to combat money laundering and give police the tools they need to take the profits out of crime. In 1996, 10 new Integrated Proceeds of Crime units were created, which combine the resources of federal and local police, Customs officials, federal prosecutors, and forensic accountants to investigate and prosecute proceeds of crime cases. The units are now located in most of Canada's major cities. Anti-gang legislation passed by Parliament in 1997 gave new power for police, prosecutors, and the courts to deal with criminal organizations. Comprehensive training programs are also being created to assist police in enforcing this law.

Marijuana

In Canada, as in the United States, marijuana remains the illegal drug of choice. Hydroponically grown Canadian marijuana has become widely used both within Canada and the United States. Despite RCMP crackdowns on such initiatives, the numbers of homegrown hydroponic operations continue to increase. Within Canadian communities, police and health agencies also face a growing problem: their resources are stretched beyond the limit.

In the face of such setbacks in the attempt to combat widespread marijuana use, some have called for radical changes to Canada's drug policy. While Canada has not been as zealous as the United States in its attempts to fight increasing marijuana use, decriminalization or even outright legalization of some "soft" drugs, such as marijuana, would represent a drastic departure from the more traditional strategy of punishing those who sell it.

The potency of marijuana in Canada has increased substantially from that used by baby boomers in the 1960s. This does not, moreover, include such potent varieties as *sinsemilla*, hash, or hashish oil. These are also much more powerful than the marijuana consumed when today's parents were young, although many are not aware of this increased potency. What has also changed is that marijuana is no longer a foreign import in Canada. Over the past few decades, both the quality and the quantity of Canadian homegrown weed operations have increased dramatically.

In 2003, official bilateral trade between Canada and the United States totaled over $394 billion. However, the true measure of cross-border trade would be much higher if marijuana trafficking were added to the equation. The United States claims that a surge of high-potency marijuana illegally smuggled into the country from Canada is fueling a drug dependency among young Americans. John Walters, director of the Office of National Drug Control, signaled several years ago Washington's ongoing irritation with what it sees as a lax attitude towards drug crimes north of the border, something that has forced it to redeploy some drug patrols from the Mexican border to its northern flank. Walters conceded that American authorities are making no dent in the flow of Canadian pot into the United States. He said Canadian police and prosecutors have told him lenient Canadian courts are at the root of the problem. And he may be right. Seizures by Edmonton Police Services, for example, show that hydroponically grown marijuana has become big business in Edmonton, and, during several periods, police were dismantling an average of one hydroponic operation a day. Some of these operations contained more than 200 high-grade plants. Across Canada in 1998, more than a million plants were seized by different police departments, and some indoor hydroponic operations were growing more than 3,000 plants. At least half the marijuana available in Canada is now grown here, and exports from Canada to the United States are increasing, especially from British Columbia.

Marijuana was first banned in Canada in 1923 under the Opium and Drug Act. Since 1997, it has been covered by the Controlled Drugs and Substances Act. In 2000, more than 30,000 Canadians were charged with simple possession of marijuana, according to the Senate Committee on Illegal Drugs. In May 2003, legislation was tabled by the Chrétien government in Parliament to amend both the Contraventions Act and the Controlled Drugs and Substances Act by decriminalizing marijuana use and possession for young adults and casual users. The marijuana reform bill would have kept cannabis possession and production illegal under the

Canadian Controlled Drugs and Substances Act, but would have introduced softer penalties for possession of small amounts of marijuana and tougher penalties for growers of marijuana. The penalties for traffickers would remain the same, with a maximum sentence of life in prison.

Legalization and decriminalization advocates say that illicit drugs should be treated as a health problem rather than an enforcement problem. One of the primary arguments for the decriminalization of marijuana is that young adults who are experimenting with different lifestyles and substances will get caught in the net cast by the War on Drugs ideology and become branded as "drug users" with a criminal record for the rest of their lives. However, others argue that enforcement does not in practice target the experimental user, but rather drug traffickers at the mid to high level, especially those involved in organized crime. The drug strategy also seeks to deprive criminals of the profits from their trade. Legislation to deal with the proceeds of crime has been in place since 1989.

Canadian public opinion on decriminalizing marijuana use has shifted over the past decade. In general, Canadians have moved from a majority opposing decriminalization to a majority supporting it. When asked about its use for health purposes, Canadians have overwhelmingly approved the idea of "medicinal marijuana" for cancer and AIDS patients, among others. In fact, in 2003 Canada was the first country in the world to approve marijuana for medicinal use. (The Netherlands also decriminalized marijuana for medicinal use in 2003. The Dutch are able to buy medicinal marijuana at the pharmacy, unlike Canadians.) The medical efficacy of marijuana versus more traditional pain-therapy medication remains in question. Positive effects may be more psychological than physical. This does not mean that the "high" is all in patients' heads, but rather that any gains in well-being may result from the well-known "placebo effect" wherein those who anticipate a positive response to a medication (even a nonexistent medication) indeed find that their condition has improved. This situation combines with the victim's sense of entitlement to compensate for suffering. For its part, in June 2005, the U.S. Supreme Court struck down a state law permitting doctors to prescribe marijuana.

Views on the decriminalization of marijuana use are certainly not shared by all groups in Canadian society. In particular, generational and gender gaps shape public opinion on this issue. The 1960s generation, the baby boomers, appear to be driving an increasingly open view of marijuana use—an attitude that is being passed on to their children.

There is currently no real consensus among Canadians about whether marijuana use should be a criminal offense. A slim majority (51 percent) favors decriminalization, while fully 45 percent believe marijuana use should remain illegal. Another 4 percent do not have an opinion one way or the other. While Canadians may not have come to any real conclusions about whether measures such as the decriminalization of soft drugs are the direction they want their drug policy to head, it is clear that Canada will not be joining its neighbor in the War on Drugs.

For the United States, of course, the issue is less the Canadian use or abuse of drugs than its position as a safe haven for drug producers, their exports to the United States, and the perception of Canadian indifference, verging on amused contempt, for the American concern over marijuana use.

Crime and Substance Abuse in the United States

U.S. CRIMINAL JUSTICE

Western democracies are built on the rule of law. Formalized systems and codes of laws, rules, and regulations separate civilization from barbarism. Historians point out such codes as benchmarks of human social development: the Code of Hammurabi; the Ten Commandments; the Roman legal system that assured its citizens of uniform treatment wherever they were in the Empire; the Napoleonic Code. At its best, the law is dispensed with equality ("without fear or favor"), overseen and administered by trained, incorruptible professionals, and enforced by skilled public officials with a careful appreciation of the rights of citizens and carefully calibrated use of force.

In technical terms, the U.S. criminal justice system (and the legal system in general) has been constructed along the same parameters as the Canadian system. The British historical experience has also strongly conditioned U.S. legal practice, although there is no equivalent to Quebec's Napoleonic Code derivatives in U.S. federal law. At the pinnacle of U.S. law stands the Constitution; at various subordinate levels are federal, state, and local laws and regulations. Canada and the United States are both highly litigious societies. As is the case for Canada, the U.S. has codified its laws; however, reflecting the federal nature of the United States, there is extensive state law as well as nationwide federal law. Although in some instances the prosecution of an accused criminal may overlap jurisdictions (in the case of murder, for example), disputes can normally be avoided.

In truth, the social reality is far closer to the ideal of equal justice under the law than the media would suggest. The high and the mighty have gone to jail for failures to adhere to the law. Doubters might imagine how unlikely it would be in most societies for Martha Stewart to pay for her peccadilloes with jail time. There is also scrupulous attention to the rights of the individual: thus OJ Simpson may have been convicted in the minds of the public of murdering his former wife, or Michael Jackson just for being certifiably odd, but they walked away from the courtroom as free men. And, many have been the cases of individuals freed on the basis of evidence that has come to light after conviction.

In the United States, "crime and punishment" are more than the title of a Russian novel. There is a strong social desire that criminals should be punished and that "the guilty" should not go free. Although the Eighth Amendment of the Constitution prohibits "cruel and unusual punishment," the baseline is still punishment. Indeed, the colonial forebears of the United States may often have been religiously motivated in venturing across the Atlantic Ocean to the New World, but their views of crime and punishment were closer to an "eye for an eye" and "a tooth for a tooth" than to New Testament injunctions to "turn the other cheek." Among the reconstructions at Colonial Williamsburg, Virginia, there is a set of stocks by which the head and hands of an accused criminal were constrained, and there the incarcerated was subjected to public abuse (what was thrown was not limited to invective) for a prescribed period of time.

And indeed, while a number of the grievances at the base of the Revolutionary War were political and economic in form, they were dressed in legalism rather than a "might makes right" set of fiats. The Declaration of Independence listed various English legal infractions, from subverting the judiciary, to refusing to implement laws, to putting British officials beyond colonial laws, and to trying American colonials in English courts. By the standards set out in the declaration, King George III was a criminal—and the American Revolution was legally justified. On the other side of the ledger, English officials charged American criminals with despoiling the tea of English merchants by throwing it into Boston Harbor. Colonial officials in Boston sheltered these criminals, so English officials punished the entire city by closing the port. On each side, the political confrontation was well dressed in formal legalism.

Following independence, while the United States never had England's long catalog of offenses for which one could be executed, it did not hesitate to hang offenders—quickly—particularly if all the urban trappings of justice were not present. For a substantial part of its history, the United States was a frontier—and frontiers collect the young, the restlessly adventurous, and those seeking to start anew (sometimes starting anew from a clouded past). There was opportunity with the availability of virtually free land and periodic gold rush mining towns that attracted the rootless. Restless and alienated former combatants immediately after the Civil War ended in 1865 added further violent strands to the frontier mix. As post-traumatic stress disorder had not been "invented" at that point in history, there were simply a lot of crazy people in the West. And, while the United States never endured boatloads of criminals being delivered from England, as was the case for Australia, massive immigration throughout the 18th, 19th, and early 20th centuries incorporated more than the totally law abiding into U.S. society. Consequently, on these frontiers, the concept of law was often a bit shaky, and in the burgeoning cities, gangs sought to extort from the weak as well as to control various "sinful" activities (which were also frequently the most profitable).

In the West, the "lawman" was the sheriff and his deputies, who enforced order (and perhaps law as a second thought) with weapons. Ordinary citizens might form a posse to pursue criminals and, upon occasion having caught them, would administer punishment by "stringing them up" rather than bothering with formal legal structures. The word "vigilante" is now a term of opprobrium, but with its origin in "committees of vigilance," such activity might well have been regarded as the duty of a responsible citizen. What is the problem with taking the law into your own hands if your own hands are clean?

While there is more than a century between this frontier era and the problems of the early 21st century (and Enron is more than a remodeled 19th-century robber baron), American attitudes, then and now, towards crime and punishment have clear parallels: criminals need punishment rather than understanding; firearms are the friend of the honest citizen (the Colt 45 revolver was "the great equalizer"); and the death penalty cures recidivism.

CULTURE, DEMOGRAPHY, AND CRIME

Observers spend considerable attention on the level of crime in the United States. And to be sure, crime is visible and persistent; like the poor, crime will always be with us. Currently among the most popular television productions in the United States are the long-running program *Law and Order* and the *CSI* franchise (popular demand has led to the expansion of the "crime scene investigation" format, with its combination of cutting-edge forensic science, edgy plots, and interchangeable characters, to multiple cities). Both *Law and Order* and the *CSI* series are the 21st-century media equivalent of mundane cops-and-robbers shows, where the bad guy is (usually) convicted, but they demonstrate that Americans find crime of high interest and punishment satisfying. These series are also highly popular in Canada, to the point that, as in the United States, they are swaying how juries think about evidence. Reportedly, a professor at St. Mary's University in Halifax is studying the "CSI-effect" and finding that it has considerable influence on juries in regard to the detail and specificity of evidence desired to convict a defendant.

But the causes of crime fall into a variety of categories, characterized according to the individual analyst:

• genetic predisposition (the sociopath);
• the large bulges of "boomer" and "echo" youth in the population;
• poverty and/or lack of economic opportunity;
• criminal immigrants;
• the drug culture and conflict over "turf," combined with other internecine fighting among criminal gangs; and
• the ubiquitous nature of guns in the USA.

And, naturally enough, when everyone has a dog in the fight, a vested interest in the outcome, and every answer is (partly) correct, there are no answers. Or at least none on which there can be general agreement.

However, faced with a burst of crime in the 1980s and 1990s, the United States responded with a renewed emphasis on punishment. There was substantial popular sentiment that judicial flexibility had resulted in idiosyncratic punishment. There was a backlash from "let the punishment fit the crime" thinking to that of "one size fits all" punishment. Consequently, in 1984, Congress passed and President Reagan signed bipartisan-mandated guidelines for specific punishment of specific crimes, substantially reducing judicial discretion. This approach was accompanied by "three strikes and you're out" legislation, requiring life sentences for a third felony conviction in many states. The former has been criticized for allowing no leeway for the hapless citizen caught up (ostensibly accidentally) in drug-related activity. The latter has generated stories of individuals with three minor thefts, which qualify as felonies, consigned to life in prison. There has been little popular sympathy with these criminals. The general attitude has been closer to "if you can't do the time, don't do the crime." .

In New York City, shortly after his successful 1994 bid for mayor, Rudy Giuliani offered the startling hypothesis that crime is indeed caused by criminals, and that allowing "minor" crime to go unpunished created contempt for the law generally. The mayor at first was derided by the chattering classes for his adoption of the "broken windows theory," which involved the intensive ticketing of jaywalkers and litterers, elimination of graffiti and broken windows in public property, cleaning up pornography in Times Square, and pursuit of vagrants and homeless, aggressive panhandlers in Central Park. Attitudes changed—or at least the chattering became whispering—when crime declined in Gotham, and young mothers with baby carriages re-inhabited Central Park. Twenty years ago, the host of a late-night show joked that many people were observed running in Central Park. This meant that "either the jogging craze had hit NYC or the muggers were running in packs." Bitterly funny at the time; almost irrelevant today.

THE U.S. PRISON SYSTEM

Doing the Time

The most obvious observation of crime in the United States over the past 20 years is that incarceration levels have risen to the point where the U.S. has the world's highest incarceration level (per capita). Both violent and property crime, however, have fallen to their lowest recorded levels.

By the end of 2001, the prison population had quadrupled since 1980; it stood at over 1.3 million at that point, and approximately 4.3 million former prisoners were still alive. Nearly a quarter of the federal and state prisoners were jailed on drug-related charges, and nearly a third of female prisoners were jailed on drug charges. Bureau of Justice statistics in 2005 showed that violent crime rates had declined 33.4 percent since 1994 to their lowest level ever recorded in 2003, and had declined 3.9 percent from 2002 to 2003. Property crime had fallen 23 percent in the same decade, and 1.2 percent from 2002 to 2003.

Naturally there is equal dispute over why crime has declined, with conservatives contending that "tough on crime" mandatory sentencing and "three strikes" legislation was putting criminals in jail—and hence they were not committing crimes. Liberals, in turn, responded that the good economy of the 1990s made crime unnecessary. Still other observers suggested that (a) the drug turf had been divided and thus "gang-bangers" no longer needed to kill each other over markets and could concentrate on selling; (b) crime is a young person's game and the overall number of those most engaged in crime (teenagers and 20-somethings) had declined; and (c) the advent of abortion on demand had substantially reduced the number of unwanted children—those who might have drifted into a life of crime.

Who Does the Crime?

Crime is often a minority occupation. Or at least the type of violent and/ or actively prosecuted crime is disproportionately associated with minorities. Hence the statistics extrapolated from the aforementioned Justice Department study indicate a one-in-three chance that a U.S. black male will go to prison during his lifetime. Such figures were one-in-six for a Hispanic male and one-in-seventeen for a white male. At one point, there was an observation that there were more African-Americans in jail or on parole than there were in college.

Nevertheless, there has been no special level of social anxiety or anguish over these statistics. To be sure there is predictable social "viewing with alarm" commentary, but that has been largely limited to those on the political left who "view with alarm" for a living. It is a cool judgment that, for whatever reason, if a high percentage of a group is being convicted of crimes, then it has committed a high percentage of the crimes. For that matter, most crime occurs within the same racial group: the victim and the victimizer are the same race. Tracking interracial crime is less easy; there is, however, a perception that there are more crimes against whites by minorities than vice versa. The statistic more frequently cited is that the death penalty is exacted against a higher percentage of blacks killing whites than against whites killing blacks.

Additionally, there has been general rejection of charges that minorities are being "profiled" for "driving while black," etc. However, to counter such accusations, law enforcement officials now are more cautious with their statistics, and regulations in some areas (for example, Washington, DC) now require roadblocks to stop every vehicle or a specific percentage rather than being selective in those they pull over for investigation.

And, notably since September 11, 2001, there has been a far greater and more active concern with illegal aliens (or "undocumented workers," or whatever the politically correct term of the day may be). These figures are as indeterminate as the numbers of U.S. citizens without health insurance, but they are characterized as being in the range of 10 to 12 million. This circumstance creates a volatile sociopolitical issue—but also a criminal concern. Although all U.S. citizens except for the American Indians were originally immigrants, and in the country's early years the national concern was filling up "empty" countryside rather than restricting access, the current reality is of an illegal alien subculture often doing marginal work at low wages but receiving social services for which they have not paid. At an absolute minimum, it makes ridiculous the efforts by diplomats in consulates and embassies to determine the *bona fides* of those applicants for visas who are adhering to the regulations for entry. Unless you are a tourist, a serious university student, or a high-end investor or professional, if you want to enter the United States, the best approach is to cross the border illegally (or come as a visitor and stay, perhaps claiming refugee status as well) and hope for a future amnesty to eradicate your illegality.

While the vast majority of those "illegals" have purely economic motivations, there is a realistic concern that terrorists will exploit illegal communities to obtain economic assistance, technical support, or "cover," and that they will not be disclosed to legal authorities. Although all 18 of the 9/11 airplane hijackers entered the United States on valid visas, the recognition that they could easily have entered the country illegally drives the concerns among immigration and law enforcement officials. A significant terrorist incident attributable to illegal immigrants would move the concern to paranoia. The basic problem is that, as a society, the United States has not come to grips with its dependence on illegal immigration any better than it has dealt with its dependence on imported petroleum. Each dependency makes life easier and more comfortable and each has clear risks.

The high-profile national and legislative discussion throughout the 2006 campaign and enduring into 2007 regarding "what to do about immigration" only accentuated the conundrums associated with illegal immigration in the U.S. The baseline, however, remains border control: if a country cannot control its borders, it simply is not a sovereign state. Without adequate control over who enters the United States, and with numerous individuals, therefore, entering the country through criminal action, there can be no expectation that such individuals will act legally in subsequent activity if it is more convenient to operate illegally.

THE DEATH PENALTY AND GUN CONTROL

The death penalty is imposed for both federal crimes and by individual states. At the local level, a few states (12) and the District of Columbia do not have the death penalty; and some impose it infrequently. The states without the death penalty are primarily small (Hawaii, Rhode Island), lightly populated (Alaska, North Dakota, Maine, Vermont), or "blue"/liberal (Massachusetts, Minnesota, Wisconsin, Iowa). Nevertheless, despite periodic campaigns against the death penalty, the U.S. population continues to support it strongly (69 percent in a 2007 Associated Press poll) and, if anything, is frustrated that it is not more widely imposed and more rapidly implemented. Not for us the soul-searching or breast beating associated with heinous crimes in other countries that leave the perpetrators to spend confined but not painful "life" prison terms (terms that often are far short of the criminal's lifespan) while their victims remain dead. The overwhelming majority of Americans were pleased that the "Oklahoma bomber" (Timothy McVeigh) was executed for having killed 168 people in 1995. With McVeigh's death, his recidivist potential was ended. Nor do we expect that there will be much grief expended when the convicted Washington sniper (John Allen Muhammad) is eventually executed. If anything, there is substantial regret that his companion shooter, Lee Boyd Malvo, will avoid execution because he was a minor while killing. Murder by minors no longer warrants a death sentence.

Although capital punishment is rarely implemented (only 59 executions in 2004, the lowest figure since 1996), the threat of the death penalty is regarded as a useful tool for the prosecutor in murder cases. An accused may be induced to plead guilty (and receive a life imprisonment sentence) to avoid a death penalty trial from a presumably unsympathetic jury, particularly when the murder victim was a law enforcement official or an obviously vulnerable person (child, young woman, elderly citizen).

This view of the death penalty extends into international relations. The United States is officially indifferent to the fact that it is one of the few advanced, democratic industrial nations (Japan is another) that imposes the death penalty. In creating the State Department's annual human rights report (*Country Reports on Human Rights Practices*), the U.S. government ignores the positions expounded by various international nongovernmental organizations against the death penalty and does not accept that capital punishment is a human rights violation, as long as the individual has received a fair trial with appropriate legal safeguards.

The modern U.S. death penalty began in 1976. Capital punishment was suspended between 1967 and 1976 as a result of several decisions of the Supreme Court, which found the application of the death penalty to be unconstitutional, on the grounds of cruel and unusual punishment in violation of the Eighth Amendment to the Constitution. However, after various refinements in legislation, in 1976 the court upheld a procedure in which the trial of capital crimes was bifurcated into the guilt versus innocence phase and the sentencing phase. Consequently, capital punishment resumed in early 1977. Between January 1977 and mid-2005, there were 972 executions in the United States, and in mid-2005, 3,455 inmates were on death row, with the largest numbers in California (639), Texas (447), and Florida (382). Executions since 1977 have been highest in Texas (345).

Most Americans do not have the slightest qualm when the death penalty is projected into international relations. President Bush's commitment that the al-Qaeda leader Osama bin Laden would be "brought to justice" is a barely concealed commitment to have him killed. Nor is there any commitment simply to capturing various terrorist leaders elsewhere in the world; if they are killed in the course of hunting them, this extrajudicial activity is regarded as a military action not subject to juridical guidelines that would apply on U.S. soil.

Consequently, Americans will leave it to Canadians to feel morally superior that Karla Homolka has been released to enjoy again the opportunity to exercise her creative sadism. Knowing the details of Mr. Bernardo's own creativity, it would probably be the rare American who would take the position adopted by a Canadian journalist who deemed it not "fair" to deprive "Paul" of human contact 23 of 24 hours each day, and not to permit him to further his education or learn a trade. In comparable circumstances in the United States, such a rationalization would prompt questions about which universe the journalist inhabited. It is almost too easy a riposte to note that Mr. Bernardo's victims are deprived of human contact 24 hours each and every day, and his previous education did not lead to socially productive ends.

If anything, the movement in criminal punishment for the United States has concentrated on "victims' rights" as still another backlash against the earlier expansion of the rights of the accused and convicted. It is a response to intense societal fatigue with clever lawyering that has resulted in nominal sentences or early releases from prison. As trials are frequently now divided into guilt-innocence and punishment stages, the friends, relatives, and associates of the victim are permitted to counter the pleas for leniency or "mitigating factors" of someone judged guilty. You are far more likely to hear "lock them up and throw away the key" than to hear extended arguments for rehabilitation and reform.

The death penalty has become another liberal versus conservative divide. Liberals will echo a Canadian journalist who said that "revenge is the antithesis of justice." Conservatives might respond that "revenge is justice" or that "justice is revenge eaten cold." Liberals contend that capital punishment doesn't prevent crime; conservatives respond that there is no way to know who is deterred from murder or for what reason. Liberals contend that the death penalty is actually more expensive than life in prison; conservatives are willing to pay that price. Liberals argue that rehabilitation is possible for anyone and/or that life in prison is a penalty worse than death. Conservatives do not believe that a life sentence is "life" (not 20 years and then parole), but they are certain that the death penalty cures recidivism.

Guns, Guns, Guns

There is no question that the United States has a defining commitment to an armed citizenry. Although other societies (Switzerland, Israel) have a citizen militia and military reserve force with light infantry combat weaponry in their homes, only the United States has built the right to possess firearms into its Constitution. The Second Amendment has withstood considerable challenge from critics who seek to restrict gun ownership; however, the flat statement that "the right of the people to keep and bear arms shall not be infringed" has not proved amenable to reinterpretation. Consequently, there is an abiding ideological divide between those who would restrict the ownership of firearms as a societal good and those for whom the bumper sticker "You will take my gun from my dead cold hand" is not hyperbole.

There is a unique coincidence between the United States and firearms. For the American colonist, a musket or a rifle was primarily a tool akin to an ax or a plow. The gunsmith sufficiently skilled to make a rifle was one of the first colonial industrialists. An imported musket was cheaper than an imported lady's dress and a standard implement on every farm where hunting and shooting game added to family protein consumption, and defense against Indian attacks was a significant concern. During the North American manifestations of European combat in the mid-18th century, American colonists were significant militia supplements to British regular forces in fighting against the French and Indians. In some instances, such as the attack on the French fortification at Louisburg, they were the principal military force. As such, the colonists maintained regular militias and local supplies of gunpowder. This militia assembly was frequently an informal exercise: troops were drilled only sporadically; military knowledge was minimal; militia officers were elected locally; and weaponry was nonstandard. But it was an armed force, albeit "a rabble in arms," and as such not under British control.

Consequently, British officials were aware that armed colonists could be a disruptive military force, and when tensions rose in 1775, the British attempted to seize local arsenals of gunpowder throughout the colonies. These excursions at Concord and Lexington prompted various iconic U.S. tales: Paul Revere's ride; the "Minuteman" response; and "the shot heard round the world." The result was the creation of an historically deep, now almost genetically imprinted, belief in the United States that an armed citizenry is a free citizenry—and the first effort by a tyrant is to disarm citizens in order to subjugate them more effectively.

The commitment to gun ownership is concomitant with persistent U.S. skepticism of government. Government is neither intrinsically trustworthy nor benign; it needs to be constantly observed, limited, checked, and balanced. Such attitudes are not axiomatically liberal or conservative; Henry David Thoreau's observation that "government is best which governs least" is as essentially skeptical as a Minnesota Militiaman who professes to believe that United Nations black helicopters hover just beneath the horizon. For such gun owners and their politically active and influential representatives, most prominently the National Rifle Association, an armed citizenry is the final defense against tyranny. Consequently, there is considerable resistance against gun control and registration, based on the assumption that once the government has registered weapons, it will move to seize them. The vast expense and indifferent results of the Canadian gun registration system is a poster child in the U.S. for ineffective gun control. The politicized argumentation has balancing absurdities: pro-gun advocates who support private ownership of unregistered machine guns versus anti-gun advocates who want bullets available only on a prescription basis.

More currently topical than the expectation of foreign invasion or federal government repression, however, are citizens who anticipate the need to defend themselves against criminals and home invasions. While as noted above, crime in general and crime against property in particular has steadily declined over the past 20 years, citizens still do not feel secure, and media coverage of violent crime accentuates this insecurity (the media maxim of "If it bleeds, it leads" makes violent crime a prominent part of television news). Moreover, there is sufficient anecdotal evidence of homeowners defending themselves with their private firearms to make it more than an urban legend. The gun control advocates cite the statistical illogic of the burglar versus homeowner confrontation during a home invasion and attempt to rebut emotion with fact by noting its infrequency; however, emotion wins.

The result is an American society in which there are over 200 million guns, with the numbers always rising, and approximately 30,000 deaths by firearms each year. Upwards of half of U.S. households own guns, and gun ownership/possession has accelerated since 9/11 as Americans took actions to provide psychological reinforcement for their security concerns. To be sure, a substantial percentage of firearms deaths are suicides (who presumably would have found some other way to end their lives) and others are criminals killing each other. Nevertheless, there are also tragic accidents on the level of a child killing a sibling while playing with a loaded gun, or murders that arguably would not have happened if a firearm were not instantly at hand. Gun owners shrug, stress the need for gun owner training and safety precautions, suggest that murders can occur with bread knives, note that over 40,000 people die each year in automobile accidents, and suspect that those who want to control their guns have a hidden agenda to reduce their freedom.

Consequently, there is a constant guerrilla war in the courts of law and public opinion over gun ownership. Following the attempted assassination of President Reagan in 1981, there was a major impetus for gun control using the badly injured and brain-damaged James Brady as the poster child for restrictions. As a consequence, with gun registration and licensing requirements varying state by state, the law-abiding citizen now must wait a period of time before obtaining a firearm and (perhaps) registering it; there are limits on numbers of weapons that can be purchased at a given time; constraints on who can be a gun dealer; and efforts to prevent gun ownership by various groups (violent criminals and the mentally impaired). At the same time, there is a counter movement in a number of states to permit "concealed carry" of pistols by citizens who apply for the privilege. Advocates argue that crime declines in such "concealed carry" areas; critics dismiss the statistics as inconclusive. The debate waxes and wanes with the proximity to the most recent atrocity—for example, the Virginia Tech shootings in April 2007.

SUBSTANCE ABUSE

Drugs and Liberty

U.S. societal debate over "substance (ab)use" is as intense as it is inconclusive. Although "substance" is often a generic description for alcohol (and even tobacco) as well as the full range of addictive narcotic drugs, the focus in this analysis will be on the "softer" drugs—those such as marijuana, cocaine, various pharmacological products—but not "hard" drugs such as heroin.

On the one hand, the number of individuals who have tried drugs rises each year. One report suggests that by 2003 there were 97 million Americans who had tried marijuana and that 15 million Americans smoked it at least monthly. (While that number is large, in a population of 300 million, it is approximately 5 percent.) Nevertheless, in some circles, marijuana or cocaine use is probably more acceptable than tobacco. On the other hand, anti-drug police activity remains intense, and de-criminalization, let alone legalization of drug use, is extremely unlikely in the near term.

Over the course of a generation, attitudes have evolved towards greater permissiveness. During the late 1960s and early 1970s, drug use (notably of marijuana and LSD) was primarily a counterculture and hippie phenomenon. Various gurus of the era called upon university youth to "tune in, turn on, and drop out"—enough did so to fill San Francisco's Haight-Ashbury district with "summer of love" enthusiasts who urged draftees headed to Vietnam to "make love, not war" (or relocate to Canada where the marijuana supposedly grew wild and the locals were friendly).

Officials were not amused. Drug use, along with sexual promiscuity (and hence social unreliability), was regarded as legally and politically unacceptable. To have been identified as a marijuana user was sufficient to deny an applicant a security clearance at a federal government agency. Evolution was slow; as late as 1987 a Supreme Court nominee (Douglas Ginsburg) withdrew when it became clear that he had used marijuana, and consequently it was charged that he would be unable to assess the legal merits of anti-drug legislation (additionally amusing to his critics was his reputation as a highly conservative jurist). Nancy Reagan's primary First Lady activity during the Reagan presidency (1981-89) was her "Just Say No" campaign against drug use, aimed particularly at school-age children. But during the 1992 presidential campaign, Bill Clinton was more a subject of ridicule than of opprobrium for his comment that he had smoked marijuana but "didn't inhale." (For those axiomatically opposed to Clinton, his drug use was only a blip on their list of indictments.)

However, by the 2000 election, Al Gore's acknowledgment that he had used marijuana when young passed largely without comment. Among the baby boomer generation the comment circulated that "If you remember the '60s, you weren't really there"—implying that the most relevant elements of the decade were associated with drug experimentation. Indeed, George W. Bush was able to transform his drug use into a joke ("When I was young and immature, I was young and immature") without formally admitting it. Bush continued to be pursued by charges that he had used cocaine during this "immature" period—charges repeatedly denied and unproved.

And as the equivalent of a U.S. government seal of approval for "experimental" drug use, United States intelligence and security agencies no longer disqualify applicants for using illegal drugs—so long as that use has ended. Such is not to suggest that a "summer of love" climate now prevails on the Potomac, but there is recognition that automatically eliminating a significant fraction of the university population from eligibility for government employment is more likely to eliminate a significant fraction of the highly qualified than to enhance the security of confidential material. Such tolerance, however, is for prior—not current—drug use, and failing a random, mandatory drug test has serious consequences. The armed forces, which were riddled with drug users during and immediately following the Vietnam War, have responded with "zero tolerance" for drug users. For the military, it is one (confirmed) strike and you're out.

For some observers, the War on Drugs is inherently unwinnable. One estimate has the U.S. market at $65 billion annually with the price of cocaine and heroin 100 times the production costs. On that basis, suppliers can lose an enormous percentage of their production to police efforts (one estimate in mid-2005 was that 400 metric tonnes of cocaine were seized worldwide in 2004, but 200 metric tonnes entered the U.S.) and still get enormously rich. As a consequence of the demand to supply ratios, inflation-adjusted prices for cocaine and heroin reportedly are half what they were 25 years ago; likewise marijuana prices have fallen and potency doubled in the past 8 years, according to other estimates. The competitive nature of the free market has increased the availability of a product, increased its effectiveness, and reduced prices. Who can argue that crime doesn't pay?

Nor does there seem to be any upper limit on the numbers of individuals who can be induced to smuggle drugs into the country. A 2005 American Enterprise Institute study reports that the number imprisoned for drug offenses has risen from 50,000 in 1980 to 450,000 in 2003; those figures do not suggest that fear of "doing the time" has deterred drug dealers or users from doing the crime.

Why then doesn't the United States just surrender? (Or just declare that "The state has no place in the hallucinations of its citizens"?) Those seeking the legalization of marijuana and other drugs contend that their personal liberties are being violated, that these drugs are used by personal choice, that decriminalization would reduce crime, that their negative effects are no worse than x, y, or z other substantives or activities, or that "it's none of your (expletive deleted) business." They reject the "nanny" state. And, to be sure, should the state take the point of view that it is simple Darwinian justice to rid the gene pool of those too stupid to seek their pleasures in less dangerous activities?

But government concern over drug use is more than the bluenose, anti-joy conclusion that bureaucratic puritans are afraid that somewhere there is someone who is having fun. Anti-drug arguments have shifted ground over a generation. There is no longer a belief in the "reefer madness" propaganda that suggested a one-puff-and-you're-hooked-forever addiction. The connectivity between marijuana use and addiction to physically damaging drugs such as heroin is far from conclusive; still, it is rare that an addict starts with heroin. He or she has experimented with multiple "gateway" drugs before graduating to hard drugs. And the damage done by hard drugs is real. In this regard, the effort to stop drug use is akin to the anti-tobacco and alcohol abolition efforts. To be sure, not every recreational use of cigarettes leads to lung cancer or emphysema, nor does every social drinker graduate to being homeless and a victim of cirrhosis of the liver. However, there are sufficient numbers of those for whom tobacco and alcohol appear to have a "lock and key" connectivity, that is, that they have a genetic predisposition to severe illness with even relatively limited exposure to such substances.

A secondary, albeit not trivial, point is that even recreational drug use has effects, akin to alcohol's, on the ability to drive a vehicle or operate equipment. The absence of quick equivalents to breath-analyser alcohol testing for marijuana use is another unresolved legal problem.

The most current analysis for the U.S. drug positions are outlined by John Walters, the White House director of the Office of National Drug Control. According to Walters in mid-2005, the bulk of illegal drug demand comes from confirmed addicts. In his view, marijuana use is a "pediatric onset" condition; if not begun during the teen years, the probability of later start-up is "very small," with much lessened likelihood of drug dependence.

Thus Walters believes that the 5 million reported users in the 12- to 17-year-old cohort are accruing the potential for future problems, particularly as today's marijuana is more potent than in the past. And Walters claims that while there are huge amounts of marijuana grown in U.S. states such as California, Kentucky, and Hawaii (where rumor calls it the state's largest cash crop), upwards of a third of the marijuana being consumed in the United States comes from Canada. In that regard, he cites reports of 10,000 growers in Ontario—an obvious potential problem for bilateral relations that is already violently demonstrated on our Mexican border. More generally, Walters and other drug warriors clearly hope to create societal attitudes towards drugs among youth that parallel or exceed the negative view of cigarette smoking or driving while intoxicated.

Society regularly shifts its grounds and chooses over time what it wants to control according to the moods of its members and its technical capabilities. At the turn of the century, various opiates, including opium and morphine, were available through drug stores. They were standard painkillers, and addiction was a secondary concern, if considered at all. Your cough syrup may well have had a heavy dose of opium or codeine. The age for consumption of alcohol has risen and fallen—and now risen again to the point where a legal adult of 18 can be licensed to kill by society as a member of the armed forces, but cannot legally consume a bottle of beer or smoke a cigarette. In contrast, what was once regarded as hard-core pornography (and as reprehensible as today's pedophile photography) is now an "R" rated movie or video.

Even the least self-aware parent knows that children will experiment with and/or rebel against their rules. A sophisticated society, like an intelligent parent, attempts to find safe rebellions for its youth and other risk-takers; challenges that expand the mind, challenge the potential, and offer memorable experiences—without significantly damaging those minds or fatally ending the potential for further learning and experience. Thus the continuing effort to discourage drug use to a point where youth have accumulated sufficient experience to recognize viscerally, as well as intellectually, that they are not immortal. U.S. society is grappling with finding such a balance.

WORLD ROLES: 7
UNILATERAL VERSUS MULTILATERAL

Whether a country acts unilaterally or multilaterally is a function of need and capability. The difference between the action of a strong country and a weak country becomes evident only when a challenge appears. Both Canada and the United States act according to their perceptions of national interest; historically, their judgments have coincided; however, at times their perceptions have differed.

Canada, for example, acted unilaterally against a Spanish trawler fishing for turbot in 1995. In mid-2005, Ottawa sought only its own opinion regarding action on the Arctic territory of Hans Island. The United States kept its own counsel publicly regarding this Canadian action. Likewise, the United States has reserved the right to take action, unilaterally if believed necessary, in pursuit of its own interests as it perceives them. Canada has frequently been less reticent in its commentary on U.S. action than the United States has been about Canadian unilateralism.

Since the end of the Cold War, the United States has been regarded as the pre-eminent global power. As such, other states wish to use U.S. power to advance their individual or organizational interests. While the United States has sought to cooperate with other states, individually and as regional groups, it has declined to be the ox to pull the United Nations plow—or to constrain its actions only to those agreed by others. To be sure, this is not a course that meets universal acclaim. There is, after all, only one United States in the United Nations and some 191 other nations—each of which (Canada among them) will have interests at variance with those of the United States.

For both Canada and the United States, our bilateral relations are of great importance: arguably they are the most extensive and intensive relations in the world, as there is no topic on which we don't meet and react with one another. It is a truism that Canada is more focused on this relationship than is the United States, and it is equally clear that, despite many positive elements, relations at the beginning of 2006 were the most strained in at least a generation. By the middle of 2007, under the Tory government, the health of the relationship might be described as "guarded."

The most prominent international organization for the past 60 years has been the United Nations. Both Canada and the U.S. have been present from and prominent in its creation. Canada's commitment to the United Nations has been steadfast; U.S. support has waxed and waned and currently is at low ebb. Indeed, the United States is now skeptical about significant elements of U.N. leadership and policy. For its part, the current configuration of the U.N. is reflexively skeptical towards U.S. foreign policies, in general; relentlessly hostile, possibly to the point of institutionalized anti-Semitism, towards Israel; paralyzed when faced with basic human rights concerns; and, until the replacement of Kofi Annan in January 2007 by Ban Ki-moon, led by a secretary-general whose personal integrity was severely compromised.

These multiple challenges are not necessarily terminal, but they are debilitating.

A Canadian Perspective

The unilateralism versus multilateralism debate has certainly caught the attention of the international affairs community across Canada. The Centre for Foreign Policy Studies at Dalhousie University in 2004 published *Independence in an Age of Empire: Assessing Unilateralism and Multilateralism*, in which 36 foreign policy experts, mostly academics, examined the topic. More specifically, the contributors replied to a 2003 article, "Canada in the Age of Terror—Multilateralism Meets a Moment of Truth," written by Michael Ignatieff, a Canadian writer then teaching at Harvard and now a sitting MP.

Ignatieff's piece argues that the multilateralists, who are clearly the overwhelming majority among both foreign policy analysts and Canadians generally, should add some realism to their perspective. He thinks Canadians are potential targets for Islamic extremists because our country also stands for many things that al-Qaeda despises. Canada must accordingly find a multilateral vision that is robust. In the case of Iraq, Ignatieff thinks Saddam Hussein's regime had "just about the worst human rights record on earth and (was) in possession of weapons of mass destruction" (the latter point was widely believed at the time of writing, in 2003).

Many European nations, the article goes on, hold to the same notion of a multilateral world that most Canadians share, in which the use of force must lie in the U.N. and national sovereignty may be overruled where human rights abuses are occurring. NATO is a Cold War alliance which Ignatieff thinks the Americans have lost interest in, in favor of "coalitions of the willing." He thinks that the leader dominates these coalitions, whereas smaller powers like Canada have more influence in alliances. On balance, I tend to agree. NATO operates on consensus; more than one might imagine, relatively small states—and particularly France—have either prevented NATO action or created circumstances in which the U.S. did not call upon NATO. At a bare minimum, the U.S. government expended enormous effort in consultation, discussion, compromise, and diplomatic interaction. The most obvious was the many years of effort associated with nuclear and conventional weapons arms control agreements with the Soviets and the Warsaw Pact. In contrast, a "coalition of the willing" is just that—a temporary ad hoc operation for a specific, usually military, mission.

The paper then contends that if Canadians are in favor of multilateralism, we must make sure that U.N. Security Council resolutions are not only passed but obeyed and enforced. The situations in Rwanda in 1994, East Timor for a period in 1999, Bosnia in the mid-1990s, Kosovo in 1999, and Darfur since 2003, however, when some permanent members of the Security Council rendered it useless as the U.N. body mandated to ensure world peace, simply shrieks for reform to the structure of the council.

Ignatieff then ventures into the debate over development assistance versus military capacity. Like probably most Canadians, I agree with him that Canada must do both well today. Reasonable military capacity is probably more necessary than ever in the post-Cold War world. Spending 1 percent of our GDP on military defense will simply no longer cut it in the currently ever-more-dangerous world. It would appear as well that there is now a near-consensus among Canadians on this. I also agree with him that the kind of benign peacekeeping for which Lester Pearson won the Nobel Peace Prize has essentially vanished. More robust peacemaking is now almost always the need of the day, most notably now in Darfur where the slaughter of African Darfurians by Arab Darfurians, planned and directed by the regime in Khartoum, has continued since April 2003 until mid-2007 as this book goes to press. Darfur remains an area of malign neglect so far as effective international action is concerned; no coalition, either U.N.-endorsed or an ad hoc assemblage of the "willing," has been willing to offer a scintilla of sacrifice to respond to what has been described by the United States as genocide.

On development, Ignatieff is part of what appears to be a strong national consensus, including all three opposition parties in the Parliament that ended in December 2005, that Canada must finally meet Lester Pearson's contribution goal from decades ago, of 0.7 percent of the GDP going to development assistance, if we are to be a responsible world citizen and leader. He's also correct that we must seek to export our rule of law far more than we are doing.

CANADA'S ROLE TODAY

An unnamed Canadian once said, only half-jokingly, that the United Nations is in the DNA of every Canadian. There is probably still a lot of truth in the quip. Our people and governments are always happy to be doing something internationally in concert with like-minded countries—and especially so when it's with some branch of the United Nations.

Some of us tend to look back at the 1950s—our halcyon years internationally—when Lester Pearson (then secretary of state for Foreign Affairs) won the Nobel Peace Prize for his leadership in negotiating a peace settlement in the Suez Canal conflict. Pearson and other Canadians were also present at the creation of the U.N. in San Francisco in 1945. A Canadian, John Humphreys, prepared the first draft of the U.N. Universal Declaration of Human Rights. Since its formation, Canada has remained a reliable ally, supporter, and bill payer of the U.N. as a whole. Canadians have also taken roles in many of its bodies, including Louise Frechette, who was appointed the first deputy secretary-general in 1998, and served in that role until 2006.

The current dilemma for Canadians, who are more than ever joined at the hip commercially to the world's only current superpower, in the debate about unilateralism and multilateralism is how we can join the debate meaningfully in an age of terrorism and weapons of mass destruction.

It's worth noting here that in an opinion survey done by the Carleton University Survey Centre and the Department of Canadian Heritage in early 2004 on what makes Canadians very proud, less than a fifth of us in all age categories said that "our political influence in the world" made us "very proud."[1] If the world needs more Canada, why are our own people so ambivalent about it?

A number of books and studies have been published in recent years about the much reduced role of Canada internationally since the end of the

---

1. Reported in *Reader's Digest*, July 2005.

Cold War in 1989. One of the best is the interim report of the External Voices Project of the Canadian Institute of International Affairs, published in 2005 by Robert Greenhill, the new president of the Canadian International Development Agency (CIDA).

The study followed discussions with 40 knowledgeable individuals from 19 countries, who are named, although no quote is attributed to anyone in particular. The major conclusions might be summarized as follows:

- Canada's international performance and reputation have both fallen significantly during the past 15 years.
- Institutions in which Canada has played a major role, such as the G8 and NATO, were felt by the persons consulted to be losing influence. Major players such as India, China, Brazil, and Mexico—along with focused niche ones like Norway—are perceived now to be assuming international roles historically filled by Canada.
- The interviewees identified three factors seen to be *absent* in Canada's current international approach: a willingness to make choices; "consistency in choices and relationships (especially with the U.S. and the United Nations) over time"; and thirdly a "determination to build world-class assets in the niche areas where Canada has chosen to lead." Greenhill also notes that nothing will improve for Canada internationally without "a major change in our mindset and our allocation of resources."[2]

The Greenhill study quite properly differentiates between making a contribution to something international and making a real difference. Greenhill notes that between 1989 and 2004, Canada spent about $243 billion of taxpayer money on diplomacy, defense, and international development. According to his sources and judgment, however, some smaller countries with far fewer resources have made a significant difference over the same period, including Sweden in development, Australia in East Timor, and Norway in peace brokering. Is it not reasonable to expect, the author asks, to make "a significant difference in at least a few areas with a quarter of a trillion dollars?" No well-informed person is likely to disagree.

Most of the experts consulted said that Canada's role has been "marginal over the past 15 years." Several interviewees could think of no example where Canada had made a real difference. Among the examples to the contrary cited by others was Canada's role in achieving majority rule in South

---

2. July 13, 2005, Reuters report from Singapore.

Africa. To do so, we leveraged our position in the G7, the Commonwealth, and *la francophonie*, lobbied international leaders, supported the Front-Line States, and engaged both the African National Congress and the South African government during the transition. It was clearly our finest hour in recent years on the continent of Africa.

Probably surprisingly to many Canadians, Greenhill's interviewees think Brian Mulroney, as prime minister from 1984–1993, was effective until 1992 in laying foundations for global trade in the WTO and regionally with NAFTA. He also demonstrated that economic integration could co-exist with political independence, developing friendship with the U.S. while pursuing Canada's own agenda on issues such as the environment, acid rain, and the declaration of full northern sovereignty. As prime minister, Mulroney also cultivated simultaneously such close relations with the United Kingdom, France, and the United States that all three of their governments later supported his candidacy for secretary-general of the United Nations. It was, however, ultimately dropped because of major national unity problems in Canada.

With the arrival of the Chrétien government in 1993 and Paul Martin's 1995 budget came severe cuts in each of our military, development, and diplomacy budgets. Canada's full retreat from international affairs had begun. As Greenhill puts it, "Externally, interviewees see Chrétien as having been conservative, risk-averse, and uninterested in international affairs except as a trade opportunity."

The subsequent refusal by Chrétien to join the "coalition of the willing" in Iraq in 2003, however, was seen as significant. An interviewee from a smaller country noted, "Canada's action was an inspiration and a comfort to us." Opinion surveys across Canada, especially since the war was prematurely declared won, indicate that a majority of Canadians share the view of Greenhill's interviewee from a smaller country.

The major international accomplishment of the Chrétien government was the Landmine Treaty, especially the process employed to achieve it, which was largely outside the U.N. forum. Over the opposition of the Clinton administration, Canada was able to assemble a successful coalition of like-minded governments and civil rights groups across the world.

The human security agenda of Minister of Foreign Affairs Lloyd Axworthy, which essentially sought to enhance the safety of the world's vulnerable peoples over the heads of reluctant governments, received a mixed response. One of those consulted by Greenhill praised the idea of humanitarian interventions. Several noted that the increase in Canadian rhetoric about the need for increased security coincided with a simultaneous reduction in our military capability to do something effective about it. A number noted that with Axworthy's departure as minister, Canada's support for human security has fallen. My own observation is that the term—if not the substance—all but disappeared in the Foreign Ministry after Axworthy left office in 2000. His successor, John Manley, did not to my knowledge ever use the term "human security" publicly, although he supported the concept in some speeches on the subject.

Axworthy's role in Peru in 2000 following the attempt by former president Alberto Fujimoro to push through his preferred election result after a very flawed election was seen as positive. Our engagement in the Organization of American States (OAS) since 1990 was also praised by Latin American observers. On the other hand, the OAS showed little interest in the putative candidacy of former Foreign Affairs minister Pierre Pettigrew to head the organization.

With respect to the New Partnership for Africa's Development (NEPAD), the Chrétien government received only a very mixed response from those Greenhill consulted. We received marks, he notes, for "pushing on a not-so-open door, particularly with the Bush administration" to get NEPAD approved at the 2002 G8 Summit in Kananaskis, Alberta. The experts were divided on NEPAD's effectiveness, and there was a consensus that Canada (which was at least the first industrial democracy to approve NEPAD) provided only fleeting leadership on the issue.

More encouragingly, we were seen to have made a difference during the period in three unconventional ways. First, we continued to produce effective internationalists and the interviewees singled out a number of individuals, including Stephen Lewis, Louise Arbour, and David Malone. The role of many Canadians in international organizations and NGOs was praised.

The second major success story for Canada was in the education of leaders in developing countries. Our International Development Research Centre (IDRC) provided research support to academics Fernando Cardoso of Brazil and Ricardo Lagos of Chile. Both became presidents of their countries during the 1990-2005 period. Singapore's ambassador to the U.N., Kishore Mahbubani, was president of the Security Council in 2001 and 2002 and studied at Dalhousie University; a number of public servants in Asia attended training courses provided jointly by CIDA and the government of Singapore.

Third, a number of interviewees from Europe and developing countries praised Canadians for our "successful, distinct socio-economic model": North American economic dynamism; European social justice; and fiscal responsibility. We also get credit for being a successful culturally pluralistic society. We seem to have demonstrated for other countries sometimes what is possible.

Despite these successes, the consensus was clearly that 1989–2004 was a period of noticeable decline for Canada internationally, especially in three major areas: our relationship with the United States; our earlier leadership in development assistance; and the importance internationally of our peace-keeping and other international activities on security.

CANADA'S BILATERAL RELATIONSHIP WITH THE UNITED STATES

Our shared economic interests with our most immediate neighbor have now reached a new phase in the movement of people, products, and services and in continental security.

Interestingly, because it is counterintuitive, none of Greenhill's interviewees indicated that Canada's independent foreign policy would affect our bilateral trade relationship. No one suggested either that a more supportive international policy would assist in the resolution of contentious trade issues such as softwood lumber. This observed lack of connectivity is interesting because other observers suggested that Prime Minister Mulroney was notably successful on issues relating to bilateral Canadian interests (for example, acid rain), based on his strong personal relations with Presidents Reagan and Bush—and these good personal relations were based on a carefully managed coincidence in foreign policies.

In Greenhill's view, NAFTA has had a major structural impact on all three nations involved over the past 15 years. Our rapid response to 9/11 with the "smart borders" initiative and tight security cooperation with the Americans allowed the common border to remain open. He cautions, however, that to keep it open we must ensure that we do not ever become a security risk. He sees no possibility of a grand bilateral bargain solving a bundle of trade issues. The NAFTA machinery, and assembling an effective coalition of players on both sides of the border to lobby the administration and Congress on case-by-case issues, will continue to be necessary for Canada.

In terms of influencing U.S. foreign policy, the study notes that the American interviewees—"Democrats, Republicans, and career officers alike—observed that Canada has become almost irrelevant to U.S. foreign policy making." One well-informed Canadian noted: "Ten years ago, we had little influence in Washington. Now we have less." Rather devastatingly, even Susan Rice, assistant secretary of state for African Affairs in the Clinton administration, noted in a recent paper, as cited by Greenhill: "While Prime Minister Chrétien and President Clinton enjoyed a warm personal relationship and met on numerous occasions, as did their respective national security advisors and foreign ministers, Canada's influence on day-to-day U.S. policy was marginal . . . . For almost a generation, the U.S. has conducted foreign policy largely without regard to Canada's perspective." Rice's suggestion that the Clinton-Chrétien relationship was "warm" may be a few degrees off. While relations were certainly better than the frozen hostility Chrétien demonstrated to Bush, Chrétien also demonstrated a level of benign contempt for Clinton (such as at a NATO Summit in 1997 when he commented dismissively about how to handle the Americans, unknowingly into an open microphone).

It has long been assumed by many that Canada's ability to influence American foreign policy was one of our major diplomatic assets. Those interviewed appear to agree that Mulroney's strong relationship with Presidents Ronald Reagan and George H. W. Bush gave Canada influence on American policy during those periods. Jean Chrétien was certainly seen as hostile to the administration of George W. Bush. In the pre-Iraq period, Tony Blair supported Canada more often than the United States on issues (especially landmines and the International Criminal Court), but Blair was thought to have transferred a close relationship from Clinton to George Bush, while Chrétien did not. From subsequent developments, this judgment seems rather indisputable.

More important, however, notes Greenhill, is the inconsistency in the way we have treated the U.S. in the period examined. Says Greenhill: "American and non-American observers noted that our attitude towards the U.S. seemed to change significantly between prime ministers and, even, during the Chrétien period, between foreign ministers. Our inconsistent attitude makes it less useful, and more risky, for U.S. decision makers to fully engage with Canada on sensitive international issues." Although there were, in my own view, changes between prime ministers and foreign ministers (for example, Andre Ouellette was far more bilaterally effective than Lloyd Axworthy), the essential change came with the Republican victory in 2000—and the administration's perception of Chrétien hostility—a hostility that became ever more pointed during Bush's first term.

Even more important than strategic consistency, concludes the study, is the use of our diplomatic assets, that is, our capabilities and the willingness to use them to help another country. According to American interviewees, many of Canada's assets useful to the United States over the past five decades have deteriorated, including:

- "Peacekeeping, but for the last 15 years you have lived off your reputation" (peacekeeping was our asset mentioned most often by Americans).
- "A bridge between the U.S. and UK . . . but the UK co-opted your strategy, positioned themselves as the bridge between the U.S. and Europe."
- "A bridge between the U.S. and the U.N. . . . As the U.N. matured, and U.S. ambivalence towards the institution grew, this approach became fragile."
- "Leaders once worth talking to, worth exchanging ideas with" (referring to Pierre Trudeau).

So far as the latter point is concerned, co-author Jones notes, it is difficult to determine when a U.S. president had a fruitful exchange with Prime Minister Trudeau. The Trudeau-Nixon relationship was poisonous; Ford was an interim president; Carter never visited Ottawa and was consumed with Iran; and Trudeau regarded Reagan with contempt.

Who then is punching above their weight with the U.S.? Interviewees, American and other, identified the UK, Australia, and France here, albeit for differing reasons. The UK has assets, including what many observers think is the best diplomatic service in the world, strong intelligence, and an effective full-service military, and has built itself into the U.S. decision making process. The UK government believes that its leverage with Washington "gives it leverage over the world," notes Greenhill.

Australia, said those interviewed, positions itself as a long-term partner and regional ally of the United States. It has a small but focused and tight military, and a willingness to use it. As Greenhill notes, Australia knows that it lives in a rough neighborhood and that only the U.S. can guarantee its security. It is also the only country that has fought alongside the United States in every war in the past century. As a result, "When Australia's PM visits, people feel a partner is coming. When Canada's PM comes, people feel it is an obligation to be fulfilled."

France is seen as having influence because it has capacity, including a Security Council veto, intelligence assets, and some of the toughest troops in the world. "All three of these countries are seen as having strategic stances which are relatively consistent over time—beyond individual chemistry and party affiliations."

For Canada, Greenhill's interviewees had various opinions on how best to increase our influence with American policymakers. The consensus was that we should be "close to the U.S., but not of the U.S." One non-American concluded: "Canada will be taken more seriously if it crafts an independent policy that focuses on different ways of making things happen than the U.S.; that leverages Canada's high level of trust with the developing world, reasonable goodwill in Europe; and historical credibility with multilateral institutions."

INTERNATIONAL SECURITY

Many of Canada's defense assets are seen as "largely irrelevant to today's real international security needs" (Greenhill), and experts say we must reform our military assets in areas that could improve security domestically and make a substantive difference internationally.

Some of the language used to describe our defense assets by interviewees were: "atrophy," "confusion," and "irrelevant." On Canada's historic role in U.N. peacekeeping, for example, we are seen to have virtually disappeared since our Somalia debacle. Greenhill: " . . . the general sense is that there is no longer the political will by Canada's leaders nor the strategic commitment by Canada's military for Canada to really make a difference in U.N. peacekeeping." The Department of National Defence website itself probably unintentionally says it all: " . . . according to the United Nations monthly summary, dated September 30, 2004, Canada is the 34th largest contributor of military troops and observers to the U.N." In 2005, Greenhill adds, Canada was "essentially gone" as a U.N. peacekeeper.

In this regard, insists co-author Jones, Canada may be selling its military contribution shorter than is necessary. Although it is no longer a significant U.N. Peacekeeping Operation (PKO) contributor, it has continued to put forces into some challenging military-related assignments in former Yugoslavia, Haiti, and particularly Afghanistan since 2001 and continuing through the present. These assignments were real and relevant—arguably more important than some of the alternative PKO exercises. Spreading forces in penny-packet portions for U.N. PKOs is a "box checking," feel-good exercise but nowhere as militarily (and politically) effective as committing larger elements in fewer spots.

The quality and discipline of our troops, the effectiveness of our officers, and our long experience with peacekeeping were well-recognized Canadian value-added to peacekeeping. In the Balkans, for example, under the U.N. and then NATO, Canada was seen to make an important contribution, especially in the provision of relief to Sarajevo. In Afghanistan, the assessment of our past role was mixed, and the results of the current, ongoing commitment and Canadian effectiveness in it are still in embryo.

Today, Greenhill notes, Canada contributes less than 2 percent of the troops engaged in U.N.-run or other internationally sanctioned security operations that exclude Iraq. Médecins Sans Frontières (MSF, or Doctors Without Borders) "consistently deploys more professions to the front lines around the world than the Canadian Armed Forces. In 2004, MSF, with a budget of only 8 percent of the Canadian military's had about 1,800 foreign professionals and 17,000 local staff deployed at any one time in critical regions around the world while Canada managed to deploy about 1,600 troops" (Greenhill). One should also note that the doctors at MSF serve on a voluntary basis, unlike our troops. In addition, we don't often use local staff except for specialized activities that only local nationals can perform, such as language translation.

To improve Canada's military effectiveness, external experts made three sets of recommendations. First and most important, we must improve the protection of our national sovereignty and increase our contribution to continental defense. This would send a message to both Canadians and Americans that Canada acknowledges its share of the burden for continental defense, and that it is ready to be a true partner in protecting the North American heartland. In practical terms, this will necessitate "superior coast guard and interdiction capabilities" (Greenhill) and "an enhanced ability to intervene quickly in case of terrorist actions within Canada and to deal effectively with large national or terrorist-caused disasters" (Greenhill). None of the Americans indicated that participation in ballistic missile defense was essential to the new level of cooperation with the U.S. such a strategy would bring.

Second, Canada must make a distinct contribution to improved international security. Interviewees recommended three areas: an air-mobile brigade with stand-alone capability; police and security training; and postconflict reconstruction. Greenhill found very strong support for the stand-alone mobile brigade because of the pressing world need for such capacity and because we have the competence and goodwill to use it in ways other nations cannot. An interviewee: "The thing we are not good at doing is reacting promptly when we see the political situation deteriorate. Canada could make a real contribution if it had a force of 5,000 that could be projected into a region, including 2,000 to 3,000 in the first weeks, that could be kept there for two months." "It could be a rapid conflict resolution force, it could provide rapid humanitarian relief, or it could provide muscular enforcement of the responsibility to protect." Other academics have advocated such an approach for many years, but to no avail.

Greenhill writes that "other like-minded countries—Norway, Belgium, Austria, and the Netherlands—were suggested as possible partners in deployment under Canadian leadership." One African leader added, "The African Union has established a security council. It has no logistics capability. Canada could provide analysts, command and control, training in peacekeeping."

European and American interviewees suggested that the RCMP, with increased personnel, is well equipped to do policing and security training abroad in postconflict situations, including future-state reconstruction. "What we need most—the West, the international community—is to deal effectively with future failed states. If I could think of someone who could provide nation-building capability, it would be Canada. Restore order, get the government system up and running, set up temporary power. Canada could play a leadership role, a distinct role."

Third, Canada must assess the relevance of all military assets and related operations from the standpoint of the 21st-century priorities. For the past half-century, Canada's high-tech, full-service conventional armed forces were part of an alliance designed to contain the Soviet Union and its threat to Western Europe. The U.S. today has such a growing superiority in high-tech conventional arms that it could last for up to 30 years.

Our current defense configuration has little support among the interviewees because it replicates assets that the West already has plenty of and is financially unsustainable since the costs of modern combat systems are mounting so quickly. We Canadians simply cannot afford the next generation of weaponry. As one American put it, " . . . defense strategy is in a state of disarray worldwide. There is less money, no clear view, and vested interests pushing for unimportant projects resulting in no boots on the ground and no money for bullets." The report concludes that our expensive assets (such as CF-18s) provided no diplomatically valuable contribution in Kosovo and the first Gulf War to what could have been provided by less expensive ones, such as special operations teams. In short, we were, says Greenhill, "a member of the force, but not to have had distinct assets or capabilities that allowed it to make a real difference."

The strong majority of the 20 experts who commented thought that our army should be the focus of our international security, with the navy and air force concentrating on continental defense. Two-thirds of them also felt it unnecessary for Canada to have its own strategic lift capacity because a combination of U.S. tactical lift and commercial could do the task. Greenhill is convinced that real human security assets, such as a mobile brigade and a will to use it, are called for and that diplomacy alone is inadequate. As he puts it, " . . . today we are the Boy Scout who stands on the corner, telling others how to help little old ladies across the street."

DEVELOPMENT LAGGARD

Developmental experts from the developing world, Europe, and the U.S. told Greenhill that, during the 1990s, Canada lost leadership on many development issues, including education and gender issues. Funding was identified as one of the major causes: our official development assistance declined to a low of 0.24 percent of GDP from 0.5 percent a decade earlier. In dollar amounts spent yearly, Canada is now only spending half as much as the Dutch.

A second reason is that Canada has had fully 10 different CIDA ministers since 1989. As soon as one gets to know the issues, he or she is replaced. "Starting about 1990, CIDA started to lose its edge: it became exceedingly bureaucratic." Another expert noted something familiar to many Canadian development professionals: "We made a proposal; a year later they [CIDA] contacted us to say that they had lost the original proposal and asked for another copy. Several months later they contacted us with an approval and said the money had to be spent by the end of the planning year—in 60 days."

On the other hand, CIDA did see some real successes in the 1990s, such as Internet interconnectiveness in Africa that joined African universities to the rest of the world. As well, in Tanzania, CIDA and the IDRC assisted in one of the best experiments anywhere in health care systems. The problem was that such successes were "sporadic and disjointed." The IDRC's budget is at the same level as 10 years ago, which, one observer added, is too small to have real impact.

Another problem is that some European countries—Sweden, Norway, the UK, and the Netherlands—are now setting higher development cooperation standards. The first two, says Greenhill, are praised for the quality and quantities of their programs, both focusing on areas such as gender equality, which has political support domestically as well as much need abroad.

To insulate its programs from political pressure, Sweden even has legislation that places development assistance at arm's length and out of reach of Swedish politicians.

In Britain, the Department of International Development has, in a decade, through good leadership, moved from the middle of the pack to what is generally considered to be the best in the world. Its former minister, Clare Short, and her leadership were, over six years, given full support by Prime Minister Tony Blair and Chancellor of the Exchequer Gordon Brown.

Greenhill's interviewees appear to agree that there are some focus areas where Canada could make a real difference: governance, health care systems, and education. On the best regions for concentration, the experts differed, depending on whether they felt human security, geographic or demographic links, or other factors were more important; those suggested included Africa, the Middle East and Afghanistan, the Caribbean and Mexico, and Ukraine.

The interviewees appear to agree that both quantity and quality are necessary in Canada's future development assistance. Five European countries have already reached Lester Pearson's goal set in the 1960s of providing 0.7 percent of GDP for international assistance, and six more have made the commitment to do so by the 2015 target for the U.N.'s Millennium Development Goals. Since Greenhill's report was published, however, then Prime Minister Paul Martin explicitly refused to set a date for Canada to reach the goal. In contrast, Prime Minister Harper specifically promised to increase funding for development in his successful election campaign—and took steps in that direction in the March 2007 budget. The budget confirmed the government would double international assistance spending by 2010-11 from 2001-02 levels, which will bring Canada's international assistance budget to CA$4.4 billion. The budget also provides an additional CA$200 million in further development assistance to support Canada's mission in Afghanistan. Initiatives will focus on creating new opportunities for women, strengthening governance, enhancing security, and addressing the challenge of combating illegal drugs. The Conservatives also pledged to focus bilateral aid on fewer countries, aiming to position Canada among the largest five donors in core countries of interest.

One interviewee concluded: "Canada needs to make a concrete commitment to the 0.7 percent if it does not want to lose all credibility in development." Greenhill clearly agrees: "Canada needs to decide if it will match the UK commitment to reach 0.7% and stay in the game, or fold."

The 2007 budget increases, however, leave Canada well short of the 0.7 percent level.

CONCLUSIONS ABOUT CANADA FROM THE STUDY

Finally, the overall conclusion of the Greenhill study is that Canada's performance since 1989 is "nothing for a country of our wealth and history of international engagement to be proud of. Our performance appears to have been well below our exaggerated rhetoric, well below our historical performance, and well below global expectations." The author correctly adds that Canada's fiscal and economic portion have strengthened and now allow us to do much more. Greenhill deserves the last word: "'The world needs more Canada' is a nice slogan. Our interviews suggest that what the world really needs is more from Canada: more commitment, more focus, more impact. Canada will spend some $100 billion on defence, development, and diplomacy over the next five years. We need to refocus that $100 billion to ensure that, in the future, we make a real difference rather than just a showing."[3] This says it all—and is probably a view shared by most Canadians from sea to sea to sea.

The United States' Role Today

THE PARAMETERS OF PRE-EMPTION

In the end, stripping aside the debates over morality and legality, the question of unilateral action versus multilateral action is one of *capability*. If you can't, you won't. A country with the strength and resolve to act unilaterally *may* elect to do so. One without such capability does not. Or at least it does not unless acting under suicidal leadership. However, even an ostensibly weak country can act unilaterally—if the object of its action is still weaker, or if the issue is not of concern to stronger states.

Some, who cannot act unilaterally but still wish to influence international events, seek other mechanisms. They may wish to avoid the consequences of action against them by those who can act unilaterally or they may join multilateral forums and alliances to promote their interests. Even those states that have the capability for unilateral action may prefer, seek, and choose to act multilaterally. At a minimum, multilateral action can reduce costs in treasure (and perhaps blood) expended. Multilateral action *may* be more

---

3. All citations from the study taken from Robert Greenhill, *External Voices: Interim Report on the External Voices Project.* Toronto: Canadian Institute for International Affairs, 2005.

efficient and reduce competing or wasteful efforts (the 2005 South Asian tsunami relief effort comes to mind). At a maximum, a global feel-goodism results when many actors are involved on a particularly worthy effort, whether it is addressing AIDS in Africa, saving the Minki whale, defeating the Central Powers in World War I or the Axis in World War II, or facing Islamic terrorism since 9/11. Nevertheless, there are idiosyncratic individuals who believe that AIDS should be handled by local faith healers, whales are simply large repositories of sushi, and the United States has created the terrorists who destroyed the Trade Center towers in 2001.

No one can logically argue that unilateral action is bad while multilateral action is good. We can assume that food for the starving, medicine to the sick, or rescue of the stranded are good, whether this assistance is delivered by one mechanism or 100. The fact that the Axis acted multilaterally against the Allies does not alleviate the opprobrium of their aggression. And if one opposed the liberation of Kuwait in 1991, let alone the liberation of Iraq in 2003, taking such action as part of a group of nations isn't an acceptable rationale to justify participation. International law has the effectiveness of a nanny (or a temp agency of nannies) attempting to control a Hells Angel biker: feckless—unless she can whistle for Robocop.

So one set of activists may say "sovereignty sucks" but international affairs are not a "one nation, one vote" activity—and certainly not subject to popular vote.

What remains important are outcomes and ends, not means. Are the results regarded as "good" rather than not (fewer AIDS victims, more whales, a free Kuwait)? And always one must reflect that the winners will determine whether the means justified the ends (or whether the means perverted the ends). In that light, let us examine the latest subelement of U.S. foreign policy: pre-emption.

What the U.S. has indicated is that it will address foreign policy problems as they occur, without an axiomatic prescription for their resolution. There will therefore be some crises that will be managed through the United Nations, some that will be managed through alliances such as NATO, others that will be addressed through ad hoc "willing" coalitions and still others that Washington will resolve by itself. This should not be a surprising statement, since it is merely the articulation of foreign policy adopted throughout U.S. history. For example, the United States unilaterally addressed the threat of the Barbary pirates in the 19th century, Spanish repression in Cuba in 1898, and various disorders in Caribbean islands such as Cuba, Haiti, and the Dominican

Republic in the 20th century. In Mexico, at the time of the American Civil War, the French installed Maximilian as its puppet emperor; subsequently the U.S. government encouraged "regime change." Prior to the First World War, the U.S. pursued Mexican guerrilla raiders across the border.

And, in passing, those familiar with British politicomilitary activity throughout the 19th and early 20th centuries will recall London's unilateral military action (described as *Queen Victoria's Little Wars* by Byron Farwell) in Africa, the Middle East, and South Asia. Nations have single-handedly taken those actions necessary to advance and support their interests—and continue to do so.

Similarly, we should not fail to recognize Canada's 1995 "Cod War," starring Brian Tobin as "Captain Canada," which provided Ottawa with a delightful frisson of unilateral, pre-emptive action against a Spanish fishing vessel. Purists might still quibble over the legality of Canadian action in international waters, but Washington didn't have a dog in that fight so there was no need to play purist. Instead, the U.S. government concluded that Canadian equities were overriding and held its public peace. The United States restricted itself to reminding Canadian officials politely and privately that, should there be a comparable problem with American fishing boats, Ottawa would be well advised to remember that the U.S. was not Spain.

SOME CASE STUDIES

Those who criticize the "Bush Doctrine" of pre-emption seem to believe that they have uncovered something as revolutionary as cold fusion. But there is nothing new under the sun, and current U.S. policy is closely linked to the past. The trail of U.S. history reveals more pre-emption and unilateral action in response to provocation than not—and when we have joined in coalitions, it has been on our own terms and our own timing. More recently, when we have led coalitions, it has been clear that we were willing to do the job ourselves, but if others wanted to come along that was fine too—but the job was going to be done.

In 1994 the United States led a coalition, including Canada, that was poised to invade Haiti and remove the military junta. Obviously, Haiti posed no threat to the United States; its leaders had no weapons of mass destruction. The primary objective was to eliminate the brutal dictatorial regime of the moment that was prompting regional instability. That the U.S.-led coalition did not, in the end, invade the island is irrelevant; the result was regime change.

In 1991, following the Iraqi invasion of Kuwait, the United States made extensive efforts through multilateral channels and unilaterally to reverse this aggression. From the moment President GHW Bush said "this will not stand," it was clear that the United States was committed to liberating Kuwait. Ultimately, Washington orchestrated a wide coalition and secured, after protracted effort, a limited U.N. mandate restricted to expelling the Iraqis but not eliminating the Saddam regime.

The United States also removed a "narco-dictator" from Panama in 1989. Manuel Noriega had no WMD, but his thugs were harassing U.S. citizens and the threat to the Panama Canal was rising. Circumstances were clearly going to get worse, so we acted with unilateral military force to end the threat. Loud were the protests that Washington had violated Panamanian sovereignty (though not, incidentally, from the Canadian government, which then supported Washington); now there is not a wet eye in the region over Mr. Noriega's incarceration. And the current Panamanian government is much better than the government that was in power in 1989.

Almost forgotten is Grenada, where, in 1983, the United States determined that an erratic leftist dictator was working closely with Cuba and a large Cuban contingent was building an airfield. The U.S. government sensed regional instability, gathered up an instant coalition of willing Caribbean partners, and removed a regional threat.

Still further back, in 1962, the United States acted unilaterally to prevent the deployment of Soviet intermediate-range nuclear missiles in Cuba. Some, including Canadians, might have been willing to live under the threat of these weapons; the United States was not.

Returning to the case of Iraq, at numerous points, including an October 7, 2002, speech, President George W. Bush made it clearer than clear that the United States did not want war, but Washington judged the threat from Iraq unacceptable. Despite extensive efforts based on the best available intelligence and calculation, the United States did not convince the United Nations to support military action against Iraq. That this lack of support was as much politicized anti-Americanism as any counter judgment on Iraqi WMD possession is a separate issue. Canadians and others did not believe that they were comparably threatened and wished to substitute their judgment of the threat for ours. Or they believed that we should act only if the United Nations judgment was substituted for our own. Washington declined to defer to the judgment of others regarding its perception of threat. The United States is bearing the consequences of its decision; it will be history's judgment whether the consequences of doing the right thing (removing a vicious dictator) for the wrong reason (belief that he had threatening WMD) justify the action—another ends and means issue.

Each nation makes choices based on priorities and capabilities. In 1995, Ottawa was ready for war with Spain over turbot; in 2003, Washington believed the safety of its citizens was as important as fish.

U.S. NATIONAL SECURITY STRATEGY

The basis for the "pre-emption" discussion was the U.S. National Security Strategy paper dating from September 2002. Rather than depending on predigested media accounts—or this commentary—a reader might wish to read it personally at: http://www.whitehouse.gov/nsc/print/nssall.html. In March 2006, the U.S. government reinforced previous policy and repeated its position on pre-emption.

Essentially, the National Security Strategy (NSS) of 2002 is a 9-part, 23-page, complex and sophisticated review of U.S. foreign policy principles, goals and objectives, and tactics for their accomplishment. It ranges from language that strikes higher notes in describing U.S. foreign policy ("Our own history is a long struggle to live up to our ideals") to pedestrian descriptions of economic objectives. It emphasizes the threat of terrorism ("The gravest danger our Nation faces lies at the crossroads of radicalism and technology"), but it repeatedly emphasizes the need for working in conjunction with friends and allies in facing each challenge. Indeed, the discussions of strengthening NATO, assisting Russia in its struggle towards democracy, addressing the challenges of China, improving intelligence collection, and many other topics, are significantly more extended than the brief discussion accorded to pre-emption. These almost standard international objectives might have been written by non-American authors.

The NSS addresses Canadian-U.S. relations several times, noting that the United States has formed flexible coalitions in the Western Hemisphere with allies, including Canada, to promote democracy and advance economic progress. It also says frankly that the United States can accomplish "little of lasting consequence" in the world without "sustained cooperation" from allies such as Canada, and it identifies as a "top priority" resolving ongoing economic disputes with Canada.

As for pre-emption, the NSS places it in the context of threats stemming from predictable terrorist action. ("The greater the threat, the greater is the risk of inaction—and the more compelling the case for taking anticipatory action to defend ourselves. . . .") The NSS carefully extrapolates long-standing international legal authority regarding pre-emption into the modern reality that recognizes the paucity of warning until the crisis is upon you. Hence there will be a need to take action upon occasion, despite uncertainty over an enemy's time and place of attack. In its phrasing and its caveats, the U.S. pre-emption policy is remarkably cautious and without the bravado that one might hypothesize from the media hype. There may be "cowboys" in Washington, but they were not drafting this language.

In the years to come, the world will see pre-emptive U.S. action—as it will see cooperative multilateral U.S. action. The United States will not limit itself in advance regarding its approach to foreign policy. No great power ever has foreclosed its option to take action according to its own counsel. In this regard, the United States will not break with historical precedent.

In late November and early December 2004, after much pointed delay, President Bush officially visited Canada (Ottawa and Halifax). In his Halifax speech, the president laid out three goals: defending U.S. security multilaterally if possible, but unilaterally if necessary; promoting democracy in the Middle East; and fighting global terrorism by relentlessly taking the fight to the terrorists. For this latter objective, Bush's adroit researchers unearthed a pertinent quote from Canada's longest-serving prime minister, William Lyon Mackenzie King, to the effect that one could not await attack but had to "go out and meet the enemy . . . defeat him before he attacks us." There was not even a touch of that famous smirk when delivering those words. Point made—but point taken? In the intervening period, U.S. government objectives have not altered one iota.

THE UNITED STATES' BILATERAL RELATIONSHIP WITH CANADA

Probably fortunately for Canada, the United States has not devoted attention to the bilateral relationship commensurate to that devoted by Canada. Historically, those countries to which Washington has devoted concentrated attention are often not happy countries—or pleased with U.S. attention.

Canada has essentially one foreign affairs concern: how to manage relations with the United States to *its* benefit (not necessarily to *mutual* benefit). In contrast, during most of the past generation, the U.S. struggled with defining global issues, the outcome of which decided the survival of Western democracy and the prevention of nuclear annihilation. It was hard, expensive, often bloody work—but the U.S. did it because no other country or combination could have done the task. Appreciation for U.S. effort has been fleeting. And, while Canada did have a share in this 50-year task, its contribution was not proportionate to the effort that it could have made.

Bilateral relations with Canada are a tertiary concern; U.S. public ignorance of the specifics of Canadian life is standard fare for Canadian humorists. Benign public ignorance, however, does not mean that U.S. specialists in Canada or technical bilateral experts are unwitting of the details of specific problems. Recent polls suggest that the U.S. now considers the UK, not Canada, as its best friend.

Consequently, while the Canada-U.S. relationship is the most intensive in the world, its depth and breadth means that even a small element of difficulty translates into many specific cases. There is a tendency to focus on the "hole" and not on the "doughnut." Niggling, tertiary economic and political differences are transmuted into the litmus test for the totality of the relationship. Since the election of George W. Bush in 2000, secondary-level economic issues (softwood lumber, "mad cow" restrictions, border security controls) have festered and become politicized. Using the old adage that the U.S. and Canada are best friends "like it or not," we are certainly in the "not" portion of that cycle.

In the post-9/11 world, the U.S. has put a premium on security to the point that it will trump economics if a choice is forced. We share a 5,500-mile undefended cliché, the porous nature of which (whether for drugs or illegal aliens) bothers Americans intensely but with less perceived seriousness by Canadians. While Canadians recognize that their economic prosperity compels action to reinforce U.S. perimeter security, their frequent public resentment blunts the popular perception of their efforts. At times, Canadian defenders of human rights convey the implicit impression that they would prefer a repeat of 9/11 than to have Canadian travelers discomfited in the least.

Canadian media have focused on a tiny handful of cases, claiming that human rights have been violated by U.S. action against these Canadian citizens while expressing virtually no appreciation for why Americans regard the rights of these individuals as secondary to U.S. security. The general attitude appears to be that Uncle Sam may have enemies but (a) he deserves them; (b) he is paranoid when he should be merely neurotic; and (c) catering to his concerns may be economically necessary but is nationally demeaning.

Hence also the clamor associated with the U.S. legal requirement to provide a secure travel/identification document to enter the country by land, beginning in 2008, baffles U.S. security specialists. Canadians have expended floods of rhetoric fighting the problem rather than pressing for an obtainable solution, such as employing smart cards or comparable technology. Even when individuals implacably hostile to the United States are identified in Canada, the professed concern that a secure travel document will significantly damage commerce and tourism appears overriding. Abstractly, Canadians should be in the forefront of those insisting on upgraded border security—to be assured that should the next terrorist attack on the U.S. originate in Canada, Americans will recognize that Canadians did all possible to forestall it.

Accentuating the negatives of substantive difference has been personalized disdain at senior levels. At their core, Canadian Liberals and U.S. Republicans are not a good psycho-political match. The ad hominem attacks by Canadian leadership immediately prior to the Iraq war inflicted wounds that have been glossed over but not healed. Despite the stakes for stability, let alone democracy in the Middle East, one can easily gain the impression that many Canadians would rather see the U.S.-led effort in Iraq fail than not. Likewise, the Canadian decision not to participate in the missile defense of the continent has led to the reluctant conclusion that Canadians have deliberately decided to be free riders for North American defense.

The decline of Canadian military capabilities has not gone unnoticed. Skeptics anticipated that proposed increases in defense funding highlighted in the final Liberal budget would no more be implemented than were previous proposals—military spending simply is not popular in comparison to health, education, or other social services. A generation-long downward spiral makes it increasingly unlikely that Canada will ever again be a militarily significant power. It is even increasingly difficult to coordinate with U.S. forces technically, regardless of good will or desire on the part of the military services.

Likewise, the current Conservative government commitments to defense fall into the "it remains to be seen" category. To be sure, lip service is better than no service, and during the 2005-06 campaign, the Conservatives (as did the Liberals) postulated increased defense spending. Defense, however, was not one of the five immediate, core commitments for the Conservatives, and it will take as long for the Canadian Forces to recover as it has taken them to decline. Nevertheless, during its first year in government, the Tories announced a series of major defense purchases in the form of helicopters and long-range transport aircraft as well as projecting increased force levels.

Any equipment purchases can take a decade or longer before the purchase order becomes wheels on the tarmac, and a Tory defeat in the next election would put all defense upgrades in question.

Recent Canadian diplomatic initiatives have frequently been unhelpful, and the Canadian position on topics such as the Anti-personnel Landmine Agreement, the Kyoto Treaty, and the International Criminal Court simply dismissed U.S. objections as misguided and irrelevant. Despite the reality that U.S. equities in each of these areas are far greater than Canada's, Ottawa abetted U.S. isolation in preference to building bridges for agreement or compromise.

At the end of 2005, Canada-U.S. bilateral relations were at a reduced decibel level (except for softwood lumber) and had settled into a slough of mutual disappointment. Prior to the 2005-06 election campaign, Prime Minister Martin better controlled public vituperation by his caucus. However, having been disappointed in its hope for regime change with "President Kerry" in 2004, Liberal Ottawa appeared simply determined to await the arrival of a deserving Democrat in the White House to resume collegial (rather than guarded) relations. Unfortunately, during the election, the Liberals campaigned on classic anti-Americanism, attempting to demonize Harper as a Bush "clone" and, *inter alia*, smearing the U.S. as lacking a "global conscience" over Kyoto as well as depicting the U.S. as wrong in virtually all of its policies, domestic and international. Then Ambassador Frank McKenna contributed to the dissonance by terming the United States a "dysfunctional" society and suggesting that Congress was akin to "535 Carolyn Parrishes in one place." McKenna was neither diplomatic nor effective.

International Security: The United Nations and Its Reform

It may well be, in John F. Kennedy's famous sobriquet, that the United Nations is the last best hope of mankind. If so, mankind is in desperate straits, as in mid-2007 never in its spotted history had the United Nations been further from political reality or closer to irrelevance.

THE BASIC PROBLEM

Essentially, the U.N. resists the reality of U.S. power. Or rather, it wishes the U.S. to use its power only for U.N.-endorsed objectives. Many of its members reject U.S. objectives, either because U.S. government objectives threaten their illegitimate regimes or because supporting American objectives would enhance further U.S. power, which is not in their national interests. Quite evidently, the United States has declined to be the ox for the U.N. plow, and it has not deferred to U.N. desires in the pursuit of its national objectives as it perceives them. These dichotomies lie at the root of U.S.-U.N. tensions. They are, however, exacerbated by the U.N.'s institutional inadequacies that are partly structural and partly personalized.

If the United Nations is to "work" as a player in global affairs in the 21st century, it must first regain stature in the eyes of the United States. This is not a clarion call of American hubris, but a pure statement of political reality. A substantial portion of the U.S. political establishment and the electorate have simply given up on the U.N.

It is not that the alphabet soup of expensive "do good" agencies will fold up shop, let alone the chatterbox General Assembly, which proclaims its irrelevance with every over-inflated oration by a marginal "world leader." These agencies, which none but aficionados or their employees can name or identify, will probably continue with their marginal efforts until "all the seas gang dry and the rocks melt with the sun." The essential requirement for a politically relevant United Nations, however, is to engage the United States.

To be sure, the USA has been affected and disaffected with the U.N. in cyclic fashion throughout the organization's history. There have been times when U.S. leadership oozed praise over the organization and others when the U.S. would have happily sent the entire structure (and its diplomats' unpaid parking tickets) to another continent. At the inception of the United Nations, the U.S. was driven by pangs of guilt (by the easily guilt-ridden) that U.S. refusal to support the League of Nations had led to its failure and the Second World War. The U.S., like Canada, threw itself into the process of creating the United Nations, and supported the design of an organization and structure that would indeed keep the peace. It was a victor's organization, reflecting the interests of the victorious allies—no matter how weakened (UK, France), battered (USSR), or faltering (the Republic of China).

This was the United Nations that the United States government rallied in 1950 to oppose North Korea's invasion of the South. The relationship, however, has been largely downhill from there. With the ever-burgeoning dimensions of the General Assembly following global de-colonization came axiomatic majorities that often railed against the United States for whatever happened to be the issue of the day espoused by always-angry third worlders. As a consequence, the U.S. largely ignored the General Assembly and worked within the Security Council to prevent the issue of the moment from gathering any steam. The U.N. was simply another Cold War forum in which inconclusive dialogue substituted for effective action (at least most of the time).

On a personal note, throughout most of my diplomatic career, ranging from 1968 to 1998, the United Nations was a ritualized sideshow where leaders met for their annual preening contests before the UNGA while more important bilateral exchanges were held in delegation embassies or quiet lounges. The U.N. was a talk shop; if there was politicomilitary heavy lifting to be done, the United States went to the NATO alliance, which was doing the serious business of keeping the Soviets from conquering Europe, or took action (in Vietnam, for example, or Grenada, Lebanon, or Panama) either unilaterally or with whatever "coalition of the willing" might be available.

During this period, however, there was a sea change in U.S. response to criticism by U.N. members. For decades, we took the "soft answer turneth away wrath" approach with the implicit hope that once former colonial states matured a bit, they would accept diplomatic norms of exchange and begin to exercise civility rather than bombast. However, playing punching bag paled during the Carter and Reagan administrations, and Ambassadors Patrick Moynihan and Jeane Kirkpatrick responded with tit-for-tat counter comment to criticism. And starting in 1970, the United States began to exercise its Security Council veto which previously it had avoided (and criticized the Soviets for employing).

With the end of the Cold War, the U.S. took another look at the United Nations. Perhaps, just perhaps, it might develop into an organization that could do something serious concerning peacekeeping. And, indeed, when faced with the Iraqi invasion of Kuwait, the most blatant act of aggression since the Nazi attack on Poland in 1939, the U.N. endorsed action to drive Iraqi forces from Kuwait, albeit while refusing to countenance an invasion of Iraq. So, Desert Storm resulted in a brilliant tactical military success that liberated Kuwait but left pending the chore of curbing future Iraqi aggression and coping with its "boxed" but still virulent dictator.

Nevertheless, if potential existed for U.N. peacekeeping following Desert Storm, it quickly ran into the sands. There was disaster in Somalia; there was utter genocidal catastrophe in Rwanda. The U.N. was unable to cope with the disintegration of former Yugoslavia. It fumbled opportunities to assist in Haiti. And, finally and most recently, in U.S. eyes, it worked to aid, abet, and assist Iraq and to thwart U.S. efforts to enforce U.N. resolutions and/or ultimately implement regime change in Baghdad. The U.N. inability to address effectively the apparently endless cycle of death in Darfur was predictable, if pathetic. Currently, the U.N.'s efforts to curb Iran's drive to develop a nuclear weapons capability manifests unwillingness to engage the realities of the Iranian activity with temporizing that simply plays to Tehran's adroit evasiveness.

No matter who mouths what platitudes, many in the United States are now convinced that the U.N. is not just the corrupt and incompetent organization that it has been so frequently, but now also a mechanism that is acting with malicious forethought to combat U.S. interests wherever they fail to align with "old Europe" and Third World desires. In particular the U.N. demonstrates relentless, axiomatic hostility to Israel that is unacceptable to the United States. It is not as if Israel is faultless—far from it. Nor is the United States blind to the generations-long plight of Palestinians, whether led by Fatah or Hamas. However, the absolute inability of most U.N. members to exercise even a scintilla of fair play on the convoluted issues of the region forces the conclusion that these members are driven more by anti-Semitism than by concern for Palestinians.

So, What Can Be Done?

In September 2005, more than 100 heads of government were scheduled to attend U.N. meetings in New York to discuss organizational reforms. It would have taken reform of the most massive and comprehensive nature to restore the U.N. to even marginal credibility. Secretary-General Kofi Annan's reform proposal (presented in March 2005) was more of an illustration of someone reading the writing on the wall when his back is up against it than a proposal that would satisfy the U.N. critics.

With "something for everyone," the Annan reform package satisfied no one sufficiently to secure the endorsement that Annan sought. By seeking, *inter alia*, agreement to a global convention against terrorism, a restructured Security Council, commitment by rich countries to provide 0.7 percent of their GDP to Third World development, and a totally revised Commission on Human Rights—by September 2005—Annan wanted the equivalent of a functional illiterate to write Nobel Prize-winning literature. If an estimated 380,000 to 400,000 dead in Darfur (at that point in the body count) were not enough to convince the U.N. that genocide was occurring, what hope was there for solving hard questions of money and national prestige?

Nevertheless, despite the febrile status of the United Nations, it could be worse. Regardless of the outcome of the 2005 Annan reform package, now under the aegis of newly selected Secretary-General Ban Ki-moon, to prevent the U.N.'s "life support" status from becoming a CSI-style political autopsy, serious steps need be taken. They cannot be delayed and they must be realistically designed.

Select a Capable and Respected Secretary-General

It may be fair; it may be unfair, but prior to his departure at the end of 2006, Secretary-General Kofi Annan was regarded as the first part of the U.N.'s problem. Annan was once the USG (Clinton administration) choice over a second term for Boutros Boutros-Ghali. However, during his tenure, Annan lost support and by 2003 was no longer regarded with any appreciation; moreover, his connection, albeit tenuous, with the vast fraud associated with the Iraq "oil for food" program cost him any residual sympathy. There was simply much too much "smoke" regarding Annan's activity in this regard to assume blithely that there was no "fire." There are those who will always "connect the dots" between his son's profiteering from oil contracts to his obstruction of U.S. efforts to gather a consensus to support Iraqi regime change. The connection is almost too obvious to be true, but...

Nevertheless, whether Kofi Annan was personally responsible for the oil-for-food corruption or profited directly from it is irrelevant. There are enough loops of fiscal cut-outs, hidden bank accounts, plausible denial, and outright deceit to make "Adscam" or "Whitewater" look puerile in comparison. But by being in command, the Secretary-General was responsible. Consequently, there was no question of another term for Annan; indeed, it was regrettable that he had to be endured until the end of his tenure in December 2006.

It is one thing to say "be gone" and another to decide on a replacement. In this regard in 2006, there was a wide range of speculation that the next SYG should be an Asian. Or an Eastern European. Or a woman. Although, in the end, South Korean Ban Ki-moon was selected, it is useful to review the listing of those who have served as secretary-general. Since 1945, there have been four Europeans, two Africans, an Asian, and a Latin American. And, with SYG Ban, there is another Asian on the list. Consequently, one can seriously argue that the next SYG should be from North America: the one continent that has never had a secretary-general. It is the turn of North America. And, in this regard, there really are two relevant "North American" countries: Canada and the United States.

If one looks for a strong Canadian candidate for SYG, either in four or eight years, the obvious 2006 candidates, Brian Mulroney, Paul Martin, and Jean Chrétien, would be effectively disqualified by age (Mulroney born in 1939, Martin in 1938, and Chrétien in 1934). Additionally, Chrétien as prime minister distinguished himself by ignorance of foreign affairs; Martin's (and Chrétien's) hostility to the United States will not be forgotten; and Mulroney is still a dirty word to many Canadians.

Nevertheless, by the time it is necessary to select the next SYG, regardless of his fate as prime minister, Stephen Harper (born in 1959) could be a viable candidate. Presumably he would not be objectionable to the United States, and he could emerge as a compromise selection.

Traditionally, the United States has been excluded from supplying senior leaders for various major institutions due to the perception that the USG already is too powerful. Thus there has never been an American pope, head of NATO, or UNSYG. But by 2010 or 2014 (assuming a second term for SYG Ban) it would be time to cast aside old paradigms and to suggest that an American SYG is the perfect device to re-engage the United States in U.N. activity and, incidentally, provide some intelligent, competent, energetic leadership to the organization.

For the United States, the obvious candidate would be former president William Jefferson Clinton, born in 1946, whose intelligence, political acuity, empathy, and energy have never been doubted—regardless of U.S. domestic questions regarding his personal moral compass. Nor would he necessarily be black-balled by a Republican administration—and a Democratic White House would probably back him strongly. Mr. Clinton has slowly been rehabilitated by good works; Monica has fallen into history. Clinton has made all the money he will ever need. For him, the attraction of the SYG position would be a huge global stage, the expectation of further domestic rehabilitation, and the desire to play a role in international issues such as Middle East peace that were major concerns during his presidency. This would be legacy building *par excellence*.

In any event, simply by advancing former president Clinton as a serious candidate for SYG, the United States would galvanize U.N. membership to seek someone of comparable stature, merit, and energy as competition. And, to be sure, reflexive U.N. hostility to any proposal presented by the U.S. might doom a Clinton candidacy; however, that rejection would be another illustration of the essential problem of the U.N.

Get Better Ambassadors

It can be argued that the U.N. has been getting the ambassadors that it deserves. And while some countries, notably those less powerful, send their best and brightest to act on the biggest available stage, other prominent countries send second-rankers. The United States has taken note of countries whose ambassadors specialize in cheap-shot politicized criticism far past any "diplomatic" requirement. One illustration, for example, highlights the 2002 Security Council debate on the International Criminal Court (ICC).

Without belaboring the substance of the ICC debate, the U.S. refused to make its military forces and civilian personnel subject to ICC authority. Others, including Canada, argued to the contrary, that is, that the U.S. had nothing to fear from the ICC, and the court is a step towards constructing an international legal and moral authority over the perpetrators of heinous war crimes. At first the U.S. sought a UNSC-endorsed exemption for its peacekeeping forces; otherwise, we said that we could not continue to support U.N. peacekeeping mandates, since our leaders could be vulnerable to legal charges regardless of whether our troops participated.

There was room for debate on this topic and the debate was heated. Having called for this debate, Canada's permanent representative to the U.N. led the charge in suggesting that U.S. concerns were frivolous and that UNSC credibility, the legality of international treaties, and the principle that all people are equal and accountable before the law, were at stake. More interestingly, he was also persistently critical of a compromise that exempted U.S. forces from ICC authority for a year. During this time, the U.S. intended to negotiate agreements with various countries where our forces were stationed or likely to operate to the effect that they would not attempt to prosecute U.S. military forces through the ICC. Without such agreements, the U.S. would not participate in U.N. peacekeeping operations. Canada took the opposing role on a subject for which the U.S. was known to have strong feelings. Although Canadian equities were nowhere as deeply engaged as those of the U.S., Ottawa in effect insisted that it knew our interests better than we did. The effort directed by the Canadian representative was designed to embarrass the United States and make it more difficult for us to protect our military personnel and civilian officials effectively. It was one of those topics where U.S. diplomats would be keeping a scorecard count of "for and against" in determining where Washington would give future support (for committee appointments, memberships, and the like). And, as the issue has evolved, the U.S. has completed exemption agreements with its allies—regardless of Canadian fulminations.

Admittedly, for the United States, the quality, political prominence, and bureaucratic weight of its ambassadors also have varied. There have been points when the U.S. ambassador to the U.N. (such as Jeane Kirkpatrick) held cabinet rank (of greater stature than a similar designation in Canada), but those of the past decade, while personally meritorious, often have faded into the NYC wallpaper.

In selecting John Bolton as U.S. ambassador to the U.N., one might say that the messenger was the message. Bolton was a severe and dedicated critic of U.N. incompetence and wrote extensively and vividly of its failures and *realpolitik* irrelevance. The extended Senate fight over Bolton's confirmation in 2005 had nothing to do with senatorial sympathy for the U.N. and everything to do with the Democratic effort to hamstring the Bush administration's effort for domestic Democratic advantage. To be sure, Bolton was a graduate of the Darth Vader School of Management, but that also meant that if he endorsed a U.N. position, it would have been viewed as having greater legitimacy. More likely, however, his blunt words and style would be the diplomatic equivalent of plucking and roasting some pigeons—not just ruffling feathers in the dovecote.

More relevant have been the persistent congressional criticism of many elements of U.N. leadership, policy direction, individual corruption, and general incompetence. In mid-2005, Congress was still considering legislation that would reduce U.S. contributions if the U.N. failed to implement specific reforms. The fate of any specific piece of legislation was less important than the obvious demonstrated hostility to the U.N.

Nevertheless, if truth is to be told, Bolton was one who could tell it. He was thoroughly familiar with the U.N., having been the assistant secretary of state for International Organizations from 1989 to 1993. In 1991, he was a major player in reversing the 1975 UNGA resolution equating Zionism with racism, thus demonstrating that he was uninterested in playing shadow games with those who opposed Israel's existence. He worked effectively within the State Department, leading arms control initiatives that ended Libya's weapons of mass destruction program and, coincident with the termination of the ABM Treaty, helped orchestrate the Treaty of Moscow that eliminated a substantial portion of U.S. and Russian strategic nuclear arsenals. At a minimum, he had Secretary Rice's endorsement as "a strong voice for reform." Although Bolton ultimately withdrew from what was judged to be an unwinnable Senate confirmation effort, until his departure from the U.N. in December 2006 he proved to be less of a bomb-thrower and more of an expert in reconstruction than his critics anticipated.

As of mid-2007, a career diplomat is "acting" as the U.S. permanent representative at the U.N. No candidate for U.N. ambassador has surfaced, and the absence of a nominee is also a message.

Get Better Staff

It is no secret that the U.N. Secretariat is hardly filled with the world's best and brightest. At best, the bureaucracy is elephantine and the struggle to overcome lethargic time servers enervating. At worst, the implicit requirement for at least token representation from all nations results in appointments of the "connected" who concentrate on enjoying the diversions of New York City.

Neither do we see the kind of senior leadership—even when presumably competent—that we should expect. Former Dutch prime minister Ruud Lubbers, as the U.N. High Commissioner for Refugees, could have been a stellar performer in a key portfolio. Instead, he seemed to have had a personal style that resulted in repeated charges of sexual harassment. These accusations were at first ignored by Secretary-General Annan, but finally they resulted in Lubbers' forced resignation in February 2005. Sexual harassment simply isn't 21st century.

There is no easy way to build a capable, honest bureaucracy; it is, however, an absolute essential for effective administration. But stage one must be to eliminate implicit hiring requirements of the marginally qualified. Stage two must be a substantial culling of peripheral (but expensive) "U.N.-crats." It would be draconian but justified to say that the 50,000-plus employees throughout the U.N. structure should be reduced by a third. In this regard, only those whose oxen stand to be gored would cavil at Annan's original proposal to streamline the U.N. Secretariat.

Eliminate the Commission on Human Rights

The commission was broken and it wasn't worth fixing. It seemed to exist only to condemn Israel and refuse to criticize any Third World state. It most recently was headed by Libya and, immediately prior to "Gulf War II," had Iraq as a prominent member. At the same time, the United States was refused a seat in 2001, as was Canada subsequently. The March 2006 agreement to replace the commission with a new Human Rights Council in

June 2006 was necessary, but hardly sufficient; as of mid-2007, the council is unfortunately living down to the expectations of its critics. Indeed, the new council does not even have the requirement of a two-thirds vote by General Assembly members for membership originally proposed by Annan. Its majority vote selection has the same "vote them off the island" limitations of an annual popularity contest, and its passage by a vote of 170 to 4 (including the U.S.) suggests that it will happily include the "usual suspects" in human rights abuse that characterized the commission.

The United States government has agreed to support the new council financially, but it is a hold-your-nose decision. It has not sought membership. And with the council focus for the first year plus of its existence being obsessively devoted to criticism of Israel (by early 2007, eight resolutions condemning Israel had been passed, and no significant attention had been paid to any other issue), positive expectations are minimal; they would be a triumph of hope over experience.

Nevertheless, there is no good answer; the U.S. does not want some human rights group, such as Amnesty International or Human Rights Watch, to be the arbiter for acceptable human rights conduct; the politicized nature of these groups currently is an ignorable irritant but giving them U.N. imprimatur would escalate their unrepresentative conduct. The commission was a noble, idealistic proposal that failed; the council is barely a sop to Cerberus.

THE SECURITY COUNCIL PROBLEM

One of the much threshed-over problems, often cited as in need of reform, is the composition and powers of the Security Council. Consisting of permanent members with veto rights (USA, UK, France, China, and Russia) and rotating non-permanent members without such power, the UNSC either is an antidemocratic device to thwart the will of the majority or a reflection of global political realities—or both. Indeed, U.S. views have evolved over the course of the U.N.'s history. At first, the U.S. was frustrated by constant Soviet vetoes of its Cold War objectives and made a fetish of how Washington didn't use the veto. Subsequently, however, the U.S. used the veto regularly—particularly to prevent invidiously unbalanced resolutions directed against Israel. Unsurprisingly, our criticism of the UNSC veto has diminished.

Nevertheless, the current composition of the UNSC does not reflect global political power. While the United States, Russia, and China remain first-rank world actors, the UK and France no longer qualify. Certainly, an argument can be made that the global power of Germany, Japan, and India is greater than that of the UK and France. Still, there is little likelihood that the UK or France will surrender their UNSC rights in a burst of gratuitous self-abnegation—or be particularly eager to have Germany join them on the UNSC. An abstract observer might raise the suggestion of a "European Community" Security Council membership, but, given the rejections of an EC constitution and its fractious internal debates over a common agricultural policy, let alone a constitution, the likelihood of comity over such a Security Council outcome is minimal.

Likewise, if one consigned the problem of UNSC representation and powers to a committee of "wise persons," the result would be a selection of reasonable, logical, fair solutions—that have as much likelihood of being adopted as you have of flying to the moon on your mental power. The Annan proposal for expanding the UNSC from 15 to 24 members, including six new permanent members, falls into this category of political theory constructs. It ignores, of course, one of the few merits of the current UNSC: it is small enough to have some coherence.

Ultimately, we may end by fiddling around the edges, for instance, by adding "permanent" reps from South Asia and Latin America, but without veto rights. Nevertheless, real UNSC reform probably belongs in the "too hard" box and is not worth the expenditure of effort necessary for tertiary changes. This will disappoint but should not surprise those who want UNSC membership as recognition of their national power.

A PERMANENT U.N. MILITARY FORCE

Currently, when the U.N. wishes to act with military force, it depends on member states to take action in accord with a resolution. Unless a major power, most specifically the United States, is willing to put military muscle into the effort, the implementation of any U.N. resolution is painfully, often pitifully, slow. The U.N. seeks contributions of forces and/or equipment (which in theory are reimbursed). All too often the forces offered are of marginal professional competence and require significant logistical, transportation, communications (etc.) support even to do the minimum required. The most disastrous case in point was the U.N.'s failure to prevent genocide in Rwanda, where, in the absence of a couple of trained combat battalions, over 800,000 people died.

Various cures have been hypothesized for this problem. One proposes that a number of states with demonstrated military competence designate specific military units that could be deployed on short order upon the personal authority of the U.N. secretary-general, or, if that power is regarded as excessive, upon the authorization of the UNSC. Such a multinational "U.N. Standing Force" might be deployed for intervention in mini-crises where the intervention of a few hundred well-trained military personnel would have a good chance of restoring order or preventing humanitarian disaster. A force along these lines, for example, might have been appropriate for Darfur where months now expanding into years have been devoted to begging the substandard-quality armed forces in the area to take action to reduce the ever-spiraling death toll—to no avail. This appeared to be the type of approach hypothesized as a "strategic" military reserve in the secretary-general's 2005 reform package.

However, the very likelihood that such a force could take effective action probably means that it would never be authorized. Those countries where a small outside intervention force could make a difference certainly don't want to make it easier for the U.N. to intervene in their domestic affairs. No nation with a combat element in the standing force would want it deployed without national agreement. Nor would any of the Perm Five on the UNSC want to restrict national freedom of action (even implicitly) by waiting on action by a U.N. force. The conclusion will likely be that those powers with significant military force will continue to act in their perceived interests—particularly if it requires relatively small military deployments. Thus the model of French Foreign Legion troops or British parachute units or U.S. Marines performing a "surgical" military exercise is too seductively efficient to pass off to the questionable competence of the United Nations.

THE MYTH OF THE PEACEKEEPER

A more basic question than the question of a standing U.N. military force is that of today's "peacekeeper." A deliberately ignored circumstance (otherwise a "dirty little secret") is that peacekeepers do not *keep* peace. In current reality, they must first *make* it. If they do not, they are only designated corpse counters and morticians with a multinational mandate. But an effective peacekeeper or peacemaker must first be a real soldier—not a civilian in a uniform. Making peace requires combat capability and an appreciation that peacemakers are going to kill people in the process. Canadians appear to be sorely troubled by this reality, as demonstrated by their reaction to Chief of Defence Staff Rick Hillier's observations in mid-2005. Likewise, when Canada expanded its commitment in Afghanistan in early 2006, there was a negative, "what are we doing *there?*" initial public reaction. Public support for the commitment appears grudging rather than profound; Prime Minister Harper's dramatic March 2006 visit to Afghanistan prompted a surge in public support that has wavered but largely endured. His subsequent visit in May 2007 had little obvious domestic effect. Consequently, the May 2006 commitment to remain in Kandahar until 2009 has the appearance of clever "gotcha" parliamentary tactics by the Tories rather than being the consequence of a thought-through national decision. The knife-edge parliamentary decision to continue the commitment only technically resolved the debate. During the Liberal leadership campaign, the contenders were clearly divided over Canada's role, and Stephane Dion's enthusiasm for stay-the-course logic was certainly muted. The interim Liberal decision appears implicitly to label Afghanistan as "Mr. Harper's War" and permit him to carry the weight of each new body bag. That Afghanistan is a NATO commitment under a U.N. mandate is an abstraction; individual deaths (56 in May 2007) are a reality. Thus a new government could easily mean a new Afghan policy.

Although it is a generalization, there were few peace*makers* throughout the Cold War, as combat in Third World areas usually continued until the proxies of the U.S. or the USSR were exhausted (or had exhausted the interest of their sponsors). There were, however, selected peace*keepers* in which the sides had separated and a U.N. force to monitor the resulting "green line" was useful. Hence, Cyprus is the classic illustration where trained professional soldiers were able to deal with the stone- and insult-throwers without panicked firing.

There were a very few countries that had good soldiers and were acceptable to both sides in the Cold War. Canada was one of these countries and filled the niche market. That is no longer the case: Canadian U.N. peacekeepers are out of this action, and now U.N. "peacekeepers" are more frequently those of marginal competence who are rented out by their countries to the U.N. for hard currency.

A NEW UNITED NATIONS

On its 50th birthday in 1995, and again at the Millennium Summit in 2000, there was considerable hope for the U.N. and its prospects. As its 60th birthday approached, however, there was general recognition that the organization was failing. There are life cycles for institutions as well as for humans and machines, and the U.N. was and still is facing the bureaucratic equivalent of mid-life crisis—and/or obsolescence. A serious argument can be made for throwing it out and starting over; however, assuming the practicalities make this approach impossible, one turns to reform—only to crash on the questions of reform what? How? When?

Fiddling around the edges of the line-and-block charts is highly unsatisfactory. Essentially, this was the content of Secretary-General Annan's 2005 package, regardless of its ultimate outcome. There are many obvious points for revision; two are prominent: we can, and should, adjust the U.N. "dues" structure; we can, and should, eliminate risible organs such as the now abolished Commission on Human Rights (and give serious consideration to dis-establishing its successor Human Rights Council). These are necessary but hardly sufficient actions. The truth remains for any organization that good people can make a badly structured organization run well, but bad people will assure that the best organizational structure fails. From top-to-bottom, the U.N. needs better personnel; until they are installed, the U.N. will continue to bleed credibility and relevance as it limps from scandal to scandal towards an end that is not a bang but a whimper.

THE MILITARY: PRIMARY OR ANCILLARY IN INTERNATIONAL RELATIONS 8

Both Canada and the United States have military forces. With this statement, the parallelism largely ends. The United States' military is large and immensely powerful; Canada's is limited and weak. Yet Canada is as likely to use its armed forces as is the United States. Indeed, Canada may use its limited forces to their fullest capability while the massive U.S. nuclear forces have served as a deterrent rather than being directly employed.

Following the Second World War, the United States moved to the front rank in defending Western (and its own) freedom and security. Canada participated in the NATO alliance and in multiple peacekeeping missions; however, Canada increasingly abdicated the defense of North America to the U.S., and Canada clearly did not contribute to the corporate military effort at a level proportionate to its potential.

Currently Canadian defense capabilities are at low ebb, the country's armed forces increasingly unable to respond to prospective challenges in any dimension—either internal security, peacekeeping, or direct combat. Proposed budget increases fall into the "it remains to be seen" category rather than anything the Canadian forces or Canada's allies can rely upon.

The end of the Cold War did not end "history" as had been implied by Francis Fukuyama's extended essay and anticipated by the self-deluded. Instead, history twisted into new-old forms with international and intranational violence no longer taking place under ideological sponsorship. The level of bloodshed is not more than the historical standard, but it is forcing new examination of old paradigms regarding peacekeeping.

The defense of North America has new dimensions. The threat is no longer Soviet bombers and missiles, but rogue states continue to prompt a U.S. missile defense program. Nevertheless, post 9/11, the demands of antiterrorism are primary, and they prompt domestic security efforts not even contemplated since the Second World War.

Although this defense is a U.S. imperative—and should be a comparable imperative for Canada—questions remain in Washington over whether Ottawa's commitment is more than lip service. The deterioration of previous bilateral comity has exacerbated the difficulties in addressing these new challenges.

The Canadian Military

THE ORIGINS OF CANADIAN DEFENSE POLICY

The history of Canada's military in recent decades has been mostly one of serious personnel shortages, aging equipment and weapons, and serious morale problems. It was not always so; from its origins in New France to the Korean War, Canada's armed forces performed duties bravely and competently. Indeed, our army, navy, and air force were among the most feared and respected during the Second World War.

In spite of the many occasions on which Canadians had cause to be proud of their military, the attitude that many now hold towards it has been one of lack of interest at best and disdain at worst. In stark contrast to the intense pride that many Americans feel about their armed forces (whether or not they agree with the cause in which they are employed), Canadian indifference towards our own armed forces has manifested itself in over four decades of severe budget and personnel cutbacks.

The root of Canada's departure from American enthusiasm for things military is thought by some to reside in our historical and continued opposition to the idea of a professional army. One of the central myths in Canada (aside from the hoariest one, that Canadians do not need an army because everyone likes us and our close cousin so much that there is no way Canada would ever be a target) is that citizens are, and should be, the primary providers of our own defense. Since our settlers and citizens of the day were enough to defend our pre-Confederation colonies against the unwanted advances of both Americans and indigenous peoples, the notion that this would be good enough to defend Canada against all threats at all times was created.

Citizen militias were certainly instrumental in repelling would-be invaders, but in view of the revolutionary changes to the geopolitical climate since the War of 1812, the construct that an untrained, volunteer citizen army is all Canada now needs to protect herself has become dangerously unsustainable. It was unsustainable by the beginning of the First World War in 1914, and is even more so today.

In an age of terrorism, questions of Canada's sovereignty and independence in matters of foreign policy have become incrementally important. Because of our geographical position next to the world's great superpower, we have had the dubious privilege of not having to maintain a large army to protect ourselves from would-be invaders. Because Canada also shares land, waterways, air, and space with the United States, in addition to a border, our neighbor has been responsible, over recent decades, for the aspects of Canadian security that are necessary to guarantee its own. Canadians and successive governments in Ottawa have been more than willing to accommodate the U.S. in this endeavor. When it comes to allowing the United States in on Canada's foreign policy views, however, Canadians have proven much more independent.

Much of the national conversation about foreign policy priorities revolves around economic and geographic relationships with the United States and their implications. Many observers argue that our bilateral relations with the U.S. are the very backbone of Canada's foreign policy. Since the events of 9/11, moreover, relations with the U.S. have become more crucial than ever, due to the ever increasing intensity of indiscriminate security threats springing from a wide variety of non-state sources.

THE UNITED STATES AND CANADA'S MILITARY

Among Canada's relations with other nations, in terms of economics and space, none approaches by a country mile the significance of our relationship with the United States. It is where the most crucial of Canada's external interests really lie. With about $2 billion in goods crossing the common border on a daily basis, Canadians simply cannot afford to take the economic and security relationship for granted. We have too much at stake. Those who are in favor of a more integrated North America assert that Canada's dependence on the United States for economic well-being and security are such that Canada simply cannot risk the closure of or disruption along the border if—or more likely when—there are future terrorist or military attacks against the continent. Like it or not, 9/11 means that continental defense has returned to the forefront of Canadian defense policy.

Since 1989, Americans have generally indulged Canada's diplomatic relations with Cuba, our opposition to landmines, and our greater tolerance (in some circles) for marijuana. In spite of a history of American acceptance of Canada's independence in the foreign policy arena, 9/11 and the War on Terror have brought a new era in bilateral relations. Canada's lukewarm response to American zeal for the War on Terror has placed new strains on the at times tense relationship between the two countries.

After Prime Minister Jean Chrétien opted not to have Canada join President Bush's "coalition of the willing" in Iraq, Bush scrapped a planned visit in 2003, although he did come in November 2004, and proceeded to call for closer relations with Mexico. When Canada, under Paul Martin's prime ministership, declined to participate in the proposed Ballistic Missile Defense (BMD) program, Secretary of State Condoleezza Rice delayed indefinitely her planned April 2005 trip to Ottawa—she finally arrived in October of that year. She was reportedly furious that Martin chose to announce his decision not to take part in BMD shortly before the Liberal party's policy convention and gave virtually no prior warning to Washington, despite earlier intimations that Canada would participate. The timing of the Martin decision gave the appearance of putting the views of Liberal party delegates ahead of good relations with a neighbor on a key bilateral issue.

With that neighbor as Canada's biggest trading partner by far and, should the situation call for it, our ultimate defender, can Canadians afford to continue to pursue and maintain an independent foreign policy and national sovereignty? The "you're either with us or against us" mantra that has defined the limits of President Bush's tolerance for opinions that differ from those of his administration presents one of the largest current challenges to Canada's foreign policy independence during a period of increasing global insecurity.

When one country depends upon another for part of its basic security needs, there are bound to be implications for the dependent's national sovereignty. At the very least, it is clear that the voice of the dependent country in foreign defense matters is less likely to be heard. It is precisely the concept of *influence* that is so problematic when it comes to Canada's foreign relations. How can Canada persuade the U.S. to accept a vision of multilateralism in dealing with the rest of the world when Canada itself is currently bringing almost nothing except essentially hollow rhetoric to the discussion?

Not surprisingly, the carrot the Canadian government held out to the United States when trying to dissuade it from its unilateralist ambitions in Iraq was woefully insufficient. Canadians could lend some much needed legitimacy to the American operations in Iraq, but so what? For President George W. Bush, his nation's support (or nonsupport, depending on whom you talk to), previous U.N. resolutions, backed up by the still glowing embers of 9/11 (so to speak) and the belief that Iraq held WMD stockpiles, as well as the world's largest military capability by far, was all the legitimacy he needed. Since Canada clearly had no corresponding stick, the Bush administration was probably not even tempted to listen to any of the justifiable concerns about a war in Iraq that were articulated by the Canadians and shared by much of the world.

For Americans, however, the point was less that Canada demurred from an invitation to join the "willing"—Canada was hardly alone in that stance—than the manner in which it rejected the U.S. views. There was a level of personalized, almost contemptuous commentary from official Canadians (as well as vituperative media) that suggested not only that the United States was wrong in its judgments, but that it had no right to take action without international sanction. In contrast, Mexico, whose opposition to the Bush administration's action against Iraq was similar to Canada's, made its points without public confrontations. As one American noted, "So much for the adage of cool heads in the North and tempestuous Latin emotionalism in the South."

CANADIAN DEFENSE STRATEGY

Canada's defense policy under its Prime Minister Stephen Harper is probably still subject to the lingering consequences of the long outdated 1994 White Paper written under the Chrétien Liberal government. The paper ranked defense policy objectives as, in descending order, protecting Canada, cooperating with the United States in the defense of North Americans, and contributing to international security. These goals were restated at least in part in Paul Martin's 2004 National Security Policy and again in his 2005 International Policy Statement.

The aims of the 1994 White Paper themselves are laudable, but Ottawa has not provided the forces before or since with enough resources to achieve the goals. The Conference of Defence Associations noted in 2002, in *A Nation at Risk*, that although Canada is "the second largest country in the world in area, with the largest coastline," Canada is "essentially incapable of defending itself against all but minimal incursions," a judgment that was reinforced by Canada's Senate Committee on National Security and Defence in a 2003 report.

Evidence for this assertion was provided by fairly recent activities by the Americans and the Danes in the Canadian Arctic. In 2003, a United States Coast Guard ship sailed the Northwest Passage in the Canadian Arctic in defiance of Canadian claims to the waterway, reaffirming the American position that the passage is an international waterway. In 2004, Danish sailors laid claim to Hans Island in the Arctic by planting a flag on the island in a bid to have it recognized as Danish territory. In both intrusions, our military were incapable of putting a halt to the incursions and were relegated to standing by, watching helplessly. Canada's efforts to assert sovereignty regarding Hans Island during 2005 were frequently characterized as belated and provocative (when they were not being dismissed as amusing "filler" for summer media reporting).

Just as worrisome is Canada's role when it comes to North American defense. If Canadian Forces can't even prevent incursions onto Canadian territory, how will they be able to stop security threats to the entire continent? This incapacity to represent a legitimate line of defense to both Canada and North America will have serious implications on the independence of Canada's foreign affairs and defense policy. If Ottawa, for lack of resources and viable alternatives, is inevitably forced to surrender the North American defense mandate to the Americans, it is inevitable that Canada's sovereignty and reputation will be severely undermined.

On international security, look no further than the limited projection, deployment, and sustainment capacities of the Canadian Forces as proof of our current national incapacity. In order to deploy troops to Afghanistan after 9/11, our military was forced to rely on American and rented strategic airlift to move personnel and equipment overseas. Had the rented and American aircraft not been available, it would have been all but impossible for Canada to transport our critical operational units to Afghanistan. If Canada cannot even respond to calls for help in the face of the worst terrorist attack on North American soil from its closest friend and neighbor without outside assistance, how can it expect to defend itself, North America, and vulnerable countries abroad substantively?

NEW WORLD ORDER

A fundamental paradigm shift seems to have occurred in the way that many Canadians view the role of our military at home and in the world, which was well summed up by Michael Ignatieff's argument: "There is something very curious about the way the military spine that was a part of the central national identity of our culture has just slipped away, so that when you make a claim in defence of national defence and military expenditure, you are ultimately regarded as some kind of foaming-at-the-mouth warmonger."

The essential bedrock that supports the idea of international law and multilateralism is the ability of the U.N., as the ultimate dispenser of the use of legitimate force, to use international law effectively to prevent the degeneration of states into conflict and to pursue and bring to justice those who violate it. The view that the United Nations is the "ultimate dispenser of the use of legitimate force" is both incorrect in law and misguided in design. International law recognizes the right of self-defense both by individual nations and alliances; the thought that a nation could not defend itself without U.N. imprimatur contradicts the very essence of state sovereignty.

In such a world order, the sovereignty of nations would not be boundless, but instead defined by a framework of human rights agreements and multilateral engagements. When nations such as Iraq and, more recently, Sudan, disregard U.N. orders, the multilateralism and international order that Canada so supports is undermined severely.

If the U.N. cannot get a national government to obey its orders peacefully, then international law and the potential for multilateralist solutions are thwarted, especially when the majority of countries in the world do not have the capacity of the United States to compel a rogue state to desist from what it is doing to its own people or others. If Canadians truly believe that there is a place for international law and cooperation between countries to enforce it in the world, then we must put our resources where our mouth is and back up an international system with a force that is adequate to stop international violence.

It is important to stress that the problem with the Canadian attitude towards our military lies not with our intentions, but with our general understanding of the new situation the world now faces. Canadians are not seeking to get away with doing less than our share, while simultaneously looking down on countries like the United States, morally self-satisfied because we are not warmongers. It is the real nature of the world that has developed in the post-Cold War years that we Canadians do not seem to have fully grasped. In fairness, Canadians have called for humanitarian intervention and the right to intervene in certain cases.

In the age of terror, the nature of international conflict has taken on a borderless dimension. Today's front lines are said to stretch from the streets of Kabul and Baghdad, to the rail tracks of Madrid and London, and across cities in Canada and the United States. It is naive to believe that, if given the means and the opportunity, terrorists would hesitate to strike in Canada. Although it is certainly safe to assume that Canadians are not targets of terror on the same level as Americans, we must also remember that no one ever thinks that the unthinkable will happen to them until it does. As America's closest neighbor and, for better or worse, "best friend," Canadians cannot afford to assume that we are not on the terrorist radar. We most certainly are—as various terrorist plans, among them those identified for the Toronto area in June 2006, clearly demonstrate.

At the same time, it is hard to blame Canadians for our assumption that we are not a target. After all, we have a well-deserved reputation as one of the best countries in the world to live in. When traveling, Canadians are warmly welcomed in almost all parts of the world, including many countries in which Americans aren't so welcome. On the other hand, after a generation of seeking to be loved and agonizing over the "ugly American" appellation, many Americans have come to the realization that nobody loves Goliath—and any Goliath in any age looks a little silly when complaining over a lack of affection.

What Canadians do not seem to understand is that we are the very rare exception, rather than the rule. If citizens of all nations in the world were welcomed, and welcomed as heartily as Canadians seem to be, Canadian attitudes towards the military would be more justifiable. In such a world of peace and harmony among nations, there would be no need for arms. Of course Canadians may be mistaking this "hearty welcome" for appreciative respect rather than the international recognition that Canada is a wealthy, non-threatening state whose citizens can be economically exploited—and whose government cannot effectively protect them. To Canada's eternal national shame, or at least that of a feeble national government at the time, nothing equivalent to the torture, rape, and murder of photojournalist Zahra Kazemi by the government of Iran, her country of origin before becoming a Canadian citizen, has ever happened to a U.S. citizen without significant U.S. government response.

What Canadians have not yet come to terms with really is that conflict is and will be a part of the global reality now and for many years to come. The conflicts that threaten the world now have grown tougher and meaner; the basic rules of war are routinely ignored, and oppressive leaders have not hesitated to resort to any means necessary, even if it means tremendous harm to massive numbers of people, as in Darfur. World conflicts really are probably no tougher or meaner than in the past. One might suggest a review of the manner in which the Communists seized control of Russia and subjugated their dissidents prior to the Second World War; the Chinese Civil

War and its aftermath; the brutality of the fighting on the Eastern Front in the Second World War, or the human losses in the Spanish Civil War. War is indeed hell.

The assumption that security goals should be focused on human security rather than state security ignores the reality that, without the latter, there can be no human security. The quaint notion that the military has no role to play in ensuring human security is a misjudgment that has had and will continue to effect a serious toll on the losses that the Canadian Forces and civilian populations in conflict-ridden areas sustain. The requirements of seemingly conventional peacekeeping operations have grown so onerous that they have now been displaced to what can be described as peace enforcement "warfare" or "war monitoring."

This leads some to the conclusion that Lloyd Axworthy's "soft power" might better be labeled "flaccid folly." As the world is now observing yet again in Darfur, diplomacy, regardless of how artful or adroit, without a military component to back it up, is futile. A population's human rights, economic progress, and social advancement cannot take place without physical security. Indeed, the first welfare objective of a "welfare state" is the defense of its people. If such cannot be secured by the resources of the state, it must be sought within alliances or collective security agreements. And the key component to such security is good weapons, not good words.

Because successive governments in Ottawa have allocated to our armed forces funds that fit budgetary requirements, rather than their operational needs, our forces were forced to face the heightened risks, with shortages in effective equipment, and not enough human resources. By far the greatest human rights challenge that Canada and the world face is providing basic existential security for civilian populations in states such as Sudan, Afghanistan, and Iraq.

Development agencies and relief workers, often considered the front lines in the struggle to provide the most basic essentials of human life, cannot even get on the ground to establish rudimentary frameworks of viability if there is no order. Humanitarian agencies continue to be squeezed out of Darfur by the government of Sudan and its Janjaweed killers, who want no foreigners with cameras present so that they can complete their elimination of African Darfurians. Electricity, communications, and other infrastructure cannot commence if there is no order. An effective government, police, and courts cannot be established if there is no order. It can probably be safely said that most Canadians, being fortunate enough to have the standard of living that they have, would agree that all of the above are indispensable to a society in which "peace, order, and good government" can reign.

In this way, peacekeeping and the "human security" policy directives that have come to define Canadian foreign affairs and defense policy informally are necessarily intertwined with a greater role for the Canadian Forces in both foreign and domestic policy. If Canada cannot back its peacekeeping, multilateralist approach with the force required to sustain it, then the independence of its foreign policy, its reputation as a leading protector of human rights, and its very sovereignty will be at stake.

THE FUTURE OF THE MILITARY

Although some Canadians would point to the fact that the Martin government ostensibly committed to boosting military and defense spending over the mid-to-long term, the new funds were primarily directed towards sustaining the fading capabilities of the forces, which are in desperate need of rescuing. For decades now, our military has had to do more with less on pitifully low budgets, which has pitted the overwhelming needs of keeping the existing army in operation against its future needs, which will be just as pressing as the present. In the end, all you can do with less is less. Ever decreasing budgets, even with brief resuscitations, are forcing military and defense officials to draw funds reserved for future military development to pay the overhead and maintenance bills of the present.

Douglas J. Bland in *Canada Without Armed Forces?* analogizes this undertaking with dumping fuel from an airplane to lighten its load to get a few more miles before it runs out of gas and crashes to the ground. In the 1990s alone, our forces went to war twice, while sustaining countless peacekeeping operations, continuing day-to-day tasks at home and abroad, and taking mounting hits to its budget. After 9/11, when all former assumptions about North American security crumbled like the Twin Towers, the campaign in Afghanistan exhausted the resources of the Canadian Forces so much that General Raymond Henault declared in 2003, "We are going to be limited in our ability to provide any sizeable land force contribution elsewhere on the international scene for the 12 months [after the Afghan deployment ended in 2004]." However, Canada renewed its Afghanistan efforts in 2004-05 and again in 2006 with force levels of approximately 2,500 in the Kandahar area by mid-2007 and a continuing, costly combat role in the region that will only become more expensive in lives and treasure.

The Harper government faces some tough policy choices regarding the direction that Canada's defense policy will take. Perhaps the most serious is the imminent collapse of the Canadian Forces core operations capabilities, which will inevitably disarm Canadian defense policy. Canada will then be forced to withdraw from international commitments for lack of adequate military resources.

Canadians need not look very far to see where a lack of adequate combat force, as opposed to "war monitoring," allowed for atrocities of horrifying proportions. In 1993, Canadian Lieutenant General Roméo Dallaire watched helplessly as, over the course of 100 days, extremist Hutu militias massacred at least 800,000 of their Tutsi countrymen. Dallaire was powerless to stop the bloodshed, as Belgian and then a small number of other U.N. forces fled the country. He later estimated that a small strike force of 3,500 soldiers would have been sufficient to stop the killing. In *Shake Hands with the Devil*, Dallaire noted that the government of Canada would not permit him to take any Canadian soldiers with him to Rwanda as he began his command of the U.N. mission.

The pledge of "No more Rwandas," a pledge given by the world and backed by Canada after the massacre, cannot be fulfilled unless Canada is ready to act where other nations lack the means or political will. Canada's reputation as a leading peacekeeper among nations cannot be sustained unless Canada can step in and lead, by example, if necessary.

Even if the Harper government raises military spending immediately and substantially, it is too late for the Canadian Forces to avoid crisis. Many blame this potential disaster on the failure of successive Canadian governments to respond appropriately to the fundamental changes to global security in the post-Cold War landscape in Canada's defense policy, which arguably occurred in the mid-1990s. If Canada is to avoid even greater problems, our government cannot afford to keep driving the Canadian Forces deeper into the ground.

Had the government taken a critical look at the state of the military in the mid-1990s and honestly reassessed its current and future needs, the forces would not be in the perilous state they are in today. In 2007 the predicament caused by Canada's seemingly intentional disarmament is upon the nation and poses a serious threat to Canada's hard-won and honorable legitimacy and influence in the international community. The 2007 budget proposals for defense expenditures and the announcements of projected equipment upgrades during the first year of the Tory government appear to be more a hostage to the continuation of the Harper government than a national commitment to revive Canadian defense structures.

Canada's sovereignty as a nation, seemingly placed absentmindedly into the hands of the United States through the neglect of the Canadian Forces for decades, could become increasingly unsure as the U.S. continues to take measures to combat terrorism and protect its homeland from external threats. Canada's very commitment to the principles of open societies and democracy could be questioned in like-minded nations worldwide as the perception grows that a very way of life is possibly at stake.

It has become fashionable to argue that, instead of increasing military expenditures, Canada needs to reduce its commitments abroad and clarify priorities in order to make the hard choices that must be made if the future of the Canadian Forces is to be salvaged. It cannot be denied that both the quantity and quality of Canada's commitments abroad have multiplied and changed rapidly over the past 30 years. At the same time, the resources for Canadian contributions overseas have declined drastically in response to the attitude of fiscal prudence that has risen on the one hand, and the principle of "health care first" on the other, both of which policies have enjoyed a high degree of popularity among Canadians.

As a result, in the absence of a well thought out consensus on where Canada's defense priorities lie, Canada's operations overseas have become many kilometers wide and a centimeter deep. The consequence of such thinly distributed resources is that the Canadian Forces have become a token of Canadian involvement in international affairs everywhere, without having a decisive impact anywhere.

In response, recent years have seen the rise of the "niche diplomacy" approach, wherein the efforts of the Canadian Forces abroad are more focused, with an emphasis on doing the most good possible. Within this type of framework, the government would be pressed to make some difficult decisions about when and where Canadians can exercise their commitment to security and humanitarian principles. There are many who now argue that Canada is already in an era of niche diplomacy, in which Canada is already placing its military not where it may be needed most, but rather where it is perceived that it can do the most good.

SWEEPING REFORM
We are not living in a world of diminishing commitments that allow for fewer, less costly operations. Instead, Canada faces a world not even dreamed of

at the conclusion of the Cold War, yet the assumptions made then continue to affect Canada's defense policy today and threaten its future tomorrow. Far from being the peaceful and diplomatic society envisioned then, the age of terror has brought Canada growing commitments which are extremely costly in equipment, weaponry, and human lives. Canada's military and security commitment have not decreased, but grown, as exponentially as terror cells across the world. While Canada's perceived obligations have grown drastically, the Canadian government's commitment to an effective, capable, and prepared military has only decreased ever more rapidly.

So what is to be done with Canada's military? Past policies have all but eliminated any reserve the Canadian Forces might have had and any new ones would cut into the military's already sparse core capabilities. One thing is for certain: the looming foreign policy crisis cannot and will not be solved by dissolving the few capabilities that still remain. Spending out of the crisis may seem like the only option for the present government, but it must be noted that during the Cold War arms buildup, it took several years for the government to match supply with demand; this measure would do nothing to resolve the immediate foreign policy crisis that faces Canadians.

Canadians ought to realize that the current military situation is a problem that only time, not money, can remedy. However, without the money, the amount of time is irrelevant. Shortly there will be no problem, because the Canadian forces will be too broken to fix. Even with money, it will take as long to repair the Canadian forces as it took them to decline—a period more akin to decades than to years.

It will take years of critical defense strategy to turn policy goals into military fact. Leaders must be trained, equipment built, and capabilities fashioned. For the time being, however, Canadians must come to terms with the fact that Canada will have to accept a diminished role in continental defense, world affairs, and perhaps even Canada's own security. Building future defense policy based on the present will only weaken Canada's national security and defense and will disable its foreign policy on many fronts. Canada's effective disarmament and all the consequences that will bring will arrive sooner, rather than later, if the current trend of defense policy is allowed to continue. Canada's military problems will only become more expensive, more time-consuming, and more difficult to reverse as time goes on. Only a sweeping reform and reassessment of Canada's defense policy now can give Canadians a glimmer of hope in rescuing the military from the void.

The United States

THE ORIGINS OF U.S. DEFENSE POLICY

- The United States as "Robocop," monster-mashing through the tulips of international relations;
- The United States as a "hyperpower" equipped with only one tool—military force—viewing world problems as nails to be hammered;
- The United States as a "rogue elephant" led by a "red-state cowboy," spending more on its armed forces than approximately the next 190 states combined.

In North America these caricatures were illustrated by the 2003 *Time* magazine choices for "Man of the Year." In its U.S. edition, the selection was The American Fighting Man; for Canada, it was the first homosexual marriage.

And, indeed, the televised images of world-ranging U.S. combat infantry in camouflage flak jackets and night vision goggles bearing infantry squad weapons of recent design look more like the science fiction vision of futuristic warriors than anything out of the history books. Likewise, the unprecedented military efficiency with which U.S. forces eliminated a previously unbeaten Afghan resistance fighter government and annihilated Iraqi conventional forces in short order has reinforced the image of the Western gunslinger with a made-in-USA tattoo on his forehead. Even those who wish to depict the United States as "bogged down" in Iraq cannot realistically project its military (versus political) defeat.

But the caricature is just that—a fragment of the reality and more akin to a figment of the imagination. It is useful to recall whence the United States has evolved regarding its view of armed forces.

In its earliest days, the United States was peopled by colonists and immigrants who were largely anti-military; for philosophical and fiscal reasons, they were hostile to a standing army of any significant dimensions. A large number of the first colonists, notably Massachusetts pilgrims and Puritans, Pennsylvania's Quakers, and other dissenting church groups, were essentially religiously motivated pacifists. If they resorted to arms, it was more in self-defense against marauding Indians or attacks by French-Canadians than as aggressive expansion. During almost 150 years of life as English subjects, the American colonies looked to English military power to protect them.

To be sure, the colonists were not unarmed sheep. They were familiar and comfortable with firearms: muskets; "fowling pieces" (shotguns); and rifles were pieces of working equipment for farmers. A gunsmith was a standard colonial craftsman, although making rifles (muskets were usually imported) was only a small part of his business, and repairing weapons absorbed most of his time. The individual colonies also had militias that were indifferently led, trained, and equipped, but were designed to counter Indian incursions and to support British forces as auxiliaries during the long series of battles with the French in Canada, which was the North American reflection of generations-long combat in Europe. During this period, the colonists began to develop a few semi-professional military leaders. Most noteworthy would be George Washington, who accompanied a British expedition to seize a French fort at Pittsburgh. The expedition was a disaster, the British commander was killed, and British redcoats were virtually annihilated by the French and the Indians firing from concealed positions while the British soldiers, in European style, stood openly in ranks. American colonists had advised against this tactic (and when the French/Indians attacked, the colonists took cover); their opinion of English military competence declined.

When the Revolutionary War started, the colonists consisted of groups of minutemen militia with only a semblance of military training and structure. They were indeed "summer soldiers" and "sunshine patriots," so when fighting left their area (or the crops needed harvesting or the going got tough), most just went home. During the winter and spring of 1777-78, 2,500 of the 11,000 remnants of the Revolutionary Army died of various causes at Valley Forge. Only intensive drills by European professional soldiers provided sufficient training and discipline to match British/Hessian professionals. And, at the end of the war in 1781, the French provided the majority of the land forces at Yorktown and the French navy defeated a British fleet coming to relieve Yorktown and prevented the evacuation of Cornwallis' forces.

In terms of the U.S. attitude towards the armed forces, the Revolutionary War left two important legacies: a conviction that a volunteer citizen soldiery is sufficient for the defense of the nation and a concomitant mistrust of a standing professional army; and an appreciation for the coincidence of military and political leadership and a recognition that military service is a basic form of service to the nation.

The Citizen in Arms

In the view of the average citizen, the minutemen had done rather well. By and large, it had been local militias that pushed the British out of Boston and provided the forces that defeated the British at Saratoga. It had been local troops that dogged the tracks of Cornwallis during his fighting in the southern colonies before being penned up in Yorktown. There was no special interest in giving the French professional soldiers credit (and after 1789 those French that had helped the struggling colonies were on their way to the guillotine).

The prototypical American hero was Washington—and Washington had in effect copied the legendary Roman leader Cincinnatus, who, after leading Romans to victory, returned to his farm.

Moreover, American colonists had a severe distaste for their experience with British professional soldiers. One complaint in the Declaration of Independence addressed the British habit of quartering troops in civilian homes; the civilians were responsible for feeding and sheltering them (and one can be sure that there were less savory concerns about soldiers' actions beyond what they ate and drank).

There also remained a substantial strain of religious pacifism in the colonies. In subsequent years, many immigrants were escaping military service in Europe. There was the generation of war that swept Europe between the beginning of the French Revolution in 1789 and Waterloo in 1812; the results of the 1848 revolutionary efforts in Germany; the Irish famine (and British military control over Ireland). None of these immigrants were enthusiastic about armies.

Additionally, a professional army is never cheap, and the armies of the 18th and 19th centuries were not manned by "the boy next door." The United States never really adopted the Chinese maxim that "just as you don't make good iron into nails, you don't make good men into soldiers," but being a soldier was often a career of last resort; without draconian discipline, soldiers were often armed alcoholics of questionable morality. Consequently, if the country could avoid a standing military force (the U.S. did not have hostile powers within immediate striking distance of its borders), it could save money and social problems by having no more than minimal military forces. And such essentially was the path that the United States followed until after the Second World War; that is, retaining as small a professional army as possible, and expanding when faced with a crisis by enlisting militia and volunteers for military action. It recognized that a cadre of professional officers was useful, but also trained these officers as civil engineers who were frequently the surveyors and construction supervisors for public works as the United States expanded into the West.

Consequently, one saw an accordion effect in the size of the U.S. Armed Forces. Swollen by volunteers during crises, they would sink precipitously during the intermissions between wars.

For example, the estimate of those who served in the Revolutionary War (217,000) and the War of 1812 (286,000) is far greater than those estimated as serving in the West for the 80 years between 1817 and 1898 (106,000) during the "Indian Wars." The war with Mexico (1846-48) involved only 78,000 servicemen. During the Civil War (1861-65), an estimated 2.2 million from both North and South served in the Union and Confederate armies, but 30 years later, at the beginning of the Spanish American War, the regular army was weak and the government called for 125,000 volunteers. Forces employed were small (17,000 in Cuba; 11,000 in the Philippines; 3,300 in Puerto Rico). Shortcomings in military performance during the war led to the creation of a general staff and, in 1902, congressional authorization of an army of 100,000.

U.S. entrance into the First World War, in April 1917, prompted a massive force increase, including conscription, ultimately totaling over 4.7 million in service. As soon as the war ended, however, force levels again dropped; the National Defense Act of 1920 authorized a regular army with a maximum enlisted strength of 280,000, but Congress soon reduced that to below 150,000. The 1920 act contemplated a National Guard of 436,000, but its actual peacetime strength stabilized at about 180,000.

Thus, on the eve of the Second World War, the U.S. was of trivial military consequence. One estimate ranked our army below Bulgaria's. The U.S. population was profoundly skeptical of foreign entanglements; it had been treated to congressional hearings outlining the massive profits of "merchants of death" during the First World War, and it believed the United States was both geographically invulnerable and morally superior to European states. Additionally, the U.S. was bound by a variety of "neutrality acts" designed to prevent involvement in foreign conflicts, making no distinction between aggressor and victim. It was only after the war began in September 1939 that the United States instituted a peacetime military draft—and that was to be for only one year. Consequently, immediately prior to the attack on Pearl Harbor in December 1941, the extension of the peacetime draft was approved by a single vote. This exceptionally close vote is excoriated as an illustration of political blindness, but it was equally based on the political commitment to a time-limited draft agreed to only one year earlier.

To be sure, even prior to Pearl Harbor, U.S. forces were expanding, reaching 1.5 million by mid-1941 and ultimately expanding to over 16 million serving between 1941 and 1945. After the war concluded, however, the focus was demobilization: by 1950, on the eve of the Korean War, the U.S. Army was the principal occupation force in Europe and in Japan, but it had a total of 591,000 soldiers in 10 divisions in Japan, Europe, and the U.S. The reserve component included 730,000 soldiers and 27 divisions.

With North Korea's communist invasion of South Korea, again U.S. force levels surged. This time, with the societal appreciation of the Soviet threat and a Cold War, they stayed high. Total armed forces personnel during the three years of the Korean War were above 5.7 million; during the long struggle in Vietnam, over 9.2 million served worldwide in U.S. forces.

U.S. DEFENSE STRATEGY

In a previous chapter, there is discussion of the issues of unilateral versus multilateral international action. U.S. strategy for the defense of North America is comparably structured: it seeks to defend the continent in co-operation with friends and allies; if necessary, however, the U.S. will act unilaterally to defend its interests and security.

Thus, in one specific instance, U.S. interests in global freedom of the seas and the right of innocent passage through straits results in its position that the Northwest Passage is international rather than Canadian domestic water. Canada's inability to patrol systematically or even comprehensively monitor (let alone defend) these waters demonstrates the point. Canadian professions of sovereignty have not been accepted by other major seafaring powers, but Ottawa has focused on U.S. refusal to accept its position as still another touchstone in negative relations. It was indicative that even before becoming prime minister, Stephen Harper stressed he would defend the Arctic against U.S. incursions. A skeptic might anticipate Hudson Bay palm trees from global warming before the projected icebreakers and Arctic base are constructed. Nevertheless, to accept the Northwest Passage as Canadian territory would provide, for example, precedent for Indonesian claims for sovereignty over international water near its territory. So, politely but firmly, the United States government will continue to emphasize that these are international waters.

On the other hand, for over 50 years, the U.S. has acted in close coopera-tion with Canada in North American Air (now Aerospace) Defense through the NORAD agreement, with its command headquartered in Colorado. The circumstances of an integrated binational staff and a commander responsible to both the president and the prime minister is unique; the cooperation has been highly effective, but NORAD, despite its renewal in May 2006 for an indefinite duration, is becoming technologically obsolete and would benefit from further organizational restructuring. Although the 2006 renewal permit-ted expansion of its responsibilities to cover maritime warning responsibilities as well as aerospace defense, maritime surveillance and control missions re-main separate from NORAD. There is still potential for expanding NORAD responsibilities to cover ground forces; the topic was considered during the re-cent renewal negotiations; however, it appeared to be a "bridge too far" given current stretched (if not stressed) bilateral relations. Specifically, Canadian re-fusal to participate in BMD has limited its missile defense role in NORAD.

Moreover, the U.S. recognizes that Canada has effectively abdicated serious continental defense to the United States. The Canadian decision is based on the conclusion that it could not defend itself against U.S. military aggression, regardless of the level of defense spending, and that any threat from outside the hemisphere sufficient to threaten Canada would also threaten the U.S.—and the U.S. would have to address it. Canadians have therefore concluded that they can be inadequately defended at great expense or inadequately defended at minimal expense. It isn't a heroic decision, but a green-eyeshade, actuarial choice to spend Canadian funds on domestic social services and not on defense. Rather than being a basic national requirement, defense for Canadians is an exercise in balancing another special interest pleader who wants expensive toys. Moreover, Ottawa's refusal to participate in continental missile defense—at zero cost to Canada, but apparently driv-en by pique at the current U.S. administration—was the political equivalent of a shin kick. U.S. observers have moved steadily towards a judgment that Canada is not just a free rider but an ungracious one as well.

The "Military Industrial Complex"

It is probably worth mentioning this old chestnut if only to dismiss it. To be simplistic, if you equip armed forces with sophisticated, modern weapon systems, you need a high-tech industrial base to do it. This is an economic fact, not a political conspiracy. If your equipment is ineffective and anti-quated (and your opponent's is not), your soldiers die and you lose battles and wars. You cannot create a defense industrial base overnight; if lost, it would take years to rebuild. The advanced manufacturing industry in the U.S. produces—at high expense—extremely capable weapons. Arguably, in most categories, they are the best weapons in the world.

To a substantial degree, the defense production also indirectly subsidizes the aerospace industry and development of information technology (the Internet, to cite a key example, was created for military interests). There are civilian benefits to at least some of the military spending and, consequently, there are vigorous political lobbies that push for production (or continued production) of various weapons. A major weapons system will be so expensive that its prime contractor can distribute subcontracts throughout many parts of the U.S., which has the effect of creating a wide range of supporters who will urge their political representatives to fund these systems.

An ancillary element of the U.S. Armed Forces is the extensive system of ports and bases across the country. One estimate for the 2003 fiscal year offered a total of 6,000 bases of all sizes (many very small) in the United States and its territories. Periodically, there are efforts to reduce and rationalize this base network; however, the process is both painful and political. Regardless of size, each base has a constituency that recognizes its economic value to the community—and closing the right base at the wrong time (Walter Reed Hospital in Washington, D.C., for example) can result in political costs that far exceed any projected economic benefit.

THE UNITED STATES AND THE CANADIAN MILITARY

The U.S. has profound respect for the quality of individual members of the Canadian Forces and a professional appreciation for its stellar history and its current qualitative level. The problem with Canadian Forces, however, is quantitative and technological. While Canada's best is well trained and organized, there is too little of it—and increasingly its equipment and technical abilities will make it less and less able to operate with comparable U.S. forces. The Harper government is planning to add 13,000 new troops to the Canadian military; however, the distance between plans and Canadians in uniform is considerable. The 2006 report of the auditor general noted that despite substantial recruitment effort, the numbers leaving the 60,000-strong Canadian military were almost as large as those entering: end strength had increased by less than 1,000 personnel. Consequently, Americans might be forgiven the classic comment of the skeptical, "I'm from Missouri" in assessing projections for expanded Canadian forces.

Thus with the best of good will and desire by both Canadian and U.S. professionals to work together (and if necessary fight together) such cooperation is becoming more and more difficult.

Clearly this circumstance is by Canadian choice. While various polls suggest domestic support for increasing spending on defense and security, it is not a priority at anywhere near the level of health, education, and social services; and there is no indication that such spending would be sacrificed for military funding. While the U.S. has quietly (and sometimes not so quietly) urged greater Canadian defense effort, even blunt and unequivocal urgings have been largely ignored.

There is also a professional recognition that the Canadian public appears unable to support any significant level of loss on active duty. Deaths or accidents in U.S. forces that would be regarded as regrettable or the consequence of a local error are escalated in Canada to national prominence and agonizing review. For example, at roughly comparable times in late 2004 and early 2005, separate U.S. and Canadian submarine accidents resulted in deaths (in each case, one sailor died). Canada dry-docked its entire subfleet for months; for the U.S., it was a problem for the individual submarine and its commander. Likewise, the outpouring of grief for individual Canadian deaths in Afghanistan suggests that the population is unwilling to accept combat losses as the equivalent of industrial accidents in a hazardous profession. No death is trivial, but one wonders if Canada could today conceive, let alone sustain, the focus that drove its army to seize Vimy Ridge in 1917. One notes, in that regard, that the total casualties at Vimy were approximately four times the current force deployed in Afghanistan.

As cited earlier, a plethora of Canadian studies have documented, sometimes in apocryphal language, the state of Canadian forces. Although there are studies arguing for comprehensive force increases, the most consistent theme appears to be the proposal that Canadian forces develop a "niche" capability. Which niche, at what cost, is the question?

For its part, the United States remains open to cooperation with Canadian forces at whatever level of capability is possible. Washington believes that military-to-military cooperation is a valid and vital facet of the national bilateral relationship. It regrets that the Canadian response to our traditional defense/security relationship is a combination of veiled hostility and indifference.

New World Order

Although it was an American academic who posited the "end of history" and an American president who spoke of a "new world order," their sanguine words did not become substance. The concept of a new world order with lions lying down with lambs (and the lambs not being replaced on a daily basis) has certainly not come into being.

To be sure, there is a new world order. In essence, the threat of catastrophic nuclear war has largely lifted. This end of ideology, if not the end of history, has released the prospects for democracy, human rights, and free market capitalism from strictures that suppressed them in large regions of the world for over 50 years. Although this is not a peaceful kingdom, the variety of recent conflicts ranging from Kosovo to Somalia to the Persian Gulf to Darfur (and the prospects of more of the same, virtually anywhere on the globe outside of North America) remind one of Byron Farwell's account of *Queen Victoria's Little Wars* wherein 19th- and early 20th-century British expeditionary forces maintained a semblance of order and advanced British interests. The losses and costs associated with such wars are never trivial to the individuals, but they would barely have qualified as "wastage" on First World War trenchlines during quiet periods.

Nevertheless, the United States is highly reluctant to become the global 911 number; local conflicts should be handled locally. There is no need for expensive starship troopers to address the equivalent of domestic disputes requiring only local constabulary. The United States will engage itself only when its national interests are involved.

Consequently, furiously stung by the 9/11 assault, the U.S. is deeply engaged in countering terrorism. The frustrations are evident; the U.S. has now been engaged in this struggle longer than it fought in the Second World War. It has become the "Long War," clearly the challenge for a generation—and clearly recognized as such. While there have been obvious successes, not the least being thwarting for over five years a repeat of the 9/11 assault, other facets are very much in play. The fate of democracy in the Middle East is the issue writ large; the fight for stability in Iraq is the issue writ small.

On a bilateral basis with Canada, the issue is one of continental security. If the world's longest undefended cliché is to continue, Washington must be convinced that Ottawa is doing all that it can to assure U.S. and Canadian security. One would think that such an imperative would be so obvious that it need not be written; however, the impression remains that Canadian concerns are half-hearted efforts undertaken only to placate the

United States. Likewise, the suggestion that Canadian hemispheric security efforts be viewed as Ottawa's military contribution appears to be an attempt to make a virtue of a necessity—and once again side-slip serious military expenditures with combat implications.

PEACEKEEPING: NEVER SIMPLE

All too often peacekeeping is confused with being the equivalent of a schoolyard crossing guard. Prior to the end of the Cold War, there were a number of cases in which the parties (sometimes surrogates for Cold War antagonists) agreed to stop fighting. These peacekeeping circumstances were relatively benign. To monitor such agreements, the concept of dispassionate, if not technically neutral, military forces evolved. Canadian Forces were the most ubiquitous and effective of these forces.

This peacekeeping, however, frequently reflected the reality that neither of the major Cold War antagonists trusted the other to provide such a force. Canada was sufficiently agreeable to both sides to be politically effective. Equally important, however, the Canadian Forces were well trained and militarily proficient. In U.S. eyes, the first requirement for a good peacekeeper is to be a good soldier—not a policeman or a social worker in a military uniform.

The diminution of Canadian military capability has concurrently diminished its potential for effective peacekeeping operations. As is noted elsewhere, much current peacekeeping is truly "peacemaking" wherein the combatants must be separated, perhaps even suppressed by force of arms, before peace is possible. If the objective is couched as a "responsibility to protect," doing so ineffectively is futile. Mistaking a funeral director for a peacemaker is more than an error in diplomacy.

FUTURE OF THE U.S. MILITARY

The future and problems of the U.S. military are entirely different than those of Canada. Defense is viewed as an essential national priority; there is no substitute for strong armed forces, and there is no political debate over the need for the U.S. to maintain military supremacy. There is debate over how much is enough and more specifically over individual weapons systems, but there is no debate that "enough" means significant military strength to prevail in any foreseeable conflict with other countries.

If anything, the problem of the U.S. Armed Forces is less a lack of capability than an excess of capability. Because the U.S. military has been so effective in its combat role, there is a tendency to want to expand this role into operations that are closer to political sociology and policing rather than combat operations. However, when you employ firefighters for rescuing kittens from trees, you may placate the SPCA, but reduce your training time for hook-and-ladder, high-building rescue.

Moreover, the expenses associated with the U.S. military are immense, virtually mind-numbing. Combined with the domestic security costs associated with 9/11 response to terrorism, the expenses have driven an economy that in 2000 anticipated open-ended surpluses into one of unprecedented deficits. While these expenditures as a percentage of GDP are not disproportionate in comparison with earlier eras, they are nevertheless gigantic. Reducing defense expenditures is a largely unnoticed objective—unnoticed because even significant cuts are lost in the massive figures of the defense budgets. More generally, the current structure of the U.S. Armed Forces has societal complications.

End of the Draft

It was Vietnam that ended the military draft and moved the United States towards an "all-volunteer" military service. In a similar manner, the involuntary call-up of military reservists during Korea, including individuals with no post-World War II reserve training, was so unpopular that such call-ups were not employed during Vietnam.

The draft was never popular in the United States (there were draft riots during the Civil War), and the French concept of universal military service as a societal binder never gained traction. In a polity that emphasizes liberty and individual freedom of choice, the military draft was the ultimate imposition—an involuntary selection with unlimited liability, frequently leading to death or injury. It could be justified only with high popular support and a societal sense that the nation was indeed at risk. The Second World War was such a circumstance. However, during the extended Cold War, "selective service" appeared more and more capricious in its selectivity. The growing size of the U.S. population made it statistically improbable that most men would serve. Even prior to the Vietnam War, the ability of the university educated to avoid military service was significant (but in the 20th century, at least, a citizen was unable to purchase a "replacement," a practice that was prevalent during the Civil War).

The intense unpopularity of the Vietnam War broke the selective service system. Levels of draft evasion and/or desertion were significant;

some estimates run into the tens of thousands. Consequently, the draft moved first to a "lottery" by birth date to make eligibility more predictable, and in July 1973, the all-volunteer force was put into effect. Except for a standby, mothballed administrative operation, the selective service boards were history.

Effects of the All-Volunteer Force (AVF)

The advantage is obvious: it accords with the U.S. national philosophy of life—other than death and paying taxes, personal choice should rule (and even assisted suicide should offer a "choice" for death). Obviously, then, there is no one in the U.S. Armed Forces who has not chosen this course. Whether for a short tour of active duty to obtain a particular kind of technical training deemed helpful in civilian life, a mechanism to acquire funds for future college study, or a commitment to a full, 20- to 30-year professional career, it is a voluntary contractual arrangement.

The senior officers of the armed forces strongly support the AVF concept. It means that there are far fewer recalcitrant and unhappy soldiers, and they are available for longer, more intensive training that matches the high-tech equipment requiring such attention. The "profession of arms" at every level is far more "professional" than ever before in history; the equipment is infinitely more expensive than the armament of 50 years ago, with a single aircraft valued in the tens of millions of dollars. Moreover, virtually the entire armed forces recognize that they accepted unlimited liability with their choice of entering military service. They are not necessarily happy when their service involves high risks—any more than the policeman is enthusiastic about pursuing an armed criminal into a dark alley—but they accept the risk as their duty. This circumstance is a little less true for those enrolled in the National Guard or the military service reserve; however, they also are all volunteers and accept the liability along with the associated pay and benefits.

The negative elements of the system are twofold, but less apparent: financial and philosophical. First, an AVF is expensive. Even years ago, anecdote associated better than 50 percent of the DOD budget with personnel costs (past, present, and future). Military personnel must receive pay and benefits commensurate with alternative civilian careers; it can no longer be a career of last resort for the individual whose skills are so low that no other job is possible. Not even an infantry "grunt" can be dumb today. Moreover, the AVF requires an expensive infrastructure to address the reality that the standard soldier will be older, married, and with children. This prototype creates a complicated personnel system avoided when the military was primarily filled with young bachelor males for two-year or three-year "hitches."

The economic element, however, means that the military is an employer in competition with other prospective employers. For much of the AVF's existence, recruiting has been easy: large pools of age-appropriate prospects (expanded to include a higher percentage of women) and a moderate economy. Under these circumstances, the quality of the individual recruit rose and, in the early 1990s, almost every new recruit had at least a high school diploma. However, when the economy is booming or when the risks associated with service rise, recruiting becomes more difficult and the quality of the recruit tends to decline. Despite a population base approaching 300 million, the United States Armed Forces must work hard to recruit approximately 170,000 to 200,000 per year to sustain armed forces of 1.4 million.

The more abstract problem is philosophical. Should a democracy require a commitment from its citizens to do more than pay taxes? Is service an essential element of citizenship? Should those who are benefiting disproportionately from a society be able to avoid any commitment to sustain it? Could an AVF become a tool of the executive branch, executing foreign policy with a "yes, sir" mentality divorced from popular support? Will an all-volunteer military eventually degrade into an equivalent of mercenaries or, worse yet, Praetorians?

An Ancillary Societal Effect

During much of the Cold War and throughout the mid-1970s, significant numbers of U.S. Foreign Service Officers (diplomats) had military experience prior to entering the Foreign Service. They were "graduates" of the Second World War, Korea, Vietnam, and—most importantly—children of the draft. These young males (as no women were drafted) anticipated they would encounter military service; the question was whether to await and/or try to dodge the draft, or embrace military service either by volunteering as an enlisted man or seeking a Reserve Officers' Training Corps (ROTC) commission as an officer. ROTC was an intelligent, logical personal decision as well as a patriotic one; the same variety of logic interested such young men in the Foreign Service. The end of the military draft reversed this logic. There was no expectation of involuntary military service; hence there was no reason to plan for it. It was now illogical to "waste" two or three years in the armed forces rather than immediately beginning a professional career, such as in the U.S. diplomatic service.

Currently, the United States, 30 years into the experiment of the AVF, is still puzzling over the question. It is perhaps indicative of the U.S. that it continues to mull over the ramifications of an AVF, when countries such as the UK apparently have no such concern over the same issue.

The Role of the Military Veteran in the United States

Born in blood, with revolutionary military officers transmuted into political leaders, the United States historically revered its civilian soldiers. The United States has, in effect, two national holidays associated with honoring its casualties in war. Decoration Day (now Memorial Day) was first observed on May 30, 1868, at Arlington National Cemetery for decorating the graves of soldiers killed in the Civil War. The second, Veterans Day (previously Armistice Day, commemorating the end of combat in the First World War) is celebrated on November 11. For many Canadians, their participation in the "Great War"—and particularly their role in the fighting over Vimy Ridge—marked their emergence as a nation. For American historians, that war is often regarded as the first appearance of the United States as a world power—and perhaps as the savior of Europe.

Canadians commemorate November 11 as Remembrance Day, while Americans mark it as Veterans Day. The difference is more than nominal. For Canadians, the day appears increasingly to be one of recalling something of dim and distant memory. The overwhelming mass of these events are so long ago and far away that they are almost the societal equivalent of looking over that box of old toys in the attic that were eventually put away. One politely listens to the tales that grandfathers (whom you cannot imagine ever being young) offer in abbreviated and sanitized form so they won't bore or shock you.

For Americans, however, the "veterans" are immediately at hand—over 25 million of them. America's wars and America's veterans are intimate parts of daily life. A long string of "little wars" and campaigns have filled the past 60 years in the United States. Although the "greatest generation" associated with the Second World War is now passing from the scene, the role of the veteran in political and social life has not declined.

It therefore shouldn't surprise that one of the most memorable political advertisements during the tumultuous 2004 election campaign was that by a group of Swift Boat veterans (the "Swift Boat Veterans for Truth") who criticized Senator John Kerry. With a passion undiminished by the passage of 30 years, they charged that Kerry had betrayed them and their comrades by his unsubstantiated accusations that U.S. soldiers were war criminals in Vietnam. There was an authenticity in their enduring outrage that deflected Kerry's effort to depict himself as a staunch defender of U.S. military security. Subsequent voting patterns indicated that a strong majority of veterans supported President Bush (and one poll suggested that 70 percent of the U.S. Armed Forces did so as well).

Reflecting this point, President Bush spoke in Arlington Cemetery on Veterans Day 2004 at the amphitheater immediately behind the Tomb of the Unknowns; it was his first significant public address following re-election. He called for dedication in meeting the challenges of the War on Terror: today in Iraq; tomorrow, who knows where. As of mid-2007, there is no expectation that Bush will change direction—and no anticipation that U.S. military will be less than loyal to political direction.

But Not War Lovers

At the same time, neither U.S. veterans nor the U.S. military are war lovers. To a degree almost unprecedented in history, the United States Armed Forces, the custodians of vast military power, are relentlessly committed to civilian control over the military. Clearly there are personal preferences among senior military officers (just as there are among university professors) over the qualities of the individuals they would prefer to lead them. However, there has never been a *coup d'état* or even revealed-long-after-the-fact planning for a military assault on U.S. civilian leadership. This point is frequently passed over as an unconscious given in U.S. politics, despite its extraordinary rarity either in historical or current terms. Likewise, the United States is almost unique in not having a national war museum—the Smithsonian museums on the Capitol Mall extol an extraordinary range of U.S. activity and accomplishment, and ethnic/racial culture, but none of them is devoted to war.

One of the prominent memorials in the Washington area is the Arlington National Cemetery. Overlooking the city and surrounding the family home of Confederate General Robert E. Lee, it holds the graves of 250,000, including those of President Kennedy, his family members, and the Tomb of the Unknowns. Less remarked is the fact that it is directly in line of sight from the Pentagon. There is no military officer who cannot directly regard the effects of even the most successful use of combat power; it is a salutary lesson that is not missed—especially as there is no comparable memorial to failed diplomatic efforts or social policies.

But to offer a little perspective. One of the abiding dividing characteristics between Canadian and U.S. history is the role of military figures in politics. A Canadian general has never become prime minister; indeed, Canada's most trusted and admired military figure from the First World War, Arthur Currie, was beleaguered in his subsequent private life by persistent libelous attacks in the media. No significant Canadian military figure emerged from the Second World War or Korea, and the most noteworthy military peacekeeper, Major-General Lewis MacKenzie, was unable to be elected an MP. Exceptions are rare. Major-General George R. Pearkes, a veteran of both world wars, served as defence minister from 1957 to 1959 and then as British Columbia's lieutenant governor. The current defence minister, Gordon O'Connor, is a retired army brigadier-general. Lieutenant-General Roméo Dallaire, of Rwanda fame, is now both a national hero and an (appointed) senator.

In contrast, a substantial majority of U.S. presidents have had military experience, and U.S. political history is replete with general-presidents. Some are obvious: Washington; Jackson; Grant. Others are more obscure: William Henry Harrison; Zachary Taylor; Rutherford Hayes; and James Garfield.

And then there is Dwight David Eisenhower—the prototype for contemporary generals who dream that their stars will lead them to political summits. Allied Commander at D-Day and Supreme Allied Commander Europe after the Second World War ended, Eisenhower was a man with a smile that could light up the world. "Ike" was everyman's instant grandfather and ostensibly so apolitical that President Truman attempted to recruit him to run as a Democrat.

But least we forget, the "I love Ike" phenomenon happened in 1952—over half a century in the past, under unique circumstances (the greatest military victory of the century and a Democrat dynasty that after 20 years in power had run out of steam). Nor did Eisenhower set any precedent for other American generals of the Second World War (in contrast to the post-Civil War, when Grant, Hayes, and Garfield wore stars, and Benjamin Harrison was a colonel). Other "five-star" officers from the Second World War—namely, Marshall, Arnold, Bradley, Nimitz, Leahy, King, and Halsey—did not enter presidential politics or seek election at any level. And, although MacArthur clearly had presidential aspirations, he did not formally enter a campaign.

Neither has recent U.S. politics offered substantial encouragement to modern general officers. Among others, Vietnam War commander William Westmoreland failed in an attempt to become governor of South

Carolina in 1974 and Peter Dawkins (Heisman Trophy winner and Rhodes Scholar) was defeated in a race for New Jersey senator in 1988. One may even recall the "boomlet" for the 1991 Gulf War hero-commander Norman Schwarzkopf, until it became clear that a grizzly bear was more amenable to political tutelage. Perhaps the most prominent "political" military officer of the past generation was General Alexander Haig. Like Eisenhower, Haig was NATO's Supreme Allied Commander Europe. Intelligent, ambitious, articulate (he gave masterful speeches), and handsome, Haig had insider political knowledge gleaned from the Nixon White House, strategic vision demonstrated while secretary of state in 1981-82, and corporate backing. Still he was an also-ran in the 1988 presidential primaries, leaving the impression that his ambition was more angry self-seeking and that he was inflexible.

Instead, while the members of the Second World War generation who entered politics and became president had military experience, it was experience as junior officers. John F. Kennedy's "PT 109" experience is most widely known, but Presidents Johnson, Nixon, Ford, Carter, and George H. W. Bush were also young naval officers. And those who have not served (or were seen as avoiding military service) have been criticized.

THE ARMED FORCES AND FOREIGN POLICY

It would be traditional but not meaningful to quote Clausewitz about war and politics. Military strength provides an option, but it is not a policy. Without the ability to resort to force at least on some level, no state can "assure domestic tranquility." Without military capability, either unique or in league with allies, a state lies vulnerable to those with such capability.

Following the Second World War, the United States found itself in a unique position of power from having led the Allied coalition against fascism and benefiting from an undamaged and vibrant economy. Subsequently, it found to its considerable disappointment that Second World War allies were those of convenience rather than conviction. The challenge of Soviet-directed communism was one that could not be ignored; indeed, to ignore it and adopt isolationism would probably have resulted in communist global control outside the Western Hemisphere. Not even nuclear weapons would have been sufficient to preserve U.S. independence against a comparably armed Soviet Union. With almost astonishing good fortune, the United States emerged unscathed from a half-century of politicomilitary challenges; it surmounted both combat confrontation with fascism and political confrontation with communism, without domestic economic damage or debilitating manpower losses.

The post-Cold War world has offered a new set of challenges. Many must be countered with military force. The absence of such force would not mitigate the problems; its presence is a necessary, albeit not sufficient, component of a solution. Whether U.S. combat power is employed to prevent "bad things" from happening or for attempting to redress the bad things that have happened, it will remain a vital facet of 21st-century U.S. foreign policy.

On the hemispheric level, fortunate circumstances continue. No nation, either North or South, poses a military threat to its neighbors. Residual issues of national borders and economic problems fall into the jaw-jaw category rather than an anticipated resort to violence. It is a rare historical circumstance that is inadequately appreciated.

HUMAN RIGHTS AND DEVELOPMENT 9

The differences between the Canadian and American approaches to human rights and development are rooted in very different histories. While Canada has evolved into the country it is today through "evolution," or slowly growing out of birth as a colony under the British monarch, America was born through the violence of revolution and set out on a path of vigor and growing confidence.

Both countries have contributed to the expansion of human rights, and both work for the betterment of the so-called developing world. Both are culturally pluralistic and diverse societies in themselves. But at the same time, Canada probably has a better reputation abroad for sincerity and respect when dealing with peoples of other cultures. Canadians behave with interest and humility when traveling abroad. The economic and foreign policies of the U.S. do not always seem to further the prosperity of all peoples. The developed world must fuse the international body of human rights legislation with our development goals, and only then will we be able to meet the Millennium Development Goals (MDGs) of the U.N.

Canada needs to set a goal for achieving the funding required by the MDGs, and prove that its commitment to these ideals is more than just words. Although Americans claim to be the "defenders of freedom and democracy," their division of our planet into "good" and "evil" will not lead to the protection and promotion of human rights for those who need it most, let alone the development of the poorest regions. Americans tend to conclude that "evil" is not an abstraction and resisting it with soft words rather than hard arms is feckless. Ideals work best when endorsed by a state or organization with real power: political, economic, and/or military.

Nevertheless, as long as nations respond to threats with fear and retaliation—and not with dialogue and understanding—and as long as economic concerns override ethical concerns, development will always be out of reach for many.

A Canadian View

Since the end of the Second World War, Canada has been involved in the promotion of human rights and international development. To cite only a few examples, former prime minister Lester B. Pearson was a key player in creating the very idea of peacekeeping, and Canada has provided leadership and involvement in numerous such missions. Canadians played an important role in the drafting of the United Nations Universal Declaration on Human Rights. More recently, we helped in the creation of the International Criminal Court and in the enactment of the Landmines Treaty.

To be certain, the Canadian role is far from spotless. Even within our own borders, a great many First Nations communities live in grinding poverty. During the Second World War, the Canadian government imprisoned Japanese-Canadians and confiscated their property. The Canadian government, through mid-2007, has maintained a policy of "constructive engagement" with a range of deeply repressive regimes such as China, Sudan, Iran, and Cuba, believing essentially that isolating the worst offenders provides no opportunity to prompt them towards even marginal improvements.

Yet the international protection and promotion of human rights have been integral to Canadian foreign policy. Respect for human rights is both a fundamental Canadian value and a critical element in the building of stable societies. And one of the centerpieces of Canadian foreign policy is to influence other states, through bilateral and multilateral tools, to respect international human rights principles. One of our most powerful tools is development.

The concept of development is constantly being rethought: human rights are being added to concerns about economic growth, poverty alleviation, and basic human needs. The Declaration on the Right to Development, the Arusha Charter on Popular Participation, and the Manila Declaration on People's Participation and Sustainable Development—all speak of people-centered development: human beings as the central element in development.

The relationship between human rights and development is still not widely understood. But to understand where it stands now, and the direction it will probably go in the future, it is worth a look at how development evolved.

APPROACHES TO DEVELOPMENT

Since the Second World War, there have been a number of theories on the most effective ways to stimulate development. These were initially purely economic and based on a Eurocentric version of development: in other words, it was thought that development everywhere should follow the same events that led to European industrial capitalism.

Keynesian economic theory was the center in which the first mainstream theory of development was rooted and was strongly interventionist in its approach. John M. Keynes valued building capital, determined by savings and investment, especially in areas such as manufacturing. Any weak area within a country's market required either state or external intervention. By the late 1960s, many realized that problems surrounding the development of the developing world were dynamic in nature and that solutions based on the European experience with primarily market-oriented issues was not very applicable to developing economies.

Neoliberal development theory was the reaction to the shortcomings of postwar Keynesianism and was based on the principles of *laissez-faire* economics. These principles assume that, as rational actors living in a world of limited resources, we all make sensible choices, and that this should be especially true in any underdeveloped economy finding itself surrounded by shortages.

The export model involved developing countries exploiting their comparative advantages—a strategy promoted by nearly all postwar development theories. It focused on one's advantage in cheap land and labor, and did lead to higher rates of economic growth until the mid-1970s. By then, neoliberalism was gaining ascendancy among government policymakers.

Import substitution also played a prominent role in changing development theory. It called for growth of product manufacturing for domestic consumption, with external dependency to be lowered while increasing self-sufficiency. This model often required more imports than first thought. There were also limitations in a domestic market demand due to high poverty levels among the population.

Export-oriented industrialization and concentration on outward-oriented growth were the next development flavors-of-the-decade to come into fashion. Along with them came International Monetary Fund and World Bank involvement in the policies of developing economies, primarily through highly painful structural adjustment policies.

Supporters of the neoliberal theory pointed at the rapid growth in the newly industrialized Asian countries and the general failure of stagnant

Latin American economies, using such examples to support their own free-market, export-led, outward-oriented development framework. They ignored authoritarianism, unequal distribution of income, gender inequality, and severe environmental damage in some of the "Asian tigers" at the time. There was in Asia also state ownership of many banks, strict import and export controls, industrial licensing, and state monopolies aplenty.

The active participation of the population in any developing country, especially the poor, in the process of development and the provision of their basic needs, was imperative to economic and societal success everywhere. The poor have the most important roles to play in the struggle to provide themselves with the means to improve their own lives. New development theories also emphasize the capability of communities to make decisions for themselves.

In 2005, through its International Policy Statement on Development, Canada committed itself to use a whole-of-government approach. There was also recognition of development as a preventative tool—using long-term development assistance to create stable societies with accountable governments, rule of law, respect for human rights, vibrant and diverse civil societies, and sustainable and healthy environments. Recent reports within the U.N. stress development as the most important mechanism in creating a global system for security. In other words, effective development helps to avoid having national populations sink into internal conflict. Canada is to focus on promoting good governance, improving health, basic education, private sector development, environmental sustainability, and women's equality.

To achieve the U.N. Millennium Development Goals, there were to be policy changes to enhance aid effectiveness. Why the outgoing Martin government did not offer a plan for our aid to increase to 0.7 percent of GDP by 2015 remained unclear to many. While its policy statement professed a number of ideals and new plans for tackling development issues, such as poverty, it did not recognize development as a human right, only a goal. This was despite an unprecedented international consensus on the issue of development, which was given a framework of targets in the MDGs.

DEVELOPMENT VERSUS HUMAN RIGHTS

There has been in recent years some improvement in the understanding of human rights among development workers. Traditionally, development workers thought of the promotion of human rights as something that was not part of their job description, although it may have been an area of concern personally. They left rights promotion and protection to human rights organizations and the foreign policies of the developed world. They believed development was focused on economic growth and providing basic needs.

The stress placed on the necessity of respect for all kinds of rights by the U.N. Declaration on the Right to Development did not always exist. Even today, the two groups tend to work in splendid isolation from one another. This has only helped to exacerbate the division between development and human rights—each failing to learn from one another—and has denied each side opportunities for collaboration in the field and professional growth.

In the development community, there has been a neglect of fundamental, economic, social, and cultural rights. Moreover, simply because statistics show there are improvements in, say, food production or building more schools, does not mean there is an equivalent improvement in the respect for the right to food or to education. Development does not automatically lead to human rights. A rights-based approach to development—the incorporation of human rights frameworks into development theory—is some guarantee that development will also bring respect for the promotion and protection of human rights. A rights-based approach also offers a good tool by which development practice can be assessed in any country.

RIGHT TO DEVELOPMENT

In 1986, the shortcomings of development efforts were given additional acknowledgment when the right to development was adopted by the U.N. General Assembly. It "brought to the fore an appreciation that development is not what happens as a result of economic growth or development planning—it is a process that allows for the exercise of the full range of rights and has as its goal the pursuit of self-actualization of people, in conditions of dignity through the exercise of their rights."[1]

The declaration itself is very much aspirational in its language, and whether realistic or not, it provided the seeds which could flower into a fair and equitable process of development for all. Article I (1) says: "The right to development (RTD) is an inalienable human right by virtue of which every human person and all peoples are entitled to participate in, contribute to, and enjoy economic, social, cultural and political development, in which all human rights and fundamental freedoms can be fully realized." Article I (2) goes on: "The human right to development also implies the full realization

---

1. Margot E. Salomon and Arjun Sengupta, *The Right to Development: Obligations of States and the Rights of Minorities and Indigenous Peoples.* London: Minority Rights Group International, 2003, p. 4.

of the right of peoples to self-determination, which includes, subject to the relevant provisions of both International Covenants on Human Rights [the 1966 U.N. Covenants on Civil and Political Rights, and Economic, Social and Cultural Rights], the exercise of their inalienable right to full sovereignty over all their natural wealth and resources."

Development is defined in the preamble as "a comprehensive economic, social, cultural and political process, which aims at the constant improvement of the well-being of the entire population and of all individuals on the basis of their active, free and meaningful participation in development and in the fair distribution of benefits resulting there from." The declaration also emphasizes that governments have a role to play. Article 3 (1) states that "States have the primary responsibility for the creation of national and international conditions favorable to the realization of the right to development."

By the late 1990s, U.N. agencies such as the U.N. Development Program (UNDP) and U.N. Children's Fund (UNICEF) had adopted human rights-based approaches to development. At the same time, development agencies were busy mainstreaming human rights in their development objectives, providing recognition of the complementary nature of the two. The declaration makes clear that the very reason for development is the realization of human rights.

However, the right to development concept continues to be one of the most debated in international law. The U.N. Working Group on the Right to Development, which was mandated to advance its implementation, is one such body. In some cases, there has been some backpedaling on this right.

The RTD has increased the debate surrounding the nature of international cooperation and responsibility in the process of development and the promotion of human rights. There is very little consensus on the roles and obligations of states in their bilateral and multilateral policies, which has made the full realization of the RTD difficult to achieve.

Although the RTD offers greater hope for marginalized and excluded groups through the promise of nondiscrimination and the equal distribution of benefits, there is still a certain unwillingness among developed countries to make a commitment to the principles of obligation and responsibility entrenched in numerous international human rights declarations. One of the best examples of this is the American Declaration of Independence, which speaks of "life, liberty, and the pursuit of happiness." "The pursuit of happiness" is no guarantee that one will realize one's personal potential; it only offers an opportunity—the point being that equality of opportunity is an obtainable objective, though equality of outcome is not. In other words, there is no right to enjoy the elements necessary for fulfillment of personal goals. This line of thinking may also be why the U.S., unlike Canada, balks at any inclusion of the idea of responsibility or obligation when it comes to resolutions in the U.N. Human Rights Commission—for instance on the rights of the child.

Critics of the RTD have opposed it for a number of reasons. They believe that it is too vague a term. In other words, it is never really clear who or what is to be developed, and who is responsible for the developing. The concept also confuses tangible rights with moral claims, and fails to offer a clear distinction between individual and collective rights. And needless to say, there is also a "cost" element: if development becomes a universal right, those who have more are obligated—perhaps legally—to give to those who have less, perhaps at unacceptable expense.

The critics are usually the same who refuse any notion of obligation or responsibility on the part of developed countries. These states are already bound to human rights obligations and international cooperation for their protection and promotion in over 100 multilateral and bilateral treaties. They fail to understand that the RTD is one which promotes a right to the development process itself, not necessarily a right to immediately "be developed"—the process of development being one in which all human rights are wholly integrated, allowing for the highest capabilities for people to realize their personal goals.

FOCUS ON NEEDS

The Canadian International Policy Statement on Development lists seven major trends that define the problem: uneven development; weak governance; health crises; lack of access to education; demographic pressure (youth without work); gender inequality; and environmental stresses/pressure on the global commons.

In any given country or situation, Canada's aid alone will not in itself be sufficient to building a sustainable democratic society. Such a development requires the initiative of citizens themselves. "Potential areas for support include the media, trade unions, peasant associations, rural cooperatives, business and professional associations, environmental advocacy groups, human rights monitors, women's organizations, legal aid groups, religious organizations, and urban popular movements."[2] You cannot have a stable, participatory democracy without a strong and vibrant civil society. The growth and empowerment of each group is one of the cornerstones for building a strong democracy, and should be prominently featured in any workable theory for development.

Increasing levels of literacy among populations is useful as a vehicle for self-development, and for increasing political awareness among the poor. There is a close relationship between personal development and political awareness, and literacy is one of the most essential components to social activity and rights awareness. Illiteracy is intimately connected with poverty and political powerlessness.

Building strong democracies requires political and developmental elements; both are mutually supportive in the advancement of human rights. The former offers political and civil rights for development of communities and individuals, the latter uses personal and communal development to advance the human condition. The two are very much interconnected, and the UNDP Human Development and Human Freedom indexes reveal a strong proportional relationship between high levels of political freedom and high levels of human development. The division between economic, social, and cultural rights (ESC rights) and civil and political rights (CP rights), and the emphasis on the latter only serves to oversimplify and confuse the issues of development.

The technical, industrial, and economic focus of past development frameworks must give way to considerations of a moral and ethical nature; the complexities and dynamics of human nature and social processes must be understood, and diversity and creativity emphasized.

WOMEN AND DEVELOPMENT

Another key component for development to be carried out along democratic and rights-based lines is gender justice. Women play such an important role in the development process and are involved in everything from food production to health care, from education to informal entrepreneurial activities.

If the discriminatory practices that inhibit women from reaching their full potential are not removed, development from a human rights perspective cannot continue in a balanced manner. It would only serve to enforce—or worse, legitimize—exploitation and violence in civil society. "The building

---

2. Clarence J. Dias and David Gillies, *Human Rights, Democracy and Development*. Montreal: International Centre for Human Rights and Democratic Development, 1993, p. 15.

of society, achieving democratic development, and realizing human rights will be meaningless if the structures and practices that diminish women's power are not abolished."[3]

Canadians recognize that women's equality is important and want to integrate women's rights—including everything from women's participation in development processes to their equal control over resources—into all areas of development. The conditions that provide equal access to the process of development, on national, political, economic, and cultural levels, must be ensured for both genders to achieve personal goals.

Women must be fully integrated in development; addressing inequalities is part of that process. They require access to education; social and political equality; involvement in organizations such as trade unions; control over reproductive rights; decision-making opportunities in corporations and development organizations; and freedom from mental and physical abuse. If these ends are addressed and actively worked towards, half of the human race will be guaranteed a fuller role in the development of their communities.

INTERNATIONAL BUSINESS, NGOs, AND DONORS

Increasing trade and investment does not necessarily lead to development. But there are business practices which ensure that investment and economic development have the most beneficial outcome for the overall population. Those companies that operate in other countries must not only ensure that their organization actively promotes human rights, but also that their business does not contribute to human rights abuses. They must ensure that they have the most positive impact possible on the country, the population, surrounding communities, and the environment. This can only be accomplished if they ensure human rights standards are respected within their own firm and by their business partners.

It has been noted by the Organization for Economic Cooperation and Development (OECD) that some firms may find the higher profitability due to cheap land and labor attractive. A repressed labor force is much more cost-advantageous than one with full rights led by trade unions. Unfortunately, there are numerous examples of Western businesses colluding with or supporting governments that systematically violate the human rights of their citizens. It can even be the commercial lobbies themselves that actively work to minimize their government's promotion of human dignity.

---

3. Dias and Gillies, p. 5.

There are a variety of ways in which a firm's activities—whether knowingly or not—may strengthen the repressive capacity of a regime. For instance, it may develop or manufacture products that increase capacity for repression; it can be a major revenue source for the regime; it may provide infrastructure such as roads, railways, power stations, and oil refineries; or its presence may give credibility internationally to an otherwise discredited regime.

However, it is possible to influence business policies. This can be done through consumers, shareholders, unions, government policies, financial and trade benefits, and lawsuits. Unfortunately, in the past, Canadian laws and policies have actually made the use of such groups and mechanisms ineffective. "Few Canadian companies with codes of conduct have any kind of guidelines on their relationship with repressive countries," says the Canadian International Policy Statement on Development, and some do not even use human rights assessments for some states, because of fear it will offend the country (for example, China), making business in that country more difficult.[4]

As Western governments and firms increasingly conduct business on an international scale, many engage in bi- or multilateral trade relations with states that fail to protect and promote human rights, either through the lack of legal expression or through weak enforcement. Separately, the Canadian government is seeking to develop a comprehensive corporate social responsibility policy for Canadian companies in the extractive industries of minerals, oil and gas. The Department of Foreign Affairs held multiple roundtable sessions with industry and civil society groups in 2006 to consult on relevant policies, particularly relating to environmental protection and human rights.[5]

The standards we live with here in Canada should be applied to the firms conducting business in countries where human rights legislation is weaker. Margot Franssen, president of The Body Shop (Canada) noted: "When you go to work you cannot leave your values at home. When you cross borders you cannot pretend the same universal human rights don't apply. We can no longer pretend it is none of our business if there are people suffering, whether it's on the other side of the world or in our own backyard. We must realize that what happens to one affects us all."[6]

---

4. Craig Forcese, *Putting Conscience into Commerce: Strategies for Making Human Rights Business as Usual*. Montreal: International Centre for Human Rights and Democratic Development, 1997, p. 31.

5. http://geo.international.gc.ca/cip-pic/library/Advisory%20Group%20Report%20-%20March%202007.pdf

6. Quoted by Forcese, p. 12.

The solution to corporate responsibility is not as easy as constructive engagement. Simply engaging in trade and investment is not sufficient, because there is absolutely no correlation between this and the liberalization of repressive regimes. There does not seem to be a relationship between increases in foreign direct investment and improvements in human rights indicators. The issues surrounding the reconciliation of trade objectives or foreign aid with human rights policies is a litmus test of our willingness to strengthen our overall sense of mutual responsibility.

It is not only the corporate community that has a role in the advancement of fair and balanced development abroad. The intellectual community and institutions of higher learning should also be more involved in the process of democratic development through the creation of policies that most effectively address the goals of the citizens. Countries such as Canada and Sweden have semi-independent institutions that conduct research in developing countries, on topics such as technology and public policy. Canada's International Development Research Centre (IDRC) has, for example, worked with governance issues in South Africa through cooperation between South African and Canadian researchers in the Macro-Economic Research Group (MERG).

The number of NGOs working internationally has also grown phenomenally. Their involvement in international institutions, such as the U.N., has increased proportionally, pointing to the increasing strength of civil society. Cooperation between Northern and Southern NGOs may lead to the creation of better measures for planning and implementing development policies. Canada has created quasi-independent mechanisms on national, regional, and continental bases. There are still large rifts between Southern NGOs, developing world governments and Western donors, as the Canadian policy statement on development notes. These turn on "issues of accountability, participation, co-optation and control, distortion of values, and financial dependency," as well as differences between Southern and Northern NGOs.[7]

OECD members could follow examples set by countries such as Canada, the U.S., Germany, and the UK. They have created quasi-independent mechanisms for democratic institution-building. The Canadian organization Rights and Democracy (formerly the International Centre for Human Rights and Democratic Development) was created by an act of Parliament in 1988. It uses Canadian official development assistance funds to build

---

7. Dias and Gillies, pp. 32-33.

grassroots organizations and promote human rights, while still being accountable to Parliament. Germany's *stiftungen*, and the UK's Westminster Foundation for Democracy, are charged with similar development goals.

The U.S. Perspective

HUMAN RIGHTS AND DEVELOPMENT: ONE WITHOUT THE OTHER?

The correlation between the United States and the championship of human rights should be unassailable. Starting in the 1600s, U.S. history is based on the search by substantial numbers of its original colonists for religious freedom and personal liberty. The Revolutionary War was fought to end the domination of a tyrannical British government over individual colonies and colonists, specifically to tax them without permitting them parliamentary representation and to rule them by the fiats of appointed governors. The Declaration of Independence is replete with language espousing individual human rights, and its most noteworthy line that individuals have the inalienable rights to "life, liberty, and the pursuit of happiness" ranks among the most memorable in world political literature.

As a political document creating a governing societal structure, the United States Constitution of 1789 and the Bill of Rights (its initial 10 amendments) proffer guarantees to U.S. citizens for free speech, assembly, religion, publication, a speedy trial by jury, and protection from self-incrimination, unreasonable searches, and "cruel and unusual punishment." The Constitution has served as a template for other nations, through the 21st century, that sought points of reference for a structure of government and protection of freedom for their citizens.

Likewise, between 1861 and 1865, the Civil War was fought not just to maintain the unity of the United States ("the Union") but to end slavery in the country and to prevent its continuation in a separate country in North America. The total of close to half a million deaths on both sides of the war remains the determining element of subsequent U.S. history.

Throughout much of the remainder of the 19th and early 20th centuries, the United States adopted a moralistic and dismissive attitude towards the power politics of Europe. Nicely sheltered behind its oceans and implicitly protected by a British fleet that controlled the seas, the U.S. was free to be contemptuous of the decaying, immoral monarchies and empires that dominated Europe. This was isolationist USA, content to "do its own thing" while dominating the Western Hemisphere as the *de facto* regional power. Thus when the First World War broke out in 1914, the U.S. had no interest in engaging itself; Washington professed neutrality, offered to sell its products to all-comers, and avoided serious reaction even to provocations such as the sinking of the *Lusitania* with the death of 124 U.S. citizen passengers. President Wilson declared that the United States was "too proud to fight" and campaigned successfully for re-election in 1916 on a motto of "He kept us out of war."

Consequently, the decision to enter the war in support of the "Allies" (UK, France, Italy) less than a year later, although prompted by unrestricted German submarine warfare against U.S. shipping, necessitated the rationale of a high moral tone. This was to be the "war to end all wars," and Wilson posited 14 points associated with U.S. participation in the war including international rights such as "self-determination," under which ethnic minorities could govern themselves in their own states, and the creation of a League of Nations that would preserve peace through agreement by its members to act collectively to maintain the security of all. The United States' ultimate refusal to support the Wilsonian ideal was highly contentious at the time, but reflected Wilson's failure of health coupled with his political failure to develop support in the Senate for U.S. participation in the League of Nations.

Nevertheless, the concept of an international organization to foster collective security ultimately evolved into the United Nations following the Second World War, and the hypothesis of self-determination for peoples drove much post-World War II decolonization. U.S. participation in the Second World War obviously was prompted by the Japanese attack on Pearl Harbor, but well prior to December 7, 1941, U.S. elite opinion was troubled by Nazi racism and Japanese atrocities in China. Such were not identified as "human rights" problems *per se*, but FDR's "Four Freedoms" speech delivered in January 1941 identified fundamental freedoms that all humans "everywhere in the world" ought to enjoy: freedom of speech; freedom of worship; freedom from want (individual economic security); and freedom from fear (world disarmament to prevent aggressive war). To be sure, one suspects that very few in the world community then paid any attention to American moralizing, just as few pay attention to comparable moralizing today.

However, following the war, these themes became more integral to U.S. foreign policy. Between 1945 and the end of the Cold War, the United States epitomized the alternative to communist dictatorial repression, military aggression, and economic stagnation. As a great power leading a coalition, the United States was supported by allies who were as committed as was the U.S. to human rights and freedoms, but the "willing" also occasionally included those who regarded the U.S. as the lesser evil when juxtaposed against Moscow's minions. Those on the margins of the Cold War were occasionally labeled as "friendly neutrals." In real terms that meant that such states were friendly to neutrals, neutral to our friends, and hostile to us—to the extent that such hostility was not economically or politically costly.

PRESENT PERSPECTIVE: THE HUMAN RIGHTS REPORT

Despite this history, which is subject to dispute by revisionists both domestic and international, the United States continues to believe in its exceptionalism. For a substantial majority of Americans, the United States remains the "shining city on the hill" as a beacon illustrating human freedom, individual liberty, and economic security.

As part of its effort to promote human rights, the United States Department of State produces a comprehensive annual Human Rights Report (HRR) officially entitled *Country Reports on Human Rights Practices.* Spawned in the Carter era in 1977 and now virtually the sole surviving child of his presidency, it was first designed to review the human rights activity of those countries that received U.S. aid. Over the years, and now over the decades, it has grown to almost 200 different reports, including non-countries such as Tibet, Hong Kong, Taiwan, Macao, and the "occupied territories" (that part of the Middle East under the control of the Israeli government following the 1967 war).

The human rights under review start with the basics from the U.S. Constitution: the right to change government in free elections; freedoms of speech, assembly, association, religion, and movement/travel. It continues in extensive detail. The HRR judges whether the government kills its opponents, tortures and abuses its citizens, or makes them "disappear." It investigates, among other things, the quality of workers' rights in their ability to organize into unions, strike, work under safe conditions, and receive a basic wage permitting a decent living for worker and family. The report examines how the investigations of snoopy nongovernmental organizations both international (Amnesty International, Human Rights Watch) and domestic are received by the government.

The report has steadily expanded into areas that might be regarded as social justice concerns: societal treatment of women, children, minorities, and Native peoples; "trafficking" in women and children; "persons with disabilities" (once just "disabled" but never "crippled"); and homosexuals (a new category beginning with the 2004 report is somewhat euphemistically labeled "Other Social Abuses" and reviews homophobic regulations and discrimination). Feminist concerns are covered extensively, notably "female genital mutilation (FGM)" or "female circumcision," which is criminalized regardless of historical, cultural, or religious connections in specific countries; it also includes child marriage. In 2004, the HRR also probed for the first time the degree to which political corruption was a problem and whether the government permitted easy access to its information (the Freedom of Information approach).

The reports are not all-encompassing. For example, because the U.S. military will enlist its own 17-year-old citizens, the "child soldier" issue is not examined. Nor is there criticism of capital punishment, since the United States holds that capital punishment accorded under rule of law and provided with a fair trial is not a human rights abuse.

Format

The reports are drafted to a rigid, pre-scripted format. As literature, they are close to being "reader hostile" in their pedestrian, formulaic prose. This is a government-bill-of-lading indictment, not evocative journalism. The events are to speak for themselves in a "nothing but the facts, ma'am," Sergeant Joe Friday style, and the drafters work devotedly to assure it is accurate—and honest—with as little "gray" and as few sins of omission as possible.

Obviously, the reports vary from "country" to country. Perhaps 100 fall into the "no problems" category. That doesn't mean they all chant in the chorus of Scandinavian angels, but that their "warts" are relatively minor. Countries of this nature would normally qualify for the gold standard of introductory language, to wit: "The Government generally respected the human rights of its citizens. . . ."

On the other end of the spectrum are the bad guys; denizens of the Axis (now Duality?) of Evil. Critics can say anything about them; nobody in the U.S. government has a dog in the fight to make North Korea or Iran look the slightest bit better. Tossing another shovel of manure on a mile-high midden may not make it smell any worse, but it is professionally proficient.

Friends Are the Problem

Obviously, the difficulty lies in Mr. In-between states—states that are U.S. allies, friends, or at a minimum useful in promoting one or another U.S. interest.

Hence we have Central Asian republics whose election practices don't pass the sniff test, but whose support and cooperation in the War on Terror have been highly important. Or Russia, whose emerging democracy doesn't seem to be doing so anymore and might be better depicted as a submerging democracy. Or China, whose gigantic economy inching towards free markets is ruled by archaic communists whose interest in the personal liberties of the citizenry is low on their "to-do" list. Or Saudi Arabia, whose oil exports are absolutely vital to Western economies, but whose government is a rigid monarchy and whose commitment to human rights is marginal—but where the alternative of radical Muslim fundamentalist government is a loathsome prospect. Or Colombia, whose government, in a desperate struggle with narco-terrorism, has handled its responses to terrorists from both right and left with less than a purist's concern for legal due process. And, of course, there are Iraq and Afghanistan, where state-directed counterterrorism and Marquis of Queensbury rules do not always coincide.

Consequently, there is intense debate within the U.S. government over labeling friends for having a "poor" human rights record (and a commensurate struggle with critics both domestic and international over the naming or non-naming of various countries and the manner in which their human rights activities are characterized).

Nor is the release of the HRR a day of glory for the U.S. government. Critics are less interested in its painstaking recount of fallen sparrows in Forgottenstan than having a chance to rip the wings off the American eagle. Their claim is that the United States is so tarnished from its post-9/11 counterterrorism actions that criticism of human rights abuses elsewhere is pure hypocrisy.

The International Religious Freedom (IRF) Report

A spinoff of the HRR is the International Religious Freedom (IRF) Report, instituted in 1998 at congressional behest and ignoring the reluctance of the Department of State to create such a document. Initially prompted by congressional concern over persecution of Christians, Tibetan Buddhists, and Baha'is, it now covers activities of the full global range of religion.

In some respects the IRF is even more volatile a report than the HRR. After all, diplomacy is the craft of the secular compromise; religion is the realm of uncompromising absolutes. A true believer cannot compromise with evil; if you represent such evil in his mind, he will die rather than negotiate with you. Thus, while the United States emphasizes its commitment to religious tolerance, it simultaneously appreciates that to others this lack of commitment to a single abiding faith, let alone to a state religion, may illustrate societal sickness and flaccid morality rather than strength. The IRF places the United States in deliberate judgment of the religious activity of others; it puts the U.S. government in the middle of an endless variety of controversies not amenable to platitudes of the "live and let live" school. The juxtaposition between the militant Muslim and the hostile nonbeliever can end explosively. Moreover, the U.S. must report each year what it has done to promote religious freedom in each of the country reports—an exercise in adroit drafting far different from reports for the original 1998 IRF, wherein some embassies said frankly that they had done nothing.

Additionally, in contrast to the rather straightforward HRR descriptions of countries, the IRF requires the identification of "countries of particular concern," with an escalating framework of sanctions to be taken against such countries if they continue with their miscreant manners. This calibrated series can range from a tap-on-the-wrist private demarche, to a wide range of security, economic, financial, and trade restrictions.

And Now the SHRD

Starting in 2003, the Supporting Human Rights and Democracy (SHRD) report is the latest entry in the library of official U.S. government reporting on human rights and political activity. In short, it is designed to emphasize the administration's conclusion that democracy is the key to human rights and that democracies, regardless of their flaws, will better protect the human rights of their citizens. Consequently, the SHRD has become another entry in the cottage industry of human rights reports, complementing the HRR and IRF by specifically itemizing federal government activity during the year to support and advance democracy.

The problem for the hard cases, both in general human rights reporting and specifically in religious freedom reporting, is how to remain true to U.S. human rights principles without damaging either our bilateral relationships or making it more difficult for countries that may be "trying" to continue to "try." A corollary is the desire to avoid providing domestic critics of U.S. bilateral relationships with additional ammunition to demand an end to our support for these governments or to provide critics of U.S. government activity, both domestic and international, with cudgels to beat administration policy by noting U.S. criticism of other countries. Maintaining perspective can be difficult, particularly in the heated and personalized atmosphere where diplomatic demurs are assailed as craven capitulation. However, the first U.S. ambassador at large for religious freedom, Robert Seiple, commented that identifying a country of particular concern (CPC) was the equivalent of a "public undressing" and that the IRF should be designed to promote religious freedom rather than to punish wrongdoers. Identifying a CPC therefore should not be an exercise in "deified testosterone" but a very carefully employed last resort.

A more general issue is the role of human rights within the framework of diplomacy. To be sure, human rights are now a substantial focus of U.S. diplomacy, and those who recall that "traditional" diplomacy had little to say about the domestic affairs of states are now *anciens* rather than current practitioners of U.S. diplomacy. Over what is now approaching 30 years, hundreds of thousands of hours have been devoted to these reports: information collection; analysis; drafting; editing; and responding to public inquiry. Diplomatic staff has not expanded commensurately and, consequently, work on human rights issues has superseded other political, economic, and cultural diplomatic work that might otherwise have been done. Moreover, the institutionalization of human rights in U.S. diplomatic demarches is rarely a positive element in bilateral state-to-state relations. At best it is a neutral element; those "good guy" states will quibble over U.S. characterizations or information and ask for rectification of any specific errors. Others, however, are aggressively critical.

Pushback from the World

The combination of the HRR/IRF—the largest annual State Department publication—generates annual, often high-decibel reaction. Some of those criticized couldn't care less (who thinks that North Korea will implement regime change because of U.S. human rights criticism?) and ignore the criticism. Some provide detailed, point-by-point rejoinders to specific issues. Others respond with "who do you think you are to criticize? (see Abu Ghraib)" ripostes. The latter delight in producing critical reports of U.S. human rights (and in a country of almost 300 million there is no shortage of shortcomings). Indeed, the publicity surrounding the 2006 HRR virtually ignored the careful, detailed case study analyses provided, and instead used the opportunity to berate U.S. policy in Iraq and Afghanistan, and its support for countries whose human rights records are less than pristine. Nevertheless, no state has broken relations with Washington over U.S. criticism stemming from human rights reporting.

The U.S. HRR also risk playing into the hands of those self-righteous professional human rights organizations, both domestic and international, who often leave the impression that they would rather see 9/11 endlessly repeated than discomfit a single individual, whether innocent or guilty. Purists and policy don't mix very well for those living in a world where the U.S. Constitution is not a suicide pact. When illegal combatants held at Guantanamo, Cuba, in accordance with U.S. jurisprudence, are characterized by an NGO as the equivalent of the millions incarcerated in Soviet-era gulags, the U.S. government loses interest in accommodating NGO whinging.

On the other hand, in truth, Goliath has no friends. And Goliath looks more than a bit silly complaining that he isn't loved (or not loved in the manner in which he wants to be loved). To those critical of the United States, our inclination is more to return a "Trudeau salute" than to bow in agreement. Or the U.S. government may offer the diplomatic equivalent of a shoulder shrug, with the suggestion that if you don't like what we are doing or how we are doing it, go forth and do it better. Frequently, both axiomatic critics and allies want U.S. assistance for one problem or another; they want the U.S. ox to pull their plow and to pass the reins to them. But that is not the Washington way, and the designs of others, regardless how selfless they are believed to be, still appear more to their interest than to general (let alone U.S.) interest.

Finally, the effort to place human rights issues subordinate to international forums or tribunals appears to have no more than ad hoc utility. To be sure, following the Second World War, the U.S. and the victorious Allies prosecuted and executed defeated Nazi and Japanese fascist military officers and officials. A skeptic may still conclude that while those executed were well deserving of death, their real crime was losing the war. And the precedent has not been entirely salutary. There are certainly U.S. citizens who were not amused to hear threats that American pilots would be tried for "war crimes" by Vietnamese who rationalized that the Nuremberg Trials were sufficient precedent. With that thought in mind, essentially, the U.S. is uninterested in consigning the fate of its citizenry to mechanisms such as the International Criminal Court (where they would not be accorded U.S. constitutional protections), and attention to the human rights of terrorists will not trump the requirement to secure the lives of U.S. citizens.

ECONOMIC ASSISTANCE

The West is beset by the problem of success: political stability; personal freedoms; economic plenty. To be sure, these problems are preferable to the problems of failure. For some, however, with these successes comes guilt (or at least concern) and they prompt the nagging question "What should we do to help others?" The question may be rooted in religious charity or *realpolitik* calculation, but it requires examination and, in turn, a judgment on an approach to the "Third World" (or whatever label is being applied to poor countries at the moment).

For the United States, the initial origins of international assistance are rooted in Christian charity. The 19th- and early 20th-century United States dispatched a steady stream of religiously motivated missionaries, who brought a combination of education, medical assistance, agricultural instruction, and theological inspiration to countries and peoples throughout the world. The parents and grandparents of today's citizens contributed pennies for missionaries, and contribution boxes for the "starving Chinese" were a church staple. They were the forerunners of televised images of starving African children with flies walking over their eyes. These missionaries were paralleled by another stream: businessmen and traders whose interest in far-flung countries was in making a profit from the relationship. (Some missionaries switched to economic interests, prompting the observation that "they came to do good and did right well.") Thus the "aid" issue has always had two components—charity and commerce.

Historically, U.S. international assistance was private: church charities or organizations such as the Red Cross managed assistance "relief" programs. In the 20th century, war-related catastrophe demanded government support. For example, using $100 million appropriated by Congress, Herbert Hoover managed the American Relief Administration immediately after the First World War and provided food for millions throughout Europe.

But it was following the Second World War that U.S. economic relief assistance turned from simply providing food to rebuilding damaged economies in response to the concern that communist aggression was threatening all Europe. The judgment was that the most adroit response to communism was economic success, and thus the 1947 Marshall Plan poured the 2005 equivalent of $100 billion in economic and technical resources into Western Europe between 1948 and 1952: victors and vanquished alike benefited. Such an effort was no longer charity, but international relations policy based on the conclusion that only economically successful Europeans would be able to be politically strong allies against the Soviet Union. In general, such economic assistance was successful. European states that had been prostrate in 1945 and staggering in 1947 revived with startling speed; of course, Europe (and

Japan) had an intellectual and financial base on which to rebuild. Having done it before, they could do it again—and knew that they could.

The Post-Colonial World

During the 30 years between 1946 and 1976, more than 90 states entered the United Nations; most were former colonies. Virtually without exception, regardless of their economic potential or previous overlords, they could be described as poor. If there was a U.S. paradigm for addressing the problems of such countries in that era, it was described by Walt Rostow in *The Stages of Economic Growth: A Non-Communist Manifesto*, which postulated the process by which countries can "take off" in economic development, a process that appeared not only reasonable but technically feasible. However, with a handful of exceptions—primarily in Asia—the problems have overwhelmed the problem-solvers. Unfortunately, combining economic growth with the socialism that appeared most attractive to many new states was particularly difficult.

The assumption was (and has been) that economic and economic-associated social problems can be addressed separately from political and social freedoms and human rights. Or, at least, the economic problems appeared more tractable than the societal restructuring necessary to sustain human rights. As a corollary, the governments of poor countries were more amenable to receiving economic assistance than to accepting political reforms that would threaten their power.

But simply addressing economic issues has hardly been simple. If the first issue was to implement sanitation and promote public health to prevent and cure disease, success in those fields quickly led to a population boom. And rising population (global population has risen from slightly over 2 billion in 1950 to 6.1 billion in 2000) creates severe pressures on all resources—starting with food production. Efforts to control population growth, however, immediately prompt resistance from many religious believers. As well, in many ethnic groups, the preference is to have large families, which are viewed as the equivalent of social security "safety nets" for the elderly.

There are other underlying, basic problems beyond fecundity control, public health, and famine relief, which, in no particular order, include:

• Should economic aid focus on the "poorest of the poor," or on countries that have taken some steps towards economic success?

- Should assistance be predicated on a recipient country's commitment to free market economics and strong efforts to eliminate corruption, or are these conditions really political preferences rather than economic concerns?
- Should aid concentrate on major "showcase" projects of the dam and airport variety or the less evident infrastructure projects such as communications or, instead, on still more basic areas such as improved agriculture, livestock, and small business management?
- Should assistance be given as straight financial grants? Should assistance be "tied" to conditions such as purchase within the granting country? Or should the assistance be in the form of loans to be repaid over an extended period?
- Should the question not be "aid" but "trade," with donors concentrating less on providing a country with products but rather on providing the country with opportunities to sell its own products (such as textiles or citrus fruit), thereby developing local industries?

For the United States, there have been no defining answers to these questions. Or, rather, there have been answers to fit the fashion of the era. Or the U.S. has attempted to endorse all of the answers, albeit in different countries. In addition, there has been recognition that while "untied" grants may be endorsed by international development specialists, they are unacceptable domestically to practical politicians.

And, most frequently, U.S. economic assistance has focused on its closest military security allies or the countries where it is facing military challenges. This circumstance is particularly true in the Middle East, where the United States provided the economic support structure for the 1979 Israel-Egypt peace agreement, and the U.S. continues to provide extensive assistance to both countries (as well as other regional allies such as Jordan). In real terms, the U.S. bought and paid for the peace agreement, and continues to pay for it on an installment plan. For example, total U.S. military and economic assistance for Israel since 1949 was estimated in 2004 to be $100 billion. Washington would be prepared to do the same for an agreement between Israelis and the Palestinians, and, indeed, expanded its economic assistance to the Palestinian Authority (PA) following the death of Yasser Arafat. This approach lies in abeyance, if not in ruins, following the January 2006 election victory of Hamas terror-connected leadership to a majority in the Palestinian legislature. As of mid-2007, the U.S. government continued to seek mechanisms to strengthen weak reeds such as PA President Mahmoud Abbas while attempting to isolate Hamas.

CURRENT OPERATION OF U.S. GOVERNMENT ECONOMIC ASSISTANCE

U.S. government economic assistance is a massive bureaucratic operation. (It is useful to note that while 20 years ago, Official Development Assistance (ODA) was the largest U.S. aid source to the developing world, currently, U.S. private aid from foundations, private and voluntary organizations, corporations, churches, and individual remittances exceed ODA—primarily because of the unique U.S. tax structure.) Official aid is administered through the U.S. Agency for International Development (USAID), which is an independent agency operating under the U.S. 1961 Foreign Assistance Act to provide economic, developmental, and humanitarian assistance to support U.S. foreign policy goals. USAID operates in cooperative accord with the Department of State, and its officials are members of U.S. embassy "country teams."

In a 2002 speech, the first presidential address concerning foreign assistance since the Kennedy administration, President Bush announced a "New Compact for Development" at the Inter-American Development Bank. He said that combating poverty is a moral imperative, made it a U.S. foreign policy priority, and proposed increased accountability for rich and poor nations; he linked greater contributions by developed nations to greater responsibility by developing nations. Bush then announced that the United States would increase its core development assistance by 50 percent over the next three years, resulting in a $5-billion annual increase over previous assistance levels.

Reflecting the government's continued effort, the 2008 federal budget requested $20.3 billion (an increase of $2.2 billion over FY 2006 enacted levels) for all State Department and USAID foreign assistance, over 50 percent of which would be directed to "Rebuilding and Developing Countries."

Separately, prior to the 2005 G8 Summit, the U.S. and the UK proposed terminating agricultural subsidies; such a move, theoretically at least, would open markets in G8 countries to imports from developing countries. European countries with highly protected farm sectors showed no enthusiasm for the proposal. It was probably a vain effort from inception—and predictably came to naught.

Despite these financial commitments and economic proposals, the United States has no interest in artificial objectives for assistance, for example, those that set specific percentages of national income to be devoted to assistance. Many in the United States, at both public and private levels, are skeptical about the effect of government-directed assistance at any level (not to mention repelled by the endless stories of kleptocratic governments/dictators that transform economic assistance into bulging Swiss bank accounts). A 1997 study suggested that the United States had provided a trillion dollars in assistance to other countries since the Second World War, without significantly advancing growth or stability in developing areas. Assistance from other states was even higher. Reports from the 2005 G8 Summit, stating that over the past 50 years Africa had benefited from a trillion dollars in assistance ($500 billion in aid and $500 billion in loan forgiveness) reinforced this skepticism. That Africa was, on the whole, worse off in relative terms than it had been 50 years earlier pointed to the assistance effort as a failure—but a failure on the part of *Africans* when compared to the relative successes enjoyed by South and East Asians over the same timeframe, with less assistance.

This explains why Prime Minister Pearson's proposal that each country should contribute 0.7 percent of its GDP to assistance efforts has no political resonance in mainstream U.S. politics. If any thought is given to the proposal, it is viewed as akin to the Kyoto Treaty, that is, another abstract, sure-to-fail proposal designed to euchre more money from the United States. Moreover, Washington regards the total amount of U.S. assistance (significantly higher than that of any other country) as both complemented by the openness of U.S. trade regulations and, in practical terms, supplemented by its global politicomilitary expenditures that contribute to international security and, thus, to economic development.

HUMAN RIGHTS VERSUS ECONOMIC DEVELOPMENT

Fortunate countries, the United States among them, have never even considered that there might be a need for choice between economic development and human rights. The U.S. has enjoyed both as its natural state of affairs; indeed, at each point in its history, the United States was probably in the front rank of both freedom and prosperity—at least as far as the status of the "common man" was concerned. The personal liberties that the colonial revolutionary enjoyed in 1776 would still be envied in many places in the world; likewise, that colonist's economic freedom from famine while being generally well clothed and housed would be quickly welcomed today by the hundreds of millions existing on $1 per day. So U.S. citizens have never had to choose; the coincidence of freedom and prosperity have been akin to the lyrics that "love and marriage go together like a horse and carriage."

Nevertheless, such a choice is the painful circumstance for many countries in the developing world, if they have any choice at all. And, while there are illustrative cases of countries moving first to relatively advanced economic development and then into greater political liberty and individual freedom, the obverse is harder to find. So far as the United States is concerned, its efforts in the Republics of Korea and Taiwan are illustrative. Between 1953 and 1974, the U.S. provided $4 billion in grant aid to the ROK, as well as military assistance. During much of this period, the ROK was ruled by former senior military officers, notably Park Chung-hee, whose "civvies" always seemed an uncomfortable fit to one accustomed to clothing with stars on his shoulders. Today, Korea is a thriving, albeit chaotic, democracy as well as a significant world economy. The case is similar for Taiwan, where the United States exerted major effort to prevent the island from being seized by mainland China. The rule of Chiang Kai-shek and his son and successor Chiang Ching-kuo, which lasted until 1988, had the trappings of democracy, but not the reality. Nevertheless, the island was prosperous, and its prosperity has continued while a vigorous democracy has also evolved.

In contrast—without belaboring the point—during the period immediately after the end of the Cold War, a number of states adopted the political structures of democracy. Having seen the success of free market capitalism (and the failures of communist economics), these societies decided that capitalism and democracy were the equivalent of a magic wand that would transmute the dross of their existing economic structures into gold. This has not always been the case, and there has been popular disappointment and disillusion with the failures of capitalism and democracy. It remains significantly easier to draft a constitution and hold an election than to implement an honest banking/financial system. Unfortunately, without the latter, the likelihood of the former surviving is limited.

WHERE ARE WE GOING? C

Having explored a selection of the multiple factors that influence Canada and the United States, we would be remiss not to examine where all of these alternative possibilities may direct us. In short, where are we going?

Historically, the question has played more heavily in Canada, conflicted by its anglophone-francophone reality and the lodestar attraction for some Canadians of the United States. There are few thoughtful Canadians today who have not deeply considered their national destiny. On the other hand, most Americans simply take it for granted that their country is great, grand, and glorious (albeit with some major fixes to make, such as rebuilding New Orleans and extracting themselves from Iraq) and will become more so with each passing year. And if in 2006, one poll suggests that 70 percent of U.S. citizens think that the country is headed in the wrong direction, it is more a transient consequence of political hostility to the Bush presidency than a conclusion that the economy or the structure of society requires radical restructuring.

More basically, some Canadians wonder about the essential artificiality of their country's borders. Specialists in international relations regularly lament over the artificial nature of many boundaries in Africa, which split communities and carved up the landmass for the benefit of surveyors from European states. Neither the Canadian provincial boundaries nor the Canada-U.S. boundary has any particular geographic logic today. A generation ago, Joel Garreau's *The Nine Nations of North America* identified the point (and the title makes it unnecessary to read the text). There could have been a Balkanized continent—or one with a single nation state.

Attraction-Repulsion

Our binational history indicates an accordion effect in the relationship—a moving closer and then a moving apart. Some psychologists have identified an "attraction-repulsion" aspect to personal relationships, that is, the closer that some personalities approach one another, the greater the individual resistance keeping them apart. Playing psychologist for nations is presumptuous at a minimum, but there are occasionally useful points. It is possible to observe a moving together in the 1980s and early 1990s, epitomized by the Free Trade Agreement (FTA) and the North American Free Trade Agreement (NAFTA) in economic terms, and the very brief "end of history" period in foreign affairs following the collapse of the Soviet Union.

Over the past several years, however, there has clearly been a moving apart. In foreign affairs, "history" blatantly has resumed, although not just with international terrorism, which the United States has identified as the "Long War" in which it is the primary target and—at least thus far, since 9/11—the primary victim. Canadians are more sanguine, less interested in fighting a "war," more inclined to believe the U.S. neurotic (if not outright psychotic) over terrorism. Canada's commitment in Afghanistan is more hesitant than heartfelt; duty rather than dedication is the driver. Elsewhere, some of the hopeful sprouts of democracy in nations throughout South America and Africa appear to have withered recently; whether democracy was oversold or its practitioners underperformed is less the question than our need to recognize that the strengthened civil societies in new and emerging democracies still need to do some intensive work, perhaps the equivalent of reinvention. And the approach to the states in the Middle East is also seriously in question. Thus the many philosophical differences between Canadian and U.S. views on international relations, muted during the Cold War (except for Trudeau's occasional flights of fancy) and subsumed for a decade after the collapse of the USSR, have re-emerged.

In bilateral economics, the FTA/NAFTA has been successful overall, despite problems such as softwood lumber and BSE. The trading relationship is the world's largest, at $2 billion per day (and steadily rising); it is hard to see or even envision an upper limit to its mutual benefits. Critics have been reduced to saying that "it would have happened anyway," but they have been forced to admit that their doomsaying did not bring doom. Canadian media prosper, Canadian health care remains "one tier," and Canadian water sits without a ripple north of the border. And yet, to a clear degree, FTA/NAFTA has become a victim of its own success. In a sense, free trade is akin to public utilities such as water, sewage, electricity, etc. When first installed, homeowners are agog over indoor plumbing and an end to flickering kerosene lamps. However, after a while, we focus on utility bills and power outages. We are unhappy with the bills for clogged plumbing and are infuriated if there is a "boil water" advisory. So it has been with NAFTA, where the advocates emphasize that 96 percent of trade takes place without incident. But 100 percent of the media attention is on the problems.

Without question, there has been a pulling away, a reviewing of the bidding, a scab-picking, cranky unwillingness to "split the difference" on issues in foreign affairs, internal security, and economics. All the little clichés about undefended borders and "best friends, like it or not" still apply. But so far as "best friends, like it or not" is concerned, we are still in the "not" portion of the cycle.

Indeed, what we may be finding is that while economics continue to haul us together, two factors—the military and social attitudes—are pushing us apart. National views on these topics appear less and less compatible, with neither political harmony nor flexibility on these topics available in the near term. This judgment goes beyond the provocatively predictive *Time* "Man of the Year" covers in 2001 juxtaposing the American Fighting Man (U.S.) and the Gay Couple (Canada), as neither nation is a caricature "red" or "blue" zone. But there are elements of a reality that need to be recognized in order to be properly appreciated.

SOME CONSTANTS

There are some immutable factors: we will continue to share the same continent and day by day we will move deeper into the 21st century. Beyond such "the sun will come up in the east" observations, our respective populations and economic dimensions are unlikely to alter significantly. Canada's will remain approximately one-tenth that of the United States, both demographically and economically.

Likewise, the "look" of our populations will remain the same. There are no populations on earth with a greater diversity of cultural, racial, ethnic, religious, social, and political communities. And virtually all groups are represented in both nations. There are proportionally more African-Americans and Hispanics in the United States and more First Nations persons and francophones in Canada, but there is no significant group that exists in one country but not in the other.

And our populations will continue to be wealthy, technologically skilled, politically engaged, and highly conscious of their social and legal rights and privileges. On the macrocosmic scale, these are societies in which the rule of law is a given, security forces defend society against criminals (rather than criminalize society), the corrupt politician is the exception not the rule, and the armed forces are committed to support and defending civilian government. On the microcosmic level, citizens use the same electric voltage and communications networks, the water on both sides of the border is potable regardless of the tendency of both societies to consume bottles of "designer water," dentists and doctors are skilled practitioners of their arts, and mechanics and repairmen fix problems correctly—usually on the first attempt.

As a consequence, the casual outside observer will indeed say "they're the same" (and many foreign ministries have a single bureau of North American affairs). But while similarities are seductive, differences are defining, and the pointed nature of these key differences does not appear subject to compromise.

NATIONAL UNITY

Canada remains at some risk; it is a political convalescent in constant fear either of relapse from old maladies (the congenital birth defect of having two nations contending within the structure of a single state) or the eruption of a possible new threat (Western separatism). In contrast the United States *is* . . . and any national unity issues are abstractions drifting into the relatively distant future and very improbably related to the political digestibility of its Hispanic population, which is regionally concentrated, in contrast to its African-American community, which is more nationally dispersed.

While the United States has no interest in a fragmented Canada and certainly emphasizes a political preference for a Canada that remains united (if only on a "devil we know" basis), it also has no lessons for national unity that Canada is able to accept. While the U.S. was willing to fight a civil war to maintain "one nation indivisible," Canadians clearly are not committed to maintaining "one Canada" by force of arms. Indeed, Canada offers a legal (complex, to be sure, but legal) mechanism for political separation; such a breakup is quite literally unconstitutional for the United States. Were the federal government of Canada clearly committed to maintaining its unity by force of arms (and maintained sufficient armed forces to do so), Washington conceivably might quietly offer military support as necessary; however, the U.S. is not going to be more committed to Canadian unity than are Canadians. Certainly, Canadians do not want to believe that they remain a single state because the U.S. so wills it; Canada has enough grievances against the United States as it stands.

As a consequence, Canadian unity is an ongoing exercise in accommodation and diplomacy. Without question, these qualities are Canadian strengths, but the need to constantly devote substantial sociopolitical energy to maintaining national integrity detracts from other priorities such as combating poverty. Should dual (or multiple) Canadas emerge in the years to come, the United States will see it as a regrettable development, albeit not a tragedy on the level of the great international wars, genocides, and unnatural disasters of the 20th century. The assumption is that any Canadian separation would reflect societal civility akin to that governing the separation of Sweden-Norway and, more recently, the Czechoslovak "velvet divorce."

DEMOCRATIC PRACTICE

The essence of Canadian-American difference lies in their varying political structures. A parliamentary structure is intended to create an efficiently operating governing structure. A party presents its policies to the electorate; if successful in obtaining a majority, it relies on predictable party discipline to transform its policies into laws, regulations, and actions. In contrast, the republican government of the United States is designed to thwart action; the multiple executive, legislative, and judicial "checks-and-balances" have prevented far more action than they have implemented. A substantial change in policy must be widely desired by the general public and many actors, over an extended period, to come to pass in the United States.

Thus, the ostensibly consensus-oriented and consultative Canadians endorse a government that is, as many Canadian observers have described it, an elected dictatorship. The citizens depend on their leaders not to abuse power. In contrast, the U.S. government reflects the suspicions of its citizens over *any* government; it must coordinate, negotiate, and compromise on virtually every significant issue. Effectively, the U.S. government is a permanent minority government—except that a defeat doesn't require an election.

This doing-democracy-differently is part of the basis for the ongoing Canadian national disunity. Quebec clings to its historical belief that Canada consists of "two founding nations" and rejects any political revision that would reduce its power. Moreover, the small provinces have no significant political representation equivalent to the U.S. Senate; they must accept what the interlock of Ontario and Quebec decides to give them—and be grateful for what they get from Ottawa (or that more isn't extracted from their provincial resources). The inability of a minority to stop majority action eliminates the frustrations of filibusters in the U.S. Senate, but it also has prompted increasing alienation in the Canadian West. The absence of any significant federal "say" for an Alberta that pays billions in taxes each year to Ottawa, with no commensurate benefit, appears inherently unstable. Some Albertans and other Western Canadians inevitably ask, "What am I getting out of this deal?"

There are many technical devices to give the disenfranchised a greater role in federal decision-making in Canada. Others have investigated, *inter alia*, innovations such as proportionate representation and devices such as the single transferable vote; these are all conceivable solutions, albeit lacking the clarity of a first-past-the-post victor. Nevertheless, it appears that remedies to national unity problems exist through improved democratic practices for Canada, despite the palatable reluctance of Canadians to grapple again with their straitjacket constitution.

ECONOMICS

There is an old maxim to the effect that if you owe the bank $10,000, you have a problem; if you owe the bank $10 million, it has a problem. When the trading relationship between the United States and Canada is such that regardless of its import to the United States, it is far more important to Canada, then Canada has the problem. This problem is unlikely to be one that goes away or even substantially alters in its ratios. The challenge for Canada is to live with less anxiety within the economic-trading relationship.

The dimensions of the trading relationship are remarkable in historical as well as economic terms. Free trade was a concept that for much of North American history appeared to be an economist's dream rather than a likely market reality—regardless of the steadily growing amounts of bilateral trade throughout the 20th century, various efforts to create free trade foundered on national political interests. The FTA (1988) and NAFTA (1994) have been, on balance, successful in their own right; however, they have created a "where do we go from here" question. Indeed, the rather cranky reaction to every free trade problem, particularly from the Canadian optic, suggests that the positive elements of free trade are seen as a given, akin to having rural electrification or potable water.

The highly politicized Canadian reactions to the percentage of the trading relationship where there are problems (softwood lumber; mad cows) suggest that Canadians deliberately chose not to recognize U.S. political problems rather than that Canada has legal justification for its complaints. Consequently, while there are theoretical "next steps" possible to deepen the trading relationship in the form of a customs union or a common currency, they are now and for the foreseeable future politically unlikely. Thus the "where do we go from here" issue may well be answered by "nowhere." This looks like more of an era for consolidation (hopefully without regression) than for innovative integration initiatives.

For a generation, the United States has been relatively indifferent (and unconscious) of the dimensions of the bilateral relationship. With the post-9/11 world and U.S. concerns over energy security, this blithe indifference is changing. However, higher levels of U.S. attention are not always a good thing for those subjected to this attention. The combination of U.S. attention to secure Albertan energy supplies and intermittent Albertan alienation from federal Canada could create bilateral political problems that currently are only hypothetical, but should not be regarded with indifference.

CULTURE, EDUCATION, AND RELIGION

The United States remains innately suspicious of public (let alone federal) support for culture or multiculturalism, national standards for education, or state support for religion. The manner in which each of these topics is handled reflects the American way of life.

If culture cannot be supported privately, it requires overwhelming public endorsement to justify taxpayer funding. There is continuing persistent skepticism among some Americans over federal funding for the Public Broadcasting System or federal grants for artists. Concurrently, privately developed U.S. culture, in the form of movies, music, and television, has proved enormously successful on a global basis; consequently, the U.S. believes that trade or regulatory barriers against these aspects of U.S. culture reflect either or both anti-Americanism and hostility to the free markets.

Moreover, institutionalized federal financial support for ethnic cultures in the U.S. is regarded as divisive rather than integrative. The global reach of modern communications encourages diversity and particularistic attitudes as much as it encourages "globalism"; consequently, the U.S. promotes national unity through implicit support for national cultural activity that ranges from students reciting the Pledge of Allegiance, to Fourth of July celebrations, to Super Bowl Sunday. Any federal attention should be directed at integrating immigrants into U.S. culture rather than encouraging traditional ties. While the U.S. is replete with ethnic, cultural, and religious heritage activity, from Welsh St. David's Day dinners to Chinese boat races, those activities are privately organized, financed, and sponsored.

American religiosity is historically derived; it is also a reflection of U.S. belief in its exceptionalism. A nation so blessed by God would be ungrateful in its hubris not to recognize and appreciate such divine attention. Many U.S. colonists and later immigrants were prompted by their search for religious freedom, and the United States has deliberately sought God's support in facing its deepest challenges—whether by Union soldiers singing "The Battle Hymn of the Republic" or in countering "godless communism." Just as recent U.S. presidents appear to require a canine companion to demonstrate their common touch, public church attendance demonstrates their commitment to the Almighty.

Battle lines are especially entrenched over same-sex marriage, as most Americans appear unwilling to accept anything beyond contractualized civil unions that provide the "game" but not the "name" of marriage—and even toleration of such civil structures is chancy. In those states during the 2004 election that had "defense of marriage" amendments to state constitutions, all were passed by substantial majorities; there were similar results for comparable legal action in another half-dozen states during the 2006 elections. The difference with Canada, now effectively the third state that legalizes same-sex marriage, is pointed.

Observers occasionally attempt to imply some level of commonality between Jihad-minded ayatollahs and U.S. religious leaders; however, that parallelism must remain illegitimate until Christian suicide bombers by the score are assaulting mosques and other Islamic facilities. Nevertheless, the U.S. government's commitment to religious freedom, as projected internationally, is not always viewed as a commitment to diversity in religious practice but often regarded instead as interference in local particular preference.

While Americans are comfortable with the quality of their culture and the strength of their religious commitments, they are dissatisfied with the U.S. education system. The remarkable diversity of decentralized education with public and private schooling produces "best in the world" outcomes, as well as mediocre and poor results. The international test results are frustrating; the ritualistic answer of "more money" appears driven by special pleading from educators, especially when school systems with lower funding per student repeatedly produce better results. Indeed, education at virtually every level appears to be a black hole, akin to health care, that will swallow unlimited amounts of funding with no guarantee of significant student improvement. It may not be a solvable problem, at least not with the existing

U.S. demographic, social, and cultural mix. Canadians seem to be obtaining better results, and certainly greater societal satisfaction, from their educational tactics and strategies.

HEALTH CARE

The health of a nation is a national concern. The difference between the best health care and the best affordable health care is an economic problem. But for Canada, a technical issue has become a defining element of the nation; paying for health care has become a spending chasm even larger and deeper than that for education and particularly poignant for its citizens since they have paid for their elder health care "up front" through a lifetime of higher taxes.

For the United States, health is, if anything, a more expensive problem; but it remains a *personal* technical problem, not a philosophical issue. While many in the United States remain convinced that health care should be a privately delivered, privately paid, and privately insured function, they appear willing to experiment with other methods for delivering medical services. Single tier; two tier; infinite tier—the delivery mechanism matters far less than the cost versus result ratio. It is conceivable that even the most efficiently delivered medical care may be so expensive that a society can afford either such medical care or effective armed forces—but not both. That would offer a gruesome choice: a society more vulnerable to external threat or a society with its citizens receiving less than optimal health care. If the choice for health care prevails in Canada, Americans might not be amused by Canadians achieving better health care while the U.S. provides for Canada's defense from American taxpayer recourse.

Canadian insistence that core medical services can only be delivered by public means places a remarkable restraint on citizens' choices in a free society. If Canadians can purchase the education, legal services, financial appraisals, and material goods of their choice, how can they be legally restricted in their choice of medical service providers? When the choice was finally put starkly to the Canadian Supreme Court in a 2005 case, the Court ruled clearly that such medical choice was indeed a protected right. To the degree that this decision is incorporated into Canadian practice, it will mean greater individual choice for Canadian citizens. It is hard to see the virtue in suffering (unless Canadians enjoy ritualized masochism) by waiting for medical services that an individual could obtain by paying for them privately. Greater flexibility in permitting private payment of medical services could also stimulate creative thinking in delivery of health services and more thoughtful exploration of other national health systems that are regarded as delivering more bandages for the buck than either the U.S. or Canada.

CRIME AND SUBSTANCE ABUSE

For the victim, any crime is too much crime. Thus the repeated admonitions that various elements of crime are falling, or at record low percentages, is only of intellectual interest; viscerally, public and individual concern is focused on local events. But currently, "local" really means national; the media follows the "if it bleeds, it leads" school of coverage; consequently, the public is intimately familiar with a variety of gruesome and vicious criminal behavior.

The persistent U.S. approach is that crime should be punished; rehabilitation gets a bow, but not the financial support that its backers claim necessary to be effective. Prison terms may indeed provide negative schooling—instruction on how to be a more effective criminal. But that argument has no resonance with most of the American population, whose motto is closer to "lock 'em up and throw away the key," as epitomized in the three-strikes-and-you're-out (or really "in" jail for the rest of your life) policy for those convicted of three felony crimes.

And punishment at its maximum—capital punishment—retains strong popular support in the United States. There are crimes that are regarded as so heinous that suffering the criminals to live would be a persistent insult to the rest of the citizenry. It would have been irrelevant to Americans if Timothy McVeigh, the Oklahoma City bomber, repented and found religion. Christians might be pleased that his faith would save him from damnation, but be no less convinced that his murder of 168 men, women, and children required his rapid dispatch to divine judgment. One cannot be sure whether the fear of capital punishment prevents criminal action; one can be sure that capital punishment prevents recidivism.

Americans are more conflicted over substance abuse and the degree to which users should be punished. The most obvious issue is addressing marijuana use—and the United States remains undecided whether pot should be handled as an equivalent to alcohol, that is, an acceptable personal choice as long as its use doesn't result in injury to others, such as driving while intoxicated. Or is marijuana a sufficiently likely gateway to more destructive drugs for which public juridical intervention is justified to prevent greater personal and societal damage, either through increased need for medical assistance or criminal activity? The many millions who have experimented with marijuana and other "soft" drugs without evident damage to health suggest the alcohol paradigm; the tens of thousands obviously damaged, often fatally, during the same period pulls one in the societal protection direction. Counted sometimes among these victims are the massive numbers jailed for drug trafficking charges; largely, however, these individuals are not unwitting innocents, but rather criminals with multiple charges, including the drug-related ones.

UNILATERALISM AND MULTILATERALISM

Countries that can act unilaterally have the choice: they can act in conjunction with international organizations, coalitions of like-minded states, or alone. Countries without military strength (or resolve) do not have the choice; if they act at all, they must act in concert with others. For the foreseeable future, the United States has both the capability and the will to act unilaterally. This is not its first preference; joint action can be cheaper and have major public relations benefits. However, the United States will act alone if it determines that its interests are at risk. It is the sole proprietor of these interests and gives a veto to no state or international organization. As a powerful state, the U.S. realizes that others wish it to act to advance their interests; however, the United States declines to be the ox for the plows of others.

This is not, to say the least, always a popular approach to international affairs. Indeed, no matter what course the United States takes, it will dissatisfy, even infuriate, a substantial element of the world community. If the U.S. were not available to be blamed, it would have to be invented. However, the United States has moved beyond embarrassment about charges of being an "ugly American"; it knows that Goliath is never popular and, indeed, looks more than a bit silly whining that he isn't loved. Respect is the most tribute that can be expected; in a pinch, fear will suffice. It was not love that induced the Libyans to terminate their WMD program or the Syrians to withdraw from Lebanon.

Historically, the United States had minimal interest in foreign affairs ("entangling alliances" was the term of opprobrium against which the iconic George Washington warned), and public support for foreign ventures has normally ranged from caution to great reluctance. Likewise, there has been no war—not even the Second World War—in which the U.S. population was universally united. This lack of unity (even when the U.S. had international endorsement, for example, in Korea, or a sizeable numbers of allies, for example, in Vietnam or Iraq) has sometimes resulted in political failures, regardless of the degree of military success. The USA has reached the point militarily where it cannot be defeated; it can only defeat itself.

As a consequence, the U.S. attitude towards the United Nations has evolved in the direction of profound skepticism. U.S. views of the U.N. have been cyclical throughout its history, vaulting from overly inflated optimism to deep pessimism. Currently, the U.S. view has moved beyond an appraisal of the U.N as flawed and incompetent to a judgment that it is actively hostile to U.S. interests, maneuvering to frustrate legitimate U.S. desires, and imbued with implacable hostility to Israel rooted less in foreign policy difference than in anti-Semitism. The likelihood that any reform program will effectively "reform" the United Nations is dubious, and pessimism must be the assessment of the proposals now in play; nevertheless, a pessimist can be pleasantly surprised, while an optimist is continually disappointed.

Given its modest weight in power equations, Canada must normally act in concert with others. However, Ottawa can act unilaterally—assuming that no greater power disagrees with Canadian action. Canada was able to act unilaterally and without apology against Spanish fishing vessels and to enforce its claim to Hans Island. In the United Nations, Canada previously played something of a bridging role between the United States and other U.N. members—a role that enhanced its own international prestige. Recently, however, Canada has found itself at odds with the U.S. on most issues of significance to the U.S.: Iraq; the Kyoto Treaty; anti-personnel landmines; the International Criminal Court. Clearly, its current influence (even in its Conservative incarnation) on the Bush administration verges on the nonexistent.

Even the most chauvinist U.S. supporter will not claim that the U.S. is always right; however, most assuredly it is not as wrong, or as frequently wrong, as its U.N. opponents portray. It is not simply American hubris to suggest the U.N.'s international relevance is directly tied to its acceptability to U.S. political leadership. If the U.N. is to play anything approaching the global role its Charter envisions, it must change from a reflexive "No," to a "Yes, but…" attitude when considering legitimate American proposals. Canada, in its own self-interest, should probably take a similar approach.

The Military and Foreign Policy

A significant portion of the world confuses military forces with foreign policy. Obviously, that is incorrect: military force, both potential and actual, is only an instrument of foreign policy. Nor does the United States regard international problems as nails to be resolved with its military hammer. However, the most adroit diplomacy, absent any military component, is unlikely to be successful unless its diplomatic objective is universally agreed. That which is universally agreed, unfortunately, is likely to be substantively irrelevant. There simply must be sticks to supplement carrots, in some instances, and occasionally a large enough stick can make even a wilted carrot appear to be a treat.

Over its national history, the United States, by necessity rather than by design, has grown to appreciate the requirements for high-quality military forces. Following the Second World War, the United States maintained military forces at a level previously unknown in peacetime, since the alternative was global domination by the USSR. In the process, the U.S. military forces reverted to the "all volunteer" nature that existed prior to the Second World War; the result has been an exceptionally capable professional force that is both responsive to executive action and substantially immune to public opinion, but also firmly committed to civilian control of the military.

The Canadian conundrum is how or if to maintain any significant military forces when the country is defended in practice by the United States. The precipitous decline of Canadian military capability over a generation has left the Canadian Armed Forces with a tiny handful of good light infantry units and relatively modern naval vessels, but with equipment that is largely antiquated—and will be very expensive to modernize. Public support for the Canadian forces is an abstraction; it appears to endorse "peacekeeping" but not military spending that would cut into societal benefits such as health, education, infrastructure, etc. Consequently, there is serious question in the U.S. whether Canadian military and foreign policy is systematically making it impossible to cooperate effectively in future with U.S. military forces.

Even the niche market of peacekeeping is one that increasingly requires trained combat forces to make rather than just keep peace. Without such capability, peacekeepers are too often in effect funeral directors rather than providers of security and stability. Canadians are writing themselves out of the key role that the country created.

It is a cruel reality of international politics that a country's voice is directly related to its military capability. Those who are doing the dying have nominal interest in "good ideas" from those with no willingness to sacrifice. Canada is rapidly descending to the level of Costa Rica in the level of politicomilitary influence it has on U.S. policy design; some Canadians, of course, are delighted with this trend. In this context, it is unclear whether the current commitment in Afghanistan will finally be judged as a worthy, extended commitment to nation building or a misguided adventure taken in support of an equally misguided U.S. War on Terror.

At a minimum, Ottawa must take action to eliminate any perception that it is indifferent to North American security. The impression remains that lip service rather than real service is Canada's motivation regarding hemispheric security. Driven by a distain bordering on hatred for the current Bush administration, the media generates the persistent impression that preventing any disadvantage or inconvenience to Canadian citizens is more important than preventing a repeat of 9/11. No one hears the voices from the grave when a Canadian is unhappy over missing a flight because of tedious security delays. Americans know now that none of the 18 hijacker terrorists originated in Canada but Canadians know that they easily could have—and still could. Persistent Canadian antipathy to tough border controls in the guise of secure travel documents is the latest bilateral irritant. It prompts the concern that a 9/11-style attack on the U.S. originating north of the border could spark a furious U.S. reaction far more economically restrictive than any currently proposed travel document.

In this regard, concrete action from Ottawa is imperative. If the next terrorist attack is sourced to Canada, no level of *mea culpa* will restore the bilateral relationship to its current, albeit stressed, comity.

HUMAN RIGHTS AND DEVELOPMENT

One would like to believe that human rights and economic development are like the song lyrics of love and marriage—they "go together like a horse and carriage." But just as modern society wryly appreciates that there is love without marriage, there can also be economic development without comparable expansion of human rights. Indeed, the current paradigm, as illustrated by Korea, Taiwan, and much of Southeast Asia, is that political freedoms have often been a somewhat tardy follow-on to economic development.

That reality does not in any manner reduce U.S. efforts to expand global respect for human rights; the annual State Department's country reports provide detailed particulars on the status of human rights in almost 200 states and political entities around the world. Human rights are a constant, if not always successful, theme in diplomatic representation to offending states. Does more need to be done? To be sure—but perhaps also with the implicit recognition that most individuals would sacrifice individual liberties for a full stomach.

With regard to assistance for developing countries, the United States is not convinced or compelled by any abstract formula. There is no magic to the "0.7 percent of GDP" proposal beyond providing a mechanism to extract more funds from wealthy countries—and create still greater opportunities for waste by recipients. By some accounts, upwards of a trillion dollars has gone to Africa in debt forgiveness and direct assistance over the past 50 years.

Corruption, incompetence, political instability, and wars have destroyed much of the possible benefits, leaving African states, in some instances, worse off overall than prior to independence. Does that mean that no assistance should be extended? Again, obviously not, but assistance should be clearly connected with good governance, free markets, vigorous action against corruption, and transparency in the use of assistance. Canadians and Americans must be bottom-line oriented in providing assistance: that assistance should not be a Lady Bountiful "feel good" distribution of alms to the many, but a specific concentration on those who can be best helped with the least effort. Canadians could most effectively focus on what is close at hand rather that which is far away. A project for a generation could be to "adopt" Haiti, which is currently a cesspool without a drain plug that the United States has attempted repeatedly and without success to stabilize. Ottawa, with its unique combination of linguistic skills and a base of Haitian refugees, including its own governor general, could take the lead in moving Haiti not to being a Caribbean Switzerland, but to the economic and political effectiveness of other regional islands.

In the End . . .

In the end, we are stuck with each other. There are next-door neighbors who realize that they could do far worse than the current side-by-side housing arrangement, but whose peccadilloes (Sam laughs too loudly; Joe whines a lot) occasionally grate. To "be-neighbor" the analogy a bit, both are pleased to be living in pleasant homes, working at good, well-paying jobs, and raising children whose prospects look promising. Although they don't spend a lot of time reflecting on the point, they appreciate that other parts of town are far less congenial to the kind of lives they wish to live.

Leaving the "neighborhood," we know that Canada and the United States have an exceptionally complex and extended relationship—one that is more likely to become "more of the same" than not. Currently, Canada's greatest challenge is inward, with the ultimate roles of Quebec and the West depressingly unresolved. For the United States, whether Iraq is *sui generis*, or just a stepping stone towards Iran, is less the question than how the nation will employ power in foreign affairs. Whether Canada is looking inward or the Unites States is gazing outward, neither is terribly comfortable with the current view. Perhaps we should take comfort in minimums: while neither of us is a solution for the problems of the other, we are far from being each other's worst problem.

ACKNOWLEDGMENTS
by DAVID T. JONES

I wish particularly to express appreciation for the protean efforts of my co-author, David Kilgour, who nurtured an embryonic idea of a collaborative effort on our nations into a reality.

Also, there is no question that without the exceptional efforts of our literary agent, Larry Hoffman, the manuscript would have wandered, perhaps indefinitely, in the wilderness of worthy but unpublished works.

Specifically, also, I want to commend the work of Joanne Lostracco, who, by providing adroit fact-checking for the text, has repeatedly aided our work.

Elements of this book appeared previously in *Policy Options*, the *Ottawa Citizen*, and *The Hill Times* (an independently owned Canadian government and politics newsweekly).

The opinions and characterizations in this book are those of the authors, and do not necessarily represent official positions of the United States government.

ACKNOWLEDGMENTS
by DAVID KILGOUR

I owe thanks to three persons, above all others, for seeing this book published. The first is Mary Cameron, a long-time senior editor at the University of Alberta Press, who encouraged and nurtured both authors in bringing the manuscript along, and offered plenty of constructive criticisms. Unfortunately, health problems required her to step aside before the manuscript could be finished, and we resolved to seek another publisher.

The second person is my co-author, David Jones, whose spirits never flagged when my own did on a number of occasions, mostly having to do with parliamentary duties and related 24/7 calls on the time of a Canadian Member of Parliament.

The third is Larry Hoffman, literary agent extraordinaire, who found publisher John Wiley & Sons quickly, at an anxious period for both authors. Our dealings with both him and John Wiley have been productive at all times.

Special thanks also go to a number of talented women and men who worked in my parliamentary office while the research and writing was going on. I hasten to say here that because their salaries, along with my own, were paid ultimately by the Canadian taxpayer—hopefully to research issues of social, economic, parliamentary, and other importance to Canadians—all of my royalties (after deduction of my out-of-pocket expenses for the fact checker and indexer) from this work will be paid directly by the publisher to the Receiver General of Canada.

In alphabetical order, I thank each of them for the following important research:

Miriam Booy, currently working in Africa, for her general work on research and for helping with the bibliography;

Paul Bure, currently working for an NGO in Ottawa, who found many important details on human rights and international development;

Margrethe Hannen, currently studying in Paris, who did research on Atlantic Canada, the North, and Western alienation, as well as ferreting out many details for the chapter on Canadian multilateralism versus American unilateralism;

Camille Renee Kam, who is completing her legal studies, who researched the chapters on the Canadian justice system and our military;

Mohan Samarasinghe, who is working in Ottawa, for his work on the bibliography; and

Nina Singh, formerly of Edmonton, who worked on Canadian education and religion.

BIBLIOGRAPHY

Preface and Introduction

Adams, Michael, *Fire and Ice: The United States, Canada and the Myth of Converging Values*. Toronto: Penguin Canada, 2003.

Binder, Sue, "Protecting American Families from Injury," *American Family Physician,* http://www.aafp.org/afp/20040515/editorials.html, on May 14, 2004.

Granatstein, J. L., *Yankee Go Home?* Toronto: A Phyllis Bruce Book, HarperCollins Publishers, 1996.

Illinois Council Against Handgun Violence, "Statistics, Facts & Quotes," February 28, 2005, http://www.ichv.org/Statistics.htm.

Lipset, Seymour Martin, *Continental Divide: The Values and Institutions of the United States and Canada*. Toronto: Routledge, 1990.

Rudmin, Floyd W., *Bordering on Aggression*. Hull, QC: Voyageur, 1993.

Wise, S. F., and Robert Craig Brown, *Canada Views the United States: Nineteenth Century Political Attitudes*. Seattle and Toronto: University of Washington Press/Macmillan Company of Canada, 1967.

Chapter 1: National Identity and Self-Image

Cooper, Robert, W., *The Breaking of Nations: Order and Chaos in the Twenty-First Century*. London: Atlantic Monthly Press, 2004.

Crowe, Harry S., J. H. Stewart Reid, and Kenneth McNaught, *Source Book of Canadian History: Selected Documents and Personal Papers*. Toronto: Longmans, 1959.

Fehrenbach, T. R., *Lone Star: A History of Texas and the Texans*. Cambridge, MA: Da Capo Press, 2000.

Foreign Affairs and International Trade Canada, *Canada's International Policy Statement: A Role of Pride and Influence: Overview.* http://www.dfait-maeci.gc.ca/cip-pic/ips/overview-en.asp, April 19, 2005.

Foreign Affairs and International Trade Canada, *Canada's International Policy Statement, A Role of Pride and Influence: Development.* http://www.acdi-cida.gc.ca/ips-development, 2005.

Kilgour, David, Elizabeth Kwasniewski, and Allan McChesney, "Human Rights Across the Commonwealth—A Joint Responsibility," *The Parliamentarian*, Vol. LXXVII(2), April 1996.

Lincoln, Abraham, "Gettysburg Address," in *A Documentary History of the United States,* Fourth Edition, Richard D. Heffner, ed. New York: New American Library, 1985.

McRoberts, Kenneth, *Misconceiving Canada: The Struggle for National Unity.* Toronto: Oxford University Press, 1997.

Stanley, Thomas J., and William D. Danko, *The Millionaire Next Door.* Atlanta: Longstreet Press, 1996.

Whelan, Susan (Canadian Minister for International Cooperation), Trade and Human Rights. Presented at Rights and Democracy Panel on Human Rights and the WTO Agenda, Cancun, Mexico, September 12, 2003.

Chapter 2: Democratic Culture and Practices

527 Group, 2004 Election Controversy, *Wikipedia*, May 31, 2005, http://en.wikipedia.org/wiki/527_groups on July 1, 2005.

Cantor, Joseph E., "Elections: The State of Campaign Finance," United States Elections 2004, International Information Programs, http://usinfo.state.gov/products/pubs/election04/campaign$.htm, on July 1, 2005.

Center for American Women and Politics, "Women in Elected Office 2005, Fact Sheet Summaries," June 2005, http://www.cawp.rutgers.edu/Facts/Officeholders/cawpfs.html on July 2, 2005.

Dizdarevic, Zlatko, *Sarajevo: A War Journal.* New York: Fromm International, 1993.

Dyck, Rand, *Canadian Politics: Critical Approaches,* Fourth Edition. Scarborough, ON: Thomson Nelson Learning, 2000.

Faler, Brian, "Census Details Voter Turnout for 2004," *Washington Post*, May 25, 2005, Washingtonpost.com.com/wp-dyn/content/article on July 3, 2005.

Morton, William L. *The Canadian Identity*. Madison, WI: University of Wisconsin Press, 1961.

Moyers, William, "NOW with Bill Moyers. Politics & Economy. Election 2004." PBS, July 5, 2004, http://www.pbs.org/now/politics/votestats.html on July 3, 2005.

Twain, Mark, *Roughing It*. New York: Signet Classics, Penguin, 1994.

Chapter 3: Economic and Resource Management

Aldonas, Grant D., "The Impact of NAFTA on the U.S. Economy," Testimony of the Under Secretary of Commerce for International Trade to the Senate Committee of Foreign Relations, Subcommittee on International Economic Policy, Export, and Trade Promotion, http://www.mac.doc.gov/nafta/AldonasTestimony.pdf on June 27, 2005.

Blum, Justin, "Congress Could Send Bush Energy Bill Today," *The Washington Post*, July 29, 2005, A4.

Blustein, Paul, "U.S. Hopes for Momentum from CAFTA," *The Washington Post*, July 29, 2005, A6.

Canadian and American Economies Compared, *Wikipedia*, http://en.wikipedia.org/wiki/Canadian_and_American_economics_compared on June 27, 2005.

Cellucci, Paul, "The Ties that Bind: The Common Borders and Uncommon Values of Canada-U.S. Relations," October 29, 2004, http://www.usembassy canada.gov/content/embconsul/cellucci_102904.pdf on June 27, 2005.

Dunbar, R. B. (Bob), *Oil Sands Supply Outlook: Potential Supply and Costs of Crude Bitumen and Synthetic Crude Oil in Canada, 2003-2017*. Calgary, AB: Canadian Energy Research Institute, 2004.

Faux, Jeff, "NAFTA at 10," Economic Policy Institute, 2005, http://www.epinet.org/content.cfm/webfeatures_viewpoints_nafta_legacy_at10 on July 24, 2005.

Friedman, Thomas, *The World Is Flat: A Brief History of the Twenty-first Century*. New York: Farrar, Straus, and Giroux, 2005.

Hart, Michael, *A Trading Nation: Canadian Trade Policy from Colonialism to Globalization*. Vancouver: University of British Columbia Press, 2002.

Innis, Harold A., *The Cod Fisheries: The History of an International Economy*. Toronto: University of Toronto Press, 1954.

Levey, David H., and Stuart S. Brown, "The Overstretch Myth," *Foreign Affairs*, March/April 2005, http://www.foreignaffairs.org/20050301facomment84201david-h-levey-stuart-s-brown/th on July 31, 2005.

Morton, William L., *The Canadian Identity*. Toronto: University of Toronto Press, 1961.

NBC News/*Wall Street Journal* Poll, "International Trade/Global Economy," taken May 12-16, 2005, PollingReport.com on June 30, 2005.

Norrie, K. H. (Kenneth Harold), *A History of the Canadian Economy*. Scarborough, ON: Thomson Nelson, 2002.

Scott, Paul, "Distorting the Record: NAFTA's Promoters Play Fast and Loose with Facts," Economic Policy Institute, 2005, http://www.epinet.org/content.cfm/issuebriefs_ib158 on July 24, 2005.

Scott, Robert E., "The High Price of 'Free' Trade: NAFTA's Failure Has Cost the United States Jobs Across the Nation," EPI Briefing Paper #147, November 27, 2003, http://www.epinet.org/content.cfm/briefingpapers_bp147.

Simpson, Jeffrey, "You Say Prosperity, I Say Productivity," *The Globe and Mail*, June 29, 2005.

Simpson, Jeffrey, "We Just Don't Get It When It Comes to Training the Workers," *The Globe and Mail*, June 28, 2005.

Thompson, John Herd, *Canada and the United States: Ambivalent Allies*. Montreal, Kingston: McGill-Queen's University Press, 2002.

U.S. Census Bureau, Foreign Trade Statistics, "Trade with NAFTA with Canada: 2005," FTD-Statistics-Country Data-U.S. Trade Balance with NAFTA with Canada, http://www.census.gov/foreign-trade/balance/c0006.html#2005.

U.S. Department of Commerce, International Trade Administration, "NAFTA 10 Years Later," Office of Industry Trade Policy, http://www.ita.doc.gov/td/industry/otea/nafta/Coverpage.pdf on June 30, 2005.

U.S. Senate Committee on Foreign Relations, Subcommittee on International Economic Policy, Export, and Trade Promotion, April 20, 2004, http://www.mac.doc.gov/nafta/speeches/reports.html on June 30, 2005.

Wayne, Anthony, "State Department Official Hails Benefits from NAFTA," April 20, 2004, http://www.usembassycanada.gov/content/can_usa/nafta_wayne_042004.pdf on June 30, 2005.

World Bank Group, Canada Data Profile, World Development Indicators Database, April 2005, http://devdata.worldbank.org/external/CCProfile. asp?SelectedCountry=CAN&CCODE=C on July 22, 2005.

Chapter 4: Culture, Education, and Religion

Axel-Lute, Paul, "Same-Sex Marriage: A Selective Bibliography of the Legal Literature," June 17, 2005, http://law-library.rutgers.edu/SSM.html on June 26, 2005.

Bauman, Kurt, "Technical Degrees Worth More," Public Information Office, U.S. Census Bureau, April 10, 2001, http://www.census.gov/Press-Release/ www/releases/archives/education/000320.html on July 13, 2005.

Bergman, Mike, "College Degree Nearly Doubles Annual Earnings," Public Information Office, U.S. Census Bureau, March 28, 2005, http://www.census.gov/Press-Release/www/releases/archives/education/ 004214.html on June 21, 2005.

Bergman, Mike, "High School Graduation Rates Reach All-Time High; Non-Hispanic White and Black Graduates at Record Levels," Public Information Office, U.S. Census Bureau, June 29, 2004, http://www.census.gov/Press-Release/www/releases/archives/education/ 001863.html on June 22, 2005.

Bergman, Mike, "Women Edge Men in High School Diplomas, Breaking 13-Year Deadlock," Public Information Office, U.S. Census Bureau, March 21, 2003, http://www.census.gov/Press-Release/www/2003/cb03-51.html on June 22, 2005.

Bibby, Reginald W., *Restless Gods: The Renaissance of Religion in Canada.* Toronto: Stoddart, 2002.

Buscher, Patricia, "Education Revenues Top $440 Billion; DC Spent the Most Per Student, Utah the Least," Public Information Office, U.S. Census Bureau, March 17, 2005, http://www.census.gov/Press-Release/www/releases/archives/ governments/004118.html on June 26, 2005.

Canadian Multiculturalism Act: An Act for the Preservation and Enhancement of Multiculturalism in Canada, July 21, 1988. http://www.pch.gc.ca/progs/multi/policy/act_e.cfm.

Canadian Association of University Teachers, "University and College Tuition in Canada Too High: Poll." CAUT News Releases, October 5, 2005, http://www.caut.ca/en/news/comms/20041125lobbyday.asp.

Chu, Jeff, "Coming Back to School," *Time*, March 20, 2006, p. 63.

College Board, "About the Midwest: Education," Economic Development, *2004 College-Bound Seniors*, National and State Reports 2004, http://midwestsites.com/stellent2/groups/public/documents/pub/mws_am_ed_00092 on June 26, 2005.

CNN, "Massachusetts Court Rules Ban on Gay Marriage Unconstitutional," February 4, 2004 (Copyright 2004 CNN).

Farhi, Paul, and Megan Rosenfeld, "American Pop Penetrates Worldwide," *Washington Post*, October 25, 1998, http://www.washingtonpost.com/wp-srv/inatl/longterm/mia/part1.htm on March 18, 2006.

Flesch, Rudolf, *Why Johnny Can't Read*. New York: Harper Paperbacks, 1986.

Fry, Richard, "High School Dropout Rates for Latino Students," ERIC Digest, 2003, http://www.ericdigests.org/2004-3/latino.html on March 18, 2006.

Howe, Julia Ward, "Battle Hymn of the Republic," *The Atlantic Monthly*, February 1862. http://womenshistory.about.com/library/etext/bl_howe_battle_hymn.htm.

Humes, Karen, and Jesse McKinnon, "2 in 5 of Asians and Pacific Islanders Have Bachelor Degrees or Higher, Census Bureau Reports," Public Information Office, Census Bureau, May 5, 2000, http://www.census.gov/Press-Release/www/releases/archives/education/000325.html on June 22, 2005.

Ipsos Canada, Canadians' National Policy Issue Agenda, *The Ipsos Trend Report Canada September/October 2004*. October 5, 2005, http://www.ipsos.ca/search.cfm.

Kohut, Andrew, "Among Wealthy Nations the U.S. Stands Alone in Its Embrace of Religion," Pew Research Center for The People & The Press, December 19, 2002, www.people-press.org on June 27, 2005.

Levitt, Steven D., and Stephen J. Dubner, *Freakonomics: A Rogue Economist Explores the Hidden Side of Everything*. New York: William Morrow, 2005.

MacIvor, Carol, "World: Culture Ministers to Create Network to Combat 'Global Monoculture,'" Radio Free Europe/Radio Liberty, Inc., July 2, 1998, http://www.rferl.org on June 21, 2005.

National Center for Education Statistics, "Enrollment Trends, Public and Private Schools," October, 5, 2005 http://nces.ed.gov/fastfacts/display.asp?id=65.

National Center for Education Statistics, "International Comparisons of Expenditures for Education," Institute of Education Sciences, U.S. Department of Education, 2005, http://nces.ed.gov/surveys/international/intlindicators/index.asp?SectionNumber=1&SubSe on June 26, 2005.

National Center for Education Statistics, "TIMSS 2003 Results," Institute of Education Sciences, U.S. Department of Education, 2005, http://nces.ed.gov/timss/Results03.asp?Quest=3.

Occupational Outlook Quarterly, "More Education Means Higher Earnings—for Life," Fall 2002, data derived from U.S. Census Bureau, www.census.gov/population/www/socdemo/educ-attn.html.

OECD, PISA 2000 Database, OECD Programme for International Student Assessment, October 5, 2005, http://pisaweb.acer.edu.au/oecd/oecd_pisa_data_s1.html.

OECD, PISA 2003 Database, OECD Programme for International Student Assessment, October 5, 2005, http://pisaweb.acer.edu.au/oecd_2003/oecd_pisa_data.html.

Peter, Katharin, and Laura Horn, "Gender Differences in Participation and Completion of Undergraduate Education and How They Have Changed Over Time," National Center for Education Statistics, Institute of Education Sciences, U.S. Department of Education, February 2005.

PISA Canada, "Measuring up: Canadian Results of the OECD PISA Study. The Performance of Canada's Youth in Mathematics, Reading, Science, and Problem Solving." PISA Canada Publications, October 5, 2005, http://www.pisa.gc.ca/brochur_e.pdf.

Progressive Policy Institute, "The United States Is the World's Top Exporter of Films and TV Shows," PPI, Trade Fact of the Week, August 25, 2004, http://www.ppionline.org/ppi_ci.cfm?knigArea on June 26, 2005.

Rosten, Leo, *The Education of Hyman Kaplan*. London: Prion Books, 2000.

Scott, Allen J., "A New James Bond Movie: Die Another Day," YaleGlobal, November 29, 2002, http://yaleglobal.yale.edu/display.article?id=479&page=2 on June 25, 2005.

Stack, Rodney, and Roger Finke, *The Churching of America, 1776-1990*. New Brunswick, NJ: Rutgers University Press, 1992.

UNESCO Institute for Statistics, Country Profile: Canada. UNESCO, October 5, 2005, http://www.uis.unesco.org/countryprofiles/html/EN/countryProfile_en.aspx?code=1240.htm.

UNESCO Institute for Statistics, Country Profile: United States. UNESCO, October 5, 2005, http://www.uis.unesco.org/countryprofiles/html/EN/ countryProfile_en.aspx?code=8400.htm.

Weiss, Rick, "9/11 Response Hurting Science, ACLU Says," *The Washington Post*, June 22, 2005, A19.

Zurita, Martha, "Improving the Education of Latino Students," Minority Student Achievement Network, Invitational Paper Series, 2005, http://www.nd.edu/~latino/ on March 18, 2006.

Chapter 5: Approaches to Health Care

Anderson, Gerard, "It's the Prices, Stupid: Why the United States Is So Different from Other Countries," *Health Affairs*, 2004, http://content. healthaffairs.org/cgi/content/full/22/3/89 on June 12, 2005.

Anderson, Gerard, "U.S. Still Spends More on Health Care than Any Other Country," Johns Hopkins Bloomberg School of Public Health, July 12, 2005. Study cited in the July/August 2005 journal *Health Affairs:* http://www.jhsph. edu/publichealthnews/press_Releases/2005/Anderson_healthspending.htm on July 13, 2005.

Glemser, Bernard, *Man Against Cancer*. New York: Funk & Wagnalls, 1969.

Grisanti, Ronald, "Iatrogenic Disease: The 3rd Most Fatal Disease in the USA," 2000-2005 Busatti Corporation, http://www.yourmedicaldetective.com/public/335.cfm on August 28, 2005.

Institute of Medicine of the National Academies, "Reducing Medical Errors Requires National Computerized Information Systems: Data Standards Are Crucial to Improving Patient Safety," The National Academies, November 20, 2003, http://www4.nas.edu/news.nsf/6a3520dc.

Leonard, Jeremy A., "How Structural Costs Imposed on U.S. Manufacturers Harm Workers and Threaten Competitiveness," Manufacturers Alliance, Manufacturing Institute of the National Association of Manufacturers, http://www.nam.org/s_nam/bin.asp?CID=227525&DOC=FILE.PDF on June 12, 2005.

MacKinnon, Janice, *Minding the Public Purse: The Fiscal Crisis, Political Trade-offs, and Canada's Future*. Montreal, Kingston: McGill-Queen's University Press, 2003.

McDonald, Heather A., "Health Care Costs, Spending Rising Faster than Wages," The National Academies, June 22, 2005, http://www.nationalacademies.org/headlines/#sh0622 on June 24, 2005.

West, Linda, *Trends and Issues in Health Care*. Toronto: McGraw Hill, 2002.

Will, George, "Health-care Costs Taxing GM," *Chicago Sun Times,* May 1, 2005, http://suntimes.com/output/will/cst-edt-geo01.hgml on June 10, 2005.

Chapter 6: Crime and Substance Abuse

"Graphical Overview of the Criminal Justice Indicators," 1999-2000/Statistics Canada, Canadian Centre for Justice Statistics.

Statistics Canada, *Graphical Overview of the Criminal Justice Indicators,1999/2000*. Canadian Centre for Justice Statistics: Ottawa. 2001, http://prod.library.utoronto.ca:8090/datalib/codebooks/cstdli/justice/2001/2001_graph_overview_e.pdf.

"Gun Control," Digital Termpapers, http://www.digitaltermpapers.com/c6928.htm on June 15, 2005.

Chaddock, Gail R., "U.S. Notches World's Highest Incarceration Rate," *The Christian Science Monitor*, www.crosswaysministries.com on June 14, 2005.

Death Penalty Information Center, "Facts About the Death Penalty," June 8, 2005, www.deathpenaltyinfo.org on June 15, 2005.

Goff, Colin H., *Criminal Justice in Canada*. Toronto: Thomson Nelson, 2004.

Gop_ryan's Xanga Site, February 12, 2006, http://www.xanga.com/gop_ryan/441921677/item.html on March 20, 2006.

Hartnagel, Timothy F., *Canadian Crime Control Policy: Selected Readings*. Toronto: Harcourt Brace Canada, 1998.

Health and Welfare Canada, *Canada's Drug Strategy*. Ottawa: Minister of National Health and Welfare, 1991.

Mirken, Bruce, "Dressing Up Failure," AlterNet, September 20, 2004, http://www.alternet.org/drugreporter/19854/ on June 17, 2005.

Pink, Joel E., and David C. Perrier, eds., *From Crime to Punishment: An Introduction to the Criminal Justice System*. Toronto: Carswell, 2003.

Rand Corporation, "Rand Finds Imprisoned Low-Level Drug Offenders in Arizona and California Typically Could Have Faced More Serious Charges," News release, Rand Corporation, June 23, 2005, http://www.rand.org/news/press.05/06.23.html on June 24, 2005.

Special Committee on Non-Medical Use of Drugs, *Policy for the New Millennium: Working Together to Redefine Canada's Drug Strategy*. Ottawa: 2002, http://www.parl.gc.ca/InfoComDoc/37/2/SNUD/Studies/Reports/snudrp02/snudrp02-e.pdf.

U.S. Department of Justice, "Crime and Victims Statistics," Bureau of Justice Statistics, Office of Justice Programs, June 9, 2005, http://www.ojp.usdoj.gov/bjs/cvict.htm on June 13, 2005.

United States Sentencing Commission, "Sentencing Reform Act" (Legislative History), http://www.ussc.gov/15_year/chapt1.pdf on June 20, 2005.

Will, George, "This War Is Worth Fighting," *The Washington Post,* June 16, 2005, A20.

Chapter 7: World Roles: Unilateral versus Multilateral

Alger, Chadwick F., *The United Nations System: The Policies of Member States*. Tokyo: United Nations University Press, 1995.

Anstee, Margaret, "What Price Peace? And United Nations Reform," *The Round Table: The Commonwealth Journal of International Affairs*, No. 346, April 1998.

Chapnick, Adam, "The Ottawa Process Revisited: Aggressive Unilateralism in the Post-Cold War World," *International Journal*, David Haglund and Joseph T. Jockel, eds., Vol. LVIII No. 3/Summer 2003, 281-294.

Farwell, Byron, *Queen Victoria's Little Wars*. New York: W.W. Norton & Company, 1972.

Fasulo, Linda M., *An Insider's Guide to the UN*. New Haven, CT: Yale University Press, 2003.

Khong, Yuen Foong, *Unilateralism and U.S. Foreign Policy: International Perspectives*, Boulder, CO: Lynne Rienner Publishers, 2003.

Greenhill, Robert, External Voices Project of the Canadian Institute of International Affairs, done by the Canadian International Development Agency (CIDA), published in early 2005.

Ignatieff, Michael, "Canada in the Age of Terror: Multilateralism Meets a Moment of Truth," *Policy Options*, February 2003.

Morris, Justin, "UNSC Reform: A Counsel for the 21st Century," *Security Dialogue*, Vol. 31(3), 2000, 265-277.

National Security Strategy of the United States of America, The White House, September 17, 2002, http://www.whitehouse.gov/nsc/nssall.html on July 5, 2005.

Newman, Dwight, "A Human Security Council? Applying a 'Human Security' Agenda to Security Council Reform," *University of Ottawa Law Review*, Vol. 31(2), Spring 2000, 213-241.

Ruggie, John Gerard, "The New United Nations: Continuous Change and Reform," *Behind the Headlines*, Vol. 56(1), Autumn 1998.

Schechter, Michael G., *Future Multilateralism: The Political and Social Framework*. New York: St. Martin's Press, 1999.

Schechter, Michael G., *Innovation in Multilateralism*. New York: United Nations University Press, 1999.

Steele, David, *UN Charter Reform and a New Global Bargain*, 2000, http://www.admin.ch/ch/d/bk/epzb/bulletin/2001/20-21wb01.pdf.

Walker, Graham F., *Independence in an Age of Empire: Assessing Unilateralism and Multilateralism*. Halifax: Centre for Foreign Policy Studies, Dalhousie University, 2004.

Chapter 8: The Military: Primary or Ancillary in International Relations

Bland, Douglas L., ed., *Canada Without Armed Forces?* Montreal, Kingston: McGill-Queen's University Press, 2004.

Canadian Department of National Defence, 1994 Defence White Paper, Canada Communication Group, 1994.

Conference of Defence Associations Institute, *A Nation at Risk: The Decline of the Canadian Forces*, Ottawa, 2002.

Granatstein, J. L., *Canada's Army: Waging the War and Keeping the Peace*. Toronto: University of Toronto Press, 2004.

Standing Committee on National Security and Defence, *Canada's Coastlines: The Longest Under-defended Border in the World*, a report of the Standing Senate Committee on National Security and Defence. Ottawa, 2003.

Stewart, Richard W., ed., *American Military History, Volume 1: The United States Army and the Forging of a Nation: 1775-1917*. Washington, D.C.: U.S. Army Center of Military History, 2005, www.army.mil/cmh-pg on July 13, 2005.

U.S. Department of Veterans Affairs, "America's Wars," VA Home Page, November 2004, http://www1.va.gov/opa/fact/amwars.html on July 8, 2005.

Walker, Graham F., *Independence in an Age of Empire: Assessing Multilateralism and Unilateralism*, Halifax: Centre for Foreign Policy Studies, Dalhousie University, 2004.

Chapter 9: Human Rights and Development

Axworthy, Lloyd, Minister of Foreign Affairs, Remarks during Consultations with Non-governmental Organizations in Preparation for the 52nd Session of the United Nations Commission on Human Rights, Ottawa, February 13, 1996.

Bandow, Doug, "Help or Hindrance: Can Foreign Aid Prevent International Crises?" CATO Institute, Policy Analysis, April 25, 1997, http://www.cato.org/pub_display.php?pub_id=1132&full=1 on July 25, 2005.

Bauer, Joanne R. and Daniel A. Bell, eds., *The East Asian Challenge for Human Rights*. Cambridge, MA: Cambridge University Press, 1999.

Brohman, John, *Popular Development: Rethinking the Theory and Practice of Development*. Oxford: Blackwell Publishers, 1996.

Carment, David, Fen Hampson, and Norman Hillmer, eds., *Canada Among Nations: Coping with the American Colossus*. New York: Oxford University Press, 2003.

Desai, Meghnad, and Paul Redfern, eds., *Global Governance: Ethics and Economics of the World Order*. London, New York: Pinter, 1995.

Dias, Clarence J., and David Gillies, *Human Rights, Democracy and Development*. Montreal: International Centre for Human Rights and Democratic Development, 1993.

Donnelly, Jack, "Human Rights, Democracy, and Development," *Human Rights Quarterly*, The Johns Hopkins University Press, Vol. 21(3), August 1999, 608-632.

Dunbar, R. B. (Bob), *Oil Sands Supply Outlook: Potential Supply and Costs of Crude Bitumen and Synthetic Crude Oil in Canada, 2003-2017*. Calgary, AB: Canadian Energy Research Institute, 2004.

Elwell, Christine, *Human Rights, Labour Standards and the New World Trade Organization: Opportunities for a Linkage: A Canadian Perspective*. Montreal: International Centre for Human Rights and Democratic Development, 1995.

Forcese, Craig, "Putting Conscience into Commerce: Strategies for Making Human Rights Business as Usual," *Rights and Democracy*, January 1997, http://www.ichrdd.ca/site/publications/index.php?subsection=catalogue&lang=en&id=1395 on March 27, 2006.

Haynes, Jeffrey, *Politics in the Developing World: A Concise Introduction* Malden, MA: Blackwell Publishers, 2002.

Herbert Hoover, *Encyclopedia Americana*, http://ap.grolier.com/article?assetid=0205570-00&templatename=/article/article.html on July 17, 2005.

Keller, Tony, "Simple Heart and Muddled Head," *University of Toronto News Digest*, July 17, 2005, http://www.news.utoronto.ca/inthenews/archive/2005_07_17.html on July 21, 2005.

Kupperman, Tamara, "State Department Critiques Human Rights," MSNBC, NBC News, March 1, 2005, http://www.msnbc.msn.com/id/7046889 on March 3, 2005.

Mark, Clyde R., "Israel: U.S. Foreign Assistance," Congressional Research Service 2004, at the Jewish Virtual Library, A Division of the American-Israeli Cooperative Enterprise, http://www.jewishvirtuallibrary.org/jsource/US-Israel/U.S._Assistance_to_Israel1.html on July 20, 2005.

McCalla, Douglas, and Michael Huberman, eds., *Perspectives on Canadian Economic History*, Second Edition. Mississauga, ON: Copp Clark Longman, 1994.

McRae, Robert Grant, *Resistance and Revolution: Vaclav Havel's Czechoslovakia.* Ottawa: Carleton University Press, 1997.

Nyamu, C. I., "How Should Human Rights and Development Respond to Cultural Legitimization of Gender Hierarchy in Developing Countries?", *Harvard International Law Journal*, Vol. 41(2), Spring 2000.

O'Manique, John, "Human Rights and Development," *Human Rights Quarterly*, Vol. 14(1), 1992, 78-103.

Pereira Leite, Sergio, "Human Rights and the IMF," *Finance & Development*, 38(4), 2001.

Rogge, Malcolm James, "Human Rights, Human Development and the Right to a Healthy Environment: An Analytical Framework," *Revue Canadienne d'etudes du developpement*, Vol. XXII(1), 2001, 33-50.

Rostow, Walt Whitman, *Stages of Economic Growth*, Second Edition. Cambridge, MA: Cambridge University Press, 1971.

Salomon, Margot E., and Arjun Sengupta, *The Right to Development: Obligations of States and the Rights of Minorities and Indigenous Peoples*. London: Minority Rights Group International, 2003, p. 4.

Sengupta, Arjun, "On the Theory and Practice of the Right to Development," *Human Rights Quarterly*. The Johns Hopkins University Press, Vol. 24(4), November 2002, 837-889.

Udombana, N. J., "The Third World and the Right to Development: Agenda for the Next Millennium," *Human Rights Quarterly*. The Johns Hopkins University Press, Vol. 22(3), August 2000, 753-787.

Uvin, Peter, *Human Rights and Development*. Bloomfield, CT: Kumarian Press, 2004.

USAID, "Statement of the Administrator," USAID Congressional Budget Justification for FY2005, http://www.usaid.gov/policy/budget/cbj2005/administrator.html on July 25, 2005.

USAID, "USAID's Fiscal Year 2006 Budget Request," Press Office/Public Information, February 8, 2005, http://www.usaid.gov/ on July 22, 2005.

U.S. Department of Army, "Foreign Economic Relations," Country Studies, http://www.country-studies.com/south-korea/foreign-economic-relations.html on July 22, 2005.

U.S. Department of State, *Country Reports on Human Rights Practices for 2004*, Washington, D.C.: U.S. Government Printing Office, 2005.

U.S. Department of State, *International Religious Freedom Report 2005*, Washington, D.C.: U.S. Government Printing Office, 2005.

U.S. Embassy in Israel, "U.S. Assistance to Israel: 1949-2004 Total," March 2004, http://www.usembassy-israel.org.il/publish/mission/amb/assistance.html on July 20, 2005.

Williams, Walter E., "Aid to Africa," *The Washington Times*, http://www.washingtontimes.com/commentary/wwilliams.htm on July 25, 2005.

Conclusion: Where Are We Going?

Garreau, Joel, *The Nine Nations of North America*. New York: Avon Press, 1989.

INDEX

official languages, 24, 28, 54, 105, 108
oil and gas industry, 79, 87–89, 192
oil sands, 87–89
Oklahoma City bomber. *See*
McVeigh, Timothy
Old North Church (Boston), 34
one-line votes, 46
Ontario, 9, 20, 22, 50, 85, 109, 173,
177, 201
OPEC (Organization of Petroleum
Exporting Countries), 88
Operation Desert Storm (1991), 228
opiates, 201
Opium and Drug Act, 184
Oregon, 9, 68
Organization of American States
(OAS), 45, 209
Organization for Economic Co-
operation and Development
(OECD), 111–12, 128, 281
organized crime, 185
Ouellette, Andre, 211
Outer Canada, 44, 50, 51, 57

P

pacifism, 254, 256
Palestinians, 15, 229,
Palestinian Authority (PA), 15, 294
Pan American Games, 12
Panama, 228
Papineau, Louis Joseph, 20
Parizeau, Jacques, 25
Park Chung-hee, 297
Parrish, Carolyn, 226
Parliament, 4, 21, 46, 47, 54–55
parliamentary secretaries, 46
parole boards, 175
Parti Quebecois, xi, 25
party discipline, 47, 48, 50, 51, 66,
303
party line, 65
party lists, 55–56
patriotism, 28–29
patronage, 44

PBS (Public Broadcasting System),
71, 123, 124, 305
peacekeeping, 205, 209, 212, 213–14,
215, 228, 232, 237–38, 241,
249–50, 251, 263, 274, 311
Pearkes, George R., 269
Pearl Harbor (Dec. 1941), 258, 274,
285
Pearson, Lester B., 27, 205, 206, 217,
296
pensions, 93, 154–55
Pentagon, 268
Penn, William, 33
Pennsylvania, 33, 134–35, 254
Pentecostal Church, 115
Perot, Ross, 67, 72
Persian Gulf, 262
Peru, 207
Pettigrew, Pierre, 209
pharmacies, online, 166
Philadelphia, Constitutional
Convention (1789), 30
Philippines, 35, 257
Plains of Abraham, battle, 20
platform documents, 65
plea bargaining, 175
Pledge of Allegiance, 28–29, 31, 154
Plymouth (Massachusetts), 33
Poland, 228
police services, 173–74, 183
political parties, US, 45, 49, 51,
65–68, 74
political spending. *See* campaign
funding
political structure, Cda/US comparisons, 4
politics
Cda, 10, 17
gender/racial distribution in, 76
military figures in, 269
minorities in, 75–76
third-rail concept, 154
US, 75–76
women in, 76

states
  and capital punishment, 193, 194
  large v. small, voting, 73
  political attitudes in, 74–75
  rights, 4, 21, 61–66
Statue of Liberty, 37
Stevens, John Paul, 63
Stewart, Martha, 187
Stockdale, James, 72
sub-Saharan Africa, 7
substance abuse, 5, 169, 172, 175,
  181–86, 198–201, 308–9
Sudan 49, 205, 247, 249, 274
Suez Canal conflict, 206
suicide, 129, 197 (*See also* assisted
  suicide)
summer of love (1967), 139, 198, 199
Sun Belt region (US), 48, 49
Supporting Human Rights and
  Democracy (SHRD), 289–90
Supreme Court (Cda), 25, 46, 53,
  139, 148–49, 150–51, 154, 307
Supreme Court (Massachusetts),
  137–38
Supreme Court (US), 29, 38, 53, 63,
  77, 133, 136, 137, 179, 185, 194,
  198
Sweden, 147, 207, 217, 282, 303
Swift Boat Veterans for Truth, 78
Switzerland, 55, 151, 152, 195
Syria, 309

T

Taiwan, 115, 128, 286, 312
Tanzania, 216
tariffs, 94, 98
taxation, 5, 23, 68, 77, 155, 160
Taylor, Zachary, 269
teachers, 127, 130–31
television, 70–71, 106, 117, 123, 124,
  188–89, 196–97, 305
10th Mountain Division (Fort Drum,
  NY), 13
territorial bloc voting, 48–49

terrorism/terrorists, xii, 15, 37, 54,
  192, 194, 204, 206, 214, 219,
  222, 223, 225, 229, 241, 246,
  242, 243, 252, 247–48, 253, 262,
  264, 268
Texas, 44, 73, 194, 288, 291, 300, 312
textile production, 90
third parties, US, 66–67
Thompson, John, 174
three-line votes, 46, 47
"three strikes and you're out" policy,
  178, 189–90, 308
Tibet, 286
Tilden, Samuel, 73
Time magazine, 254, 301
time zones, 11
tobacco, 5, 75, 78, 90, 169, 198, 200,
  201
Tobin, Brian, 220
Tomb of the Unknowns, 29, 268
Toronto, 50, 248
Toronto–Montreal–Ottawa triangle.
  See Inner Canada
town meetings, 61
trade agreements, 84–87
trade, Cda/US, 79, 125, 210, 243,
  244, 304–5 (*See also* exports/im-
  ports; Free Trade Agreement;
  NAFTA; trade agreements)
travel, to US (documents), 224–25,
  312
Treasury notes/bonds, 92
Treaty of Moscow, 233
Treaty of Paris, 20
Treaty of Utrecht, 20
Trends in International Mathematics
  and Sciences Study, 128
Tropic of Cancer (Miller), 38
Tropic of Capricorn (Miller), 38
Trudeau, Pierre, 13, 23–24, 26, 60, 89,
  212, 300
Truman, Harry S., 269
tsunami (2005), 113–14, 219
tuition, 133